1979

Beginnings in Poetry

William J. Martz Ripon College

Beginnings in Poetry 2nd edition

Scott, Foresman and Company
Glenview, Illinois   Brighton, England

for

Nedra, Bruce, and Bill

Acknowledgments

Cover Art: Mickey Stanzler

W. H. AUDEN   "O What Is That Sound" copyright 1937 and renewed © 1965 by W. H. Auden.
"Musée des Beaux Arts" and "The Unknown Citizen" copyright 1940 and renewed © 1968 by
W. H. Auden. Reprinted from *Collected Shorter Poems 1927-1957,* by W. H. Auden, by permission
of Random House, Inc., and Faber and Faber Ltd.   ROBERT BLY   "Love Poem" and "Solitude
Late at Night in the Woods" reprinted from *Silence in the Snowy Fields,* Wesleyan University Press.
Copyright © 1962 by Robert Bly, reprinted with his permission. "Watching Television" from *The
Light Around the Body* by Robert Bly. Copyright © 1963 by Robert Bly. Reprinted by permission
of Harper & Row, Publishers.   LOUISE BOGAN   "The Crossed Apple" reprinted with the per-
mission of Farrar, Straus & Giroux, Inc., from *Blue Estuaries* by Louise Bogan. Copyright 1954,
© 1968 by Louise Bogan.   PHILIP BOOTH   "First Lesson" from *Letter from a Distant Land* by
Philip Booth. Copyright © 1957 by Philip Booth. Reprinted by permission of The Viking Press, Inc.
"Deer Isle" from *Margins* by Philip Booth. Copyright © 1962 by Philip Booth. Reprinted by permis-
sion of The Viking Press, Inc.   GWENDOLYN BROOKS   "The Lovers of the Poor" from *Selected
Poems* by Gwendolyn Brooks. Copyright © 1960 by Gwendolyn Brooks. Reprinted by permission of
Harper & Row, Publishers.   GEOFFREY CHAUCER   "The Portrait of the Knight," "The Portrait
of the Friar," "The Portrait of the Wife of Bath," "The Portrait of the Pardoner," and "The Pardoner's
Tale" from Geoffrey Chaucer, *The Canterbury Tales,* translated by Nevill Coghill. Copyright Nevill

Preface

The Second Edition of *Beginnings in Poetry* is, like the First, an introductory text for the college student about to undertake a study of poetry. Retained from the First Edition in revised form is the introductory "Essay on How to Read a Poem," and most of the original table of contents numbering approximately one hundred poems. The introductory essay has now become Chapter 1, "Overview." I continue to be convinced of the value of offering a fairly comprehensive introductory essay that can be read through in about an hour, thus giving the student an overview of poetry and allowing the instructor to discuss a point when it comes up without being forced to develop it from scratch. Beyond this, the Second Edition is very much a new book and reflects some conclusions I have reached about the teaching of poetry since the publication of the First Edition.

Perhaps the most important of these conclusions relates to language. I often find that my students can well appreciate a whole poem without knowing at all the meaning of some of its parts. And yet anyone who teaches poetry knows that a genuinely full experience of a poem requires a close awareness of the language the poet is using. So in the Second Edition I have included full facing-page notes for a selection of poems of the kind likely to be taught in most beginning courses. These poems are part of Chapter 2, "The Uses of Language," and are preceded by a discussion of the process of definition. The facing-page notes begin with the humble function of telling what the possibly unfamiliar words and references mean, but more largely, and perhaps cumulatively, they are intended to suggest the nature and quality of the poetic experience and hence to complement the introductory essay in a vital way. The facing-page notes are, however, explanatory rather than interpretive, so the student ought to feel encouraged to synthesize his own response to the poem, even though he is offered relatively full information and range of allusion. The poems in Chapter 2 could be regarded themselves as a core group or could easily be combined with other poems to make a core group suited to a particular instructor's needs. In addition, but not confined to Chapter 2, I have included in facing-page arrangement the excellent Nevill Coghill translation for a selection of Chaucer's portraits of the Canterbury pilgrims.

A second of my conclusions is that within some obvious limits an introductory anthology should permit as much choice and flexibility as possible. This conclusion has its application in two basic areas. The first involves the elements of poetry. Following Chapter 2 and the poems with facing-page notes are six additional chapters which parallel in organization the points developed in the introductory essay. These chapters, "The Rhythm of Song," "Characterization," "Description," "Tone and Point of View," "The Poem of Ideas," and "Pleasure and Judgment," offer a combination of text, poems, and study questions and suggestions. Although they are intended to complement the introductory essay, they are independent of it and may be taken up in any order the instructor chooses. There is, in fact, no ultimate necessity to begin with the introductory essay. I can imagine a class which is completing a discussion of the short story appropriately beginning with "Characterization," or a class which is completing a discussion of the essay appropriately beginning with "The Poem of Ideas." The plain fact is that there is no per-fect "system" for teaching poetry. A flexible stance, combined with an awareness of the nature of the poetic experience, is a necessity.

The second area to which the principles of choice and flexibility apply is the selection of poems. In the Second Edition the number of poems has been increased to over three hundred. The poems themselves range in length from a few lines to several hundred. There is no attempt to do with some three hundred poems a job of historical coverage that might require nine hundred, and yet, for those who wish it, the present collection ranges from Chaucer to living contemporaries and includes representative work of the major literary figures likely to come to mind in a "first round" of historical choice emphasizing excellence. Substantial emphasis is given to the modern period, broadly con-strued, with Emily Dickinson, Thomas Hardy, Gerard Manley Hopkins, A. E. Housman, William Butler Yeats, Robert Frost, Wallace Stevens, William Carlos Williams, T. S. Eliot, E. E. Cummings, Theodore Roethke, and Dylan Thomas represented with a fullness that ought to be sufficient to allow some study in depth. Thirty-two poets born in the twen-tieth century are represented, nearly all by two or more poems. Poets of stature from previous centuries substantially represented are Chaucer, Shakespeare, Campion, Donne, Jonson, Milton, Pope, Blake, Burns, Wordsworth, Shelley, Keats, Tennyson, Browning, and Whitman—and also anonymous ballads of the Middle Ages and the King James Version of the Bible. I have also included a couple of contemporary song lyrics, but I have not attempted a full representation because it would be virtually obsolete before the book could be brought to print. Also, the contemporary student has his own favorites which he is ready to bring to class, and in greater number than could ever be practically included in an introduction to poetry. The poems in the Second Edition represent, as one would expect, a wide variety of subject matter and verse form. I hope I have struck a reasonable balance.

Finally, the Second Edition offers some useful appendix material, including Bio-graphical Notes, a Note on Listening, a full Glossary of Critical Terms, and Indexes by Theme, Verse Form, and Author, Title, and First Line. The Biographical Notes are brief and in a simple, factual format which includes the poet's chief works; sweeping generali-zations are avoided. A special effort has been made to provide a usable Glossary, which I have come increasingly to feel is needed in an introductory anthology.

I hope, then, that the Second Edition of *Beginnings in Poetry* will serve its purpose as an introductory anthology. I trust that it will encourage and comprehend many differ-ent approaches to poetry, and I am confident that those of us who teach poetry have the same end in mind, the experience of the poem itself, the experience of poetry itself, and, in one way or the other, the celebration of life by poetry's special kind of confrontation with its richness, wonder, and complexity.

William J. Martz

General Table of Contents

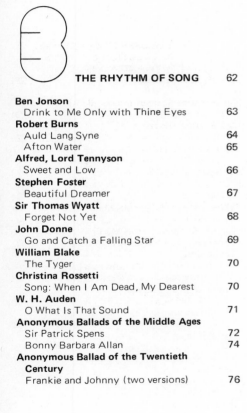

5

DESCRIPTION 110

6

TONE AND POINT OF VIEW 126

Chronological Table of Contents

Beginnings in Poetry

Overview: An Essay on How to Read a Poem

Hippolyta. This is the silliest stuff that ever I heard.

Theseus. The best in this kind are but shadows; and the worst are no worse, if imagination amend them.

William Shakespeare, *A Midsummer Night's Dream,* V, i, 212-14

A poem is an individuality. It has to have, to use a vague and omnibus word, *style.* A poem is an imaginative act done in words. We read it; we enter into the imaginative act, for pleasure, to know life better, to expand our share in its mystery and wonder. The question becomes, how?—how does anyone, particularly someone new to poetry, go about reading it? Since a poem is usually composed of sentences, we might go back a step and ask ourselves what kind of sentences we are most used to hearing and to reading. One answer is bound to be sentences of overt or explicit statement, and such we find in poems in relative abundance. Observe the explicitness of the following, all from famous poems:

> They who one another keep
>   Alive, ne'er parted be.

Donne, **Sweetest Love, I Do Not Go**

>   Therefore am I still
> A lover of the meadows and the woods,
> And mountains; and of all that we behold
> From this green earth;

Wordsworth, **Tintern Abbey**

> Be secret and exult
> Because of all things known
> That is most difficult.

Yeats, **To a Friend Whose Work Has Come to Nothing**

>   Earth's the right place for love:
> I don't know where it's likely to go better.

Frost, **Birches**

In each case the speaker is obviously making no effort to be oblique or to hold back meaning; from the explicitness of his statement we assume that he wants to communicate much as we communicate in everyday life. How then may we describe the style or the individuality of these sentences?

First, let us suggest the difference between these sentences and the kind of sentences we ordinarily use by comparing them with samples of our more everyday expression. In the same order, here are everyday equivalents for the four poem sentences:

Physical separation cannot part a man and a woman who are one in spirit.

I still love meadows, woods, mountains, and the whole green earth.

Keeping things to yourself is hard but rewarding.

The best place to live is right here on earth.

The equivalents are patently lacking in vitality. The two kinds of explicit statement, the the poetic and the prosaic, make a contrast that points to the difference between the imaginative and the dull. But what more precisely is meant by *poetic?*

One quality immediately discernible in the poem sentences, read with the natural emphasis of speech, is their pronounced regularity of accent or stress—their measuring of emphasis or iambic meter, a basic pattern of *ta bum / ta bum / ta bum* abstracted from them. Three such units, or feet, to a line are conveniently called, after the Greek, iambic *trimeter*; four, iambic *tetrameter*; five, iambic *pentameter*; six, iambic *hexameter*. But individualizing variations are more important than the basic pattern, which without variation would be pure monotony. In each of Donne's four-accent lines, for example, we are struck by such variations. In the first line the light accent in the opening *ta bum* is omitted, so that the meter is

    bum / ta bum / ta bum / ta bum

or   They who one another keep.

In the second line a pause (or cesura) falls after the first *ta bum* and the light accent is omitted in the second two feet, so that the meter is

    ta bum / pause / bum / bum / ta bum

or   Alive, ‖ ne'er parted be.

Thus, in part, individuality is achieved *first* from the fact of meter and *then* from the fact of metrical variation. The lines from the other poems would easily submit to a similar analysis, but the everyday equivalents do not. For example, the first equivalent, given a natural speech accent, might look like this:

    Physical separation cannot part a man and a woman in love.

Of course the prose sentence does not altogether lack rhythm, but it does not have the distinct, relatively regular rhythm of the poetry sentence. Moreover, this description of meter, though useful to make a distinction between poetry and prose, is rudimentary and oversimplified; we can hardly abstract *ta bum's* from lines of poetry without a certain sense of absurdity.

One aspect of oversimplification is to assume accents of two strengths, strong and weak, when actually the ear discerns with ease at least three—strong, medium, and weak, or primary (/), secondary (\ ), and light (⌣)—with all manner of delicate gradations possible and normal in the natural accent of speech. Another aspect of oversimplification is to assume a basic pattern of a weak stress immediately followed by a stronger one. The rhythm of some verse, such as the following lines from "Hurrahing in Harvest" by Gerard Manley Hopkins, achieves a regularity which distinguishes it as poetry by a control of accent or stress with no regard to iambic alternation or to what may be described as substituting a different foot—such as a *bum ta* (trochee) or a *ta ta bum* (anapest)—for an iambic foot:

Summer ends now; now, barbarous in beauty, the stooks arise

Around; up above, what wind-walks!   what lovely behavior

Of silk-sack clouds!   has wilder, wilful-wavier

Meal-drift moulded ever and melted across skies?

The control of accent or stress is roughly numerical: there are eight stresses in the first two lines, seven in the second two.

Still another aspect of oversimplification is to assume that the poet may not mix an iambic pattern with other patterns. In fact, we are drawn to the possible closeness of prose and verse. Here is the first paragraph of Ernest Hemingway's novel *The Old Man and the Sea* broken into line lengths that emphasize such mixing; accent marks are placed in those lines that read like poetry, with the contrast between prose and iambic meter labeled for emphasis:

He was an old man who fished alone   *iambic*

in a skiff in the Gulf Stream

and he had gone eighty-four days now without

taking a fish. In the first forty days a boy

had been with him.   *prose*

But after forty days without a fish   *iambic*

the boy's parents had told him   *iambic*

that the old man was now   *iambic* definitely and finally *salao*,

which is the worst form of unlucky,

and the boy had gone at their orders in another

boat which caught three good fish the first week. *prose*

It made the boy sad to see *iambic*

the old man come in each day *iambic*

with his skiff empty

and he always went down to help him carry

either the coiled lines or the gaff and harpoon

and the sail that was furled around the mast. *iambic*

The sail was patched with flour sacks and, furled, *iambic*

it looked like the flag of permanent defeat. *iambic*

Such writing is a cross between poetry and prose but on the whole has a rhythm that demands the name of poetry, a name which it does not generally get in the novel but does get when it is presented as poetry, as in the work of Walt Whitman. The final aspect of oversimplification—which applies to both metrical and stress-controlled lines—is to assume that all sounds have the same *length*. One suspects, for example, that Donne intended *ne'er* and *parted* to be spoken slowly, dwelled upon, as it were, and you can easily imagine giving singular emphasis to *Alive* while reading the preceding line with great rapidity and with fairly light stress on each word.

All of this leads us naturally to a second individualizing quality in the poem sentences. For reasons linked particularly to their rhythm, whether metrical or stress-controlled, they excite our curiosity to know who is speaking them and under what circumstances. The poem sentences hint at character, draw us into a situation or into an aspect of a situation. Rather than being like the four everyday equivalents—rational, dry, platitudinous, and detached from a specific reality—the poem sentences suggest all the intriguing interest of life as we experience it. Observe that the first few lines of Donne's poem put us directly into the dramatic situation of a tender farewell of a man to his wife:

Sweetest love, I do not go
  For weariness of thee,
Nor in hope the world can show
  A fitter love for me;

The sentence quoted previously from this poem (p. 1) is the man's last assurance to his wife, significantly preceded by specific reference to their marriage bed:

> But think that we
> Are but turned aside to sleep;
> They who one another keep
>   Alive, ne'er parted be.

Thus in *context* the sentence of the last two lines is descriptive of a marriage that has known the deepest possible sexual contentment.[1] Returning to the opening statement, we are now aware that the speaker wants to dispel from his wife's mind any thought that another woman could attract him, could be "a fitter love." Such specific and delicate reference to their total relationship keeps his farewell from being sentimental, as ordinary speech might be in the same situation—"I'll miss you, my one and only." The poem thus brings to us the emotional quality, the emotional reality, of a specific and individual experience that is at the same time universal—known, at least as a possibility, to all men.

The act of reading a poem as an individuality may be summed up thus far as follows:

1. Read the poem as you would anything else, with the natural emphasis of speech, for its natural sense and its natural rhythm. The natural emphasis of speech may not always coincide with the demands of metrical pattern—a situation analogous to the use of counterpoint in music, where one melody is combined with another.
2. You will have small if any difficulty understanding explicit statements made in the poem, since such statements are the common coin of everyday communication. Yet the explicit statements attract us not for themselves, for their rational content, but rather for the excitement of their speaker's experience.

Now we may examine some more sentences from famous poems. Like the first group, they are poetic in the sense of having a distinct rhythmic regularity and in the sense of exciting our curiosity to know who is speaking them and under what circumstances:

This flea is you and I, and this   *iambic tetrameter*

Our marriage bed and marriage temple is;   *iambic pentameter*

Donne, **The Flea**

                              such stuff

Was courtesy, she thought, and cause enough   *iambic pentameter*

For calling up that spot of joy.

Browning, **My Last Duchess**

---

1. *Context* is everything surrounding a given unit (word, phrase, line, or more) of the poem and modifying that unit's meaning while in turn being modified by it. More simply, context refers to the situation in which a phrase or line is spoken.

⏑ ⁄⏑ ⁄ ⏑ ⁄ ⏑ ⁄ ⏑ ⁄
Forth issue then in copious golden jets,

⁄ ⏑ ⁄ ⏑ ⁄
Sparkles from the wheel.

*iambic pentameter
and trimeter
in a free verse poem*

Whitman, **Sparkles from the Wheel**

⏑ ⁄⏑ ⁄ ⏑⏑ ⁄ ⏑ ⁄ ⏑⏑⏑ ⁄ ⁄
The only emperor is the emperor of ice-cream.

iambic hexameter?

Stevens, **The Emperor of Ice-Cream**

Whereas the meaning of the first group of poem sentences was explicit—that is, to a considerable extent immediately understandable—the meaning of these last sentences is implicit, or implied. The flea, the spot of joy, the sparkles, and the emperor of ice-cream are too particular to have equivalents in the kinds of sentences we are used to hearing every day. It becomes imperative to examine the context in which they occur if we are to understand them at all. We are drawn now to a poetic individuality that requires a particular kind of reading. We must be aware of the poet's use of *symbol,* an object which suggests meaning beyond itself.

Here is Robert Browning's "My Last Duchess," a dramatic monologue—a poem in which a speaker who is distinctly not the poet gradually reveals his situation and his character. Browning tells us first that the scene is Ferrara, which he expects us to know is a Renaissance Italian city-state.

Ferrara

That's my last Duchess painted on the wall,
Looking as if she were alive. I call
That piece a wonder, now: Frà Pandolf's hands
Worked busily a day, and there she stands.
5 Will't please you sit and look at her? I said
"Frà Pandolf" by design, for never read
Strangers like you that pictured countenance,
The depth and passion of its earnest glance,
But to myself they turned (since none puts by
10 The curtain I have drawn for you, but I)
And seemed as they would ask me, if they durst,
How such a glance came there; so, not the first
Are you to turn and ask thus. Sir, 'twas not
Her husband's presence only, called that spot
15 Of joy into the Duchess' cheek: perhaps
Frà Pandolf chanced to say, "Her mantle laps
Over my lady's wrist too much," or "Paint
Must never hope to reproduce the faint
Half-flush that dies along her throat:" such stuff
20 Was courtesy, she thought, and cause enough
For calling up that spot of joy. She had
A heart—how shall I say?—too soon made glad,

Too easily impressed; she liked whate'er
She looked on, and her looks went everywhere.
25   Sir, 'twas all one! My favor at her breast,
The dropping of the daylight in the West,
The bough of cherries some officious fool
Broke in the orchard for her, the white mule
She rode with round the terrace—all and each
30   Would draw from her alike the approving speech,
Or blush, at least. She thanked men,—good! but thanked
Somehow—I know not how—as if she ranked
My gift of a nine-hundred-years-old name
With anybody's gift. Who'd stoop to blame
35   This sort of trifling? Even had you skill
In speech—(which I have not)—to make your will
Quite clear to such an one, and say, "Just this
Or that in you disgusts me; here you miss,
Or there exceed the mark"—and if she let
40   Herself be lessoned so, nor plainly set
Her wits to yours, forsooth, and made excuse,
—E'en then would be some stooping; and I choose
Never to stoop. Oh, sir, she smiled, no doubt,
Whene'er I passed her; but who passed without
45   Much the same smile? This grew; I gave commands;
Then all smiles stopped together. There she stands
As if alive. Will't please you rise? We'll meet
The company below, then. I repeat,
The Count your master's known munificence
50   Is ample warrant that no just pretence
Of mine for dowry will be disallowed;
Though his fair daughter's self, as I avowed
At starting, is my object. Nay, we'll go
Together down, sir. Notice Neptune, though,
55   Taming a sea-horse, thought a rarity,
Which Claus of Innsbruck cast in bronze for me!

"My Last Duchess" reads easily, is not a difficult poem. It is clear in the first two lines that the speaker is a duke whose duchess has died. He is standing before a painting of his dead wife and is speaking to a "stranger" who is later specifically identified as an envoy from a Count with a marriageable daughter. The age is clearly one in which marriages were arranged and dowries were important. What interests us is how the Duke feels about his former wife, what their relationship was like, and how he feels about a new marriage. It is for him a time of transition, a situation we always find interesting. We are quickly aware that the Duke speaks with a coldness and an impersonality toward the person we would normally presume he would have loved. There is no fixed point at which we become aware of this attitude, although the possibilities available for Browning to exploit may be seen *as possibilities* in the first few words: stress *my* and you might have an egocentric Duke; stress *last* and you might have a man who exults in the arithmetic of a succession of wives. Surely the first four lines arouse our suspicions about the Duke's character, and by line eleven his egocentricity is pronounced—"to myself they turned," "none puts by The curtain . . . but I," "as they would ask me." We are now prepared for a remark that must be taken as snide: " 'twas not Her husband's presence only, called that spot Of joy into the Duchess' cheek." The Duke seems to hate his late wife for the blush on her cheek, which perhaps he takes as suggestive of a kind of happiness that he himself cannot have. The contrast he feels between himself and the Duchess is strong and explicit: "such stuff Was courtesy, *she* thought" (my italics). And when in the next line he reiterates the phrase "that spot of joy," we suspect that it tortures him, that it has more meaning for him than a simple "blush" (note this repetition of the motif in line 31) would normally have. In other words, to him the spot of joy is a symbol. But to know more specifically what additional meaning the poet intends, we must consider the poem as a whole.

Browning exploits, as we have said, his speaker's coldness and impersonality. Thus the colder the Duke gets the warmer is the author, by implication, toward the Duchess. Browning could, if he wished, show the Duchess to be at fault no matter how callous and guilty (perhaps of his wife's murder) the Duke. But Browning is careful to stack the cards of possibility, for the Duchess is presented as wholly a person of love and joy. This is an extreme *contrast*, a device by which the poet informs us of his intention. He is, in fact, seeing life in terms of a contrast between good and evil; but since his final emphasis is on character—and what interests us in the poem is revelation of character—the spot of joy is finally a symbol not merely of good but of an individual's dignity, which is inviolable. At the end of the poem we have a Duke who has gradually revealed himself as a bitter and unhappy man. The last word of the poem is the egocentric *me*, but by the last word we know that this *me* is pitiful, jealous, unable to love, and above all unable to find satisfaction in hate, since not even death can destroy that spot of joy in the Duchess' cheek. Her dignity lives and burns in him as a reminder of what he is not, and in the depths of his being he is aware of what he is.

Here is Wallace Stevens' "The Emperor of Ice-Cream," a poem of great individuality but more difficult to read and to comprehend than "My Last Duchess":

> Call the roller of big cigars,
> The muscular one, and bid him whip
> In kitchen cups concupiscent curds.
> Let the wenches dawdle in such dress
> 5 As they are used to wear, and let the boys
> Bring flowers in last month's newspapers.
> Let be be finale of seem.
> The only emperor is the emperor of ice-cream.
>
> Take from the dresser of deal,
> 10 Lacking the three glass knobs, that sheet
> On which she embroidered fantails once
> And spread it so as to cover her face.
> If her horny feet protrude, they come
> To show how cold she is, and dumb.
> 15 Let the lamp affix its beam.
> The only emperor is the emperor of ice-cream.

Two devices obviously draw us to the line "The only emperor is the emperor of ice-cream": its *placement* at the end of each of the two eight-line stanzas of the poem and its *repetition*, suggestive of a refrain. Moreover, the sense of the line teases us, for its two objects, an emperor and ice-cream, are in fact disparate in character, the great yoked with the small.[2] Apparently the speaker intends some comedy or perhaps an element of mockery. His imperative and energetic opening is a general summons for, absurdly, a figure identified in a literal way as a roller of big cigars, perhaps a storekeeper. But then the speaker shocks us by identifying him as one who whips "concupiscent curds." The curds are literal, suggesting a milk product such as ice-cream; but when the speaker attributes the quality of lust to the product of the roller of big cigars, we want to know why—particularly since the next two lines suggest a scene of flirtatious girls (who are usually near a neighborhood store) and the next two seem to allude to the boys bringing flowers to these girls. But the allusion is mocking because the flowers are to be brought in "last month's newspapers" rather than the normal tissue paper wrappings of the florist. Moreover, since the newspapers are last month's rather than this morning's, we are aware that the speaker has temporality on his mind, is perhaps suggesting that life is short. This concern is confirmed abstractly in the next line by the *be* and *seem* relationship. If *be* refers to bringing flowers (an everyday symbol of beauty or life) and *seem* to last month's newspapers, then the speaker is emphasizing that life is to be fully lived even though it is cradled by reminders of death—by whatever is past in time and has therefore lost its moment of life (flowers, moreover, must wilt). Only now does the speaker by indirect statement identify the roller of big cigars as an emperor, an emperor who as an emperor is a patent absurdity. The emperor must be a figure of death, which rules over the moments of our life, but an absurd and ineffectual figure. The speaker's recognition of him is ambiguous; he is the *only* emperor in the sense that he does have real power, but he is also the only emperor in the contemptuous sense that he is nothing for us to worry about.

The second stanza confirms that the real subject of the poem is life and death. The *she* of the horny feet is cold and dumb and needs a shroud. Nothing can be done about death other than to accept it; yet the speaker does *not* accept it, for when in conclusion

---

2. The yoking of the great and the small for a comic purpose is typical of a type of poem known as the *mock heroic*, which treats an apparently trivial subject in a grand manner. The grand manner usually imitates characteristics of the classical epic—such as heroes making brave speeches or the poet's lofty descriptions of battle dress. Compare the following from Alexander Pope's *The Rape of the Lock* with the line from Stevens. Note how Pope yokes the Bible with trivial objects of a dressing table, a cup of chocolate with the sea, counsel with tea, husbands with lap-dogs:

Here files of pins extend their shining rows,
Puffs, Powders, Patches, Bibles, Billet-doux. (I, 137-38)

[The spirit who neglects his charge]
In fumes of burning Chocolate shall glow,
And tremble at the sea that froths below! (II, 135-36)

Here [Hampton Court] thou, great ANNA! whom three realms obey,
Dost sometimes counsel take—and sometimes Tea. (III, 7-8)

Not louder shrieks to pitying heaven are cast,
When husbands, or when lap-dogs breathe their last. (III, 157-58)

he repeats the line about the emperor he means it in the ambiguous sense we have noted. The question becomes, of course, does he have a final emphasis? This can only be answered by returning to the fact that he yokes the great and the small in such a way as to mock the emperor, or death. The poem as a whole, in other words, acts as an asser- tion of humorous defiance. Death gloats, but despite his muscles we can affirm our own being.

To our two previous statements on the act of reading a poem as an individuality we may add a third:

3. The nature and quality of the speaker's experience is often communicated through emphasis on objects that in context carry a symbolic meaning. A symbol may be thought of as an implicit statement.

We have emphasized the fact that a poem brings us the feeling or the emotional quality of an experience and have discussed symbol as a means or a device to this end. Other devices mentioned include rhythm, development of situation and character, contrast, placement, repetition, and yoking. When we speak of means, we are speaking of what is commonly known as *technique.* It is time to put in perspective the relationship between style and technique.

We have said that a poem is an individuality. It is obvious that the general subject of all poems is human experience, a fact which triggers the question of how the poet is to communicate his particular experience. The answer, *in general*, is obvious: by a process of selection and arrangement, by organizing and shaping his subject matter so that the ele- ments of technique are exploited for the individual purpose. The answer, *specifically*, is incredibly complex, as we have suggested by examining the complexity of but one element of technique, rhythm. The fact is that just as we have no infallibly correct way to read a poem, so the poet has no infallibly correct way to write one. No amount of technique assures him success, and—to echo a thought of Archibald MacLeish—no amount of ingenuity can fake individuality. One problem in reading a poem is to keep from being captivated by technique, while always observing technique as it functions in the creation of an individuality, a style. With this in mind we may consider other basic means or techniques that the poet normally uses to make a poem.

Earlier we asked what kind of sentences we are most used to hearing and to reading and suggested that one answer is bound to be sentences of explicit statement. Another obvious answer is sentences of comparison, since it is completely natural for us to think in terms of similarities and differences. We may, of course, compare two like objects, such as two buildings in terms of their size, but it is generally a little more interesting to compare two unlike objects and thus to express ourselves in *metaphor*. Our everyday speech abounds with metaphors, especially (and unfortunately) those that are vague or exhausted from overuse—"I felt like a million dollars," "she was pretty as a picture," "that story is as old as the hills." But here are two poets describing trees:

You may see their trunks arching in the woods
Years afterwards, trailing their leaves on the ground
Like girls on hands and knees that throw their hair
Before them over their heads to dry in the sun.

Frost, **Birches**

The pear tree lets its petals drop
Like dandruff on a tabletop.

Snodgrass, **April Inventory**

Here in one serious and one humorous example we have precision and vitality. In both cases the comparison is introduced by the word *like*, which makes them *as comparisons* somewhat self-consciously explicit. But Yeats is hardly less explicit when he writes:

An aged man is but a paltry thing,
A tattered coat upon a stick . . .

Sailing to Byzantium

or Donne when he exclaims:

I can love both fair and brown;

. . . .

And her who is dry cork and never cries.

The Indifferent

The first kind of comparison, using *like* or *as*, is sometimes called a *simile* and the second a *metaphor*, but the distinction is seldom pressed and the word *metaphor* is now generally used to comprehend both types. What is important is the linguistic distinctiveness which the four examples have in common—the original way of looking and thinking. They also have in common a strong pictorial quality; we are able quickly and directly to *see* girls drying their hair, dandruff on a tabletop, a scarecrow, and a dry cork.
  Compare this to Ben Jonson in a song to Celia:

Kiss, and score up wealthy sums
On my lips, thus hardly sundered,
While you breath.

or to Andrew Marvell:

    But at my back I always hear
Time's wingèd chariot hurrying near;
And yonder all before us lie
Deserts of vast eternity.

To His Coy Mistress

Jonson and Marvell both require that we supply something to the picture. Jonson requires our own image of *wealthy sums*, which we then associate with the strength (from the verb *sundered*) and with the sensuality of kissing; Marvell requires the picture and sound of a chariot imagined to have wings (an object less common to our experience, incidentally, than girls or cork) as well as the image of time as a person (the device is *personification*) and then the association of the staggering abstraction of eternity with our experience of deserts. Jonson and Marvell have precision and vividness of a different kind than our previous examples. They are precisely suggestive—that is, precise and yet a little indeterminate as they attempt to link the general, or the abstract, to the concrete. Jonson, in fact, goes so far as to describe the fairly specific kiss in terms of the more general *wealthy sums* and of some unspecified game to score, thus reversing the normal process of describing the abstract in terms of the concrete (such as time in terms of a chariot and charioteer or eternity in terms of a desert).

Metaphor ranges in its function, then, from a pictorial distinctness to an invitation to the reader to build on a picture suggestion. Of course, since no word *is* a picture the reader in a sense is always required to supply his own; the question is essentially one of degree. Consider now this passage from John Ciardi's "The Gift":

> Josef Stein, poet, came out of Dachau
> like half a resurrection, his other
> eighty pounds still in their invisible grave.

We must first know that Dachau was one of the infamous Nazi concentration camps built for genocide.[3] If we then ask what a resurrection *looks like*, the most we can probably say is a dead person, cold, stiff, ashen, who has just come alive. This is in fact the poet's emphasis, but he has another emphasis in *half*, a rhetorical one, a deliberate exaggeration (the device of *hyperbole*). The miracle of the fictional Stein's survival is so great as to defy belief beyond the normal defiance of belief which resurrection would involve anyway.[4] In a similar way the invisible grave refers not to something we can see but to something we have to imagine; its referent is the total nightmare experience, the living death, of the concentration camp.

Now look at Randall Jarrell's famous war poem "The Death of the Ball Turret Gunner":

> From my mother's sleep I fell into the State
> And I hunched in its belly till my wet fur froze.
> Six miles from earth, loosed from its dream of life,
> I woke to black flak and the nightmare fighters.
> When I died they washed me out of the turret with a hose.

3. The device of referring to something outside the poem itself—such as a person, place, or historical event—is *allusion*.

4. A simple example of hyperbole is Robert Burns' "And I will love thee still, my dear, Till a' the seas gang dry." That's a lot of evaporation, to say the least.

We have first to imagine that the speaker is a dead man commenting on his own death. We have to think of the State personified as a woman with a child in her belly, a child who is the gunner. The final picture of a dead man being washed out of a turret with a hose is horrible in its own right, but the horror is compounded because the speaker is thinking of the turret as the belly of the State, as if perhaps the gunner were an embryo, denied his chance for life by war and disposed of with incredible impersonality.

To our previous statements about the act of reading a poem as an individuality we may now add a new one:

4. The poet often seeks to search out the quality and meaning of his experience by use of metaphor, which is usually visual but ranges from the pictorially distinct to the precisely suggestive.

"The Death of the Ball Turret Gunner" shows us metaphor as a technique functioning to characterize a speaker who is, with good reason, profoundly bitter. Our other examples, although not whole poems, also suggest the character of a speaker and the way in which he is addressing his subject. Ciardi's rhetoric is that of a man sickened by man's inhumanity to man, sickened perhaps to bitterness. Frost speaks in an intimate, personal (to a *you*), meditative way, his thoughts trailing, as it were, one after another in his metaphor: first girls, then their posture, then the action of throwing their hair, then where they throw it, then the function of drying, then the place, in the sun. Snodgrass is witty, employing a shock technique; his manner is casual, but his matter, the dandruff comparison, strikes hard. Yeats, if we assume (as is the case) that the speaker is old, is reflective. Donne seems severe in comparing one he can love to a dry cork. Jonson is admiring, flattering, determined. Marvell speaks smoothly, but like Snodgrass his subject matter is in a tense relationship to his metrical manner, since time and eternity are threatening. Each speaker is expressing how he feels about his experience or about his subject. He adopts a *tone*, which is to say a tone of voice. He expresses his attitude. He treats his experience or his subject from a certain *point of view.*

Tone and *point of view* are overlapping terms that are both useful in poetry criticism. Although *point of view* may be thought of as the complex of attitudes that the author has toward his subject—and thus as larger in scope than *tone*—the term is perhaps most useful in inviting us to begin with certain mechanical distinctions, particularly with three possibilities: (1) The first-person speaker who need not be distinguished from the author, although obviously not every such poem is distinctly biographical in character. (2) The first-person speaker who *must* be distinguished from the author, as is usually true of the dramatic monologue (it is completely obvious, for example, that the poet Browning is not a duke whose duchess has died). (3) The third-person or, as it is sometimes called, the objective point of view.

The third-person point of view is often used for purposes of description. Here are a few lines from Tennyson's "Mariana":

> She saw the gusty shadow sway.
> But when the moon was very low,
>   And wild winds within their cell,
>   The shadow of the poplar fell
> Upon her bed, across her brow.

The *mood*, or pervasive emotional condition, is one of dreariness, starkness, solitude. But the poet is detached from his subject; his attitude is difficult to fix. Now look at the opening stanza of Housman's "Loveliest of Trees," in which beyond the objective point of view you might sense an attitude of appreciation, even of reverence:

> Loveliest of trees, the cherry now
> Is hung with bloom along the bough,
> And stands about the woodland ride
> Wearing white for Eastertide.

It is an attitude that the poet breaks, as he switches point of view in the next stanza from third-person to first-person: "Now, of my threescore years and ten." Robert Bly switches point of view in the same way. Here is the first stanza of "Solitude Late at Night in the Woods":

> The body is like a November birch facing the full moon
> And reaching into the cold heavens.
> In these trees there is no ambition, no sodden body, no leaves,
> Nothing but bare trunks climbing like cold fire!

The speaker's attitude is not easy to define, but perhaps we may infer what it is by observing the technique of his description. He uses metaphor—"the body is like a November birch," the "trunks climbing like cold fire"—and a negative personification, trees with no ambition. The speaker's emphasis is twofold. *Reaching* and *climbing* suggest that if the body is his body he feels desire, is animated, has life. Yet in contrast to this is the coldness of the heavens and a feeling of *departing* from life and its normal ambitions, its normal warmth. The twofold emphasis is summarized in the phrase *cold fire. Cold fire* is a *paradox,* or a seeming contradiction that is nevertheless in some significant sense true.[5] The speaker's attitude seems to be an appreciation of life *through* an awareness of death. But his use of personification insists that life dominates even the deathlike scene. Solitude may be coldness, but even such coldness has its own life. The speaker seems, then, to love the solitude of the woods and certainly not to fear it. The next stanza, switching point of view, snaps us to everyday reality: "My last walk in the trees has come." The line implies that the speaker has a deep relation to the woods, which the rest of the poem confirms. The final lines, returning to the third-person point of view, illustrate the speaker's "joy" in walking in the woods through an image that is visual, olfactory, and tactile:

> The leaves are down, and touching the soaked earth,
> Giving off the odor that partridges love.

---

5. Certain familiar paradoxes underlie many poems. Such paradoxes are: victory is defeat (or defeat is victory), sanity is insanity, strength is weakness, morality is immorality, life is death. The paradox central to Yeats' "To a Friend Whose Work Has Come to Nothing" is that of victory in defeat. Ciardi's "The Gift" uses the paradox of living death. A paradox such as "cold fire," "sweet sorrow," or "silent sound" is technically called an *oxymoron*, a somewhat abrupt or compressed combination of contradictory terms.

As with the partridges so with the speaker, who, by implication, imagines himself in solitude feeling a total involvement with nature.

It should be clear that the objectivity of the third-person point of view is far from emotionally neutral. Similarly, as we have seen in our examination of "My Last Duchess," the author, as distinct from the fictional speaker in a dramatic monologue, comes to have emotional involvement even though he is detached from his subject. In fact, in such a dramatic monologue as "My Last Duchess" we see the fictional speaker simultaneously in two ways, from two points of view—his own and the author's. At some point that is not fixed but is potential from the very beginning of the poem, we sense the presence of the author's view, in Browning's case an attitude of great warmth toward the Duchess. But such a descriptive phrase as *great warmth* leads us to note, or to confess, that English as a language is word weak for the gamut of emotions that constitute the possibilities of attitude, tone, or mood. Such words as *sympathetic, unsympathetic, personal, impersonal, formal, informal, warm, cool, serious, humorous, excited, angry, firm, harsh, depressed, bitter, hopeful,* and, perhaps above them all, *ironic* always leave us with a feeling of vagueness when compared to the precision of the poem. Yet they are helpful in acting as a bridge between the precisely articulated experience of the poet and our own personal experience.

A majority of the poems we read are written from the point of view of the first person who need not be distinguished from the author, a person concerned not so much with an apparent objectivity as with a direct response to experience. This is true, for example, of the Shakespearean sonnet "My Mistress' Eyes":

My mistress' eyes are nothing like the sun;
Coral is far more red than her lips' red:
If snow be white, why then her breasts are dun;
If hairs be wires, black wires grow on her head.
5   I have seen roses damask'd, red and white,
But no such roses see I in her cheeks;
And in some perfumes is there more delight
Than in the breath that from my mistress reeks.
I love to hear her speak, yet well I know
10   That music hath a far more pleasing sound:
I grant I never saw a goddess go;
My mistress, when she walks, treads on the ground:
    And yet, by heaven, I think my love as rare
    As any she belied with false compare.

The speaker is reacting to love conventions that are worn-out and false, cataloguing them in the context of his reaction. His attitude is one of contempt for such conventions. Thus the opening line (metrically a line whose sense demands but *one* primary accent, even though the basic iambic pattern is present) explodes on the word *nothing*, for the beginning of the sentence—"My mistress' eyes are"—is normal, disarming, and conventional. The speaker is, moreover, *ironic*, for even as early as the first line we have the possibility that he wants to affirm his lady's value in truer terms than the conventional. He *says* that his mistress' eyes are nothing like the sun, but while seeming to mean that they are less, he actually means that they are more. This discrepancy between what he seems to be saying and what he is actually saying is an ironic one.[6] His irony continues. In the third line the word *then* is particularly strong in its ironic function: since snow *is* white it is absurd to make that fact into a conditional proposition; the logician's *then* is thus part of what must be a mock ironic argument. It is mock because it imitates and derides a love convention and ironic because it means other than what it says—it means that his mistress' breasts are really a lovely dun, or grayish brown, rather than an unflattering dun, if the whiteness of the snow is the standard of comparison. Moreover, *dun* suggests "gloomy," a suggestion which the speaker is using ironically to say what is not the nature of his experience in love. The mockery continues with a second conditional proposition, one which mocks the conventional comparison of hairs to *golden* wires.

The fourth line is the first to reveal a positive fact about his love's physical appearance, a fact that is framed by a mock argument which introduces a modulation of tone from defiant rejection of conventions to modest unassuming assertion of fact. In lines five and six we have the distinct possibility that the speaker's tone is still harsh and defiant, but at the same time he is simply resigned to the fact that his love's complexion is neither of an ideal blush nor of an ideal paleness. Line eight confirms the fact that he is modulating his tone. The verb *reeks* explodes in a manner similar to the opening explosion on the noun *nothing*, yet the explosion tends, ironically, to deny its own meaning, to be no explosion but more a matter-of-fact acceptance. The speaker's ironic comment on perfume and his mistress' breath is, moreover, an *understatement* (the device opposite to hyperbole).[7] By ironically preferring a girl with a slight case of halitosis, the speaker is affirming her value in truer terms than the conventional comparisons. We have the sense that, for purposes of argument, he is *determined* to love her as she is. By line nine it is apparent that he has spent a good deal of his anger and that his anger, in turn, has been mock ironic anger. Lines nine through twelve reverse the emphasis of the two disparate tones: the tone of modest, unassuming assertion of fact becomes dominant and that of defiant rejection recedes. Neither his comment on his mistress' voice nor his statement that she treads the ground is particularly unfavorable. This suggests a suppression of his mock irony, as does the wry use of the conventional *treads* in contrast to the realistic *walks*. The closing couplet unites the defiant assertion or mock ironic tone of the speaker's opening with a tender and matter-of-fact assertion of his love's worth—all to make us think and feel about what his experience of love really is.

We may now add yet another statement about the act of reading a poem as an individuality:

6. Irony is often classified in two ways, *irony of situation* and *irony of statement*. Irony always involves a discrepancy of some kind. The situation, for example, that for want of a horseshoe nail a kingdom was lost involves the discrepancy between the smallness of a nail and the largeness of a kingdom. In irony of statement the discrepancy is between what is said and what is intended. Everyone is familiar with irony that is expressed by tone of voice; an example is the student weary of institutional food who exclaims, "Ah, delicious." Often, a description of situation is necessary to understand what meaning is intended. Imagine a lover saying, "I'll love you until the ocean evaporates." If, unlike Robert Burns, the lover is not being serious, ironic meaning must be intended; but to know what that ironic meaning is, a description of situation would be needed. All irony ultimately involves situation, but some irony *depends* on an intonation or a verbal twist. See Chapter 6 for a further discussion of irony.

7. *Understatement* is a key device used to achieve irony. You will often have occasion in poetry criticism to use the term *ironic understatement*. Frost's "I don't know where it's likely to go better" is an ironic understatement. Browning's Duke speaks in ironic understatement when he says " 'twas not her husband's presence only" that called the spot of joy into the Duchess' cheek.

5. A close awareness of the poet's point of view and of the tone of voice in which he is probably speaking are crucial to our participation in the quality and meaning of his experience.

With this statement our argument seems to draw full circle. We notice that the couplet which completes "My Mistress' Eyes" is an explicit statement, yet its meaning lies not so much in its rational content as in the excitement of the speaker's individual experience, his individuality being his style. The excitement of the poem focuses on the spending of mock anger, so that the explicit statement is probably spoken at a low energy level or is an understatement of the intensity with which its rationally clear meaning is felt. Probably, we say, but not necessarily—so able is the complex poem, as human experience itself is able, to comprehend varied interpretation.

To speak of a rationally clear meaning is to speak of *theme*. Although the term is often used in the sense of *subject*, it is better defined as a *one-sentence statement of the central idea* of the poem. Such a statement, as we have seen in "My Mistress' Eyes," may be explicit in the poem. Theme is also explicit in Donne's "They who one another keep Alive, ne'er parted be." To *select* such statements as *the* themes is, of course, to see the poems whole, to offer a judgment on their intent, to read them purposefully. Yet we should remember that any such statement has a severe limitation: out of context, the meaning emphasized tends to be the rational meaning. In "Sweetest Love," clearly more important than the rational statement is the effect on us of a speaker tenderly saying good-by to his wife, an effect of quietly expressed anguish at the fact of departure coupled with firm assurance of continuing love.

The difficulty of selecting the theme becomes even more severe when the poet avoids explicit statement in favor of implicit statement. How flat it is to take a poem like "My Last Duchess" and state the theme like this, "Real human dignity is inviolable." And yet the poet *is* concerned with such abstractions as human dignity and its inviolability. Similarly, it hardly does justice to "The Emperor of Ice-Cream" to state its theme like this, "Although death is a gloating fact of life, by humorous defiance we can assert our being." Yet the subject of the poem is, finally, the relationship of life and death. To see a poem, then, in terms of its theme is natural to the poem and natural to us—it is part of the ordering of experience which takes place in the poem and part of the craving for order that we have as human beings. We readily affirm that art is not idea, but nevertheless we need idea in order to enter into the imaginative act that is the poem.

We may take a workmanlike view of theme statement and describe its characteristics. It is good to emphasize that theme is a sentence needing a *distinct* subject and a *distinct* predicate. Following the definition we have stipulated, you cannot fairly say that the theme of poem X is love, for this would be to use theme in the sense of subject rather than in the sense of subject and predicate, and although you have written a sentence it would not be a sentence that deals wholly with the theme. If, however, you were to write, "Physical separation cannot part a man and a woman who are one in spirit," you would be making a statement of theme. Your statement would comprehend the total action or situation—sometimes we say *plot*—of the poem.[8] It would be, moreover, a statement of

---

8. *Plot* is a selection and arrangement of incidents or aspects of an incident. *Plot* is a term usually used in reference to the short story, novel, and drama—but it is also useful for poems. One of the most familiar plots is boy meets girl, boy wants girl, girl's father objects, boy wins over girl's father, boy marries girl. Nothing precludes a short poem from using this plot, but in the poem the immediate focus would be upon some particular and probably urgent aspect of the triangular relationship of father, daughter, and lover.

the theme of the poem, its central idea, rather than merely a statement of *a* theme that occurs in the poem. Your statement would involve the relationship between the specific and the general. The general subject of all poems is human experience. The action, situation, or plot of a poem may be quite specific, as the mere title of "Stopping by Woods on a Snowy Evening" would suggest. Your theme statement should not be so general that it takes as its distinct subject the mere fact of human experience. To be sure, "physical separation" as a subject is still quite general, but it is at least more specific than "human experience." On the other hand, your theme statement should not be so specific that it merely summarizes the action of the poem. Thus the statement, "A man who stops by the woods on a snowy evening decides that he has promises to keep," would not be a satisfactory theme statement. Your goal in framing a theme statement is rather to state the specific generalization which best captures what we may see as the poem's unified intent. This generalization may be reduced to a simple formula: take a specific abstraction and see it operating in terms of action and conclusion. Yet a formula must never become an end in itself, nor dare we let ourselves be beguiled by mere abstraction, mere rational content.

We may, then, add a final statement on the act of reading a poem as an individuality:

6. Since a poem by nature is an organization and a unification of human experience, it can be reduced to formulation as a theme, but a poem is always an individual rendering of the not-so-individual theme.

We have thus accumulated in something of a systematic order six statements on the act of reading a poem as an individuality. These statements may finally be reduced to two:

1. Taking pleasure in rhythm, read with the natural emphasis of speech.
2. Taking pleasure in organization or form, read for the quality and excitement of the speaker's particular experience as it is also universal, or thematic.

A good poem is a complicated thing. It invites us to *know* in the deepest sense of the word, to know life better and to expand our share in its mystery and wonder. Less cosmically, it invites us into the delight of cultivating individual taste.

TEN QUESTIONS
For Any Poem
or
For Comparing Poems

1. What is the rhythm of the poem? Make a preliminary estimate of its effect.
2. Does the poem make explicit statements? If so, do they seem central to the poet's intent?
3. What are the main objects in the poem? Are they symbols? Are they formulaic symbols or symbols complexly related to the context?
4. Who is the poem's speaker? What is his situation? How would you summarize the plot of the poem?
5. What is the poet's point of view and tone? Does it change significantly during the poem? Why is the change important to the development of the poem?
6. Is metaphor dominant in the poem? How visual is the metaphor? Can you relate it to point of view and tone?
7. Does the poem assume, contain, or depend upon some paradox or group of paradoxes?
8. Is the poem ironic? Ironic in situation, in point of view and tone, or in both?
9. What additional means does the poet use to achieve his total effect? Does he use repetition, contrast, hyperbole, understatement, personification, or a discrepancy between the seriousness of what he is saying and the lightness with which he says it?
10. What is the theme of the poem? Remember that theme is a one-sentence statement of the central idea of the poem and comprehends its total action. Expand your one-sentence statement to a short paragraph, and tell what you think is the importance or value of the theme as the poem expresses it.

2

The Uses of Language:
A Selection of Poems
with Facing-Page Notes

Words strain,
Crack and sometimes break, under the burden,
Under the tension, slip, slide, perish,
Decay with imprecision, will not stay in place,
Will not stay still.

T. S. Eliot, "Burnt Norton," ll. 152-56

The following selection of poems is accompanied by complete facing-page notes which give the meanings of words, phrases, and allusions, at least some of which are likely to be unfamiliar to you. The purpose of these notes is to suggest, graphically perhaps, that a genuinely full experience of a poem depends upon knowing what the words it uses mean or how they are being used. The poems following are, of course, of the kind that require such notes. Most poems, though not necessarily less complex, do not require them and are noticeably easier to comprehend in a first encounter; to name but a few, Housman's "Loveliest of Trees" (p. 363), Frost's "Stopping by Woods on a Snowy Evening" (p. 84), Ben Jonson's "Epitaph on Elizabeth L. H." (p. 134), Blake's "The Little Black Boy" (p. 265), Yeats' "For Anne Gregory" (p. 148). The assumption behind the selection of poems in this chapter is that a good poem is worth an extra effort. But this is true of *any* good poem and is not just a function of a poem's diction, "easy" or "hard." A poem is a word-structure, and whatever the nature of its complexity, and whether we read it aloud or silently, that is what it is and what it remains.

The Process of Definition

First, however, it is well to remind ourselves of the process of definition. A word is a sound or a combination of sounds, or its representation in writing, that symbolizes and communicates a meaning or meanings. Although the process of definition is enormously complex, it is useful to think of a definition as having two parts. The first is the *class* of objects to which the term being defined belongs. The second is the *differentiation* of the term being defined from other objects. Thus a *car,* for example, belongs to a class of objects known by the word *vehicle.* Every car is a vehicle, but not every vehicle is a car. What distinguishes or differentiates a car from other vehicles is that it is self-propelled, moves on land, has four wheels (usually!), and is mainly used to carry passengers. Such differentiations quickly begin to multiply. What actually propels the car? Of course we know that it is an internal combustion engine, but someone who had never seen a car would not automatically know this. What are the wheels made of? Of course we know that a car moves on rubber tires (natural or synthetic) inflated with air to some thirty pounds of pressure. We also know that the steering wheel is round rather than square and that the car may be stopped by pressing a brake pedal rather than by throwing an anchor out the door (a car, incidentally, has doors!). The point is that we know a great deal, if we think about it, about what a car is, and the knowledge we have about it *is* our full definition of it. Our everyday use of words takes such definition for granted. So it is, to a considerable extent, when we read a poem. A poem requires, however, an extra measure of sensitivity and concentration, since as a word-structure it is reaching for the *quality* of some aspect of human experience. It must, moreover, be freely recognized that for their unique purposes poets must often do things with words that require our close attention.

One of the most important things that a poet does with words is to play with the process of definition, to exploit the meaning which a word has in order better to comprehend the nature or quality or complexity of human experience. Milton's sonnet on his blindness, "When I Consider How My Light Is Spent" (p. 40), is, in fact, essentially built on such word play, particularly his pun on *talent* in the sense of poetic ability and in the sense of a variable unit of weight and money used in the ancient world. Milton is also alluding to the parable of the talents as told in Matthew 25:14−30, which is quoted in the footnote to the poem. If you happened not to know the parable of the talents, you could not possibly understand what Milton is doing in the poem. If you knew the word *talent* only in the sense of "superior ability," you would miss the reference to the unit of weight and money. *Talent* in the sense of superior ability is the definition that is probably as automatic as our awareness of what a car is. However, it is typical of the poem not to stop there, but rather to make a fuller use of words as its way of getting at experience.

Two terms often used in the process of definition are *denotation* and *connotation*. In logic *denotation* refers to a class of objects and *connotation* to a set of attributes. Thus Washington, Lincoln, Roosevelt (both Theodore and Franklin), Truman, and Eisenhower denote "presidents" of the United States, but the connotation of "president" is leader, power, responsibility, great historical significance, and so on. In general usage *denotation* has come to mean explicit meaning and *connotation* has come to mean suggestion. A good example of this is the word *home*, which explicitly refers to a place where one lives, but which is often used to suggest warmth, love, joy, security, parents, brothers, and sisters; in other words, *home* is a word that has positive connotations. You should note that a dictionary definition of *home* includes *both* denotative and connotative meanings. There is no definite line that can be drawn between denotation and connotation; what *home* suggests is, in fact, explicit.

The distinction between denotation and connotation is nevertheless often a useful one. For one thing, the word *home* is a clear-cut instance in which the dictionary definition of the word includes both denotative and connotative meaning. But consider now the word *test*. The dictionary definition says a means of examination, trial, or proof, a set of questions, problems, or exercises to determine a person's knowledge. It does *not* say, as many of us have felt at one time or another, either an exciting challenge or a source of mental anguish. The latter are connotations that are certainly widespread. They are meanings that the word *test* suggests rather than states, and since the dictionary does not tell us these connotations we simply have to appeal to our experience to know them. Such an appeal to experience raises a serious question; my experience may not be the same as yours, meaning that your experience is one that I may miss, and vice-versa. To return to our original example, what does the word *car* suggest to you? Independence, time payments, freedom, fun, something to take apart and put together again, mechanical mystery, careful craftsmanship, poor craftsmanship, color, speed, power? If you grant that *car* does not connote all of these things to all people, then you will readily be able to see that a poet must take into account what a word may or may not suggest. You might, in fact, enjoy turning at this time to Karl Shapiro's poem "Buick" (p. 406) as an example of one possibility of a treatment of *car*.

The notes to the poems that follow attempt to give a graphic suggestion of the connotations as well as the denotations of various words and phrases.

Anonymous Lyric of the Middle Ages
Sumer Is Icumen In

Sumer is icumen in,
   Lhude sing, cuccu!
Groweth sed, and bloweth med,
   And springth the wude nu—
         Sing cuccu!

5 Awe bleteth after lomb,
   Lhouth after calve cu;
  Bulluc sterteth, bucke verteth,
   Murie sing cuccu!

  Cuccu, cuccu, well singes thu, cuccu:
10   Ne swike thu naver nu;
  Sing cuccu, nu, sing cuccu,
   Sing cuccu, sing cuccu, nu!

	Sumer Is Icumen In	Spring has come, spring is here.
2	*Lhude sing, cuccu*	Sing loud, cuckoo bird, or more generally, sing loud as the cuckoo bird sings, exult in the advent of spring. The name *cuckoo* is an imitation of the call of the male of the species during the spring mating season.
3	*Groweth sed*	The seed grows, the seed blossoms.
	bloweth med	The meadow blooms.
4	*springth the wude nu*	The wood springs to life anew.
5	*Awe bleteth after lomb*	The ewe bleats after the lamb. The *ewe* is a female sheep. The cry of a sheep, goat, or calf is called a *bleat*. The sense here is that the mother is looking after her young.
6	*Lhouth after calve cu*	The cow lows after the calf. The *low* is the sound made by cattle, their deep bellowing or mooing. The sense is again that of the mother looking after her young.
7	*Bulluc sterteth*	The bullock leaps. A *bullock* is a young bull or bull calf.
	bucke verteth	The buck breaks wind, emits intestinal gas, farts. The buck is a male deer. The speaker humorously regards the buck breaking wind as a sign of the joy of spring.
8	*Murie sing*	Sing merrily.
9	*well singes thu*	You sing well.
10	*Ne swike thu naver nu*	Never stop singing, sing on forever. Literally, cease thou never now.
11	*Sing cuccu, nu*	Sing cuckoo, now. As in line 2, two senses are possible here. The first, and perhaps "normal" one, is that the speaker is addressing the cuckoo and asking it to begin singing. The second is the more general sense of an exhortation to everyone to sing with or as the cuckoo sings. Since the cuckoo was known as the herald of spring, both senses suggest the kind of exultation that accompanies the advent of spring.

Sir Thomas Wyatt   (1503–1542)
My Galley Chargèd with Forgetfulness

My galley chargèd with forgetfulness
Through sharp seas, in winter nights, doth pass
'Tween rock and rock; and eke mine enemy, alas,
That is my lord, steereth with cruelness;
5   And every hour a thought in readiness,
As though that death were light in such a case.
An endless wind doth tear the sail apace
Of forcèd sighs and trusty fearfulness;
A rain of tears, a cloud of dark disdain,
10   Hath done the wearèd cords great hinderance.
Wretched with error and eke with ignorance,
The stars be hid that led me to this pain;
Drownèd is reason that should me comfort,
And I remain despairing of the port.

Galley	A low sea-going vessel of ancient and medieval times, propelled by oars and sails and commonly used in the Mediterranean both as merchantship and warship. Wyatt's reader would know at once that he is not talking literally of a galley, but intends to develop a figurative comparison.
Chargèd	Heavily loaded, burdened. The difference between these two synonyms is instructive. *Heavily loaded* is literal. *Burdened* is literal but also strongly figurative—or one could say connotative. In and of itself it distinctly carries the sense of "psychologically burdened." *Chargèd* is like burdened in suggesting by itself the sense of "charged with care."
Forgetfulness	The condition of forgetting everything, that is, the feeling that one is in a state of oblivion, detached from or unaware of reality. The speaker is describing a condition of mental shock, an awareness of severe loss of meaning in his life.
2 *sharp*	Rough, violent, piercingly cold.
3 *eke*	Also. This word was archaic, no longer in wide use, even at the time Wyatt was writing this poem, which was published in *Tottel's Miscellany* (1557).
4 *my lord* *steereth*	The speaker is referring in a conventional way to his ladylove. Steers, guides the course of the galley. The speaker is referring figuratively to his ladylove guiding the course of their relationship.
5 *every hour a thought in readiness*	To the speaker every hour seems to promise more depression. The reading in *Tottel's Miscellany* for *hour* is *oar*. [*Tottel's Miscellany* (1557) is the earliest and most famous of numerous sixteenth-century English song collections. It is known by the name of its publisher, Richard Tottel (d. 1594), rather than its actual title, *Songs and Sonnets,* and contain 271 poems.]
6 *As though that* *light*	As though. The speaker probably intends a pun here, *light* in the sense of having little weight (death not mattering to him) and in the sense of illumination, a beneficent comfort, a glimpse of divine reality.
7 *apace*	Rapidly, swiftly.
8 *Of forcèd sighs* *trusty fearfulness*	The syntactical construction is loose here. *Of forcèd sighs* refers to "an endless wind" (l. 7); thus, an endless wind of forcèd sighs. The sighs are those of the speaker's ladylove. A fearfulness that may be relied upon. The speaker is complaining that his lady will not yield to him sexually.
9 *a cloud of dark disdain*	The reference here is to the expression of scorn or contempt on the lady's face.
10 *wearèd cords*	The worn ropes (that hold the sail in place). *Tottel's Miscellany* reads *wearied.*
11 *Wretched* *eke*	Living in a state of misery; unhappy. Also, contemptible. Also, as in line 3.
12 *The stars be hid*	The stars are hidden, the causes are hidden. *Stars,* which means planets as well as stars, refers to astrology, which holds that the position of the heavenly bodies has an influence on the activities of men.
13 *comfort*	*Tottel's Miscellany* reads *consort*, which means to accompany or to escort, as one ship would accompany or escort another.
14 *despairing of the port*	The speaker's ladylove here becomes the port toward which he as the galley sails. The image is conventional and specifically sexual, but *port* is more broadly suggestive of all of the emotional comfort, the safety and security of love, which the speaker feels he needs, but which he is unable to reach ("despairs of").

William Shakespeare (1564—1616)
Sonnet 30

When to the sessions of sweet silent thought
I summon up remembrance of things past,
I sigh the lack of many a thing I sought,
And with old woes new wail my dear time's waste:
5 Then can I drown an eye, unused to flow,
For precious friends hid in death's dateless night,
And weep afresh love's long since cancelled woe,
And moan the expense of many a vanished sight:
Then can I grieve at grievances foregone,

1 *sessions* — A *session* is the state of being seated. The speaker either is or imagines himself as being seated. *Session* also means the sitting of any deliberative body and the sitting of a judge or judges in order to determine causes, that is, a judicial investigation or a judicial trial; the speaker is thus making a self-examination of some kind.

   sweet silent thought — The figure of speech in which several words are used where one or a few will do is called *periphrasis*. Since thought is by definition silent, the speaker does not need, except for emphasis, to say that it is. *Sweet* means pleasing to the sense of taste, hence pleasing in general, but also precious. In addition, sweet means pleasing to the ear or melodious, which might apply here in a paradoxical sense, namely, that silence is pleasing sound. Compare this with Keats' "Heard melodies are sweet, but those unheard Are sweeter" ("Ode on a Grecian Urn," ll. 11-12).

2 *summon up* — Call up, call forth with authority or with urgency. To *summon* also means specifically to call by authority to appear before a court or a judge in order to answer a charge or give evidence; *summon up* is consistent with *sessions* as a legal metaphor.

   remembrance — Memory, recollection. Perhaps a *remembrance* or a keepsake.

   things past — Past events, what has happened to me.

3 *sigh the lack* — Lament the absence in my life; long for experiences I missed.

4 *woes* — Miseries, misfortunes, griefs, mental anguish.

   new wail — Newly wail, wail anew. To *wail* is to express pain or sorrow by prolonged cries, to complain or to lament bitterly.

   my dear time's waste — The precious time I wasted, the destruction by time of what was precious to me.

5 *drown an eye* — Cry profusely, cry limitless tears.

   unused to flow — Unaccustomed to the flow of tears. The speaker is drawing a contrast of extremes between not crying at all and crying profusely, between not expressing his emotions and expressing them freely.

6 *For* — On account of, that is, in memory of.

   hid — Hidden.

   dateless night — Endless night, eternal darkness.

7 *love's long since cancelled woe* — *Cancelled* here suggests that the debt of grief occasioned by the death of friends has been paid in full. Even though the speaker is realistically adjusted to the loss of friends through death, he nevertheless can "weep afresh."

8 *expense* — Cost, high cost, that is, loss.

   many a vanished sight — The speaker's friends lost through death.

9 *grieve at grievances* — Feel deep sorrow on account of the loss of friends through death, feel deep sorrow on account of my sufferings.

   foregone — Past, in the past; also, neglected, given up.

10   And heavily from woe to woe tell o'er
     The sad account of fore-bemoanèd moan,
     Which I new pay as if not paid before.
         But if the while I think on thee, dear friend,
         All losses are restored and sorrows end.

John Donne   (1572–1631)
The Canonization

For Godsake hold your tongue and let me love,
    Or chide my palsy or my gout,
My five gray hairs or ruin'd fortune flout,
    With wealth your state, your mind with Arts improve,

10	*heavily*	Several meanings are appropriate here. *Heavily* means in a heavy manner, ponderously, and relates to the act of counting ("tell o'er"). It also means with sorrow, as well as forcibly, violently, intensely.
10-11	*tell o'er The sad account*	Count up again the charges of grief. The speaker is comparing his griefs to a money reckoning. An *account* is a statement of moneys received and paid, with a calculation of the balance. *Tell* means to count, reckon up, or calculate. It also means to give a description of and to announce, to proclaim.
11	*fore-bemoanèd moan*	The grief which I have already expressed or experienced.
12	*new*	Newly.
	as if not paid before	As if the charges of grief had not been paid already, as if my suffering for the loss of friends through death had not occurred.
13	*the while*	The time to which the speaker is referring in the previous lines, the time during which his thoughts take their direction.

	Canonization	The action of placing formally in the canon or list of saints. In the ecclesiastical definition, a saint is a person formally recognized by the Church as having attained, by living an exceptionally holy life, an exalted station in heaven and as being entitled to the veneration of the faithful.
1	*For Godsake*	An exclamation of impatience or irritation. Literally, for God's sake, that is, acting in a way assumed to be pleasing to God.
	love	Express love, show love in action, make love (in a sexual sense).
2	*chide*	Find fault with, scold me because of.
	palsy	Paralysis resulting from a disorder in the nervous system, sometimes accompanied by involuntary tremors. An enfeebled condition, helplessness.
	gout	A disease characterized by painful inflammation of the smaller joints, especially that of the big toe. It often spreads, however, to the larger joints and to the internal organs. Gout is a disturbance of the uric-acid metabolism, occurs in fits, and may be precipitated by excessive intake of food and alcoholic drink.
3	*My five gray hairs*	That is, a clear sign that the speaker is aging, with just enough gray hair to be visible.
	ruin'd fortune	Loss of prosperity, with chance, accident, or bad luck regarded as the cause.
	flout	A verb meaning to "scorn" with compound direct object "hairs" and "fortune." The speaker is saying, chide my palsy, flout my five gray hairs, etc. Inversion of normal word order, subject followed by verb, is common in the poem.
4	*your state*	Your condition in life, your social status; also, how you feel toward life (your state of mind). *State* also means one's existence as a spiritual being.
	Arts	Skills, learning, with particular reference to areas of experience in which taste is an important factor, such as music, painting, poetry, or architecture.

5   Take you a course, get you a place,
         Observe His Honour, or His Grace,
Or the King's real, or his stamped face
    Contemplate, what you will, approve,
    So you will let me love.

10 Alas, alas, who's injur'd by my love?
     What merchant's ships have my sighs drown'd?
Who says my tears have overflow'd his ground?
    When did my colds a forward spring remove?
    When did the heats which my veins fill
15   Add one more to the plaguey Bill?
Soldiers find wars, and Lawyers find out still
    Litigious men, which quarrels move,
    Though she and I do love.

     Call us what you will, we are made such by love;
20   Call her one, me another fly,
    We are tapers too, and at our own cost die,

5 *Take you a course*
Follow a particular course of study (as at a university) and, more generally, choose for yourself a direction in life that suits you.

a place
An appointment at court, a high-ranking position.

6 *Observe*
Regard with attention, study closely.

His Honour . . . His Grace
Honorific or respectful terms applied to people of high rank or social standing. *Grace* (His Grace, Her Grace, Your Grace) is commonly used with reference to or in addressing the king or queen.

7 *his stamped face*
The likeness of the King stamped on coins.

8 *what you will, approve*
Prove, or put to the test of experience, whatever you wish to find out. *What you will* may also be read as a separate thought: do what you will, do whatever you wish to do, thus making *approve* in turn a separate thought.

11 *drown'd*
Overwhelmed, caused to sink. The figure of speech here is a hyperbole, the speaker comparing in a negative sense his lover's sighs to a wind strong enough to cause a sailing vessel to sink. To imagine a lover's sighs as strong enough to sink a ship was conventional love rhetoric, that is, a cliché, in Donne's time.

12 *overflow'd*
Flooded.

13 *colds*
Chills, depression of spirit (that a lover at one time or another is bound to feel).

a forward spring remove
Cause the water of an onrushing spring to stop flowing by freezing it. *Forward* means eager, energetic. A *spring* is a flow of water rising naturally out of the earth, hence a desirable source of water supply.

14 *the heats*
The fevers, the lover's passions. In the old physiology a person's temperament was thought to be determined by a combination of such qualities in the fluids of the body as cold, hot, moist, and dry.

15 *one more*
One more name.

the plaguey Bill
The list of people who died of the plague. In Donne's time epidemic diseases such as bubonic plague were responsible for so many deaths that it was necessary to have a method of keeping track of those who died. Weekly lists were compiled for each parish.

16 *find out still*
Continue to discover.

17 *Litigious*
Fond of disputes, quarrelsome, fond of going to the law to settle quarrels.

which quarrels move
Whom quarrels move to go to the law.

20 *fly*
Any winged insect, here probably the moth because the moth would be attracted to and perhaps burned by a candle flame and, as in the next line, at its "own cost die."

21 *tapers*
Candles.

at our own cost die
There is a play on words here. The tapers or candles are consumed as they burn, but in Donne's time to *die* also meant to consummate the sexual act, to have an orgasm.

And we in us find th' Eagle and the Dove.
The Phoenix riddle hath more wit
By us, we two being one, are it.
25 So to one neutral thing both sexes fit,
We die and rise the same, and prove
Mysterious by this love.

We can die by it, if not live by love,
And if unfit for tombs and hearse
30 Our legend be, it will be fit for verse;
And if no piece of Chronicle we prove,
We'll build in sonnets pretty rooms;

22	*in us*	In ourselves.
	th' Eagle and the Dove	The eagle is here a symbol of earthly strength and the dove of heavenly meekness. *Eagle* and *dove* are also terms from alchemy, the aim of which was to transmute base metals into gold. The terms refer to processes leading to such transmutation.
23	*The Phoenix riddle*	The phoenix was a mythological bird, only one of which existed at any one time. After living a thousand years it lit its own funeral pyre, was consumed by it while singing its own funeral song, and was then reborn from its own ashes. It was thus a symbol of immortality and of rebirth. The "riddle" applied to the sexes is that they are consumed in the fire of their own passion but are reborn to new desire.
	wit	Sense, meaning, wisdom.
24	*By us*	Through us, because of us.
25	*one neutral thing*	The phoenix is described as neither male nor female. Also, the oneness of a sexual union gives the sexes the same identity rather than continuing the identity of male as male and female as female. *Neutral* implies that the sexes are normally at odds with each other —in a battle—but that love dissolves their differences.
	fit	Harmonize with, but the reference here is also specifically to the sexual act.
26	*die*	Die in the manner of the phoenix bird, and consummate the sexual act, as in line 21.
	rise the same	Are reborn, are regenerated sexually, are resurrected, with perhaps an allusion to the Resurrection of Christ.
27	*Mysterious*	Beyond human knowledge or comprehension, related to religious truth or religious rite (such as the mystery of the Eucharist).
28	*die by it*	That is, die for it, assert with finality the meaning and the value of our love, renounce the world. See also notes to lines 21 and 26.
29	*tombs and hearse*	A *tomb* is a place of burial, often an above-ground structure. *Hearse* has several meanings which fit the context here: a coffin; a permanent framework of iron or other metal fixed over a tomb to support rich coverings; a temple-shaped structure of wood used in royal and noble funerals, decorated with banners and often with short poems or epitaphs pinned upon it. The current meaning of *hearse*, a carriage or car for carrying the coffin at a funeral, probably also applies. In any case, the speaker's emphasis is clearly on the contrast between worldly show and true meaning.
30	*legend*	Story, inscription, or motto, story of the life of a saint.
31	*Chronicle*	A detailed chronological record of historical events. Chronicles were a common literary form in the sixteenth century. Some well-known examples are the works of Richard Grafton (1568), Raphael Holinshed (1577), and John Stow (1580).
	prove	Prove to be.
32	*sonnets*	A general term for love poems as well as specifically the fourteen-line poem usually in iambic pentameter and with a relatively fixed rhyme scheme.

As well a well-wrought urn becomes
The greatest ashes, as half-acre tombs,
35   And by these hymns, all shall approve
Us *Canoniz'd* for Love:

And thus invoke us; You whom reverend love
    Made one another's hermitage;
You, to whom love was peace, that now is rage;
40   Who did the whole world's soul contract, and drove
        Into the glasses of your eyes
        (So made such mirrors and such spies
That they did all to you epitomize,)
    Countries, Towns, Courts: Beg from above
45   A pattern of your love!

33	*a well-wrought urn*	An *urn* is an earthenware or metal vase used by the ancient Greeks and Romans and others to preserve the ashes of the dead, but *well-wrought urn* refers also to an excellent poem that would serve as a fit and permanent memorial to the lovers.
	becomes	Is appropriate or suitable to.
34	*The greatest ashes*	The ashes of great people.
35	*hymns*	Songs of praise to God, specifically metrical compositions adapted to be sung in a religious service. The speaker is referring to the "sonnets" which he and his love would write.
	all	All who follow us, posterity.
36	*Canoniz'd*	Placed formally in the list or canon of saints, consecrated. See note to poem title.
37	*invoke*	Appeal to for aid, as in prayers directed to a saint in heaven.
	reverend love	Love worthy of deep respect or reverence.
38	*hermitage*	A solitary dwelling place. Hermits typically chose a life of solitude for religious reasons.
39	*that now is rage*	What we are now experiencing is animal desire, mere sexual passion. The speaker imagines those who invoke the sainted lovers as aware of a lack of spirituality in their sexual relationships.
40	*Who*	You (that is, the sainted lovers) who.
	contract	Cause to shrink. The sainted lovers are regarded as a microcosm or representation in their small world of the soul of the entire universe. The power of their love is so great that it concentrates all of the meaning, value, and spirituality in the universe.
40-41	*drove Into the glasses of your eyes*	The lovers are imagined as seeing the world ("Countries, Towns, Courts," which are the objects of the verb "drove") and forcing it to be contained inside their own eyes. *Glasses* are looking glasses, glass mirrors, and also lenses.
42	*So made*	So you made.
	such mirrors and such spies	The eyes of the lovers became like mirrors reflecting the events of the world and like spies uncovering all knowledge of the world.
43	*they*	The eyes of the lovers (mirrors and spies).
	did all to you epitomize	Summarized or concentrated all of the world for you.
44-45	*Beg from above A pattern of your love*	Those who invoke the sainted lovers ask them to beg from Heaven a pattern of their love so that others might be enabled to follow it.

Sonnet 9

If poisonous minerals, and if that tree
Whose fruit threw death on else immortal us,
If lecherous goats, if serpents envious
Cannot be damn'd, alas, why should I be?
5   Why should intent or reason, born in me,
Make sins, else equal, in me more heinous?
And mercy being easy and glorious
To God, in his stern wrath why threatens he?
But who am I that dare dispute with thee
10   O God? O! of thine only worthy blood
And my tears make a heavenly Lethean flood,
And drown in it my sins' black memory.
That thou remember them, some claim as debt;
I think it mercy if thou wilt forget.

1	*minerals*	Any natural substances, either animal or vegetable, but specifically mineral medicines or poisons. The speaker is referring to those minerals which by their own nature are poisonous.
	that tree	The tree of knowledge of good and evil. "And the Lord God commanded the man [Adam], saying, Of every tree of the garden thou mayest freely eat: But of the tree of the knowledge of good and evil, thou shalt not eat of it: for in the day that thou eatest thereof thou shalt surely die" (Genesis 2:16-17).
2	*Whose fruit*	"And when the woman saw that the tree *was* good for food, and that it *was* pleasant to the eyes, and a tree to be desired to make *one* wise, she took of the fruit thereof, and did eat, and gave also unto her husband with her; and he did eat" (Genesis 3:6).
	on else immortal us	On us who would have been immortal had the fruit of the forbidden tree not been tasted.
3	*lecherous goats*	Goats were commonly associated with lechery. *Goat* is still used figuratively to refer to a licentious man. The speaker may also have in mind the satyr, a creature of Greek mythology, part goat, part man, and regarded as a symbol of lechery or lustfulness.
	serpents envious	In tempting Eve to eat the forbidden fruit, the Devil assumed the form of a serpent, that is, a reptile or a poisonous snake (Genesis 3: 1-5). A serpent is a symbol of envy, jealousy, malice, deceit.
5	*intent or reason*	*Intent* is purpose formed in the mind, that which is willed, an act of the mind, a thought of any kind. *Reason* is the intellectual power employed in adapting thought or action to some end. The two terms are closely related, or one could say that some of the differences between them are merely nominal, but the crucial point of difference seems to be in the fact that reason is a capacity for complex thought, for intricate argument, that which so markedly distinguishes man from the lower animals.
	born in me	Natural characteristics, for which the speaker is not personally responsible.
6	*else equal*	Otherwise the same. Why, for example, should intent or reason make lechery in a man different from lechery in a goat?
	in me	Committed by me.
	heinous	Hateful, vile, outrageously wicked.
8	*To God*	For God to grant or show.
	wrath	Violent anger, especially that displayed by way of demanding punishment; also, righteous indignation (of God).
9	*dispute*	Argue, debate heatedly, oppose.
10	*thine only worthy blood*	The blood of Christ, the Son of God, whose blood was shed on the cross for the salvation of man.
11	*And my tears*	And of my tears. The metaphor "tears of repentance" is implied here, but the speaker is deliberately more general.
	Lethean	In Greek mythology, Lethe was a river in Hades whose water produced forgetfulness of the past or oblivion in those who drank it.
12	*my sins' black memory*	The black memory which I have of my sins, the pangs of conscience which I suffer, or your (God's) view of me as a sinner.
13	*them*	The sins.
	debt	The debt which as sinners they owe to God, or the debt which God owes to them not to overlook their sins.

John Milton   (1608–1674)
When I Consider How My Light Is Spent[1]

When I consider how my light is spent
Ere half my days in this dark world and wide,
And that one talent which is death to hide
Lodged with me useless, though my soul more bent
5 To serve therewith my Maker, and present
My true account, lest He returning chide,
"Doth God exact day-labor, light denied?"
I fondly ask. But Patience, to prevent
That murmur, soon replies, "God doth not need
10 Either man's work or His own gifts. Who best
Bear His mild yoke, they serve Him best. His state
Is kingly: thousands at His bidding speed,
And post o'er land and ocean without rest;
They also serve who only stand and wait."

1. In this poem Milton is alluding to the parable of the talents in Matthew 25:14-30:

> For the kingdom of heaven is as a man travelling into a far country who called his own servants, and delivered unto them his goods. And unto one he gave five talents, to another two, and to another one; to every man according to his several abilities; and straightway took his journey. Then he that had received the five talents went and traded with the same, and made them other five talents. And likewise he that had received two, he also gained other two. But he that had received one went and digged in the earth, and hid his lord's money. After a long time the lord of those servants cometh, and reckoneth with them. And so he that had received five talents came and brought other five talents, saying, Lord, thou deliveredst unto me five talents: behold, I have gained beside them five talents more. His lord said unto him, Well done, thou good and faithful servant: thou hast been faithful over a few things, I will make thee ruler over many things: enter thou into the joy of thy lord. He also that had received two talents came and said, Lord, thou deliveredst unto me two talents: behold, I have gained two other talents beside them. His lord said unto him, Well done, good and faithful servant; thou hast been faithful over a few things, I will make thee ruler over many things: enter thou into the joy of thy lord. Then he which had received the one talent came and said, Lord I knew thee that thou art an hard man, reaping where thou hast not sown, and gathering where thou hast not strawed: And I was afraid, and went and hid thy talent in the earth: lo, there thou hast that is thine. His lord answered and said unto him, Thou wicked and slothful servant, thou knewest that I reap where I sowed not, and gather where I have not strawed: Thou oughtest therefore to have put my money to the exchangers, and then at my coming I should have received mine own with usury. Take therefore the talent from him, and give it unto him which hath ten talents. For unto every one that hath shall be given, and he shall have abundance: but from him that hath not shall be taken away even that which he hath. And cast ye the unprofitable servant into outer darkness: there shall be weeping and gnashing of teeth.

My Light	His eyesight; Milton was blind at the time he wrote this sonnet. Also, his poetic genius, his talent as a poet, the illumination of his soul by divine truth.
Is Spent	Was spent, has been spent, meaning used up, paid out, exhausted.
2 *Ere half my days*	Milton was forty-three years old when, in 1651, he became blind. *Ere* means before. The sense here is, before half of the days of my life have passed.
in this dark world	The syntactical relationship of this phrase to the rest of the sentence is not altogether clear. The likely sense of the line is, before half of the days of my life have passed in this wicked world. *Dark world* would thus be a general reference to the condition of life as evil or devoid of spiritual illumination. The emphasis on the opening line would then be on a contrast between the spiritual illumination offered by the poet and a world distinctly lacking it. There is also an immediate allusion to the Puritan Revolution as a time of great stress. And on the literal level, it is a dark world because he is blind.
3 *that one talent*	Milton is punning here on *talent* in the sense of poetic ability and in the sense of a variable unit of weight and money used by the Assyrians, Babylonians, Greeks, Romans, and other peoples of the ancient world. He alludes specifically to the parable of the talents told by Jesus.
4 *Lodged with me*	Placed inside me, contained within me. From the French *loge,* hut, cottage.
more bent	Is more bent.
5 *To serve therewith my Maker*	To serve by means of that (talent) my Maker, to use my talent to serve God.
6 *My true account*	An account of the deeds of my life. Note the use of *account* here as a money reckoning in accord with the parable of the talents.
lest He returning chide	An allusion to the second coming of Christ, as well as to the return of the lord in the parable of the talents. Note that "chide" marks the end of the temporal clause begun by the first word of the poem.
8 *fondly*	Foolishly.
prevent	Forestall, intercept, outrun. A theological meaning of *prevent* is go before with spiritual help, with God's grace, as an anticipation of human action or human need.
10 *His own gifts*	The gifts which God gives to men, such as Milton's poetic talent.
11 *His mild yoke*	Probably an allusion to Jesus' saying: "Come unto me, all ye that labour and are heavy laden, and I will give you rest. Take my yoke upon you, and learn of me; for I am meek and lowly in heart: and ye shall find rest unto your **souls.** For my yoke is easy, and my burden is light" (Matthew 11:28-30).
12 *thousands*	Thousands of angels.
bidding	Command.
13 *post*	Travel with speed.
14 *They also serve*	The angels of the highest order were those who served God in contemplation.
wait	Keep watch, be in readiness to receive orders. Also, look forward to with desire, be in a state of continuing expectation.

Samuel Taylor Coleridge   (1772–1834)
Kubla Khan
Or, A Vision in a Dream. A Fragment

In Xanadu did Kubla Khan
A stately pleasure-dome decree:
Where Alph, the sacred river, ran
Through caverns measureless to man
5   Down to a sunless sea.
So twice five miles of fertile ground
With walls and towers were girdled round:
And there were gardens bright with sinuous rills,
Where blossomed many an incense-bearing tree;
10 And here were forests ancient as the hills,
Enfolding sunny spots of greenery.

	A Vision in a Dream	Coleridge writes in a note on a manuscript copy of the poem: "This fragment with a good deal more, not recoverable, composed, in a sort of reverie brought on by two grains of opium, taken to check a dysentery, at a farmhouse between Porlock and Linton, a quarter of a mile from Culbone Church, in the fall of the year, 1797."
1	*Xanadu*	A city, region, or province in China, and Kubla Khan's capital, probably located near what is now Peking.
	Kubla Khan	Mongol emperor (c. 1215-1294) who founded the Yüan dynasty (a succession of rulers from the same family or line) in China. His grandfather was Genghis Khan, who conquered Mongolia, China, and other lands. *Khan* is a title of respect for rulers; its Turkish root simply means sovereign or ruler.
2	*A stately pleasure dome*	Royal palace. In his preface to the poem Coleridge describes himself as falling asleep in his chair at the moment he was reading a sentence from Samual Purchas' *Purchas His Pilgrimage* (1613). Purchas writes of the palace: "In Xamdu did Cublai Can build a stately palace, encompassing sixteen miles of plain ground with a wall, wherein are fertile meadows, pleasant springs, delightful streams, and all sorts of beasts of chase and game, and in the midst thereof a sumptuous house of pleasure."
	decree	Command to be built.
3	*Alph*	The river Alph, or Alpheus, is actually in Greece. In Greek mythology its waters were said to flow under the sea and to emerge as the fountains of Arethusa at Syracuse in Sicily. J. L. Lowes suggests that Coleridge associated the river Alph with the Nile, which according to myth flowed underground from Asia to Africa.
4	*Through caverns*	Through a network of underground caverns or caves.
	measureless to man	Unable to be measured by man because of their inaccessibility and extent; also, beyond rational comprehension.
5	*a sunless sea*	An underground sea, a sea that is sunless because it is underground. *Sunless* also suggests certain qualities, such as cheerlessness, and thus perhaps the dark regions of experience.
6	*twice five miles*	Ten miles (*twice* does not modify *girdled*).
7	*walls and towers*	Normally towers would be part of a wall enclosing a given area. The image suggested here is probably that of a wall that is essentially continuous.
	girdled	Surrounded, enclosed. *To girdle* means to surround as with a girdle or belt worn around the waist.
8	*gardens bright*	Bright gardens. *Bright* does not modify *sinuous rills.*
	sinuous rills	A *rill* is a brook or small stream. *Sinuous* means winding, abounding in turns and curves.
9	*Where*	In which (gardens).
	incense-bearing tree	*Incense* is an aromatic gum, or mixture of gums and spices, that burns with a fragrant odor; such gums are sometimes obtained from certain species of trees, as, for example, is the case with frankincense. The burning of incense is particularly associated with religious ceremony.
11	*Enfolding*	Enclosing, embracing.

But oh! that deep romantic chasm which slanted
Down the green hill athwart a cedarn cover!
A savage place! as holy and enchanted
15 As e'er beneath a waning moon was haunted
By woman wailing for her demon-lover!
And from this chasm, with ceaseless turmoil seething,
As if this earth in fast thick pants were breathing,
A mighty fountain momently was forced:
20 Amid whose swift half-intermitted burst
Huge fragments vaulted like rebounding hail,
Or chaffy grain beneath the thresher's flail:
And 'mid these dancing rocks at once and ever
It flung up momently the sacred river.
25 Five miles meandering with a mazy motion
Through wood and dale the sacred river ran,
Then reached the caverns measureless to man,

12	*romantic chasm*	A *chasm* is a deep crack in the earth's surface, an abyss. *Romantic* means having the qualities of a romance, that is, suggestive of things remote from ordinary life, fabulous, imaginary, beyond what is rational, marked by imaginative appeal; it also suggests adventurousness. A *romance* is a narrative dealing with the adventures of a hero of chivalry in the age of knighthood, and, more generally, a narrative whose scenes and incidents are remote from ordinary life, are extravagant.
13	*athwart*	Across, from one side to the other.
	a cedarn cover	A concentration of cedar trees. *Cedarn* is a poetic term meaning pertaining to cedar trees.
14	*enchanted*	Endowed with magical powers.
15	*waning*	Declining (as from full to half to crescent to new moon), growing dim.
16	*demon-lover*	Perhaps a cruel lover. A *demon* is a supernatural being intermediate between gods and men, an evil spirit.
17	*turmoil*	Extreme agitation, commotion. *Turmoil* is an abstract word; it does not have a concrete referent. Consider, however, the possibility of sexual connotations in lines 17 to 28.
	seething	Boiling, churning and foaming as if boiling, in a state of violent agitation.
18	*fast thick pants*	Rapid heavy breaths, a close succession of gasps.
19	*momently*	Every instant; that is, a rapid succession of eruptions of the water.
20	*Amid*	In the middle of.
	half-intermitted	Momentarily interrupted.
21	*vaulted*	Leaped, shot up.
	rebounding	Springing back from the force of impact, leaping.
22	*chaffy grain*	Grain mixed with chaff. *Chaff* refers to the husks of grain which are separated from the grain by threshing (by mechanical means).
	the thresher's flail	The *thresher* is one who threshes grain by beating it, for example, with a *flail,* a hand instrument consisting of a wooden handle at the end of which a club is hung so as to swing freely.
23	*'mid*	Amid, as in line 20.
24	*It*	The chasm.
	momently	See note to line 19.
25	*meandering*	Winding.
	mazy	Full of windings and turnings, resembling a maze or baffling network of winding and crossing paths.
26	*dale*	Valley. From the old Teutonic word *dalom,* a deep or low place. In literary English *dale* is considered poetic, that is, not a word normally used in writing or speaking.
27	*measureless to man*	See note to line 4.

And sank in tumult to a lifeless ocean:
And 'mid this tumult Kubla heard from far
30 Ancestral voices prophesying war!
   The shadow of the dome of pleasure
   Floated midway on the waves;
   Where was heard the mingled measure
   From the fountain and the caves.
35 It was a miracle of rare device,
A sunny pleasure-dome with caves of ice!

   A damsel with a dulcimer
   In a vision once I saw:
   It was an Abyssinian maid,
40   And on her dulcimer she played,
   Singing of Mount Abora.
   Could I revive within me
   Her symphony and song,
   To such a deep delight 'twould win me,
45 That with music loud and long,
I would build that dome in air,
That sunny dome! those caves of ice!
And all who heard should see them there,
And all should cry, Beware! Beware!
50 His flashing eyes, his floating hair!
Weave a circle round him thrice,
And close your eyes with holy dread,
For he on honey-dew hath fed,
And drunk the milk of Paradise.

28	*tumult*	Noisy movement, agitation, commotion.
	a lifeless ocean	An underground sea, lifeless probably in the obvious sense of the absence of wind and marine life, but also in the figurative sense of dull, depressing, lacking in the vitality associated with life.
29	*'mid*	In the middle of, as in line 20.
30	*Ancestral voices*	See note to line 1.
	prophesying	Predicting.
32	*on the waves*	Of the sacred river Alph.
33	*the mingled measure*	*Measure* means poetic rhythm, beat, musical quality. *Mingled* means mixed and refers to the combination of sounds from the two different sources, *fountain* and *caves*.
35	*a miracle of rare device*	A perfect creation, a work of art.
37	*damsel*	A young unmarried woman, originally one of noble birth.
	dulcimer	A musical instrument with strings of graduated lengths stretched over a sound box and either struck with two padded hammers held in the hands or plucked.
38	*a vision*	See note to poem title.
39	*an Abyssinian maid*	*Abyssinia* is another name for Ethiopia, a country in east central Africa; it includes the regions of the upper Nile (see note to line 3). A *maid* is a young unmarried woman.
41	*Mount Abora*	A name coined by Coleridge probably to suggest an earthly paradise and possibly the same earthly paradise as Milton's Mount Amara (*Paradise Lost,* IV, 281).
43	*symphony*	Harmony of sound, harmonious music; specifically, a passage for a single instrument occurring in a vocal composition, an accompaniment to a song.
46	*in air*	That is, in his imagination.
49	*Beware! Beware!*	The reason for this cry, as becomes clear in the following lines, is that the poet takes on the identity of a magician, particularly the kind who would inspire awe or dread.
50	*his floating hair*	Pointing in all directions, as if blown by the wind or because of rapid movements of the body.
51	*Weave a circle round him thrice*	To ward off any evil spirit which might possess him.
53	*honey-dew*	A sweet sticky substance found on the leaves and stems of trees and plants and excreted by various insects, especially aphids; an ideally sweet or luscious substance.
54	*the milk of Paradise*	The milk found in Paradise, that is, that (food) which is perfect or ideal, inspiration.

Lewis Carroll (Charles Lutwidge Dodgson)   (1832–1898)
Jabberwocky[1]

'Twas brillig, and the slithy toves
    Did gyre and gimble in the wabe;
All mimsy were the borogoves,
    And the mome raths outgrabe.

5 "Beware the Jabberwock, my son!
    The jaws that bite, the claws that catch!
Beware the Jubjub bird, and shun
    The frumious Bandersnatch!"

He took his vorpal sword in hand:
10   Long time the manxome foe he sought,—
So rested he by the Tumtum tree,
    And stood awhile in thought.

And as in uffish thought he stood,
    The Jabberwock, with eyes of flame,

1. This is a nonsense poem in which Lewis Carroll invents words for fun. To *jabber* means to talk rapidly and indistinctly or unintelligibly. *Wocky* is Carroll's own coinage, though he does say in a letter to the fourth class of the Girls' Latin School in Boston that he found that "the Anglo-Saxon word 'wocer' or 'wocor' signifies 'offspring' or 'fruit.'" The following conversation between Alice and Humpty Dumpty about the first stanza of the poem appears in Chapter Six of *Through the Looking Glass*. The reader should also consult *The Annotated Alice,* ed. Martin Gardner (New York: Clarkson N. Potter, 1960), for a full treatment of the language of the poem.

"You seem very clever at explaining words, Sir," said Alice. "Would you kindly tell me the meaning of the poem called 'Jabberwocky'?"

"Let's hear it," said Humpty Dumpty. "I can explain all the poems that ever were invented—and a good many that haven't been invented just yet."

This sounded very hopeful, so Alice repeated the first verse:—

  "'Twas brillig, and the slithy toves
    Did gyre and gimble in the wabe:
  All mimsy were the borogoves,
    And the mome raths outgrabe."

"That's enough to begin with," Humpty Dumpty interrupted: "there are plenty of hard words there. *'Brillig'* means four o'clock in the afternoon—the time when you begin *broiling* things for dinner."

"That'll do very well," said Alice: "and *'slithy'*?"

"Well, *'slithy'* means 'lithe and slimy.' 'Lithe' is the same as 'active.' You see it's like a portmanteau—there are two meanings packed up into one word."

8 *frumious*

In his preface to "The Hunting of the Snark" Carroll writes: "This also seems a fitting occasion to notice the other hard words in that poem ['Jabberwocky']. Humpty-Dumpty's theory, of two meanings packed into one word like a portmanteau, seems to me the right explanation for all. For instance, take the two words 'fuming' and 'furious.' Make up your mind that you will say both words, but leave it unsettled which you will say first. Now open your mouth and speak. If your thoughts incline ever so little towards 'fuming,' you will say 'fuming-furious'; if they turn, by even a hair's breadth, towards 'furious,' you will say 'furious-fuming'; but if you have that rarest of gifts, a perfectly balanced mind, you will say 'frumious.'"

9 *vorpal*

Carroll wrote on December 18, 1877, to a child friend, Maud Standen, "I am afraid I can't explain 'vorpal blade' for you—nor yet 'tulgey wood.'"

10 *manxome*

"Manx" is the Celtic name for the Isle of Man.

11 *Tumtum*

An imitation of the sound of a stringed instrument, especially when strummed monotonously. Variant forms are tum-a-tum and tum-ti-tum.

13 *uffish*

Carroll continues in his letter of December 18, 1877, to Maud Standen, "but I did make an explanation once for 'uffish thought' —It seems to suggest a state of mind when the voice is gruffish, the manner roughish, and the temper huffish."

"I see it now," Alice remarked thoughtfully: "and what are *'toves'*?"

"Well, *'toves'* are something like badgers—they're something like lizards—and they're something like corkscrews."

"They must be very curious-looking creatures."

"They are that," said Humpty Dumpty: "also they make their nests under sundials—also they live on cheese."

"And what's to *'gyre'* and to *'gimble'*?"

"To *'gyre'* is to go round and round like a gyroscope. To *'gimble'* is to make holes like a gimlet."

"And *'the wabe'* is the grass-plot round a sundial, I suppose?" said Alice, surprised at her own ingenuity.

"Of course it is. It's called *'wabe'* you know, because it goes a long way before it, and a long way behind it——"

"And a long way beyond it on each side," Alice added.

"Exactly so. Well then, *'mimsy'* is 'flimsy and miserable' (there's another portmanteau for you). And a *'borogove'* is a thin shabby-looking bird with its feathers sticking out all round—something like a live mop."

"And then *'mome raths'*?" said Alice. "I'm afraid I'm giving you a great deal of trouble."

"Well, a *'rath'* is a sort of green pig: but *'mome'* I'm not certain about. I think it's short for 'from home'—meaning that they'd lost their way, you know."

"And what does *'outgrabe'* mean?"

"Well, *'outgribing'* is something between bellowing and whistling, with a kind of sneeze in the middle: however, you'll hear it done, maybe—down in the wood yonder—and, when you've once heard it, you'll be *quite* content."

15 Came whiffling through the tulgey wood,
        And burbled as it came!

    One two! One two! And through and through
        The vorpal blade went snicker-snack!
    He left it dead, and with its head
20   He went galumphing back.

    "And hast thou slain the Jabberwock?
        Come to my arms, my beamish boy!
    O frabjous day! Callooh! Callay!"
        He chortled in his joy.

25 'Twas brillig, and the slithy toves
        Did gyre and gimble in the wabe;
    All mimsy were the borogoves,
        And the mome raths outgrabe.

Gerard Manley Hopkins   (1844–1889)
The Windhover
To Christ Our Lord

I caught this morning morning's minion, king-
    dom of daylight's dauphin, dapple-dawn-drawn Falcon, in his riding

15	*whiffling*	Moving lightly as if blown by a puff of air, fluttering; also, making a light whistling sound. Martin Gardner writes that this word "usually had reference to blowing unsteadily in short puffs, hence it came to be a slang term for being variable and evasive," and also that in an earlier century it meant "smoking and drinking" (*The Annotated Alice,* p. 196).
	tulgey	See note to line 9.
16	**burbled**	To *burble* means to bubble and is a word that imitates a sound; thus the suggestion here could be "made a bubbling sound." Martin Gardner suggests that the word is a combination of "burst" and "bubble."
18	*snicker-snack*	Apparently a humorous imitation of a sound.
20	*galumphing*	The *Oxford English Dictionary* defines this word as Carroll's combination of "gallop" and "triumphant" and meaning "to march on exultantly with irregular bounding movements."
22	*beamish*	Beaming, shining brightly or radiantly, smiling expansively.
23	*Callooh! Callay*	The *calloo* is a species of arctic duck that winters in northern Scotland, so named for its evening call, "Calloo! Calloo!" *Callay* seems to be a playful variation of the sound.
24	*chortled*	This word, coined by Lewis Carroll, is now part of the English language. It combines chuckled and snorted and means chuckled gleefully.

	Windhover	A name for the kestrel, a species of small hawk, the name derived from its habit of hovering in the air with its head to the wind; that is, *wind* plus *hover.* To *hover* means to fly, soar, or float as if suspended, to hang or remain suspended in the air over or about a particular spot.
1	*I caught this morning morning's minion*	This morning I caught morning's minion, but the context does not preclude the first *morning* from being an adjective modifying *morning's. A minion* is a loved object, a darling, a favorite, especially the favorite of a sovereign, an obsequious or servile dependent; also, a lover or ladylove, especially a mistress or paramour.
1-2	*kingdom of daylight's dauphin*	The dauphin of the kingdom of daylight (in apposition to minion). *Dauphin* was the title of the eldest son of the king of France from 1349 to 1830; hence here the figurative meaning is that of heir to a kingly state, to a condition of splendor. *Dauphin* was a proper name which was the same word in French as *dolphin,* the sea mammal which is sometimes called "porpoise."
2	*dapple-dawn-drawn*	*Dapple* means spotted or mottled. The senses of *drawn* which seem to fit here are traced, sketched, or outlined (by the *dawn*), and pulled (in the direction of the dawn).

Of the rolling level underneath him steady air, and striding
High there, how he rung upon the rein of a wimpling wing
5 In his ecstasy! then off, off forth on swing,
As a skate's heel sweeps smooth on a bow-bend: the hurl and gliding
Rebuffed the big wind. My heart in hiding
Stirred for a bird,—the achieve of, the mastery of the thing!

Brute beauty and valor and act, oh, air, pride, plume here
10 Buckle! And the fire that breaks from thee then, a billion
Times told lovelier, more dangerous, O my chevalier!

No wonder of it: shéer plód makes plough down sillion
Shine, and blue-bleak embers, ah my dear,
Fall, gall themselves, and gash gold-vermilion.

3 *the rolling level under-
neath him steady air*

The simplest way to read this phrase is to take *rolling, level, under-
neath him,* and *steady* as adjectives modifying air. But other
combinations fit the context; for example, *rolling* could modify
level and *level* in turn could be either an adjective or a noun. *Steady
air* could be read in apposition to *rolling level,* with *underneath him*
adverbial and modifying *rolling level.*

striding

Walking with long steps or advancing the foot beyond the usual
length of a step. *Striding* does not have a meaning that would
normally be used to describe the flight of a bird.

4 *rung upon the rein of a
wimpling wing*

To *ring,* in speaking of a hawk, means to rise spirally in flight. A *rein*
is a long narrow strap or thong of leather, attached to the bridle on
each side of the head, by which a horse is guided; and any similar
device used for the same purpose, or any means of guiding, con-
trolling, or governing. *Wimpling* means enveloping, covering,
rippling. A *wimple* is a garment of linen or silk formerly worn by
women and so folded as to envelop the head, chin, and sides of the
face and neck, retained in the dress of some nuns today and typical
of the dress of nuns in Hopkins' day; also, a fold or wrinkle, a turn
or twist.

5 *on swing*

With a swinging movement. *Swing* means a sweep or swoop,
freedom and scope of movement, a rhythmic or graceful motion.

6 *As a skate's heel sweeps
smooth on a bow-bend*

The image here is that of an ice skate in a long sweeping motion.
The phrase *on a bow-bend* describes the motion of the skate in
terms of the curve of an archer's bow, with *on* equivalent to "in
the manner of."

the hurl

The motion of the bird as it seems to be thrown, flung, or cast.

7 *Rebuffed*

To *rebuff* means to refuse bluntly or contemptuously, to snub;
also, to repel or drive back.

8 *for a bird*

By analogy, for Christ, to whom the poem is addressed.

achieve

Achievement.

10 *Buckle*

Fasten together, join closely, equip for battle; also, collapse,
crumple. *Buckle* may be read as either indicative (they buckle)
or imperative, the speaker directing beauty, valor, etc., to buckle
(you buckle).

11 *told*

Counted, reckoned; also, narrated, made known, communicated.

lovelier

The sense here is probably "*lovelier* each new time it is told."

chevalier

A knight (i.e., a horseman or mounted soldier), a chivalrous,
gallant man, a defender or champion of a cause or principle.

12 *No wonder of it*

It is nothing to wonder at.

shéer plód

Sheer means a swerving or deviating course, specifically an abrupt
deviation of a ship from the line of its course; also, the upward
curve of a ship's deck as viewed from the side. *Plod* means trudging,
moving heavily and slowly, and laborious or monotonous work.

plough down sillion

A ploughed furrow. *Sillion* (selion) means furrow, or a narrow strip
of land lying between two furrows.

13 *blue-bleak embers*

Embers are the smoldering ashes of a fire. *Bleak* means pale and
wan, sickly, ashen, depressing, cheerless.

14 *gall*

Rub, chafe, abrade.

gash

Make a gash or gashes of, cut or slash. A *gash* is a long and deep cut
or slash made in the flesh or in any object.

gold-vermilion

Vermilion is a bright red or scarlet.

T. S. Eliot (1888–1965)
The Love Song of J. Alfred Prufrock

*S'io credesse che mia risposta fosse
A persona che mai tornasse al mondo,
Questa fiamma staria senza piu scosse.
Ma perciocche giammai di questo fondo
Non torno vivo alcun, s'i'odo il vero
Senza tema d'infamia ti rispondo.*

Let us go then, you and I,
When the evening is spread out against the sky
Like a patient etherized upon a table;
Let us go, through certain half-deserted streets,
5   The muttering retreats
Of restless nights in one-night cheap hotels
And sawdust restaurants with oyster-shells:
Streets that follow like a tedious argument
Of insidious intent
10 To lead you to an overwhelming question. . . .
Oh, do not ask, "What is it?"
Let us go and make our visit.

In the room the women come and go
Talking of Michelangelo.

15 The yellow fog that rubs its back upon the window-panes,
The yellow smoke that rubs its muzzle on the window-panes,
Licked its tongue into the corners of the evening,
Lingered upon the pools that stand in drains,
Let fall upon its back the soot that falls from chimneys,
20 Slipped by the terrace, made a sudden leap,
And seeing that it was a soft October night,
Curled once about the house, and fell asleep.

And indeed there will be time
For the yellow smoke that slides along the street,
25 Rubbing its back upon the window-panes;
There will be time, there will be time
To prepare a face to meet the faces that you meet;
There will be time to murder and create,
And time for all the works and days of hands
30 That lift and drop a question on your plate;
Time for you and time for me,
And time yet for a hundred indecisions,
And for a hundred visions and revisions,
Before the taking of a toast and tea.

S'io . . . rispondo

The epigraph is from Dante's *Inferno,* spoken by the fraud Guido da Montefeltro in the eighth circle of hell, Canto XXVII, ll. 61-66: "If I thought my answer were to one who could ever return to the world, I would not reply; but since no one ever did return alive from this depth, I answer you without fear of infamy."

1 *you and I*

The form of the poem is that of a dramatic monologue. The possibilities here are that Prufrock is talking to himself (is assuming two separate identities in his single self), to the reader, and to an unidentified second person.

7 *sawdust restaurants*

Cheap restaurants, with sawdust sprinkled on the floor to absorb spillage.

14 *Michelangelo*

Italian artist (1475-1564) and one of the greatest figures of the Renaissance. As the *Encyclopaedia Britannica* puts it, "the greatest monumental painter of the Renaissance and certainly the most famous of all sculptors since the time of the Greeks."

15 *yellow fog*

In a note to line 60 of his poem "The Waste Land"—"Under the brown fog of a winter dawn"—Eliot himself refers us to Baudelaire's poem "The Seven Old Men," which describes an infernal group of seven old men in a yellow fog. The *yellow fog* connotes an infernal gloom.

29 *works and days*

Title of a poem by Hesiod, Greek poet of the eighth century B.C., praising hard work on the farm.

33 *visions*

That which is seen, intelligent foresights, mental images, imaginative conceptions, and mystical experiences of supernatural truth.

35 In the room the women come and go
    Talking of Michelangelo.

    And indeed there will be time
    To wonder, "Do I dare?" and, "Do I dare?"
    Time to turn back and descend the stair,
40 With a bald spot in the middle of my hair—
    (They will say: "How his hair is growing thin!")
    My morning coat, my collar mounting firmly to the chin,
    My necktie rich and modest, but asserted by a simple pin—
    (They will say: "But how his arms and legs are thin!")
45 Do I dare
    Disturb the universe?
    In a minute there is time
    For decisions and revisions which a minute will reverse.

    For I have known them all already, known them all:
50 Have known the evenings, mornings, afternoons,
    I have measured out my life with coffee spoons;
    I know the voices dying with a dying fall
    Beneath the music from a farther room.
      So how should I presume?

55 And I have known the eyes already, known them all—
    The eyes that fix you in a formulated phrase,
    And when I am formulated, sprawling on a pin,
    When I am pinned and wriggling on the wall,
    Then how should I begin
60 To spit out all the butt-ends of my days and ways?
      And how should I presume?

    And I have known the arms already, known them all—
    Arms that are braceleted and white and bare
    (But in the lamplight, downed with light brown hair!)
65 Is it perfume from a dress
    That makes me so digress?
    Arms that lie along a table, or wrap about a shawl.
      And should I then presume?
      And how should I begin?

              . . . . .

70 Shall I say, I have gone at dusk through narrow streets
    And watched the smoke that rises from the pipes
    Of lonely men in shirt-sleeves, leaning out of windows? . . .

    I should have been a pair of ragged claws
    Scuttling across the floors of silent seas.

39	*descend the stair*	Probably an allusion to Dante's figure of a stairway from Hell to Heaven. In the *Purgatorio* (XXVI, 145-48) the troubador Arnaut Daniel (flourished c. 1180-1210), speaking from the purgatorial flames, implores Dante by the goodness that guides him to the summit of the stairs to be mindful of his suffering. Prufrock's suffering is that of a man who desires to ascend (be at peace with himself), but who lacks, and knows he lacks, the strength to do so.
43	*a simple pin*	A necktie pin or ornament fastened to a necktie by means of a pin or clasp.
52	*the voices dying with a dying fall*	The opening lines of Shakespeare's *Twelfth Night* are spoken by Duke Orsino:

If music be the food of love, play on;
Give me excess of it, that, surfeiting,
The appetite may sicken, and so die.
That strain again! it had a dying fall.

56	*The eyes that fix you in a formulated phrase*	Cf. Alexander Pope's description of life at Hampton Court in *The Rape of the Lock* (III, 15-16):

A third interprets motions, looks, and eyes;
At every word a reputation dies.

63-64	*Arms that are braceleted . . . light brown hair*	Cf. John Donne's poem "The Relic" (ll. 1-12):

When my grave is broke up again
Some second guest to entertain
(For graves have learned that woman-head,
    To be to more than one a bed)
        And he that digs it spies
A bracelet of bright hair about the bone,
    Will he not let us alone,
And think that there a loving couple lies,
Who thought that this device might be some way
To make their souls, at the last busy day,
Meet at this grave, and make a little stay?

. . . . .

75 And the afternoon, the evening, sleeps so peacefully!
    Smoothed by long fingers,
    Asleep . . . tired . . . or it malingers,
    Stretched on the floor, here beside you and me.
    Should I, after tea and cakes and ices,
80 Have the strength to force the moment to its crisis?
    But though I have wept and fasted, wept and prayed,
    Though I have seen my head (grown slightly bald) brought in upon
        a platter,
    I am no prophet—and here's no great matter;
    I have seen the moment of my greatness flicker,
85 And I have seen the eternal Footman hold my coat, and snicker,
    And in short, I was afraid.

    And would it have been worth it, after all,
    After the cups, the marmalade, the tea,
    Among the porcelain, among some talk of you and me,
90 Would it have been worth while,
    To have bitten off the matter with a smile,
    To have squeezed the universe into a ball
    To roll it toward some overwhelming question,
    To say: "I am Lazarus, come from the dead,
95 Come back to tell you all, I shall tell you all"—
    If one, settling a pillow by her head,
        Should say: "That is not what I meant at all.
        That is not it, at all."

    And would it have been worth it, after all,
100 Would it have been worth while,
    After the sunsets and the dooryards and the sprinkled streets,
    After the novels, after the teacups, after the skirts that trail along the floor—
    And this, and so much more?—
    It is impossible to say just what I mean!
105 But as if a magic lantern threw the nerves in patterns on a screen:
    Would it have been worth while
    If one, settling a pillow or throwing off a shawl,
    And turning toward the window, should say:
        "That is not it at all,
110   That is not what I meant, at all."

. . . . .

    No! I am not Prince Hamlet, nor was meant to be;
    Am an attendant lord, one that will do
    To swell a progress, start a scene or two,
    Advise the prince; no doubt, an easy tool,

82 *my head . . . brought in upon a platter*

The head of John the Baptist was brought to Salome on a platter to reward her for dancing for Herod. See Matthew 14:1-12 and Mark 6:14-28. "But when Herod's birthday was kept, the daughter of Herodias danced before them, and pleased Herod. Whereupon he promised with an oath to give her whatsoever she would ask. And she, being before instructed of her mother, said, Give me here John Baptist's head in a charger. And the king was sorry: nevertheless for the oath's sake, and them which sat with him at meat, he commanded it to be given her. And he sent, and beheaded John in the prison. And his head was brought in a charger, and given to the damsel: and she brought it to her mother" (Matthew 14:6-11).

83 *prophet*

John the Baptist. "And when he would have put him to death, he feared the multitude, because they counted him as a prophet" (Matthew 14:5). "And others said, that it is a prophet, or as one of the prophets" (Mark 6:15).

85 *the eternal Footman*

Death. Cf.: "Think then, my soul, that death is but a groom, Which brings a taper to the outward room" (John Donne, "The Second Anniversary," ll. 85-86).

92 *into a ball*

Let us roll all our strength and all
Our sweetness up into one ball,
And tear our pleasures with rough strife
Through the iron gates of life.

Andrew Marvell, "To His Coy Mistress" (ll. 41-44)

94 *Lazarus*

Refers to both the Lazarus of Luke 16:19-31, and to the Lazarus of John 11:1-44. The former was not permitted to return from the dead to warn the wealthy about hell. The latter, the brother of Mary and Martha, was resurrected from the grave by Christ.

111-19 *No! I am not Prince Hamlet . . . Fool*

The allusion to the character of Shakespeare's Hamlet is general but emphasizes Hamlet's noble character in contrast to Prufrock. An "attendant lord" (l. 112) probably refers to the inept Rosencrantz and Guildenstern, and to the fop Osric, although several others in the play, such as Polonius, are possible. There is no "Fool" (l. 119) in *Hamlet,* but the fool was a character typical of Elizabethan drama. Shakespeare's most famous Fool is in *King Lear.*

115   Deferential, glad to be of use,
Politic, cautious, and meticulous;
Full of high sentence, but a bit obtuse;
At times, indeed, almost ridiculous—
Almost, at times, the Fool.

120   I grow old. . . . I grow old. . . .
I shall wear the bottoms of my trousers rolled.

Shall I part my hair behind? Do I dare to eat a peach?
I shall wear white flannel trousers, and walk upon the beach.
I have heard the mermaids singing, each to each.

125   I do not think that they will sing to me.

I have seen them riding seaward on the waves
Combing the white hair of the waves blown back
When the wind blows the water white and black.

We have lingered in the chambers of the sea
130   By sea girls wreathed with seaweed red and brown
Till human voices wake us, and we drown.

117 *Full of high sentence*

In the General Prologue to *The Canterbury Tales* Chaucer describes the speech of the Clerk of Oxford as "ful of hy sentence" (l. 305), that is, full of cogent meaning.

121 *rolled*

Cuffed, a new fashion in the years just before the poem was published in 1915.

129-31 *We have lingered . . . drown*

In Greek myth the sirens were creatures part bird and part woman who lured mariners to their destruction by their sweet song, but in later folklore they sometimes appear as part fish and part woman, with the power to lure men to chambers beneath the sea, where the men drown when the sirens stop singing.

The Rhythm of Song

Music resembles song, in each
Are nameless graces which no methods teach.

Alexander Pope, *An Essay on Criticism,* II. 143-44

The *Oxford English Dictionary* defines a song as a metrical composition adapted for singing, especially such a composition having a regular verse form. In plain terms, words and music combine but the combination seems to go better when metrical rhythms invite, as it were, the step into musical expression. Most of us know what it feels like to burst into song, to want to burst into song, or at least to enjoy a pulsing rhythm for its own sake. Man by his nature has an impulse to sing, to use song as an outlet for his emotions. Following are some metrical compositions set to music that has become so familiar as to be all but inseparable from the words.

Ben Jonson (1573–1637)
Drink to Me Only with Thine Eyes

Drink to me only with thine eyes,
   And I will pledge with mine;
Or leave a kiss but in the cup
   And I'll not look for wine.
5 The thirst that from the soul doth rise
   Doth ask a drink divine;
But might I of Jove's nectar sup,
   I would not change for thine.

I sent thee late a rosy wreath,
10 Not so much honoring thee
As giving it a hope that there
   It could not withered be.
But thou thereon didst only breathe
   And sent'st it back to me;
15 Since when it grows and smells, I swear,
   Not of itself but thee.

Questions and Suggestions

1. The predominant metrical pattern of the poem is iambic tetrameter alternating with iambic trimeter:

$$\smile / \, | \, \smile / \, | \, \smile / \, | \, \smile /$$

$$\smile / \, | \, \smile / \, | \, \smile /$$

What are the variations in the metrical pattern? Do they make a difference in the poem as a poem, or in the poem as it would be sung?

2. How does the poem as a poem appeal to your ear? Are you aware of the rhyme scheme as you read it? Is there a reason why the rhyming words are mainly monosyllables? In addition to using rhyme, does Jonson repeat vowel and consonant sounds?

3. Does the speaker's idea seem sentimental to you? If not, how does he make himself convincing? Can you describe the second stanza as a variation of the idea of the first stanza?

4. Notice the use of the word *smells* in line 15. It has a connotation today that it did not have in Jonson's day. Look up the word *smell* in the dictionary. Is the connotative meaning listed?

Robert Burns   (1759–1796)
Auld Lang Syne

Should auld acquaintance be forgot,
  And never brought to mind?
Should auld acquaintance be forgot,
  And auld lang syne!

5   For auld lang syne, my jo,
        For auld lang syne,
      We'll tak a cup o' kindness yet
        For auld lang syne.

And surely ye'll be your pint-stowp!
10   And surely I'll be mine!
And we'll tak a cup o' kindness yet
  For auld lang syne.

We twa hae run about the braes,
  And pu'd the gowans fine;

Auld Lang Syne Literally, old long since; hence, long ago, the good old days.   **9** *be your pint-stowp* Be able to consume your three-pint measure.   **13** *twa hae* Two have.   *braes* Small hills.   **14** *pu'd the gowans* Pulled the wild daisies.

15 But we've wander'd mony a weary fitt
      Sin auld lang syne.

We twa hae paidl'd i' the burn,
  Frae morning sun till dine;
But seas between us braid hae roar'd,
20 Sin auld lang syne.

And there's a hand, my trusty fiere!
  And gie's a hand o' thine!
And we'll tak a right guid-willie-waught,
  For auld lang syne.

15 *mony* Many.   *fitt* Foot.   **16** *Sin* Since.   **17** *paidl'd i' the burn* Paddled in the brook.   **18** *Frae* From.   **19** *braid* Broad.   **21** *fiere* Comrade.   **22** *gie's* Give us.
23 *guid-willie-waught* Long and hearty draught (of beer).

Afton Water

Flow gently, sweet Afton, among thy green braes,
Flow gently, I'll sing thee a song in thy praise;
My Mary's asleep by thy murmuring stream,
Flow gently, sweet Afton, disturb not her dream.

5 Thou stock-dove whose echo resounds thro' the glen,
Ye wild whistling blackbirds in yon thorny den,
Thou green-crested lapwing, thy screaming forbear,
I charge you disturb not my slumbering fair.

How lofty, sweet Afton, thy neighbouring hills,
10 Far mark'd with the courses of clear winding rills;
There daily I wander as noon rises high,
My flocks and my Mary's sweet cot in my eye.

How pleasant thy banks and green valleys below,
Where wild in the woodlands the primroses blow;
15 There oft as mild ev'ning weeps over the lea,
The sweet-scented birk shades my Mary and me.

Thy crystal stream, Afton, how lovely it glides,
And winds by the cot where my Mary resides;
How wanton thy waters her snowy feet lave,
20 As gathering sweet flow'rets she stems thy clear wave.

1 *braes* Slopes, small hills.   **16** *birk* Birch tree.

> Flow gently, sweet Afton, among thy green braes,
> Flow gently, sweet river, the theme of my lays;
> My Mary's asleep by thy murmuring stream,
> Flow gently, sweet Afton, disturb not her dream.

Questions and Suggestions

1. Does the metrical pattern of "Auld Lang Syne" resemble that of "Drink to Me Only with Thine Eyes"? What are the differences? Notice the repetition of the phrase "auld lang syne." Does this repetition fit the emotion of the poem? A phrase, line, or lines recurring regularly in a poem is called a *refrain*. The second stanza (indented) of "Auld Lang Syne" is the refrain.
2. The metrical pattern of "Afton Water" may be described as anapestic tetrameter. Does the longer line (that is, longer than iambic tetrameter) seem to reinforce the idea of "flow gently"? Notice that "flow gently" is a refrain phrase.
3. Do you think that one of Burns' poems is either poetically or musically better than the other? Can the question be meaningfully discussed, or is it simply a question of taste?

Alfred, Lord Tennyson   (1809–1892)
Sweet and Low

> Sweet and low, sweet and low,
>   Wind of the western sea,
> Low, low, breathe and blow,
>   Wind of the western sea!
> 5 Over the rolling waters go,
> Come from the dying moon, and blow,
>   Blow him again to me;
> While my little one, while my pretty one, sleeps.
>
> Sleep and rest, sleep and rest,
> 10   Father will come to thee soon;
> Rest, rest, on mother's breast,
>   Father will come to thee soon;
> Father will come to his babe in the nest,
> Silver sails all out of the west
> 15   Under the silver moon;
> Sleep, my little one, sleep, my pretty one, sleep.

Questions and Suggestions

1. Assume that the metrical pattern of "Sweet and Low," except for the last line of each stanza, is iambic tetrameter. Then describe the metrical pattern of the poem

in terms of substitutions made for a number of the iambic feet. How many metrical feet can you count in the last line of each stanza? What is the metrical pattern of the last line of each stanza? Can you see a reason for a change in metrical pattern from the first seven lines to the eighth line of each stanza? Can you describe the rhythm of the poem in terms of rhythmic phrases rather than of metrical feet? Do the vowel sounds—for example, of *sweet, low, blow, sleep, soon*—make a difference in the rhythm of the poem?

2. If you know the music to "Sweet and Low," explain how it is appropriate to what the speaker is expressing.

A song as a metrical composition adapted for singing is generally distinguished from "song lyrics," which are the words to any song that we might sing but which, apart from their music, *may or may not* involve the pleasure of poetry. In fact, it must be said that song lyrics often look like prose and are typically full of trite language such as, "You Belong to My Heart," "It's All in the Game," "You're Driving Me Crazy," "Tomorrow's Gonna Be Another Day," "It's a Fine Life," to mention just a few titles. Here is Stephen Foster's "Beautiful Dreamer." It offers little of the pleasure of poetry, but if you know the music, it's a lovely serenade:

Stephen Foster   (1826–1864)
Beautiful Dreamer

Beautiful dreamer, wake unto me,
Starlight and dewdrops are waiting for thee.
Sounds of the rude world heard in the day,
Lulled by the moonlight, have all passed away.

5   Beautiful dreamer, queen of my song,
List while I woo thee with soft melody.
Gone are the cares of life's busy throng,
Beautiful dreamer, awake unto me.
Beautiful dreamer, awake unto me.

10   Beautiful dreamer, out on the sea
Mermaids are chanting the wild lorelie.
Over the streamlet vapors are borne,
Waiting to fade at the bright coming morn.

Beautiful dreamer, beam on my heart,
15   E'en as the morn on the streamlet and sea.
Then will all clouds of sorrow depart,
Beautiful dreamer, awake unto me.
Beautiful dreamer, awake unto me.

11 *lorelie*   Lorelei, in folklore a siren who sits on the echoing rock of Lorelei and lures boatmen to their destruction. The Lorelei is a rock, famous for its echo, midway between Coblenz and Bingen on the right bank of the Rhine River.

Questions and Suggestions

1. Identify some contemporary song lyrics you think are terrible, but which neverthe-
   less are set to music you like. Identify some contemporary song lyrics you think are
   very good, but which are set to music you do not like particularly well.
2. Is "soft melody" a fair description of Foster's intent in "Beautiful Dreamer"? Can
   you identify some contemporary song lyrics whose intent is similar?

The song is a subdivision of the lyric poem. In ancient Greece a *lyric* was a poem
intended to be sung or recited in accompaniment to a lyre (a stringed instrument resem-
bling a harp), but *lyric* is now a general term for any poem that combines musicality and
strong emotion, particularly emotion that is personal or subjective. A *song* is often
defined as a lyric poem that is particularly adapted to musical expression, but what is
at stake in such identification is clearly a matter of degree, for there is no way to fix
which poems will adapt to music and which poems will not. Chance, moreover, will
have it that some will be adapted to music and some will not. Since prose is often effec-
tively put to music, one would suspect that any metrical composition with a regular verse
form, and thus a rhythmic headstart, could be put to music if someone musically talented
decided to do so. The question of what words adapt to music is really an academic one,
since the pleasure we find in the poem we call a song relates to the pleasure of music, but
does not *necessarily* involve music itself; conversely, as we have noted, the words (lyrics)
to many songs that we enjoy singing do not necessarily involve the pleasure of poetry.
Following are some strongly rhythmical songs which give us a pleasure related to music,
but which are not known for having been set to music.

Sir Thomas Wyatt   (1503–1542)
Forget Not Yet

Forget not yet the tried intent
Of such a truth as I have meant;
My great travail so gladly spent
           Forget not yet.

5 Forget not yet when first began
The weary life ye know, since whan
The suit, the service none tell can;
           Forget not yet.

Forget not yet the great assays,
10 The cruel wrong, the scornful ways,
The painful patience in denays,
           Forget not yet.

6 *whan* When.   **9** *assays* Trials.   **11** *denays* Denials.

Forget not yet, forget not this,
How long ago hath been and is
15 The mind that never meant amiss;
    Forget not yet.

Forget not then thine own approved,
The which so long hath thee so loved
Whose steadfast faith yet never moved;
20   Forget not this.

John Donne (1572–1631)
Go and Catch a Falling Star

Go and catch a falling star,
 Get with child a mandrake root,
Tell me where all past years are,
 Or who cleft the devil's foot,
5 Teach me to hear mermaids singing,
 Or to keep off envy's stinging,
   And find
   What wind
Serves t' advance an honest mind.

10 If thou be'st born to strange sights,
 Things invisible to see,
Ride ten thousand days and nights
 Till age snow white hairs on thee;
Thou, when thou return'st, wilt tell me
15 All strange wonders that befell thee,
   And swear
   Nowhere
Lives a woman true, and fair.

If thou find'st one, let me know;
20   Such a pilgrimage were sweet;
Yet do not, I would not go
 Though at next door we might meet.
Though she were true when you met her,
And last till you write your letter,
25   Yet she
   Will be
False ere I come, to two or three.

---

2 *mandrake root* The root of an herb. The root was forked like the lower part of the human body and was said to shriek when it was pulled up.

William Blake   (1757–1827)
The Tyger

Tyger! Tyger! burning bright
In the forests of the night,
What immortal hand or eye
Could frame thy fearful symmetry?

5 In what distant deeps or skies
Burnt the fire of thine eyes?
On what wings dare he aspire?
What the hand dare seize the fire?·

And what shoulder, & what art,
10 Could twist the sinews of thy heart?
And when thy heart began to beat,
What dread hand? & what dread feet?

What the hammer? what the chain?
In what furnace was thy brain?
15 What the anvil? what dread grasp
Dare its deadly terrors clasp?

When the stars threw down their spears,
And water'd heaven with their tears,
Did he smile his work to see?
20 Did he who made the Lamb make thee?

Tyger! Tyger! burning bright
In the forests of the night,
What immortal hand or eye,
Dare frame thy fearful symmetry?

Christina Rossetti   (1830–1898)
Song: When I Am Dead, My Dearest

When I am dead, my dearest,
  Sing no sad songs for me;
Plant thou no roses at my head,
  Nor shady cypress tree.
5 Be the green grass above me
  With showers and dewdrops wet;
And if thou wilt, remember,
  And if thou wilt, forget.

I shall not see the shadows,
10   I shall not feel the rain;
I shall not hear the nightingale
   Sing on as if in pain.
And dreaming through the twilight
   That doth not rise nor set,
15   Haply I may remember,
   And haply may forget.

W. H. Auden   (1907–   )
O What Is That Sound

O what is that sound which so thrills the ear
   Down in the valley drumming, drumming?
Only the scarlet soldiers, dear,
   The soldiers coming.

5   O what is that light I see flashing so clear
   Over the distance brightly, brightly?
Only the sun on their weapons, dear,
   As they step lightly.

O what are they doing with all that gear,
10   What are they doing this morning, this morning?
Only their usual manoeuvres, dear,
   Or perhaps a warning.

O why have they left the road down there,
   Why are they suddenly wheeling, wheeling?
15   Perhaps a change in their orders, dear.
   Why are you kneeling?

O haven't they stopped for the doctor's care,
   Haven't they reined their horses, their horses?
Why, they are none of them wounded, dear,
20   None of these forces.

O is it the parson they want, with white hair,
   Is it the parson, is it, is it?
No, they are passing his gateway, dear,
   Without a visit.

25   O it must be the farmer who lives so near.
   It must be the farmer so cunning, so cunning?
They have passed the farmyard already, dear,
   And now they are running.

O where are you going? Stay with me here!
30   Were the vows you swore deceiving, deceiving?
No, I promised to love you, dear,
        But I must be leaving.

O it's broken the lock and splintered the door,
        O it's the gate where they're turning, turning;
35   Their boots are heavy on the floor
        And their eyes are burning.

We began this chapter with some metrical compositions set to music that has become so familiar as to be all but inseparable from the words. The group just concluded consists of strongly rhythmical songs whose central pleasure for us is that of poetry, but which seem to take us to the threshold of musical expression, to make us want to sing them out. Following are some folk or popular ballads. A *ballad* is a song that tells a story, a narrative poem intended to be sung. The folk or popular ballad is usually anonymous and was originally transmitted orally. It is distinguished from the literary ballad, which is usually the work of a single author deliberately using the popular ballad as a model; Tennyson's "Northern Farmer, New Style" (p. 316) is an example of a literary ballad. Popular ballads are plentiful, as you may see by a look at Francis J. Child's superb collection of 305, *The English and Scottish Popular Ballads* (1882-1898), reprinted in five volumes (New York: Dover Publications, 1965). The music to Child's ballads may be found in Bertrand H. Bronson's *The Traditional Tunes of the Child Ballads,* four volumes (Princeton: Princeton University Press, 1959-1971).

Anonymous Ballads of the Middle Ages
Sir Patrick Spens

1

The king sits in Dumferling town,
    Drinking the blude-reid wine:
"O whar will I get guid sailor,
    To sail this ship of mine?"

2

5   Up and spak an eldern knicht,
        Sat at the king's richt knee:
"Sir Patrick Spens is the best sailor
        That sails upon the sea."

1 *Dumferling* Dunfirmline, a town fourteen miles northwest of Edinburgh and a favorite residence of many Scottish kings.   **2** *blude-reid* Blood-red.   **3** *whar* Where.   *guid* Good.
5 *spak* Spoke.   *eldern knicht* Old knight.   **6** *richt* Right.

3

The king has written a braid letter
10   And signed it wi' his hand,
And sent it to Sir Patrick Spens,
    Was walking on the sand.

4

The first line that Sir Patrick read,
    A loud lauch lauched he;
15 The next line that Sir Patrick read,
    The tear blinded his ee.

5

"O wha is this has done this deed,
    This ill deed done to me,
To send me out this time o' the year,
20   To sail upon the sea?

6

"Mak haste, mak haste, my mirry men all,
    Our guid ship sails the morn."
"O say na sae, my master dear,
    For I fear a deadly storm.

7

25 "Late, late yestre'en I saw the new moon
    Wi' the auld moon in hir arm,
And I fear, I fear, my dear master,
    That we will come to harm."

8

O our Scots nobles were richt laith
30   To weet their cork-heeled shoon,
But lang or a' the play were played
    Their hats they swam aboon.

9 *braid* Broad.   **14** *lauch* Laugh.   **16** *ee* Eye.   **17** *wha* Who.   **21** *Mak* Make.
mirry Merry.   **22** *the morn* In the morning.   **23** *na sae* Not so.   **25** *yestre'en* Yesterday
evening.   **26** *auld* Old.   *hir* Her.   **29** *richt laith* Right loath.   **30** *weet* Wet.   *shoon*
Shoes.   **31** *lang or a'* Long before all.   **32** *aboon* Above (that is, above them in the water,
since they were drowned).

9

> O lang, lang may their ladies sit,
>   Wi' their fans into their hand,
> 35 Or ere they see Sir Patrick Spens
>   Come sailing to the land.

10

> O lang, lang may the ladies stand
>   Wi' their gold kems in their hair,
> Waiting for their ain dear lords,
> 40   For they'll see them na mair.

11

> Half o'er, half o'er to Aberdour
>   It's fifty fadom deep,
> And there lies guid Sir Patrick Spens
>   Wi' the Scots lords at his feet.

38 *kems* Combs.   **39** *ain* Own.   **40** *na mair* No more.   **41** *Aberdour* A village on the north shore of the Firth of Forth ten miles northeast of Edinburgh.   **42** *fadom* Fathom.

Bonny Barbara Allan

1

> It was in and about the Martinmas time,
>   When the green leaves were a falling,
> That Sir John Græme, in the West Country,
>   Fell in love with Barbara Allan.

2

> 5 He sent his man down through the town,
>   To the place where she was dwelling:
> "O haste and come to my master dear,
>   Gin ye be Barbara Allan."

3

> O hooly, hooly rose she up,
> 10   To the place where he was lying

Bonny Comely, attractive, healthy.   **1** *the Martinmas time* November 11, the feast of St. Martin, Pope Martin I, who died in 655, the last pope to die a martyr.   **8** *Gin ye be* If you are. **9** *hooly* Slowly, gently.

And when she drew the curtain by:
   "Young man, I think you're dying."

4

"O it's I'm sick, and very, very sick,
   And 'tis a' for Barbara Allan."
15 "O the better for me ye s' never be,
   Though your heart's blood were a-spilling.

5

"O dinna ye mind, young man," said she,
   "When ye was in the tavern a drinking,
That ye made the healths gae round and round,
20   And slighted Barbara Allan?"

6

He turned his face unto the wall,
   And death was with him dealing:
"Adieu, adieu, my dear friends all,
   And be kind to Barbara Allan."

7

25 And slowly, slowly raise she up,
   And slowly, slowly left him,
And sighing said, she could not stay,
   Since death of life had reft him.

8

She had not gane a mile but twa,
30   When she heard the dead-bell ringing,
And every jow that the dead-bell geid,
   It cried, "Woe to Barbara Allan!"

9

"O mother, mother, make my bed!
   O make it saft and narrow!
35 Since my love died for me today,
   I'll die for him tomorrow."

---

14 *a'* All.   **15** *ye s'* You shall.   **17** *dinna ye mind* Don't you remember.   **19** *gae* Go.
29 *gane* Gone.   *twa* Two.   **31** *jow* Stroke.   *geid* Gave.   **34** *saft* Soft.

Questions and Suggestions

1. The most common stanza in which ballads are written is called the *ballad stanza.* It is defined as a four-line stanza alternating iambic tetrameter and iambic trimeter, usually rhyming *a b c b.* Which of these two ballads is the more clear-cut example of the use of this stanza pattern? Describe their similarities and differences in the use of the ballad stanza.
2. Look again at Jonson's "Drink to Me Only with Thine Eyes" (p. 63) and Burns' "Auld Lang Syne" (p. 64). Is the ballad stanza flexible? Does it seem to be a form that is somehow helpful in bringing us in words to the threshold of musical expression?
3. Comment on the story value of "Sir Patrick Spens" and "Bonny Barbara Allan." Are enough details given to make each story interesting? Do you prefer one to the other? If so, why?

Since the popular ballad was originally transmitted orally, it often appears in more than one version. The early twentieth-century American ballad "Frankie and Johnny," or "Frankie and Albert," exists in hundreds of versions, the Robert A. Gordon collection numbering some three hundred variants. In his book *Frankie and Johnny* (1930, reissued in 1968 by Benjamin Blom, Inc.), containing his own play based on the ballad, as well as a discussion and several versions of the ballad, John Huston cites evidence that the story of Frankie and Johnny is based on an actual incident that took place in St. Louis on October 15, 1899. Frankie Baker, aged twenty-seven, shot Allen Britt (or Albert, as he liked to be called), aged seventeen, on a Sunday night in the hallway of the old Phoenix Hotel when he was with a girl named Alice Pryar, an eighteen-year-old prostitute. Albert had gone after Frankie with a knife. She gave herself up and, after the inquest, was released on the coroner's decision of justifiable homicide. Huston quotes the St. Louis *Post-Dispatch* account of the story and also the City Hospital Record. Music for the ballad may be found in *American Ballads and Folk Songs,* collected and compiled by John A. Lomax and Alan Lomax (New York: The Macmillan Co., 1934), and in Alan Lomax's *The Folk Songs of North America* (New York: Doubleday & Company, Inc., 1960).

Following are two versions of the ballad.

Frankie and Johnny
First Version

Frankie and Johnny were lovers, O Lordy, how they could love.
Swore to be true to each other, true as the stars above.
He was her man, but he done her wrong.

Frankie she was his woman, just like everyone knows,
5 She spent a hundred dollars for a suit of Johnny's clothes.
He was her man, but he done her wrong.

Frankie and Johnny went walking, Johnny in his bran' new suit,
"O good Lawd," says Frankie, "but don't my Johnny look cute?"
He was her man, but he done her wrong.

10 Frankie went down to Memphis, she went on the evening train.
She paid one hundred dollars for Johnny a watch and chain.
He was her man, but he done her wrong.

Frankie went down to the corner to buy a glass of beer.
She says to the fat bartender, "Has my lovingest man been here?
15 He was my man, but he's doing me wrong."

"Ain't going to tell you no story, ain't going to tell you no lie,
I seen your man 'bout an hour ago with a girl named Alice Pry.
If he's your man, he's doing you wrong."

Frankie went down to the hotel, she didn't go there for fun,
20 Under her long red kimono she toted a forty-four gun.
He was her man, but he done her wrong.

Frankie went up the stairway, looked in the window so high,
There was her lovin' Johnny a-lovin' up Alice Pry.
He was her man, but he done her wrong.

25 Frankie threw back her kimono, she took out her forty-four,
Roota-toot-toot three times she shot right through that hotel door.
She shot her man, 'cause he done her wrong.

Johnny grabbed off his Stetson, "O good Lawd, Frankie, don't shoot."
But Frankie pulled the trigger, and the gun went roota-toot-toot.
30 He was her man, but she shot him down.

First time she shot him he staggered, second time she shot him he fell,
Third time she shot him, O Lordy, there was a new man's face in hell.
She killed her man who had done her wrong.

"Roll me over easy, roll me over slow,
35 Roll me over on my left side, for the bullet hurt me so.
I was your man, but I done you wrong."

Frankie heard a rumbling away down in the ground.
Maybe it was Johnny where she had shot him down.
He was her man, and she done him wrong.

22 *the window so high* The transom.   **28** *Stetson* A stylish hat with high crown and wide brim, designed by American hatmaker John Stetson (1830-1906).

40 "O, bring on your rubber-tired hearses, bring on your rubber-tired hacks,
They're takin' my Johnny to the buryin' ground but they'll never bring him back.
He was my man, but he done me wrong."

The judge he said to the jury, "It's plain as plain can be.
This woman shot her man, it's murder in the second degree.
45 He was her man, though he done her wrong."

Now it wasn't murder in the second degree, it wasn't murder in the third.
Frankie simply dropped her man, like a hunter drops a bird.
He was her man, but he done her wrong.

"Oh, put me in that dungeon. Oh, put me in that cell.
50 Put me where the northeast wind blows from the southwest corner of hell.
I shot my man 'cause he done me wrong."

Frankie walked up the scaffold, as calm as a girl could be,
She turned her eyes to heaven and said, "Good Lord, I'm coming to thee.
He was my man, and I done him wrong."

40 *hacks* Carriages, coaches.

Frankie and Johnny
Second Version

Frankie was a good woman, everybody knows,
She'd give the tailor a hundred dollar bill to make her man a suit of clothes.
He was her man, but he done her wrong.

Frankie was a good woman, everybody knows,
5 Every time she gave Johnny a hundred dollar bill, he'd spend it on those parlor
house whores.
He was her man, but he done her wrong.

Frankie went down to the barroom and called for a glass of gin.
She asked the man called the bartender, "Has my cheatin' man been in?
He's my man, I believe he's doin' me wrong."

10 Says, "Frankie, I'll tell you no story, good gal, I'll tell you no lie,
I saw your man pass here an hour ago with a girl called Alice Fry.
He's your man, I believe he's doin' you wrong."

5 *parlor house* A brothel with a parlor or lounge was considered elegant. **13** *crib house*
A small building.

Frankie went back to the crib house, this time she didn't go for fun.
Under her blue silk kimono she brought her Johnny's forty-four gun
15 To kill her man, 'cause he done her wrong.

Frankie went down to the hop joint and knocked on the hop joint door,
She says, "Open up, you Chinese ——, or you'll run this joint no more.
I'm lookin' for my man, 'cause he's done me wrong."

Frankie went down to the coke joint and she rung the coke joint bell.
20 She says, "If I find that mistreatin' bastard in here, I'm going to kill him sure as hell,
Because he's my man, and he's been doin' me wrong."

She crept up an old dark alley, she heard her pet bulldog bark.
Lookin' up the stairway, she spied Johnny sneaking through the dark.
He was her man, but he's done her wrong.

25 Now when Johnny he saw Frankie, the poor boy started to run.
She says, "You might as well stop, you ——, I'm going to shoot you with your
    own gun,
Because you was my man, but you done me wrong."

When Johnny saw Frankie meant it, he started off as fast as he could,
But she squeezed that forty-four four times, and he dropped like a stick of wood,
30 'Cause he was her man, but he done her wrong.

"Turn me over Frankie, turn me over slow,
Turn me over on my left side, baby, your bullet wound me so.
I was your man, but I done you wrong."

Now the cops they got Frankie and put her in a cell.
35 The very first word I heard her say, "I wonder will my man get well?
I love my man, though he done me wrong."

The doctor was to operate on Johnny with a great big surgeon's knife.
Frankie offered the doctor a thousand dollars cold to save her Johnny's life,
'Cause he was her man and he done her wrong.

40 Frankie went to the hospital about three o'clock next day.
She got there just five minutes late, Johnny had passed away.
He was her man and he done her wrong.

Frankie went to Johnny's mother, and she fell down on her knees,
And she cried, "Mother, mother, forgive me, won't you please!
45 He was your son and the only one."

---

16 *hop joint* An opium den.   **19** *coke joint* An establishment selling "coke," a slang term
for cocaine.

Mother says, "Frankie, I forgive you, but forget I cannot,
You killed my one and only son, the only support I got.
He was my son and the only one."

The judge he says to Frankie, "Here you stand before me,
50 We've got you charged with an awful crime, murder in the first degree,
You shot your man, 'cause he done you wrong."

Frankie says, "Judge, I'm sorry this thing has come to pass,
I never shot him in the first degree, I shot him in his trifling ——,
'Cause he done me wrong, 'cause he done me wrong."

55 The jury went out on Frankie and sat under an electric fan,
Come back and said, "You're a free woman, go kill yourself another man,
If he does you wrong, if he does you wrong."

Rubber tire the buggies, rubber tire the hacks,
Frankie even rubber tire the horses' feet to bring poor Johnny back,
60 Though he was her man and he done her wrong.

Frankie went out to the graveyard and fell down on her knees,
And she prayed to the good Lord to give poor Johnny ease
Because he was her man, now he's dead and gone.

I looked down the street, Lord, far as I could see,
65 All I could hear was a two-string bow playing *Nearer, My God, to Thee.*
He was her man, and he done her wrong.

58 *hacks*   Carriages, coaches.

Questions and Suggestions

1. Describe the key similarities and differences between the two versions. Which do you prefer? Why?
2. For contrast with the ballad you might wish to read some narrative poems such as Chaucer's *The Pardoner's Tale* (p. 184), Pope's *The Rape of the Lock* (p. 242), Browning's *The Pied Piper of Hamelin* (p. 319), and James Dickey's "Cherrylog Road" (p. 425), or perhaps a sample of Byron's very long narrative poem *Don Juan* (p. 284).

Characterization

All I will do is to state a possibility. If human nature does alter it
will be because individuals manage to look at themselves in a new way.

E. M. Forster, *Aspects of the Novel*

It is fair to describe the rhythm of song as one of the fundamental experiences of poetry. The poems which we call songs may be thought of as rhythmic heightenings of language to the point of bringing us to the threshold of musical expression. There is also a sense in which any poem with a strong poetic rhythm at least heads us in the direction of musical expression; in other words, poetry by its nature has a quality of musicality about it. And yet our experience tells us that not all poems are songs or songlike. What, then, is the fundamental difference between a song and a poem emphasizing characterization and dramatic situation, especially in light of the fact that a song could easily intrigue us in terms of who the speaker is and the sheer interestingness of the speaker's experience? The answer to this question lies in an emphasis on *purpose.* For example, the opening line of Robert Frost's "Stopping by Woods on a Snowy Evening" is strongly iambic and has a strong poetic rhythm:

      Whose woods these are I think I know,

as does the rest of the opening stanza and, indeed, the rest of the poem. It could easily be argued on the basis of rhythm that "Stopping by Woods" brings us to the threshold of musical expression, but what dissuades us from calling it a song is that its purpose is clearly a dramatic one. Although this is not to say that a song is without dramatic purpose, it is to say that a poem's function—to sing, to narrate, to characterize—is, generally speaking, identifiable. Frost's speaker in "Stopping by Woods" is reflective. He scarcely desires to break into song, and one reason that we do not is that he does not.

      Poems which emphasize characterization might remind you of your experience with the short story. As in the short story, you look at the stature of the character, at whether or not you can identify with his thoughts and feelings, with the quality of his experience, with his problems, or whether, by contrast, you view him in a relatively detached way. As in the short story, you want to know whether he is a static or a dynamic character, whether he is more or less fixed as a person or is changing or acting and reacting in relation to challenge. As in the short story, you want to know what his motives are, whether or not there are cause-and-effect patterns to ponder. And as in the short story, you want character to be shown in action, not just talked about. The difference between a poem and a short story lies, of course, in the fact that the poem typically focuses on a dramatic moment, a high point or possibly a crisis in the speaker's experience, and is not concerned (except for narrative poems) with telling a story in the usual sense. A poem strong in characterization and dramatic situation typically *implies* a story, however, and is thus strong in the kind of interest a story has.

The poem, like the short story, creates a fictional character or characters. In fact, some poets stay with the same fictional character from poem to poem and end up creating a single fictional identity, sometimes called a *mythic* character, a complex imaginative realization of the individual experience of self and even of country. Two great practitioners of this art are Walt Whitman and Robert Frost. Whitman created a character he simply called by his own name—"I am Walt Whitman"—who was not unlike the real-life Walt Whitman, a poet whose aim was to celebrate the unity of man and nature and to be the voice of democracy. Frost created a character often referred to as the New England Yankee, who was not at all like the real-life Robert Frost, as Lawrance Thompson's definitive biography of Frost so vividly demonstrates. The New England Yankee, in plain terms, is a relatively "nice guy," while the real-life Robert Frost was not nearly so nice as his fictional creation. The discrepancy between a biographical reality and a fictional reality reminds us that our pleasure in a poem's characterization is a pleasure in a *fictional* characterization, in the kind of truth for which fictional characterization reaches. By the same token, even if the speaker is virtually identical with the real-life poet it is wise to regard him as a fictional character, because any shaping of a poem necessitates the manipulation of detail and suggestion for the purpose of the poem as distinct from the purpose of biography. What a poet concerned with characterization does is either to create a fictional character or, as it is sometimes expressed, to use the device of a *persona,* to assume a mask of fictional identity.

Following are Frost's "Stopping by Woods on a Snowy Evening" and Section 21 from Whitman's *Song of Myself.* If you find yourself engrossed by the character of the speakers, keep in mind that both poets are substantially represented elsewhere in this anthology.

Robert Frost   (1874–1963)
Stopping by Woods on a Snowy Evening

Whose woods these are I think I know.
His house is in the village though;
He will not see me stopping here
To watch his woods fill up with snow.

5   My little horse must think it queer
To stop without a farmhouse near
Between the woods and frozen lake
The darkest evening of the year.

He gives his harness bells a shake
10 To ask if there is some mistake.
The only other sound's the sweep
Of easy wind and downy flake.

The woods are lovely, dark and deep,
But I have promises to keep,
15 And miles to go before I sleep,
And miles to go before I sleep.

Questions and Suggestions

1. Consider each stanza as a phase of the action of the poem and describe how the
    character of the speaker is progressively revealed. Does the speaker have reasons for
    stopping or, once he has stopped, reasons for pausing to reflect, and, finally, reasons
    for deciding to depart?
2. Is the poem effective in showing character in action even though there is little
    action in the sense of movement in the poem? Explain.

Walt Whitman   (1819–1892)
21: I Am the Poet of the Body and I Am the Poet of the Soul
From SONG OF MYSELF

I am the poet of the Body and I am the poet of the Soul,
The pleasures of heaven are with me and the pains of hell are with me,
The first I graft and increase upon myself, the latter I translate into a new tongue.

I am the poet of the woman the same as the man,
5   And I say it is as great to be a woman as to be a man,
And I say there is nothing greater than the mother of men.

I chant the chant of dilation or pride,
We have had ducking and deprecating about enough,
I show that size is only development.

10 Have you outstript the rest? are you the President?
It is a trifle, they will more than arrive there every one, and still pass on.

I am he that walks with the tender and growing night,
I call to the earth and sea half-held by the night.

Press close bare-bosom'd night—press close magnetic nourishing night!
15 Night of south winds—night of the large few stars!
Still nodding night—mad naked summer night.

Smile O voluptuous cool-breath'd earth!
Earth of the slumbering and liquid trees!

Earth of departed sunset—earth of the mountains misty-topt!
20   Earth of the vitreous pour of the full moon just tinged with blue!
Earth of shine and dark mottling the tide of the river!
Earth of the limpid gray of clouds brighter and clearer for my sake!
Far-swooping elbow'd earth—rich apple-blossom'd earth!
Smile, for your lover comes.

25   Prodigal, you have given me love—therefore I to you give love!
O unspeakable passionate love.

Questions and Suggestions

1. What devices does the speaker use to suggest that his personality is dynamic?
    Consider, for example, the directness of his assertion of what he is and what he
    does and his use of repetition. What other devices can you identify?
2. Describe in your own words the dramatic situation of the poem. How much
    "story" does the poem imply? How does the speaker's conception of himself
    as one who sings a "song of myself" reinforce character and dramatic situation
    rather than taking emphasis away from them? Note the speaker's use of "chant"
    (l. 7).

Although the speaker of the Frost poem or of the Whitman poem is best regarded
as a fictional character, such a speaker is also normally regarded at least as relating to the
actual personality or to an aspect of the personality of the poet who creates him. Poets
also create fictional characters who are distinctly separate people from themselves, much
like the characters created in a play—the doctor, the lawyer, the businessman, the house-
wife, the careerwoman, the young man or young woman, the old man or old woman, the
extrovert, the introvert, the hero, the villain, the intelligent person, the simple person,
the educated person, the uneducated person, the strong-willed person, the weak-willed
person, and so on to a virtually infinite number of possibilities or combinations. Such
characterization ranges, of course, from simple stereotypes to multi-dimensional com-
plexity. Refer back to T. S. Eliot's "Love Song of J. Alfred Prufrock" (p. 54) and study
Eliot's fictional creation, J. Alfred Prufrock. The form of the poem is that of the dramatic
monologue, in which the speaker speaks in his own voice and gradually reveals his char-
acter and situation. There is little chance that in a general as opposed to a psychologically
subtle way you would mistake Prufrock for the poet, T. S. Eliot.

Questions and Suggestions

1. Is Prufrock essentially a static or a dynamic character? If you think he is a static
    character, how does Eliot keep us interested in him? If you think he is a dynamic
    character, what makes him dynamic?

2. Describe in your own words Prufrock's problem. How well does he understand himself and his problem? Do you sympathize with him? Why or why not? In his own terms has he done what he can do to solve his problem?

3. The poem moves by means of a shift-of-association technique, just as the mind itself moves, without observing an ordered movement in time and space. Imagine yourself sketching a plot for a short story about Prufrock. Write your plot sketch on the assumption that you will tell the story of Prufrock in a straight narrative manner with a movement ordered in time and space. Allow yourself the liberty of one flashback, that is, one movement from present time to past time and then back to present time.

Following are some further examples of fictional characters who are distinctly separate people from the poet who creates them, but rather than being characters who, like Prufrock, reveal themselves in the first person, they are characters created by a third-person speaker; note, however, that in "Mr. Flood's Party" E. A. Robinson combines the use of first person and third person.

Geoffrey Chaucer   (c. 1343—1400)

The Portrait of the Knight
From THE GENERAL PROLOGUE OF THE CANTERBURY TALES
*Translation by Nevill Coghill**

    A Knyght ther was, and that a worthy man,
    That fro the tyme that he first bigan
    To riden out, he loved chivalrye,
    Trouthe and honour, fredom and curteisye.
5 Full worthy was he in his lordes werre,
    And therto hadde he riden, no man ferre,
    As wel in Cristendom as in hethenesse,
    And evere honoured for his worthynesse.
      At Alisaundre he was whan it was wonne.
10 Ful ofte tyme he hadde the bord bigonne
    Aboven alle nacions in Pruce;
    In Lettow had he reysed, and in Ruce,
    No Cristen man so ofte of his degree.
    In Gernade at the seege eek hadde he be
15 Of Algezir, and riden in Belmarye.
    At Lyeys was he, and at Satalye
    Whan they were wonne; and in the Grete See
    At many a noble armee hadde he be.
    At mortal batailles hadde he been fiftene,
20 And foughten for oure feith at Tramyssene
    In lystes thries, and ay slayn his foo.
    This ilke worthy knyght hadde been also
    Somtyme with the lord of Palatye
    Agayn another hethen in Turkye.
25 And everemoore he hadde a sovereyn prys;
    And though that he were worthy, he was wys,
    And of his port as meeke as is a mayde.
    He nevere yet no vileynye ne sayde
    In al his lyf unto no maner wight.
30 He was a verray, parfit, gentil knyght.
      But for to tellen yow of his array,
    His hors were goode, but he was nat gay.
    Of fustian he wered a gypon
    Al bismotered with his habergeon,
35 For he was late ycome from his viage
    And wente for to doon his pilgrymage.

*Note: The translation is *not* always line for line.

There was a *Knight,* a most distinguished man,
Who from the day on which he first began
To ride abroad had followed chivalry,
Truth, honor, greatness of heart and courtesy.
5   He had done nobly in his sovereign's war
And ridden into battle, no man more,
As well in christian as in heathen places,
And ever honored for his noble graces.
    He saw the town of Alexandria fall;
10 Often, at feasts, the highest place of all
Among the nations fell to him in Prussia.
In Lithuania he had fought, and Russia,
No christian man so often, of his rank.
And he was in Granada when they sank
15 The town of Algeciras, also in
North Africa, right through Benamarin;
And in Armenia he had been as well
And fought when Ayas and Attalia fell,
For all along the Mediterranean coast
20 He had embarked with many a noble host.
In fifteen mortal battles he had been
And jousted for our faith at Tramissene
Thrice in the lists, and always killed his man.
This same distinguished knight had led the van
25 Once with the Bey of Balat, doing work
For him against another heathen Turk;
He was of sovereign value in all eyes.
And though so much distinguished, he was wise
And in his bearing modest as a maid.
30 He never yet a boorish thing had said
In all his life to any, come what might;
He was a true, a perfect gentle-knight.
    Speaking of his appearance, he possessed
Fine horses, but he was not gaily dressed.
35 He wore a fustian tunic stained and dark
With smudges where his armor had left mark;
Just home from service, he had joined our ranks
To do his pilgrimage and render thanks.

Questions and Suggestions

1. In the short story expository passages often get us interested in a character by describing him. This in turn involves the problem of the *selection* of detail, especially vivid detail, and its *arrangement.* Comment on the selection and arrangement of detail in the portrait of the Knight.
2. What *type* of character is the Knight? What details emphasize him as a type and what details tend to individualize him?

Edwin Arlington Robinson   (1869—1935)
Mr. Flood's Party

Old Eben Flood, climbing alone one night
Over the hill between the town below
And the forsaken upland hermitage
That held as much as he should ever know
5 On earth again of home, paused warily.
The road was his with not a native near;
And Eben, having leisure, said aloud,
For no man else in Tilbury Town to hear:

"Well, Mr. Flood, we have the harvest moon
10 Again, and we may not have many more;
The bird is on the wing, the poet says,
And you and I have said it here before.
Drink to the bird." He raised up to the light
The jug that he had gone so far to fill,
15 And answered huskily: "Well, Mr. Flood,
Since you propose it, I believe I will."

Alone, as if enduring to the end
A valiant armor of scarred hopes outworn,
He stood there in the middle of the road
20 Like Roland's ghost winding a silent horn.
Below him, in the town among the trees,
Where friends of other days had honored him,
A phantom salutation of the dead
Rang thinly till old Eben's eyes were dim.

25 Then, as a mother lays her sleeping child
Down tenderly, fearing it may awake,

---

8 *Tilbury Town*   A fictitious name for Gardiner, Maine.   **11** *the poet*   Omar Khayyám. See stanza 7 of *The Rubáiyát* (p. 308).   **20** *Roland*   The hero of the medieval French romance *The So of Roland.*

He set the jug down slowly at his feet
With trembling care, knowing that most things break;
And only when assured that on firm earth
30   It stood, as the uncertain lives of men
Assuredly did not, he paced away,
And with his hand extended paused again:

"Well, Mr. Flood, we have not met like this
In a long time; and many a change has come
35   To both of us, I fear, since last it was
We had a drop together. Welcome home!"
Convivially returning with himself,
Again he raised the jug up to the light;
And with an acquiescent quaver said:
40   "Well, Mr. Flood, if you insist, I might.

"Only a very little, Mr. Flood—
For auld lang syne. No more, sir; that will do."
So, for the time, apparently it did,
And Eben evidently thought so too;
45   For soon amid the silver loneliness
Of night he lifted up his voice and sang,
Secure, with only two moons listening,
Until the whole harmonious landscape rang—

"For auld lang syne." The weary throat gave out,
50   The last word wavered; and the song being done,
He raised again the jug regretfully
And shook his head, and was again alone.
There was not much that was ahead of him,
And there was nothing in the town below—
55   Where strangers would have shut the many doors
That many friends had opened long ago.

42 *auld lang syne*   Literally, old long since; hence, long ago, the good old times.

Questions and Suggestions

1. Do you enjoy Mr. Flood as a comic character? What is there about his character
   or his situation that makes you laugh?
2. Can you see some reasons *why* Robinson combines third person and first person
   in this poem?

Wilfred Owen   (1893–1918)
Disabled

He sat in a wheeled chair, waiting for dark,
And shivered in his ghastly suit of grey,
Legless, sewn short at elbow. Through the park
Voices of boys rang saddening like a hymn,
5 Voices of play and pleasures after day,
Till gathering sleep had mothered them from him.

About this time Town used to swing so gay
When glow-lamps budded in the light blue trees,
And girls glanced lovelier as the air grew dim,—
10 In the old times, before he threw away his knees.
Now he will never feel again how slim
Girls' waists are, or how warm their subtle hands;
All of them touch him like some queer disease.

There was an artist silly for his face,
15 For it was younger than his youth, last year.
Now, he is old; his back will never brace;
He's lost his colour very far from here,
Poured it down shell-holes till the veins ran dry,
And half his lifetime lapsed in the hot race,
20 And leap of purple spurted from his thigh.

One time he liked a blood-smear down his leg,
After the matches, carried shoulder-high.
It was after football, when he'd drunk a peg,
He thought he'd better join.—He wonders why.
25 Someone had said he'd look a god in kilts,
That's why; and may be, too, to please his Meg;
Aye, that was it, to please the giddy jilts
He asked to join. He didn't have to beg;
Smiling they wrote his lie; aged nineteen years.
30 Germans he scarcely thought of; all their guilt,
And Austria's, did not move him. And no fears
Of Fear came yet. He thought of jewelled hilts
For daggers in plaid socks; of smart salutes;
And care of arms; and leave; and pay arrears;
35 *Esprit de corps;* and hints for young recruits.
And soon he was drafted out with drums and cheers.

Some cheered him home, but not as crowds cheer Goal.
Only a solemn man who brought him fruits
Thanked him; and then inquired about his soul.

40 Now, he will spend a few sick years in Institutes,
    And do what things the rules consider wise,
    And take whatever pity they may dole.
    To-night he noticed how the women's eyes
    Passed from him to the strong men that were whole.
45 How cold and late it is! Why don't they come
    And put him into bed? Why don't they come?

Questions and Suggestions

1. What details of the poem identify the disabled man as a casualty of World War I?
   In what basic ways does the author suggest a general concern for anyone who is the
   victim of war?
2. Is the poem at all sentimental? Explain.

W. H. Auden (1907–   )
The Unknown Citizen

(To JS/07/M/378
This Marble Monument
Is Erected by the State)

He was found by the Bureau of Statistics to be
One against whom there was no official complaint,
And all the reports on his conduct agree
That, in the modern sense of an old-fashioned word, he was a saint,
5 For in everything he did he served the Greater Community.
Except for the War till the day he retired
He worked in a factory and never got fired,
But satisfied his employers, Fudge Motors Inc.
Yet he wasn't a scab or odd in his views,
10 For his Union reports that he paid his dues,
(Our report on his Union shows it was sound)
And our Social Psychology workers found
That he was popular with his mates and liked a drink.
The Press are convinced that he bought a paper every day
15 And that his reactions to advertisements were normal in every way.
Policies taken out in his name prove that he was fully insured,
And his Health-card shows he was once in hospital but left it cured.
Both Producers Research and High-Grade Living declare
He was fully sensible to the advantages of the Instalment Plan
20 And had everything necessary to the Modern Man,
A phonograph, a radio, a car and a frigidaire.

Our researchers into Public Opinion are content
That he held the proper opinions for the time of year;
When there was peace, he was for peace; when there was war, he went.
25 He was married and added five children to the population,
Which our Eugenist says was the right number for a parent of his generation,
And our teachers report that he never interfered with their education.
Was he free? Was he happy? The question is absurd:
Had anything been wrong, we should certainly have heard.

Questions and Suggestions

1. What details would you choose in order to characterize the unknown citizen as
    he might exist today? Auden's poem is some thirty years old. In what specific ways
    is it still up-to-date?
2. What Auden's Unknown Citizen is implies what he is not. Write a paragraph
    sketching what the Unknown Citizen is not.

Gwendolyn Brooks   (1915—   )
The Lovers of the Poor

                    arrive. The Ladies from the Ladies' Betterment League
Arrive in the afternoon, the late light slanting
In diluted gold bars across the boulevard brag
Of proud, seamed faces with mercy and murder hinting
5   Here, there, interrupting, all deep and debonair,
The pink paint on the innocence of fear;
Walk in a gingerly manner up the hall.
Cutting with knives served by their softest care,
Served by their love, so barbarously fair.
10 Whose mothers taught: You'd better not be cruel!
You had better not throw stones upon the wrens!
Herein they kiss and coddle and assault
Anew and dearly in the innocence
With which they baffle nature. Who are full,
15 Sleek, tender-clad, fit, fiftyish, a-glow, all
Sweetly abortive, hinting at fat fruit,
Judge it high time that fiftyish fingers felt
Beneath the lovelier planes of enterprise.
To resurrect. To moisten with milky chill.
20 To be a random hitching-post or plush.
To be, for wet eyes, random and handy hem.
                    Their guild is giving money to the poor.
The worthy poor. The very very worthy
And beautiful poor. Perhaps just not too swarthy?

25   Perhaps just not too dirty nor too dim
     Nor—passionate. In truth, what they could wish
     Is—something less than derelict or dull.
     Not staunch enough to stab, though, gaze for gaze!
     God shield them sharply from the beggar-bold!
30   The noxious needy ones whose battle's bald
     Nonetheless for being voiceless, hits one down.
                But it's all so bad! and entirely too much for them.
     The stench; the urine, cabbage, and dead beans,
     Dead porridges of assorted dusty grains,
35   The old smoke, *heavy* diapers, and, they're told,
     Something called chitterlings. The darkness. Drawn
     Darkness, or dirty light. The soil that stirs.
     The soil that looks the soil of centuries.
     And for that matter the *general* oldness. Old
40   Wood. Old marble. Old tile. Old old old.
     Not homekind Oldness! Not Lake Forest, Glencoe.
     Nothing is sturdy, nothing is majestic,
     There is no quiet drama, no rubbed glaze, no
     Unkillable infirmity of such
45   A tasteful turn as lately they have left,
     Glencoe, Lake Forest, and to which their cars
     Must presently restore them. When they're done
     With dullards and distortions of this fistic
     Patience of the poor and put-upon.
50   They've never seen such a make-do-ness as
     Newspaper rugs before! In this, this "flat,"
     Their hostess is gathering up the oozed, the rich
     Rugs of the morning (tattered! the bespattered. . . .)
     Readies to spread clean rugs for afternoon.
55   Here is a scene for you. The Ladies look,
     In horror, behind a substantial citizeness
     Whose trains clank out across her swollen heart.
     Who, arms akimbo, almost fills a door.
     All tumbling children, quilts dragged to the floor
60   And tortured thereover, potato peelings, soft-
     Eyed kitten, hunched-up, haggard, to-be-hurt.
           Their League is allotting largesse to the Lost.
     But to put their clean, their pretty money, to put
     Their money collected from delicate rose-fingers
65   Tipped with their hundred flawless rose-nails seems . . .
          They own Spode, Lowestoft, candelabra,

---

36 *chitterlings* Hog intestines, especially as used for food.   **41** *Lake Forest, Glencoe*
Wealthy suburbs of Chicago.   **66** *Spode, Lowestoft* Fine English china, Spode is named for Josiah
Spode (1754–1827), who made chinaware in the latter part of the eighteenth century; Lowestoft ware
is named for the town in East Suffolk which manufactured it.

Mantels, and hostess gowns, and sunburst clocks,
Turtle soup, Chippendale, red satin "hangings,"
Aubussons and Hattie Carnegie. They Winter
70   In Palm Beach; cross the Water in June; attend,
When suitable, the nice Art Institute;
Buy the right books in the best bindings; saunter
On Michigan, Easter mornings, in sun or wind.
Oh Squalor! This sick four-story hulk, this fibre
75   With fissures everywhere! Why, what are bringings
Of loathe-love largesse? What shall peril hungers
So old old, what shall flatter the desolate?
Tin can, blocked fire escape and chitterling
And swaggering seeking youth and the puzzled wreckage
80   Of the middle passage, and urine and stale shames
And, again, the porridges of the underslung
And children children children. Heavens! That
Was a rat, surely, off there, in the shadows? Long
And long-tailed? Gray? The Ladies from the Ladies'
85   Betterment League agree it will be better
To achieve the outer air that rights and steadies,
To hie to a house that does not holler, to ring
Bells elsetime, better presently to cater
To no more Possibilities, to get
90   Away. Perhaps the money can be posted.
Perhaps they two may choose another Slum!
Some serious sooty half-unhappy home!—
Where loathe-love likelier may be invested.
                    Keeping their scented bodies in the center
95   Of the hall as they walk down the hysterical hall,
They allow their lovely skirts to graze no wall,
Are off at what they manage of a canter,
And, resuming all the clues of what they were,
Try to avoid inhaling the laden air.

68 *Chippendale*   Furniture made by Thomas Chippendale (c. 1718-1779), known for its
beautiful proportions, strength, and durability, and very valuable as antiques.   **69** *Aubussons*   Fine
tapestries, named for a town in central France where they have been made for hundreds of years.
Hattie Carnegie   Fashionable clothes by Hattie Carnegie (1889-1956), a well-known couturière (one
who designs, makes, and sells fashionable women's clothing).   **70** *cross the Water*   Travel to Europe.
71 *Art Institute*   The Art Institute of Chicago.   **73** *Michigan*   Michigan Avenue in Chicago, well-
known for its luxurious stores.

Questions and Suggestions

1.   This poem is a characterization both of The Lovers of the Poor and of the life which
     the poor live in slum or ghetto. The contrast is stark. Do you find it convincing, or
     too simple?

2. Consider the poem as a structure. What are its basic parts or divisions? How do the parts relate to one another and move toward a conclusion?

The examples given thus far ought at least to suggest that characterization is one of the fundamental things we experience in poetry, with possibilities as rich and varied as life itself and virtually without limit. Following is a group of examples emphasizing what we might call character and dramatic moment. We have suggested that poems (other than narrative poems) do not tell a story in the usual sense. The following poems "break in" to a dramatic situation. Somewhat suddenly, though briefly, we are there, which is very commonly what poems do, the way they work. Each is in the first person, the poet creating a fictional character, or a persona, a mask.

Percy Bysshe Shelley   (1792–1822)
Ode to the West Wind

1

O wild West Wind, thou breath of Autumn's being,
Thou, from whose unseen presence the leaves dead
Are driven, like ghosts from an enchanter fleeing,

Yellow, and black, and pale, and hectic red,
5 Pestilence-stricken multitudes: O thou,
Who chariotest to their dark wintry bed

The wingèd seeds, where they lie cold and low,
Each like a corpse within its grave, until
Thine azure sister of the spring shall blow

10 Her clarion o'er the dreaming earth, and fill
(Driving sweet buds like flocks to feed in air)
With living hues and odours plain and hill;

Wild Spirit, which art moving everywhere;
Destroyer and preserver; hear, Oh hear!

2

15 Thou on whose stream, 'mid the steep sky's commotion,
Loose clouds like earth's decaying leaves are shed,
Shook from the tangled boughs of Heaven and Ocean,

Angels of rain and lightning: there are spread
On the blue surface of thine airy surge,
20 Like the bright hair uplifted from the head

Of some fierce Mænad, even from the dim verge
Of the horizon to the zenith's height
The locks of the approaching storm. Thou dirge

Of the dying year, to which this closing night
25   Will be the dome of a vast sepulchre,
Vaulted with all thy congregated might

Of vapours, from whose solid atmosphere
Black rain, and fire, and hail will burst: Oh hear!

3

Thou who didst waken from his summer dreams
30   The blue Mediterranean, where he lay,
Lulled by the coil of his crystalline streams,

Beside a pumice isle in Baiæ's bay,
And saw in sleep old palaces and towers
Quivering within the wave's intenser day,

35   All overgrown with azure moss and flowers
So sweet, the sense faints picturing them! Thou
For whose path the Atlantic's level powers

Cleave themselves into chasms, while far below
The sea-blooms and the oozy woods which wear
40   The sapless foliage of the ocean, know

Thy voice, and suddenly grow gray with fear,
And tremble and despoil themselves: Oh hear!

4

If I were a dead leaf thou mightest bear;
If I were a swift cloud to fly with thee;
45   A wave to pant beneath thy power, and share

The impulse of thy strength, only less free
Than thou, O uncontrollable! If even
I were as in my boyhood, and could be

---

21 *Mænad* An attendant of Dionysus, Greek god of wine.   **32** *Baiæ's bay* Baiæ was an ancient city in southwest Italy.

The comrade of thy wanderings over heaven,
50 As then, when to outstrip thy skiey speed
Scarce seemed a vision; I would ne'er have striven

As thus with thee in prayer in my sore need.
Oh! lift me as a wave, a leaf, a cloud!
I fall upon the thorns of life! I bleed!

55 A heavy weight of hours has chained and bowed
One too like thee; tameless, and swift, and proud.

5

Make me thy lyre, even as the forest is:
What if my leaves are falling like its own!
The tumult of thy mighty harmonies

60 Will take from both a deep autumnal tone,
Sweet though in sadness. Be thou, spirit fierce,
My spirit! Be thou me, impetuous one!

Drive my dead thoughts over the universe
Like withered leaves to quicken a new birth!
65 And, by the incantation of this verse,

Scatter, as from an unextinguished hearth
Ashes and sparks, my words among mankind!
Be through my lips to unawakened earth

The trumpet of a prophecy! O, wind,
70 If Winter comes, can Spring be far behind?

Questions and Suggestions

1. Suggest how the dynamism of the speaker's personality helps make him seem like a believable character. Are you prompted, as some have been, to make fun of the speaker for the line, "I fall upon the thorns of life! I bleed!" (l. 54)?
2. Describe the movement of the poem from Part 1 through Part 5.

William Butler Yeats   (1865–1939)
Sailing to Byzantium

1

That is no country for old men. The young
In one another's arms, birds in the trees
—Those dying generations—at their song,
The salmon-falls, the mackerel-crowded seas,
5 Fish, flesh, or fowl, commend all summer long
Whatever is begotten, born, and dies.
Caught in that sensual music all neglect
Monuments of unageing intellect.

2

An aged man is but a paltry thing,
10 A tattered coat upon a stick, unless
Soul clap its hands and sing, and louder sing
For every tatter in its mortal dress,
Nor is there singing school but studying
Monuments of its own magnificence;
15 And therefore I have sailed the seas and come
To the holy city of Byzantium.

3

O sages standing in God's holy fire
As in the gold mosaic of a wall,
Come from the holy fire, perne in a gyre,
20 And be the singing-masters of my soul.
Consume my heart away; sick with desire
And fastened to a dying animal
It knows not what it is; and gather me
Into the artifice of eternity.

4

25 Once out of nature I shall never take
My bodily form from any natural thing,
But such a form as Grecian goldsmiths make
Of hammered gold and gold enamelling
To keep a drowsy Emperor awake;
30 Or set upon a golden bough to sing
To lords and ladies of Byzantium
Of what is past, or passing, or to come.

Byzantium Ancient city on the Bosporus, formerly Constantinople, today Istanbul. Byzantium
was the capital of the Eastern Roman Empire, a center of culture, religion, and art.   **19** *perne in a
gyre* Spiral.

Questions and Suggestions

1. The speaker is an old man. How is he like an old man as you usually think of an old man? How is he different?
2. What is the speaker's view of himself? Why would he be gathered into the artifice of eternity rather than into eternity itself?

Theodore Roethke   (1908–1963)
Elegy for Jane
My Student, Thrown by a Horse

I remember the neckcurls, limp and damp as tendrils;
And her quick look, a sidelong pickerel smile;
And how, once startled into talk, the light syllables leaped for her,
And she balanced in the delight of her thought,
5 A wren, happy, tail into the wind,
Her song trembling the twigs and small branches.
The shade sang with her;
The leaves, their whispers turned to kissing;
And the mold sang in the bleached valleys under the rose.

10 Oh, when she was sad, she cast herself down into such a pure depth,
Even a father could not find her:
Scraping her cheek against straw;
Stirring the clearest water.

My sparrow, you are not here,
15 Waiting like a fern, making a spiny shadow.
The sides of wet stones cannot console me,
Nor the moss, wound with the last light.

If only I could nudge you from this sleep,
My maimed darling, my skittery pigeon.
20 Over this damp grave I speak the words of my love:
I, with no rights in this matter,
Neither father nor lover.

Questions and Suggestions

1. An elegy inevitably characterizes both the person mourned for and the person doing the mourning. Roethke did not actually know his student Jane very well. Does this fact make his emotion less legitimate, his characterization of her less believable? Does it enhance your understanding of the last three lines of the poem?
2. Notice the speaker's references to birds and to song. How do these references reveal his character and emotion? What other devices does he use to project character and feelings?

Robert Lowell   (1917–   )
Skunk Hour
(For Elizabeth Bishop)

Nautilus Island's hermit
heiress still lives through winter in her Spartan cottage;
her sheep still graze above the sea.
Her son's a bishop. Her farmer
5 is first selectman in our village;
she's in her dotage.

Thirsting for
the hierarchic privacy
of Queen Victoria's century,
10 she buys up all
the eyesores facing her shore,
and lets them fall.

The season's ill—
we've lost our summer millionaire,
15 who seemed to leap from an L. L. Bean
catalogue. His nine-knot yawl
was auctioned off to lobstermen.
A red fox stain covers Blue Hill.

And now our fairy
20 decorator brightens his shop for fall;
his fishnet's filled with orange cork,
orange, his cobbler's bench and awl;
there is no money in his work,
he'd rather marry.

25 One dark night,
my Tudor Ford climbed the hill's skull;
I watched for love-cars. Lights turned down,
they lay together, hull to hull,
where the graveyard shelves on the town. . . .
30 My mind's not right.

A car radio bleats,
"Love, O careless Love. . . ." I hear
my ill-spirit sob in each blood cell,
as if my hand were at its throat. . . .

1 *Nautilus Island*   An island just south of Castine, Maine, at the mouth of the Bagaduce River in Penobscot Bay.   15-16 *an L. L. Bean catalogue*   L. L. Bean is a Maine mail-order house and specializes in items for sportsmen.   18 *Blue Hill*   A town on the coast of Maine southeast of Bangor.   26 *Tudor Ford*   A two-door Ford car of the 1930s and '40s.

35   I myself am hell;
     nobody's here—

     only skunks, that search
     in the moonlight for a bite to eat.
     They march on their soles up Main Street:
40   white stripes, moonstruck eyes' red fire
     under the chalk-dry and spar spire
     of the Trinitarian Church.

     I stand on top
     of our back steps and breathe the rich air—
45   a mother skunk with her column of kittens swills the garbage pail.
     She jabs her wedge-head in a cup
     of sour cream, drops her ostrich tail,
     and will not scare.

Questions and Suggestions

1. The term "confessional" has been applied to this and to other Lowell poems. Do you find the term apt? Explain.
2. The speaker defines his problem as "hell"—"I myself am hell" (l. 35). Do you find him convincing? Is the problem of modern life as a psychological hell one which you have seen before, in movies, on television, in magazines? How does what you know of the problem compare with what you find in the poem?
3. Although the speaker feels what hell is like, is he also affirmative?

In poetry there is no greater achievement of characterization than that to be found in the plays, that is, in the poetic drama, of William Shakespeare. It thus seems appropriate to conclude this chapter with two soliloquies from *Hamlet,* the third and the fourth. They are, of course, part of a very long play, almost 4000 lines, a play probably as complex as any ever written, but the soliloquies may nevertheless be appreciated as separate poems, especially if one knows the basic outline of the plot. Hamlet's father has been murdered by his Uncle Claudius, who marries Hamlet's mother and becomes King of Denmark. The Ghost of Hamlet's father reveals the fact of the murder to Hamlet and enjoins him to take revenge. But Hamlet has doubts, for the Ghost may be an apparition or a devil in disguise. At the time of the third soliloquy, having decided to test Claudius with a play representing Claudius' murder of his father, Hamlet is meditating on the meaning of life. At the time of the fourth soliloquy he is on his way to England, sent there by Claudius, who plans to have him murdered there. Hamlet sees the army of Fortinbras on its way to Poland and the fourth soliloquy follows.

For both soliloquies full facing-page notes are included. Shakespeare's language merits close attention.

William Shakespeare   (1564–1616)
To Be or Not to Be
From HAMLET (III, i, 56-88)

    Enter Hamlet.

Hamlet. To be, or not to be, that is the question:
    Whether 'tis nobler in the mind to suffer
    The slings and arrows of outrageous fortune
    Or to take arms against a sea of troubles
5   And by opposing end them. To die, to sleep—
    No more—and by a sleep to say we end
    The heartache, and the thousand natural shocks
    That flesh is heir to. 'Tis a consummation
    Devoutly to be wished. To die, to sleep—
10   To sleep, perchance to dream, ay there's the rub,
    For in that sleep of death what dreams may come
    When we have shuffled off this mortal coil
    Must give us pause. There's the respect
    That makes calamity of so long life.
15   For who would bear the whips and scorns of time,
    Th' oppressor's wrong, the proud man's contumely,
    The pangs of despised love, the law's delay,
    The insolence of office, and the spurns
    That patient merit of th' unworthy takes,
20   When he himself might his quietus make

1	*To be, or not to be*	To live or to die, but also to have a meaningful personal identity or none at all.
3	*slings*	Stones thrown by a sling, a weapon for hurling stones by hand with great force.
	outrageous fortune	Hamlet here personifies *fortune* as a warrior. *Outrageous* means excessive, violent, cruel.
4	*a sea of troubles*	A great mass of troubles, an immense quantity of problems. To take arms against a sea is technically a mixed metaphor, since one does not normally use a weapon against water, but as C. H. Herford notes, the action of rushing against the waves of the sea with weapons in hand was a custom attributed to the Celts.
5	*by opposing end them*	By the act of fighting one's problems to end them.
8	*consummation*	A perfection, a fulfillment, an end, or death. Hamlet may also have in mind a sexual consummation as a symbol of a desired peace of mind.
10	*rub*	Obstacle. The term derives from the game of bowls and refers to anything that diverts the wood bowl, or ball, from its proper course as it rolls along the ground, and also to the bowl's actual meeting with such an obstacle.
12	*shuffled off this mortal coil*	It is difficult to say how visual a metaphor this is meant to be. *Shuffled* means cast off. *Coil* is usually glossed abstractly as turmoil, but its obvious meaning is a coil of rope. If Hamlet is thinking of a coil of rope, then coil must refer to the body. Thus *this mortal coil* could refer simply to the human body as it is known to suffer turmoil, or the technical term today would be *anxiety,* fear without an object. Perhaps the coil metaphor is essentially impressionistic, which would not be inconsistent with "to take arms against a sea of troubles."
13	*give us pause*	Cause us to hesitate.
	respect	View, consideration, the thing taken into account (rather than esteem).
14	*makes calamity of so long life*	Makes a calamity out of a long life.
15	*scorns*	Jeers. Hamlet uses a simple personification of time as something given to both physical and verbal abuse.
16	*contumely*	Contemptuous language or treatment.
17	*despised love*	A love that is received with contempt, or scorned.
	the law's delay	The slowness of judicial procedure, the long time it takes before a case is actually heard.
18	*insolence of office*	The contempt for the rights of others shown by men holding official positions.
	spurns	Kicks (physical blows) and the contempt that goes with them.
19	*patient merit*	Patient men of merit.
	of th' unworthy takes	Endures from the unworthy.
20	*quietus*	A legal term referring to debt settlement and here used in the sense of final debt settlement, or death.

With a bare bodkin? Who would fardels bear,
To grunt and sweat under a weary life,
But that the dread of something after death,
The undiscovered country, from whose bourn
25   No traveller returns, puzzles the will,
And makes us rather bear those ills we have
Than fly to others that we know not of?
Thus conscience does make cowards of us all,
And thus the native hue of resolution
30   Is sicklied o'er with the pale cast of thought,
And enterprises of great pitch and moment
With this regard their currents turn awry
And lose the name of action.

How All Occasions Do Inform Against Me
From HAMLET (IV, iv, 32-66)

Exeunt all but Hamlet.

How all occasions do inform against me
And spur my dull revenge! What is a man,
If his chief good and market of his time
Be but to sleep and feed? A beast, no more.
5   Sure he that made us with such large discourse,
Looking before and after, gave us not
That capability and godlike reason
To fust in us unused. Now, whether it be
Bestial oblivion, or some craven scruple
10   Of thinking too precisely on th' event—
A thought which, quartered, hath but one part wisdom
And ever three parts coward—I do not know
Why yet I live to say, 'This thing's to do,'
Sith I have cause, and will, and strength, and means

21	*bare bodkin*	A *bodkin* is a dagger or a pointed instrument used for such things as piercing holes in cloth or fastening up a woman's hair. In addition to meaning unsheathed, *bare* means mere. Hamlet's emphasis is on how little it takes to end a life.
	fardels	Packs or burdens, often in the figurative sense of burdens of sin or sorrow.
24	*bourn*	A boundary or limit.
28	*conscience*	In addition to the usual sense of the faculty that decides on the right or wrong of our actions, *conscience* here is inmost thought or deep reflection. It also carries the sense, etymologically, of self-knowledge (*cum scientia,* Latin for *knowing with*), or, to put it another way, the term identifies the relationship between thought and action as a central issue of the play.
29	*native hue*	Natural color, healthy complexion.
30	*sicklied o'er*	Becomes sick looking all over.
	cast	Tinge, hue.
31	*pitch*	Height. *Pitch* is also more specifically a term from falconry referring to the height to which the falcon soars before swooping down on its prey.
	moment	Importance, weight.
32	*currents*	Directions, courses. Note the consistency of this with *pitch* in the falconry metaphor.
	awry	To one side, off course.

1	*inform against me*	Take shape against me, accuse me.
2	*dull*	Sluggish, delayed.
3	*market of his time*	That for which he sells his time, the profit of his time.
5	*Sure*	Surely.
	discourse	Power of thought, breadth of comprehension.
6	*Looking before and after*	Able to look at past and future, reasoning from cause to effect.
8	*fust*	Grow mouldy or musty. A *fust* is a wine cask. The verb *fust* means to taste of the cask.
9	*Bestial oblivion*	Animal-like forgetfulness, unconscious disregard.
	craven scruple	Cowardly hesitation. A *scruple* is a doubt or hesitation in regard to right and wrong, especially such a doubt or hesitation that is overly refined.
13	*to do*	To be done, still not done.
14	*Sith*	Since.

15 To do't. Examples gross as earth exhort me.
Witness this army of such mass and charge,
Led by a delicate and tender prince,
Whose spirit, with divine ambition puffed,
Makes mouths at the invisible event,
20 Exposing what is mortal and unsure
To all that fortune, death, and danger dare,
Even for an eggshell. Rightly to be great
Is not to stir without great argument,
But greatly to find quarrel in a straw
25 When honor's at the stake. How stand I then,
That have a father killed, a mother stained,
Excitements of my reason and my blood,
And let all sleep, while to my shame I see
The imminent death of twenty thousand men
30 That for a fantasy and trick of fame
Go to their graves like beds, fight for a plot
Whereon the numbers cannot try the cause,
Which is not tomb enough and continent
To hide the slain? O, from this time forth,
35 My thoughts be bloody, or be nothing worth!   *Exit.*

15	*gross*	Large, heavy, conspicuous in magnitude, obvious.
	exhort	Urge, incite.
16	*mass and charge*	Size and burdensome cost.
17	*delicate and tender*	Sensitive and refined. *Tender* also means youthful and immature.
18	*with divine ambition puffed*	Inflated with godlike ambition. *Puffed* implies (as does *inflated*) that Fortinbras' ambition is an expression of vanity, is absurd.
19	*Makes mouths at the invisible event*	Mocks or scorns the unknown future, shows contempt for the risk involved.
21	*dare*	Threaten.
22	*Rightly*	Truly.
23	*argument*	Motive.
24-25	*greatly to find quarrel in a straw When honor's at the stake*	Eagerly to quarrel over a trifle for the sake of honor, to recognize the importance of and to fight for principle even in a trifling matter. *At the stake* means either risking the loss of, as in a wager, or threatened with death, as persons bound to a stake or post for execution, especially by burning. The latter possibility is made more cogent by Hamlet's reference to *a straw,* which as a material that burns easily is readily associated with the stake. The effect of this reading is to make Hamlet more bitter and to emphasize the utter necessity of fighting for principle.
26	*a father killed*	A father who has been killed.
	stained	Morally corrupted.
27	*Excitements*	Powerful feelings or motives.
30	*fantasy and trick of fame*	Illusion and trifle that hold the promise of fame.
31	*like*	As if they were.
	plot	Small piece of ground.
32	*Whereon the numbers cannot try the cause*	Which cannot even hold the number of soldiers fighting over it.
33	*continent*	Of sufficient capacity.

Description

The rose is a rose,
And was always a rose.
But the theory now goes
That the apple's a rose,
And the pear is, and so's
The plum, I suppose.

The dear only knows
What will next prove a rose.
You, of course, are a rose—
But were always a rose.

Robert Frost, "The Rose Family"

The poet is typically a creator of visual images, and to create visual images he must be able to describe, with sensitivity, with precision, with vividness. It is not so much a matter of the creation of poems of pure description, but rather of description as a vital element of poetry. Obviously some poems will be more descriptive or have more of a descriptive purpose than others. It is natural for a poet, as for any of us, to revel in the senses, and what could be more natural than for a poet to want to record his sense-revelling in words? What the poet sees becomes, moreover, part of his commitment to reality, his celebration of the universal through the particular. We thus come to take pleasure in what the poet describes, whether a person, the natural world, the world of man, or whatever combination his response to reality seems to dictate.

There is a large body of poetry sometimes called "nature poetry" and a number of poets sometimes called "nature poets." The terms on the surface are rather neutral, but they nevertheless sometimes carry the unfortunate suggestion of a sentimental response to the natural world. Good poets are not sentimentalists. Their emotions, rather, are deep, honest, and genuine. Consider, for example, the following short poems, which it would be fair to call nature poetry, and which reach rather beautifully for the descriptive moment.

Samuel Taylor Coleridge   (1772—1834)
Sea-Ward, White Gleaming

Sea-ward, white gleaming thro' the busy scud
With arching Wings, the sea-mew o'er my head
Posts on, as bent on speed, now passaging
Edges the stiffer Breeze, now, yielding, drifts,
5 Now floats upon the air, and sends from far
A wildly-wailing Note.

Walt Whitman   (1819–1892)
The Dalliance of the Eagles

Skirting the river road, (my forenoon walk, my rest,)
Skyward in air a sudden muffled sound, the dalliance of the eagles,
The rushing amorous contact high in space together,
The clinching interlocking claws, a living, fierce, gyrating wheel,
5   Four beating wings, two beaks, a swirling mass tight grappling,
In tumbling turning clustering loops, straight downward falling,
Till o'er the river pois'd, the twain yet one, a moment's lull,
A motionless still balance in the air, then parting, talons loosing,
Upward again on slow-firm pinions slanting, their separate diverse flight,
10   She hers, he his, pursuing.

T. S. Eliot   (1888–1965)
V. Cape Ann
From LANDSCAPES

O quick quick quick, quick hear the song-sparrow,
Swamp-sparrow, fox-sparrow, vesper-sparrow
At dawn and dusk. Follow the dance
Of the goldfinch at noon. Leave to chance
5   The Blackburnian warbler, the shy one. Hail
With shrill whistle the note of the quail, the bob-white
Dodging by bay-bush. Follow the feet
Of the walker, the water-thrush. Follow the flight
Of the dancing arrow, the purple martin. Greet
10   In silence the bullbat. All are delectable. Sweet sweet sweet
But resign this land at the end, resign it
To its true owner, the tough one, the sea-gull.
The palaver is finished.

Cape Ann   A cape or promontory located northeast of Boston.   **5** *Blackburnian warbler*
A North American warbler or singing bird.

Each leaves us with a strong visual impression, a strong visual image. Each is, if you will, dynamic. Each grasps reality by describing. And do you notice that metaphor—in the sense of a comparison between two normally unrelated objects—is used quite sparingly, Whitman's comparison of the eagles to a gyrating wheel being the one prominent metaphor in the three poems?

What matters in the poem with a strong descriptive purpose or with a strong element of description is, as I have implied, sensitivity, precision, and vividness. Whether or not such qualities are achieved *through* metaphor is essentially a technical matter. It is not, however, a minor technical matter for the simple reason that the resources of metaphor—of vivid comparison of objects normally unrelated—are often the necessary means for a poet to use in capturing a "just right" visual image. Following are some examples of strongly descriptive poems that are both literal, calling a bird a bird, a city a city, a bat a bat, and metaphoric, describing faces as rain-beaten stones, a city as a hog butcher, auto wrecks as empty husks of locusts. The questions and suggestions following each poem focus on objects mentioned or described in literal terms and on the use of metaphor as part of an overall descriptive process.

William Wordsworth (1770–1850)
Composed upon Westminster Bridge, September 3, 1802

Earth has not anything to show more fair:
Dull would he be of soul who could pass by
A sight so touching in its majesty;
This City now doth, like a garment, wear
5 The beauty of the morning; silent, bare,
Ships, towers, domes, theaters, and temples lie
Open unto the fields, and to the sky;
All bright and glittering in the smokeless air.
Never did sun more beautifully steep
10 In his first splendor, valley, rock, or hill;
Ne'er saw I, never felt, a calm so deep!
The river glideth at his own sweet will:
Dear God! the very houses seem asleep;
And all that mighty heart is lying still!

Questions and Suggestions

1. Comment on the poet's use of personification for purposes of description. How many uses of personification can you identify in this sonnet? (Reminder: *Personification* is a figure of speech in which human characteristics are attributed to inanimate objects, abstract ideas, or anything nonhuman.) Collect or invent a short list of personifications that seem to have a strongly descriptive purpose.
2. Comment on the level of generality of the speaker's description of London. Is it quite general, quite specific, or both? Does the sonnet have visual impact? Describe a city you have seen from a certain vantage point.

William Butler Yeats (1865–1939)
The Magi

Now as at all times I can see in the mind's eye,
In their stiff, painted clothes, the pale unsatisfied ones
Appear and disappear in the blue depth of the sky
With all their ancient faces like rain-beaten stones,

5 And all their helms of silver hovering side by side,
And all their eyes still fixed, hoping to find once more,
Being by Calvary's turbulence unsatisfied,
The uncontrollable mystery on the bestial floor.

Questions and Suggestions

1. Who were the Magi? Did you carry with you to this poem a visual image of them? Does the phrase "Calvary's turbulence" suggest a visual image to you?
2. Strike the metaphor "like rain-beaten stones" from line 4 and substitute a literal description for it. What is the effect of such a substitution?

Carl Sandburg (1879–1967)
Chicago

Hog Butcher for the World,
Tool Maker, Stacker of Wheat,
Player with Railroads and the Nation's Freight Handler;
Stormy, husky, brawling,
5   City of the Big Shoulders:

They tell me you are wicked and I believe them, for I have seen your painted
     women under the gas lamps luring the farm boys.
And they tell me you are crooked and I answer: Yes, it is true I have seen the
     gunman kill and go free to kill again.
And they tell me you are brutal and my reply is: On the faces of women and
     children I have seen the marks of wanton hunger.
And having answered so I turn once more to those who sneer at this my city,
     and I give them back the sneer and say to them:
10 Come and show me another city with lifted head singing so proud to be alive
     and coarse and strong and cunning.
Flinging magnetic curses amid the toil of piling job on job, here is a tall bold
     slugger set vivid against the little soft cities;
Fierce as a dog with tongue lapping for action, cunning as a savage pitted against
     the wilderness,
     Bareheaded,
     Shoveling,
15   Wrecking,
     Planning,
     Building, breaking, rebuilding,
Under the smoke, dust all over his mouth, laughing with white teeth,
Under the terrible burden of destiny laughing as a young man laughs,
20 Laughing even as an ignorant fighter laughs who has never lost a battle,
Bragging and laughing that under his wrist is the pulse, and under his ribs the heart
     of the people,
          Laughing!

Laughing the stormy, husky, brawling laughter of Youth, half-naked, sweating,
    proud to be Hog Butcher, Tool Maker, Stacker of Wheat, Player with Railroads
    and Freight Handler to the Nation.

Questions and Suggestions

1. Sandburg, in the manner of Whitman, uses a technique of cataloguing in his description. Does his cataloguing, which might appear random, actually represent a careful selection and arrangement of detail? Explain.
2. How much metaphor does Sandburg use before line 12 and the phrase "Fierce as a dog"? Is the city personified? Does the personification seem easy and natural or strained?
3. Write a brief description of Chicago as if you were the Wordsworth of "Composed upon Westminster Bridge," and a brief description of Wordsworth's London as if you were Sandburg.

Karl Shapiro   (1913–   )
Auto Wreck

Its quick soft silver bell beating, beating,
And down the dark one ruby flare
Pulsing out red light like an artery,
The ambulance at top speed floating down
5 Past beacons and illuminated clocks
Wings in a heavy curve, dips down,
And brakes speed, entering the crowd.
The doors leap open, emptying light;
Stretchers are laid out, the mangled lifted
10 And stowed into the little hospital.
Then the bell, breaking the hush, tolls once,
And the ambulance with its terrible cargo
Rocking, slightly rocking, moves away,
As the doors, an afterthought, are closed.

15 We are deranged, walking among the cops
Who sweep glass and are large and composed.
One is still making notes under the light.
One with a bucket douches ponds of blood
Into the street and gutter.
20 One hangs lanterns on the wrecks that cling,
Empty husks of locusts, to iron poles.

Our throats were tight as tourniquets,
Our feet were bound with splints, but now,

       Like convalescents intimate and gauche,
25 We speak through sickly smiles and warn
       With the stubborn saw of common sense,
       The grim joke and the banal resolution.
       The traffic moves around with care,
       But we remain, touching a wound
30 That opens to our richest horror.
       Already old, the question Who shall die?
       Becomes unspoken Who is innocent?
       For death in war is done by hands;
       Suicide has cause and stillbirth, logic;
35 And cancer, simple as a flower, blooms.
       But this invites the occult mind,
       Cancels our physics with a sneer,
       And spatters all we knew of denouement
       Across the expedient and wicked stones.

Questions and Suggestions

1. Imagine yourself as a reporter writing up this accident. What details would you
    include or exclude from your report and why? What words would you definitely
    use, what words might you use, and what words would you definitely not use?
    Explain.
2. Does the poem make a strong use of metaphor? Where does metaphor in the poem
    seem to have its strongest visual impact?

Randall Jarrell   (1914–1965)
Bats

       A bat is born
       Naked and blind and pale.
       His mother makes a pocket of her tail
       And catches him. He clings to her long fur
5 By his thumbs and toes and teeth.
       And then the mother dances through the night
       Doubling and looping, soaring, somersaulting—
       Her baby hangs on underneath.
       All night, in happiness, she hunts and flies.
10 Her high sharp cries
       Like shining needlepoints of sound
       Go out into the night and, echoing back,
       Tell her what they have touched.
       She hears how far it is, how big it is,
15 Which way it's going:
       She lives by hearing.

The mother eats the moths and gnats she catches
In full flight; in full flight
The mother drinks the water of the pond
20 She skims across. Her baby hangs on tight.
Her baby drinks the milk she makes him
In moonlight or starlight, in mid-air.
Their single shadow, printed on the moon
Or fluttering across the stars,
25 Whirls on all night; at daybreak
The tired mother flaps home to her rafter.
The others all are there.
They hang themselves up by their toes,
They wrap themselves in their brown wings.
30 Bunched upside-down, they sleep in air.
Their sharp ears, their sharp teeth, their quick sharp faces
Are dull and slow and mild.
All the bright day, as the mother sleeps,
She folds her wings about her sleeping child.

Questions and Suggestions

1. As description this poem is relatively simple and matter-of-fact. Write a paragraph explaining how simplicity and matter-of-factness are *suggestive*.
2. Look up an encyclopedia article on bats. Does the article lead you to a new perspective on the poem? Do both article and poem get you interested in bats? Explain.

John Logan   (1923–   )
White Pass Ski Patrol

His high-boned, young face is so brown
from the winter's sun,
the few brief lines in each green eye's
edge as of a leaf
5 that is not yet gone from the limb—
as of a nut which is gold or brown.

For he has become very strong
living on the slopes.
His belly and thighs are newly
10 lean from the thin skis.
Tough torso of the man, blue wooled.
Thin waist. White, tasseled cap of the child.

   White Pass A winter sports area in the Cascades (l. 27) about thirty miles west of Yakima, Washington.

Beneath the fury of those great,
dyn dark panes of glass, that

15 seem to take a man out of grace,
his gentle eyes wait.
(We feel their melancholy gaze
which is neither innocent nor wise.)

Like those knights of the winter snows—
20 with a healing pack
(sign of the cross on breast and back)—
serene, snow-lonely,
he patrols the beautiful peaks
and the pale wastes that slide like a beast.

25 Sometimes still blind from his patrol,
you'll see him pull down
from the dangerous Cascades his
heavy sledge of pain,
its odd, black-booted, canvas-laced
30 shape alive or dead, without a face.

Colors blooming in the sun, he
caroms down his own
path, speeds (bending knees), dances side
to side, balancing.
35 Under-skis glow golden in the
snow spume around his Christiana.

And as he lifts away from us,
skis dangle like the
outstretched limbs of a frog in spring.
40 He swings gently in
the air, vulnerable, so much
the "poor, bare, forked" human animal.

And now he slowly rises up
over trees and snow.
45 He begins to grow more thin, and then
vanishes in air!
as, high in the lithe boughs of pines,
the silver leaves flake silently down.

---

27 *Cascades* A mountain range extending from northern California to British Columbia.
36 *Christiana* A skiing turn effected by shifting the weight to one advanced ski and turning its tip
outward.   **42** *"poor, bare, forked"* "Unaccommodated man is no more but such a poor, bare,
forked animal as thou art," spoken by King Lear to the disguised Edgar in Shakespeare's *King Lear*
(III, iv, 111-12).

There are the shadow tracks he left
50 down the long, white hill
beside the lift. Wait! Look up! Cloud
trails in the bright sky!
Breathing a wake of snow ribbons,
something has just flown over the mountain!

Questions and Suggestions

1. Comment on the speaker's use of color. Is his use of color both direct and indirect? Explain.
2. The focus of the poem is on the description of a single person. Does this seem to intensify the visual impact of the poem? Does the description of the ski patroller move in any way in ordered stages?

We have thus far emphasized description that is literal and description that is metaphorical in the restricted sense of vivid comparisons of objects normally unrelated. Our emphasis has been on metaphor as a technical means serving the ends of description, but metaphor is also used more broadly as a synonym for *symbol,* an object or a description that suggests meaning beyond itself. The idea of a symbol is implicit in the whole concept of a poem that creates a strong visual image. A poem that describes is rather likely to have a symbolic purpose, a meaning beyond itself. A poet's accuracy is of a different kind from scientific or clinical description, and the suggestion of meaning beyond the object itself *is* the accuracy of the poet's description. This is another way of saying that a poet's aim is to be faithful to the quality and complexity of experience. A poem may be considered an ordered or structured use of symbols and is itself thought of, finally, as a symbol (or metaphor, in the broad sense). A poem is made up of words, and each word is a symbol in that it signifies an object, an event, an idea, or the like. Metaphor in the restricted sense of comparison of objects normally unrelated is an aspect of language as a symbolic process. The whole poem becomes a complex symbol.

It would be false to minimize the complexity of the poem as symbolic process. But the poet as a creator of visual images is creating something to which most of us can respond immediately and directly, as we do to pictures of all kinds, to television, to movies. Despite a basic complexity, the symbolic suggestiveness of a description is often perceived immediately and directly, easily and naturally. For example, Wordsworth looks at London and sees it as a symbol of a certain kind of beauty; he is, as a matter of fact, explicit in telling us his purpose. Whitman's eagles in their "dalliance" come to suggest a relationship in a symbolic way. Shapiro's auto wreck is quickly felt as a symbol of irrational horror. One reason that as human beings we like to describe the things we see and experience—the grisly things as well as the beautiful—is that in deep and mysterious ways what we describe and how we describe it are reality for us.

Following, without question or comment, is a final group of poems that are strongly descriptive, that are poetry as a visual art.

John Keats   (1795–1821)
To Autumn

1

Season of mists and mellow fruitfulness,
  Close bosom-friend of the maturing sun;
Conspiring with him how to load and bless
  With fruit the vines that round the thatch-eaves run;
5 To bend with apples the mossed cottage-trees,
  And fill all fruit with ripeness to the core;
    To swell the gourd, and plump the hazel shells
With a sweet kernel; to set budding more,
And still more, later flowers for the bees,
10 Until they think warm days will never cease,
    For Summer has o'er-brimmed their clammy cells.

2

Who hath not seen thee oft amid thy store?
  Sometimes whoever seeks abroad may find
Thee sitting careless on a granary floor,
15 Thy hair soft-lifted by the winnowing wind;
Or on a half-reaped furrow sound asleep,
  Drowsed with the fume of poppies, while thy hook
    Spares the next swath and all its twinèd flowers:
And sometimes like a gleaner thou dost keep
20 Steady thy laden head across a brook;
  Or by a cider-press, with patient look,
    Thou watchest the last oozings hours by hours.

3

Where are the songs of Spring? Aye, where are they?
  Think not of them, thou hast thy music too—
25 While barrèd clouds bloom the soft-dying day,
  And touch the stubble-plains with rosy hue;
Then in a wailful choir the small gnats mourn
  Among the river sallows, borne aloft
    Or sinking as the light wind lives or dies;
30 And full-grown lambs loud bleat from hilly bourn;
  Hedge crickets sing; and now with treble soft
The redbreast whistles from a garden-croft;
  And gathering swallows twitter in the skies.

---

15 *winnowing* Blowing the chaff away from the grain.   **17** *hook* Scythe.   **19** *gleaner*
One who gathers reaped grain.   **28** *sallows* Willows.   **30** *bourn* Region.   **32** *garden-croft*
Enclosed garden.

Gerard Manley Hopkins   (1844—1889)
Pied Beauty

Glory be to God for dappled things—
   For skies of couple-colour as a brinded cow;
     For rose-moles all in stipple upon trout that swim;
Fresh-firecoal chestnut-falls; finches' wings;
5   Landscape plotted and pieced—fold, fallow and plough;
     And áll trádes, their gear and tackle and trim.
All things counter, original, spare, strange;
   Whatever is fickle, freckled (who knows how?)
    With swift, slow; sweet, sour; adazzle, dim;
10 He fathers-forth whose beauty is past change:
                  Praise him.

2 *brinded*   Brindled, streaked, spotted.

William Carlos Williams   (1883—1963)
The Yachts

contend in a sea which the land partly encloses
shielding them from the too heavy blows
of an ungoverned ocean which when it chooses

tortures the biggest hulls, the best man knows
5 to pit against its beating, and sinks them pitilessly.
Mothlike in mists, scintillant in the minute

brilliance of cloudless days, with broad bellying sails
they glide to the wind tossing green water
from their sharp prows while over them the crew crawls

10 ant-like, solicitously grooming them, releasing,
making fast as they turn, lean far over and having
caught the wind again, side by side, head for the mark.

In a well guarded arena of open water surrounded by
lesser and greater craft which, sycophant, lumbering
15 and flittering follow them, they appear youthful, rare

as the light of a happy eye, live with the grace
of all that in the mind is feckless, free and
naturally to be desired. Now the sea which holds them

is moody, lapping their glossy sides, as if feeling
20 for some slightest flaw but fails completely.
Today no race. Then the wind comes again. The yachts

move, jockeying for a start, the signal is set and they
are off. Now the waves strike at them but they are too
well made, they slip through, though they take in canvas.

25 Arms with hands grasping seek to clutch at the prows.
Bodies thrown recklessly in the way are cut aside.
It is a sea of faces about them in agony, in despair

until the horror of the race dawns staggering the mind,
the whole sea become an entanglement of watery bodies
30 lost to the world bearing what they cannot hold. Broken,

beaten, desolate, reaching from the dead to be taken up
they cry out, failing, failing! their cries rising
in waves still as the skillful yachts pass over.

Archibald MacLeish   (1892-   )
Immortal Autumn

I speak this poem now with grave and level voice
In praise of autumn, of the far-horn-winding fall.

I praise the flower-barren fields, the clouds, the tall
Unanswering branches where the wind makes sullen noise.

5 I praise the fall: it is the human season.
                                        Now
No more the foreign sun does meddle at our earth,
Enforce the green and bring the fallow land to birth,
Nor winter yet weigh all with silence the pine bough,

But now in autumn with the black and outcast crows
10 Share we the spacious world: the whispering year is gone:
There is more room to live now: the once secret dawn
Comes late by daylight and the dark unguarded goes.

Between the mutinous brave burning of the leaves
And winter's covering of our hearts with his deep snow
15 We are alone: there are no evening birds: we know
The naked moon: the tame stars circle at our eaves.

It is the human season. On this sterile air
Do words outcarry breath: the sound goes on and on.
I hear a dead man's cry from autumn long since gone.

20 I cry to you beyond upon this bitter air.

Richard Wilbur   (1921—   )
A Baroque Wall-Fountain in the Villa Sciarra

            Under the bronze crown
Too big for the head of the stone cherub whose feet
        A serpent has begun to eat,
Sweet water brims a cockle and braids down

5   Past spattered mosses, breaks
On the tipped edge of a second shell, and fills
        The massive third below. It spills
In threads then from the scalloped rim, and makes

            A scrim or summery tent
10 For a faun-ménage and their familiar goose.
        Happy in all that ragged, loose
Collapse of water, its effortless descent

            And flatteries of spray,
The stocky god upholds the shell with ease,
15   Watching, about his shaggy knees,
The goatish innocence of his babes at play;

            His fauness all the while
Leans forward, slightly, into a clambering mesh
        Of water-lights, her sparkling flesh
20 In a saecular ecstasy, her blinded smile

            Bent on the sand floor
Of the trefoil pool, where ripple-shadows come
        And go in swift reticulum,
More addling to the eye than wine, and more

Villa Sciarra Formerly a private estate in Rome but now public property, located southeast of the Vatican and on the west bank of the Tiber. The villa residence and the park surrounding it are bounded on three sides by the Wall of the Janiculum Hill; there are fountains in the wall at various points.   **4** *cockle* A plant or weed.   **22** *trefoil* Of a three-part design.   **23** *reticulum* Netlike structure, network.

25   Interminable to thought
Than pleasure's calculus. Yet since this all
Is pleasure, flash, and waterfall,
Must it not be too simple? Are we not

More intricately expressed
30   In the plain fountains that Maderna set
Before St. Peter's—the main jet
Struggling aloft until it seems at rest

In the act of rising, until
The very wish of water is reversed,
35   That heaviness borne up to burst
In a clear, high, cavorting head, to fill

With blaze, and then in gauze
Delays, in a gnatlike shimmering, in a fine
Illumined version of itself, decline,
40   And patter on the stones its own applause?

If that is what men are
Or should be, if those water-saints display
The pattern of our areté,
What of these showered fauns in their bizarre,

45   Spangled, and plunging house?
They are at rest in fulness of desire
For what is given, they do not tire
Of the smart of the sun, the pleasant water-douse

And riddled pool below,
50   Reproving our disgust and our ennui
With humble insatiety.
Francis, perhaps, who lay in sister snow

Before the wealthy gate
Freezing and praising, might have seen in this
55   No trifle, but a shade of bliss—
That land of tolerable flowers, that state

As near and far as grass
Where eyes become the sunlight, and the hand
Is worthy of water: the dreamt land
60   Toward which all hungers leap, all pleasures pass.

30 *Maderna*   Carlo Maderna (1556-1629), chief architect of St. Peter's Church in Rome from 1603 until his death.   **43** *areté*   A Greek word meaning excellence, virtue, the sum of good qualities that make character.   **52** *Francis*   St. Francis of Assisi (c. 1182-1226).

Sylvia Plath   (1932–1963)
Blue Moles

1

They're out of the dark's ragbag, these two
Moles dead in the pebbled rut,
Shapeless as flung gloves, a few feet apart—
Blue suede a dog or fox has chewed.
5   One, by himself, seemed pitiable enough,
Little victim unearthed by some large creature
From his orbit under the elm root.
The second carcase makes a duel of the affair:
Blind twins bitten by bad nature.

10   The sky's far dome is sane and clear.
Leaves, undoing their yellow caves
Between the road and the lake water,
Bare no sinister spaces. Already
The moles look neutral as the stones.
15   Their corkscrew noses, their white hands
Uplifted, stiffen in a family pose.
Difficult to imagine how fury struck—
Dissolved now, smoke of an old war.

2

Nightly the battle-shouts start up
20   In the ear of the veteran, and again
I enter the soft pelt of the mole.
Light's death to them: they shrivel in it.
They move through their mute rooms while I sleep,
Palming the earth aside, grubbers
25   After the fat children of root and rock.
By day, only the topsoil heaves.
Down there one is alone.

Outsize hands prepare a path,
They go before: opening the veins,
30   Delving for the appendages
Of beetles, sweetbreads, shards—to be eaten
Over and over. And still the heaven
Of final surfeit is just as far
From the door as ever. What happens between us
35   Happens in darkness, vanishes
Easy and often as each breath.

Tone and Point of View

We know the truth, not only by the reason,
but also by the heart.

Blaise Pascal, *Pensées,* no. 282

Think of *tone* as the attitude expressed by an inflection of the voice, what we often refer to as "tone of voice." We usually know from hearing and from the situation we are in whether or not a speaker is sympathetic or unsympathetic to us, to himself, or to his circumstances, whether he is personal or impersonal, formal or informal, warm or cold, happy or angry, affirmative or negative, pleasant or unpleasant, literal or ironic, and so on to just about all of the possibilities or contrasts one might name. We also know that when it comes to indicating what tone of voice a speaker is using, words often fail us. In describing tone, the best words we have are mere pointers to something too delicate, elusive, or complex for a mere word or handful of words. The complexity of tone relates, of course, to the total complexity of human character and to the total complexity of all of the situations and relationships which human beings get themselves involved in.

Now imagine the problem of the poet with regard to tone. The words which the poet writes may be—indeed will be—spoken, but what he leaves on a page of paper is sent off without a spoken voice to indicate his precise intent. In fact, the assumption that he has a precise tonal intent is absurd, for he himself will seldom read one of his own poems twice in precisely the same way. The poem which he leaves on a page of paper represents, then, a vehicle for interpretation; we may tone it as we please. But with some limits, for lots of things suggest to us certain possibilities that are more likely, more reasonable, than others—the obvious factors such as the identity of the speaker, the nature of his situation, his intent, the quality of his diction, particularly the connotation or suggestiveness of his words, and metrical urgency. So we may think of what the poet does to create tone on a silent and forbidding piece of paper as a balancing of implicit suggestions to give us a consistent range of possibilities. Or we could say that the total design of a poem will manage to suggest its overall tone and, of course, changes or modulations of tone within the overall design.

If we think of *tone* as the complex of attitudes an author has toward his subject, it may be useful to call it *point of view.* The terms overlap, but since tone is so frequently thought of in relation to "tone of voice" it is usually thought of as narrower in scope than point of view. Point of view, moreover, indicates certain mechanical distinctions, particularly the distinction between first-person speaker and third-person; thus we commonly speak of the first-person point of view or the third-person point of view, but we do not speak of first-person tone or third-person tone.

Perhaps somewhere at the center of both tone and point of view is the concept of *irony;* it is natural for us to speak of both ironic tone and ironic point of view. The simplest definition of irony is the use of words to convey the opposite of their literal meaning. We are readily familiar with this use of irony as it is expressed by tone of voice, as, for example, in the sentence, "You're a real friend," spoken to the person who has failed to be of any help at all. But irony has many shades, so it is more broadly defined as an expression marked by a deliberate contrast between the literal or apparent meaning and the intended meaning. Instead of saying to the person who failed to be of any help at all, "You're a real friend," we could also say directly, literally, "You were not of any help at all." Thus the phrase "real friend" is important in the ironic statement. Such irony is *verbal* in its orientation or is in some way dependent upon the specific character of the statement made.

Verbal irony or irony of statement can be distinguished from *irony of situation,* which occurs when the development of a situation in and of itself involves a discrepancy or is contrary to our expectations, to the point of view which we have assumed. When for want of a horseshoe nail a kingdom is lost, we have a discrepancy between the smallness of a nail and the largeness of a kingdom. When we do everything that we are supposed to do in order to achieve a given end and the result is that we still do not achieve it, the situation created is usually regarded as ironic. For example, one may study hard for an examination and still not do well on it, or vice versa. Such irony of situation easily compounds; for example, the football player who trains all summer to get into excellent condition but breaks his leg during the first practice may then watch—as the irony of his situation compounds—his rival who ignored preseason training have a brilliant season. Such things, though not likely or usual, do happen with persistent regularity in real life, which constantly involves us in an awareness of and a confrontation with irony. So important is this fact of real life to the writer that we have a special instance of situational irony called *dramatic irony,* which involves a discrepancy between what a character says and the author's point of view toward him, with the reader or spectator coming to share the author's point of view, an ironic point of view. Keep in mind that, although some irony depends upon an intonation or a verbal twist, all irony involves situation.

Following are four groups of poems. The first group is intended to suggest some varieties of irony, both of statement and of situation. Each of the next three groups consists of poems that have a certain tonal kinship with each other and are offered as an illustration of some of the basic tonal directions a poet might take. These tonal directions may or may not involve the spectrum that ranges from a delicate hint of irony to a central ironic intent. The poems in the first of these three groups have a quality of tenderness, softness, sympathy, some kind of pointer we use for relationship, for love. The tone of the second of the three groups takes us into the arena that includes protest, anger, bitterness, in general a sense of life as intensely serious business. The third group, offered without question or comment, consists of poems whose tone or point of view is soon if not at once recognized as humorous.

Percy Bysshe Shelley   (1792—1822)
Ozymandias

I met a traveler from an antique land
Who said: Two vast and trunkless legs of stone
Stand in the desert. Near them, on the sand,
Half sunk, a shattered visage lies, whose frown,
5   And wrinkled lip, and sneer of cold command,
Tell that its sculptor well those passions read
Which yet survive, stamped on these lifeless things,
The hand that mocked them and the heart that fed;
And on the pedestal these words appear:
10   "My name is Ozymandias, king of kings:
Look on my works, ye Mighty, and despair!"
Nothing beside remains. Round the decay
Of that colossal wreck, boundless and bare
The lone and level sands stretch far away.

Ozymandias   The Egyptian pharaoh Ramses II (1304-1237 B.C.), who erected hundreds of monuments throughout Egypt and Nubia, including colossal statues of himself.   **1** *antique* Ancient.
4 *visage* Face.   **8** *mocked* Imitated, that is, shaped in sculpture.   *the heart that fed* The pharaoh, who ordered the sculpture done.

Questions and Suggestions

1. Explain why the basic situation of the poem may be fairly described as ironic. Suggest some changes that the ravages of time normally effect in our lives and comment on whether or not such changes are likely to suggest irony of situation.
2. How does the characterization of Ozymandias intensify the irony of situation? How does the relationship between Ozymandias and the sculptor also intensify the irony of situation?
3. Explain the ironic effect of the words that appear on the pedestal. May they be taken in more than one way? If so, does this fact complicate the irony of the poem?

Arthur Hugh Clough   (1819—1861)
The Latest Decalogue

Thou shalt have one God only; who
Would be at the expense of two?
No graven images may be
Worshipped, except the currency:

Decalogue   Ten Commandments.

5   Swear not at all; for, for thy curse
Thine enemy is none the worse;
At church on Sunday to attend
Will serve to keep the world thy friend:
Honor thy parents; that is, all
10 From whom advancement may befall:
Thou shalt not kill; but needst not strive
Officiously to keep alive:
Do not adultery commit;
Advantage rarely comes of it:
15 Thou shalt not steal; an empty feat,
When it's so lucrative to cheat:
Bear not false witness; let the lie
Have time on its own wings to fly:
Thou shalt not covet; but tradition
20 Approves all forms of competition.
The sum of all is, thou shalt love,
If any body, God above:
At any rate shall never labor
More than thyself to love thy neighbor.

12 *to keep alive*   To keep others alive.

Questions and Suggestions

1. Taking this poem as an example of irony of statement, explain what makes so obvious the discrepancy between what the speaker says and what he intends. What makes the title of the poem particularly appropriate to its ironic content?
2. Suggest some possibilities for the tone of voice in which this poem might be recited. Explain how possible choices of tone of voice relate to the poem's ironic content.
3. Summarize the basic ideas of the poem in a short paragraph that is *not* ironic.

Robert Frost   (1874—1963)
Fire and Ice

Some say the world will end in fire,
Some say in ice.
From what I've tasted of desire
I hold with those who favor fire.

1 *end in fire*   Heraclitus, a Greek philosopher of the sixth and fifth century B.C., thought that the world had its origin in fire and would end in fire. See also Revelation 20; e.g., 20:9, "and fire came down from God out of heaven, and devoured them."

5 But if it had to perish twice,
   I think I know enough of hate
   To say that for destruction ice
   Is also great
   And would suffice.

Questions and Suggestions

1. Robert Frost is known as a poet who makes frequent use of understatement. In this poem the speaker is speaking lightly about a serious subject, the end of the world; there is thus a discrepancy between what he is saying and the manner in which he is saying it. Suggest how the speaker *maintains* his manner throughout the poem by careful selection of word and phrase.
2. What is underneath the casual manner of the speaker? How does he really feel? Consider especially the line, "I think I know enough of hate."
3. Make up some examples of your own of ironic understatement. Can you give some examples of ironic understatement which you have seen or heard?

Archibald MacLeish   (1892–   )
Dr. Sigmund Freud Discovers the Sea Shell

Science, that simple saint, cannot be bothered
Figuring what anything is for:
Enough for her devotions that things are
And can be contemplated soon as gathered.

5 She knows how every living thing was fathered,
   She calculates the climate of each star,
   She counts the fish at sea, but cannot care
   Why any one of them exists, fish, fire or feathered.

   Why should she? Her religion is to tell
10 By rote her rosary of perfect answers.
   Metaphysics she can leave to man:
   She never wakes at night in heaven or hell

Dr. Sigmund Freud   The founder of psychoanalysis (1856-1939). He received his M.D. from the University of Vienna in 1881. "Psycho-analysis," writes Freud, "has been reproached time after time with ignoring the higher, moral, supra-personal side of human nature. The reproach is doubly unjust, both historically and methodologically" ("The Ego and the Id," *The Standard Edition of the Complete Psychological Works of Sigmund Freud,* ed. James Strachey, London: Hogarth Press, 1961, XIX, p. 35). Freud also writes, "Science, in her perpetual incompleteness and insufficiency, is driven to hope for her salvation in new discoveries and new ways of regarding things" ("The Resistances to Psycho-analysis," *Standard Edition,* XIX, p. 213).

Staring at darkness. In her holy cell
There is no darkness ever: the pure candle
15   Burns, the beads drop briskly from her hand.

Who dares to offer Her the curled sea shell!
She will not touch it!—knows the world she sees
Is all the world there is! Her faith is perfect!

And still he offers the sea shell. . . .
What surf
20   Of what far sea upon what unknown ground
Troubles forever with that asking sound?
What surge is this whose question never ceases?

Questions and Suggestions

1. The irony of this poem is based upon a contrast between science and religion, or between an attitude of mind that can be said to be represented by science and an attitude of mind that can be said to be represented by religion. Summarize briefly in your own words both basic attitudes of mind or outlooks on life. Which of the two best suits your own disposition?
2. The speaker is clearly against science because, he asserts, "it cannot be bothered Figuring what anything is for." Do you think that it is possible for science to concern itself with ultimate purposes as well as its own immediate purposes? Do you think that the scientist ought to have a strong sense of social responsibility, a constant questioning about the meaning and value of what he does?
3. Does your response to the poem depend upon whether you favor science or religion? If you favor science, can you still enjoy the speaker's irony?

William Stafford   (1914—   )
Traveling Through the Dark

Traveling through the dark I found a deer
dead on the edge of the Wilson River road.
It is usually best to roll them into the canyon:
that road is narrow; to swerve might make more dead.

5   By glow of the tail-light I stumbled back of the car
and stood by the heap, a doe, a recent killing;
she had stiffened already, almost cold.
I dragged her off; she was large in the belly.

My fingers touching her side brought me the reason—
10   her side was warm; her fawn lay there waiting,
alive, still, never to be born.
Beside that mountain road I hesitated.

The car aimed ahead its lowered parking lights;
under the hood purred the steady engine.
15 I stood in the glare of the warm exhaust turning red;
around our group I could hear the wilderness listen.

I thought hard for us all—my only swerving—
then pushed her over the edge into the river.

Questions and Suggestions

1. Describe the basic conflict in the mind of the speaker at the time of his discovery
    of the dead deer. Is this conflict ironic? Explain.
2. The speaker is talking about an event that has already taken place. How does this
    narration in the past tense—the fact that he is looking back on a past experience—
    contribute to the irony of the poem?
3. Does the speaker's situation and the choice it involves remind you of the speaker
    and his choice in "Dr. Sigmund Freud Discovers the Sea Shell"? Explain.

In the following poems you will recognize a quality of tenderness, softness,
sympathy, some kind of pointer we use for relationship, for love.

Thomas Campion   (1567—1620)
My Sweetest Lesbia

My sweetest Lesbia, let us live and love,
And though the sager sort our deeds reprove,
Let us not weigh them. Heaven's great lamps do dive
Into their west, and straight again revive,
5   But soon as once set is our little light,
Then must we sleep one ever-during night.

If all would lead their lives in love like me,
Then bloody swords and armor should not be;
No drum nor trumpet peaceful sleeps should move,
10 Unless alarm came from the camp of love.
But fools do live, and waste their little light,
And seek with pain their ever-during night.

Lesbia   Name of a lady celebrated by the Roman poet Catullus (c. 84-54 B.C.) in a poem
which Campion here imitates. The name has no connection with the word *lesbianism*, which is derived
from Lesbos, an island in the Aegean Sea.

When timely death my life and fortune ends,
Let not my hearse be vexed with mourning friends,
15 But let all lovers, rich in triumph, come
And with sweet pastimes grace my happy tomb;
And Lesbia, close up thou my little light,
And crown with love my ever-during night.

Questions and Suggestions

1. When the speaker says, "Let us live and love," his intent is clear. How persuasive is he on a rational basis? Describe the quality of his appeal to his lady on an emotional basis.
2. Comment on the significance of *light* as it appears in each of the three stanzas. What is the effect of the "light"—"night" rhyme and of its repetition? Does the rhyme scheme of each stanza seem to relate to the speaker's tone? Explain.

Ben Jonson   (1573—1637)
Epitaph on Elizabeth, L. H.

Wouldst thou hear what man can say
In a little? Reader, stay.
Underneath this stone doth lie
As much beauty as could die;
5 Which in life did harbor give
To more virtue than doth live.
If at all she had a fault,
Leave it buried in this vault.
One name was Elizabeth,
10 Th' other let it sleep with death;
Fitter, where it died to tell,
Than that it lived at all. Farewell.

Questions and Suggestions

1. Write an epitaph for a public figure who has died in recent years. In writing the epitaph, what problems do you have in controlling tone? Is it difficult not to be sentimental?
2. Comment on the quality of Jonson's diction, particularly on the simplicity of the words he uses.

1 Corinthians, Chapter 13
From THE KING JAMES VERSION OF THE BIBLE

Though I speak with the tongues of men and of angels, and have not charity, I am become *as* sounding brass, or a tinkling cymbal.

2 And though I have *the gift of* prophecy, and understand all mysteries, and all knowledge; and though I have all faith, so that I could remove mountains, and have not charity, I am nothing.

3 And though I bestow all my goods to feed *the poor,* and though I give my body to be burned, and have not charity, it profiteth me nothing.

4 Charity suffereth long, *and* is kind; charity envieth not; charity vaunteth not itself, is not puffed up,

5 Doth not behave itself unseemly, seeketh not her own, is not easily provoked, thinketh no evil;

6 Rejoiceth not in iniquity, but rejoiceth in the truth;

7 Beareth all things, believeth all things, hopeth all things, endureth all things.

8 Charity never faileth: but whether *there be* prophecies, they shall fail; whether *there be* tongues, they shall cease; whether *there be* knowledge, it shall vanish away.

9 For we know in part, and we prophesy in part.

10 But when that which is perfect is come, then that which is in part shall be done away.

11 When I was a child, I spake as a child, I understood as a child, I thought as a child: but when I became a man, I put away childish things.

12 For now we see through a glass, darkly; but then face to face: now I know in part; but then shall I know even as also I am known.

13 And now abideth faith, hope, charity, these three; but the greatest of these *is* charity.

Questions and Suggestions

1. It is generally recognized that in this chapter where the word *charity* is used *love* would be more accurate. For each use of *charity* substitute *love* and then comment on the difference in tone which the substitution makes.

2. The full title of 1 Corinthians is "The First Epistle of Paul the Apostle to the Corinthians." What is an epistle? What do you know about the life of St. Paul? Who were the Corinthians? Do any of these facts make a difference in how you might think of the tone of the passage?

Walt Whitman   (1819–1892)
To You

Stranger, if you passing meet me and desire to speak to me, why
    should you not speak to me?
And why should I not speak to you?

Questions and Suggestions

1. Does Whitman in so short a poem succeed in establishing a tone? If so, how would you describe his tone?
2. Write a few sentences in which you try to establish a distinct tone quickly and efficiently for each. Label each sentence according to its tone and compare your sentences and their labels with those of your classmates.

Robert Frost   (1874—1963)
The Pasture

I'm going out to clean the pasture spring;
I'll only stop to rake the leaves away
(And wait to watch the water clear, I may):
I shan't be gone long.—You come too.

5   I'm going out to fetch the little calf
That's standing by the mother. It's so young
It totters when she licks it with her tongue.
I shan't be gone long.—You come too.

Questions and Suggestions

1. What is the relationship between the speaker and the "you" of the poem? What assumptions do you make about this relationship, and what assumptions might you then make about the speaker's tone?
2. Does the speaker seem to have an attitude toward nature? If so, how does his attitude toward nature relate to the "you" of the poem?

Hyam Plutzik   (1911—1962)
To My Daughter

Seventy-seven betrayers will stand by the road
And those who love you will be few but stronger.

Seventy-seven betrayers, skilful and various,
But do not fear them: they are unimportant.

5   You must learn soon, soon, that despite Judas
The great betrayals are impersonal

(Though many would be Judas, having the will
And the capacity, but few the courage).

You must learn soon, soon, that even love
10 Can be no shield against the abstract demons:

Time, cold and fire, and the law of pain,
The law of things falling, and the law of forgetting.

The messengers, of faces and names known
Or of forms familiar, are innocent.

Questions and Suggestions

1. In what sense is this poem "to" the speaker's daughter?
2. Explain how "You must learn" (ll. 5 and 9) takes its tone from the context in which it is spoken.

Robert Hayden   (1913—   )
Frederick Douglass

When it is finally ours, this freedom, this liberty, this beautiful
and terrible thing, needful to man as air,
usable as earth; when it belongs at last to all,
when it is truly instinct, brain matter, diastole, systole,
5 reflex action; when it is finally won; when it is more
than the gaudy mumbo jumbo of politicians:
this man, this Douglass, this former slave, this Negro
beaten to his knees, exiled, visioning a world
where none is lonely, none hunted, alien,
10 this man, superb in love and logic, this man
shall be remembered. Oh, not with statues' rhetoric,
not with legends and poems and wreaths of bronze alone,
but with the lives grown out of his life, the lives
fleshing his dream of the beautiful, needful thing.

Questions and Suggestions

1. Who was Frederick Douglass? If you do not know, look up his life in an encyclopedia.
2. What is your own attitude toward Frederick Douglass and how does it compare with that of the speaker?
3. What is your estimate of the content of this poem? Since it is a tribute to Frederick Douglass and since it celebrates the ideal of freedom, does it need a great amount of hard fact? If it moves you the first time you read it, does it move you the second and third time? If so, why?

Philip Booth (1925–   )
First Lesson

Lie back, daughter, let your head
be tipped back in the cup of my hand.
Gently, and I will hold you. Spread
your arms wide, lie out on the stream
5 and look high at the gulls. A dead-
man's float is face down. You will dive
and swim soon enough where this tidewater
ebbs to the sea. Daughter, believe
me, when you tire on the long thrash
10 to your island, lie up, and survive.
As you float now, where I held you
and let go, remember when fear
cramps your heart what I told you:
lie gently and wide to the light-year
15 stars, lie back, and the sea will hold you.

Questions and Suggestions

1. Compare this poem to Plutzik's "To My Daughter." What are the similarities and differences in the way each speaker approaches the same subject?
2. Why is the sea important to the speaker in relation to what he has to say to his daughter? What feelings about the sea do you carry with you to the poem?

Galway Kinnell (1927–   )
First Song

Then it was dusk in Illinois, the small boy
After an afternoon of carting dung
Hung on the rail fence, a sapped thing
Weary to crying. Dark was growing tall
5 And he began to hear the pond frogs all
Calling upon his ear with what seemed their joy.

Soon their sound was pleasant for a boy
Listening in the smoky dusk and the nightfall
Of Illinois, and then from the field two small
10 Boys came bearing cornstalk violins
And rubbed three cornstalk bows with resins,
And they set fiddling with them as with joy.

It was now fine music the frogs and the boys
Did in the towering Illinois twilight make
15 And into dark in spite of a right arm's ache
A boy's hunched body loved out of a stalk
The first song of his happiness, and the song woke
His heart to the darkness and into the sadness of joy.

Questions and Suggestions

1. Does the use of the word *song* in the title begin to suggest how the speaker feels toward his subject? Why is "First Song" a better title than "The First Song of His Happiness" (l. 17) or "The First Song of a Boy's Happiness"?
2. Why does the first song of his happiness wake the heart of the boy "to the darkness and into the sadness of joy"? Do you think that joy generally carries sadness with it, and that sadness sometimes carries joy with it?

The tone or point of view of the following group of poems takes us into an arena that includes protest, anger, bitterness, in general a sense of life as intensely serious business.

William Shakespeare   (1564–1616)
Sonnet 129

The expense of spirit in a waste of shame
Is lust in action; and till action, lust
Is perjur'd, murd'rous, bloody, full of blame,
Savage, extreme, rude, cruel, not to trust;
5 Enjoy'd no sooner but despisèd straight,
Past reason hunted, and no sooner had
Past reason hated, as a swallowed bait
On purpose laid to make the taker mad;
Mad in pursuit and in possession so;
10 Had, having, and in quest to have, extreme;
A bliss in proof, and prov'd, a very woe;
Before, a joy propos'd; behind, a dream.
  All this the world well knows; yet none knows well
  To shun the heaven that leads men to this hell.

Questions and Suggestions

1. Notice the pun on "waste" (waist) in the first line. Does the pun make a difference in what you might assume to be the speaker's tone? Explain.

2. What is the contrast between the first twelve lines and the last two? Does the contrast change or modify the speaker's tone?

John Donne   (1572–1631)
The Flea

Mark but this flea, and mark in this
How little that which thou deny'st me is;
   It suck'd me first, and now sucks thee,
And in this flea our two bloods mingled be.
5   Thou know'st that this cannot be said
A sin, nor shame, nor loss of maidenhead;
   Yet this enjoys before it woo,
And pamper'd, swells with one blood made of two,
And this, alas, is more than we would do.

10   O stay, three lives in one flea spare,
Where we almost, yea more than married are.
   This flea is you and I, and this
Our marriage bed and marriage temple is;
   Though parents grudge, and you, we're met
15 And cloister'd in these living walls of jet.
   Though use make you apt to kill me,
Let not to that, self-murder added be,
And sacrilege: three sins in killing three.

   Cruel and sudden, hast thou since
20 Purpled thy nail in blood of innocence?
   Wherein could this flea guilty be,
Except in that drop which it suck'd from thee?
   Yet thou triumph'st, and say'st that thou
Find'st not thyself nor me the weaker now.
25   Tis true. Then learn how false fears be
Just so much honor, when thou yield'st to me,
Will waste, as this flea's death took life from thee.

Questions and Suggestions

1. What words in the poem work particularly to create the speaker's tone? What words might you substitute for them, keeping the sense but losing the tone?
2. Why does the speaker choose to focus on the flea? Does he see it as a symbol? Explain.

John Milton   (1608–1674)
On the Late Massacre in Piedmont

Avenge, O Lord, thy slaughtered saints, whose bones
Lie scattered on the Alpine mountains cold;
Ev'n them who kept thy truth so pure of old,
When all our fathers worshipped stocks and stones,
5 Forget not: in thy book record their groans
Who were thy sheep, and in their ancient fold
Slain by the bloody Piedmontese, that rolled
Mother with infant down the rocks. Their moans
The vales redoubled to the hills, and they
10 To heav'n. Their martyred blood and ashes sow
O'er all th' Italian fields, where still doth sway
The triple Tyrant that from these may grow
A hundredfold, who, having learnt thy way,
Early may fly the Babylonian woe.

1 *thy slaughtered saints*   Members of the Protestant sect, the Waldensians, who in 1655 were massacred by Italian soldiers. Cromwell protested. As his secretary, Milton wrote the protest as well as several other official letters to the Continent.   **12** *triple Tyrant*   The Pope.   **14** *Babylonian woe* See Revelation 14:8, 17:5, 18:2.

Questions and Suggestions

1. Imagine yourself as the speaker of this poem. Would you shout it out or say it quietly? Could you do both and still be faithful to the speaker's emotion?
2. Write a short response to an atrocity, either real or imagined.
3. Describe Milton's appeal to our senses in this poem. How does this appeal help suggest his attitude toward the atrocity?

William Wordsworth   (1770–1850)
The World Is Too Much with Us

The world is too much with us; late and soon,
Getting and spending, we lay waste our powers;
Little we see in Nature that is ours;
We have given our hearts away, a sordid boon!
5 This Sea that bares her bosom to the moon,
The winds that will be howling at all hours,
And are up-gathered now like sleeping flowers,
For this, for everything, we are out of tune;
It moves us not.—Great God! I'd rather be
10 A Pagan suckled in a creed outworn;

So might I, standing on this pleasant lea,
Have glimpses that would make me less forlorn;
Have sight of Proteus rising from the sea;
Or hear old Triton blow his wreathèd horn.

13 *Proteus* In Greek mythology, the prophetic "Old Man of the Sea" who had the power to assume any shape he chose.   **14** *Triton* In Greek myth, Triton, the son of Poseidon, the god of the sea, was the trumpeter of the sea, and the sound of his conch-shell horn calmed the waves.

Questions and Suggestions

1. Explain in what ways this poem applies to the contemporary world. Were Wordsworth alive today, do you think that he would be interested in ecology?
2. Write a paragraph either agreeing or disagreeing that the world is too much with us. What is the tone of your paragraph, and how does it compare with that of the poem?

Thomas Hardy   (1840–1928)
Channel Firing

That night your great guns, unawares,
Shook all our coffins as we lay,
And broke the chancel window-squares,
We thought it was the Judgement-day

5 And sat upright. While drearisome
Arose the howl of wakened hounds:
The mouse let fall the altar-crumb,
The worms drew back into the mounds,

The glebe cow drooled. Till God called, "No;
10 It's gunnery practice out at sea
Just as before you went below:
The world is as it used to be:

"All nations striving strong to make
Red war yet redder. Mad as hatters
15 They do no more for Christés sake
Than you who are helpless in such matters.

"That this is not the judgment-hour
For some of them's a blessed thing,

Channel The English Channel.   **9** *glebe cow* Cow pastured on the glebe, a plot of land belonging to a parish church.

For if it were they'd have to scour
20 Hell's floor for so much threatening. . . .

"Ha, ha. It will be warmer when
I blow the trumpet (if indeed
I ever do; for you are men,
And rest eternal sorely need)."

25 So down we lay again. "I wonder,
Will the world ever saner be,"
Said one, "than when He sent us under
In our indifferent century!"

And many a skeleton shook his head.
30 "Instead of preaching forty year,"
My neighbor Parson Thirdly said,
"I wish I had stuck to pipes and beer."

Again the guns disturb the hour,
Roaring their readiness to avenge,
35 As far inland as Stourton Tower,
And Camelot, and starlit Stonehenge.

35 *Stourton Tower* Stour Head, a town in Staffordshire on the river Stour.   36 *Camelot* In Arthurian legend, the seat of King Arthur's court.   *Stonehenge* A circular setting of large standing stones surrounded by an earthwork, about eight miles north of Salisbury, Wiltshire, England, built during the late Neolithic or Early Bronze Age (1800-1400 B.C.).

Questions and Suggestions

1. This poem uses the dramatic device of imagining that the speakers are dead. What effect does this device have on the tone of the poem?
2. How does the characterization of God beginning at line 9 help make the poem bitterly ironic? Consider, for example, the phrase "Red war yet redder" (l. 14).
3. Do stanzas seven and eight add a touch of humor to the poem? If so, is the humor appropriate? Explain.

Wilfred Owen   (1893–1918)
Mental Cases

Who are these? Why sit they here in twilight?
Wherefore rock they, purgatorial shadows,
Drooping tongues from jaws that slob their relish,
Baring teeth that leer like skulls' teeth wicked?
5 Stroke on stroke of pain,—but what slow panic,
Gouged these chasms round their fretted sockets?
Ever from their hair and through their hands' palms

Misery swelters. Surely we have perished
Sleeping, and walk hell; but who these hellish?

10   —These are men whose minds the Dead have ravished.
Memory fingers in their hair of murders,
Multitudinous murders they once witnessed.
Wading sloughs of flesh these helpless wander,
Treading blood from lungs that had loved laughter.
15   Always they must see these things and hear them,
Batter of guns and shatter of flying muscles,
Carnage incomparable, and human squander,
Rucked too thick for these men's extrication.

Therefore still their eyeballs shrink tormented
20   Back into their brains, because on their sense
Sunlight seems a blood-smear; night comes blood-black;
Dawn breaks open like a wound that bleeds afresh.
—Thus their heads wear this hilarious, hideous,
Awful falseness of set-smiling corpses.
25   —Thus their hands are plucking at each other;
Picking at the rope-knouts of their scourging;
Snatching after us who smote them, brother,
Pawing us who dealt them war and madness.

18 *Rucked*   Gathered into heaps.   **26** *rope-knouts*   Whips used to flog criminals.

Questions and Suggestions

1. How does the phrase "purgatorial shadows" (l. 2) set the tone for this poem?
2. What are the principal images which Owen uses to create a sense of horror?
3. Compare "Mental Cases" with Milton's sonnet "On the Late Massacre in Piedmont" (p. 141). In what ways are the feelings of each speaker similar, in what ways different?

Countee Cullen   (1903–1946)
Incident

Once riding in old Baltimore,
    Heart-filled, head-filled with glee,
I saw a Baltimorean
    Keep looking straight at me.

5   Now I was eight and very small,
    And he was no whit bigger,
And so I smiled, but he poked out
    His tongue, and called me "Nigger."

      I saw the whole of Baltimore
10   From May until December;
      Of all the things that happened there
      That's all that I remember.

Questions and Suggestions

1. Explain how the incident suggests how the speaker feels rather than stating how he feels.
2. Why is it important that the point of view is that of a mature man looking back at his childhood rather than, for example, the child himself speaking of what happened to him?

Sylvia Plath   (1932–1963)
Daddy

You do not do, you do not do
Any more, black shoe
In which I have lived like a foot
For thirty years, poor and white,
5 Barely daring to breathe or Achoo.

Daddy, I have had to kill you.
You died before I had time—
Marble-heavy, a bag full of God,
Ghastly statue with one grey toe
10 Big as a Frisco seal

And a head in the freakish Atlantic
Where it pours bean green over blue
In the waters off beautiful Nauset.
I used to pray to recover you.
15 Ach, du.

In the German tongue, in the Polish town
Scraped flat by the roller
Of wars, wars, wars.
But the name of the town is common.
20 My Polack friend

Says there are a dozen or two.
So I never could tell where you

13 *Nauset* An area of the Cape Cod National Seashore facing the Atlantic.   **15** *Ach, du* German for "Ah, you."

Put your foot, your root,
I never could talk to you.
25   The tongue stuck in my jaw.

It stuck in a barb wire snare.
Ich, ich, ich, ich,
I could hardly speak.
I thought every German was you
30   And the language obscene.

An engine, an engine
Chuffing me off like a Jew.
A Jew to Dachau, Auschwitz, Belsen.
I began to talk like a Jew.
35   I think I may well be a Jew.

The snows of the Tyrol, the clear beer of Vienna
Are not very pure or true.
With my gypsy ancestress and my weird luck
And my Taroc pack and my Taroc pack
40   I may be a bit of a Jew.

I have always been scared of *you,*
With your Luftwaffe, your gobbledygoo.
And your neat moustache
And your Aryan eye, bright blue.
45   Panzer-man, panzer-man, O You—

Not God but a swastika
So black no sky could squeak through.
Every woman adores a Fascist,
The boot in the face, the brute
50   Brute heart of a brute like you.

You stand at the blackboard, daddy,
In the picture I have of you,
A cleft in your chin instead of your foot
But no less a devil for that, no not
55   Any less the black man who

27 *ich*   German for "I."   33 *Dachau, Auschwitz, Belsen*   Concentration camps in which
Jews were put to death by the Nazis during World War II. Dachau is north of Munich, Auschwitz in
southwest Poland, and Belsen northeast of Hannover.   36 *Tyrol*   A province in western Austria
lying almost wholly within the Alps.   39 *Taroc pack*   A deck of cards for a game called "taroc"
(also "tarok") developed in Italy in the fourteenth century and played mainly in Germany and
central Europe. Some of the cards called "tarots" are used in fortune-telling.   42 *Luftwaffe*   The
German air force before and during World War II.   44 *Aryan*   In Nazi ideology, member of a race
of supermen, specifically gentile, of Nordic stock.   45 *Panzer-man*   A man given to the use of ar-
mored tanks. The German army of World War II made heavy use of panzer or armored tank divisions.

Bit my pretty red heart in two.
I was ten when they buried you.
At twenty I tried to die
And get back, back, back to you.
60   I thought even the bones would do.

But they pulled me out of the sack,
And they stuck me together with glue.
And then I knew what to do.
I made a model of you,
65   A man in black with a Meinkampf look

And a love of the rack and the screw.
And I said I do, I do.
So daddy, I'm finally through.
The black telephone's off at the root,
70   The voices just can't worm through.

If I've killed one man, I've killed two—
The vampire who said he was you
And drank my blood for a year—
Seven years, if you want to know.
75   Daddy, you can lie back now.

There's a stake in your fat black heart
And the villagers never liked you.
They are dancing and stamping on you.
They always *knew* it was you.
80   Daddy, daddy, you bastard, I'm through.

65 *Meinkampf*   Adolf Hitler's book *Mein Kampf (My Struggle),* first published in 1925, became the bible of the Nazi party.

Questions and Suggestions

1.   Write a brief summary or paraphrase of the relationship between the speaker and her father.
2.   Note the allusions in the poem to World War II (1939–1945), the years when Sylvia Plath was growing from a girl of seven to a girl of thirteen. To what does she allude that was crucial to her emotional development?
3.   Is the anguish and hatred which the speaker feels intense enough to suggest mental breakdown or madness? Describe the fundamental conflict or tension in the speaker's mind.

Following, without question or comment, is a group of poems whose tone or point of view is soon if not at once recognizable as humorous. For longer poems distinctly humorous see the selection from Byron's *Don Juan* (p. 284) and Browning's *The Pied Piper of Hamelin* (p. 319) and *Fra Lippo Lippi* (p. 327).

William Butler Yeats   (1865–1939)
For Anne Gregory

"Never shall a young man,
Thrown into despair
By those great honey-coloured
Ramparts at your ear,
5   Love you for yourself alone
And not your yellow hair."

"But I can get a hair-dye
And set such colour there,
Brown, or black, or carrot,
10   That young men in despair
May love me for myself alone
And not my yellow hair."

"I heard an old religious man
But yesternight declare
15   That he had found a text to prove
That only God, my dear,
Could love you for yourself alone
And not your yellow hair."

T. S. Eliot   (1888–1965)
Macavity: The Mystery Cat

Macavity's a Mystery Cat: he's called the Hidden Paw—
For he's the master criminal who can defy the Law.
He's the bafflement of Scotland Yard, the Flying Squad's despair:
For when they reach the scene of crime—*Macavity's not there!*

5   Macavity, Macavity, there's no-one like Macavity,
He's broken every human law, he breaks the law of gravity.
His powers of levitation would make a fakir stare,
And when you reach the scene of crime—*Macavity's not there!*
You may seek him in the basement, you may look up in the air—
10   But I tell you once and once again, *Macavity's not there!*

Macavity's a ginger cat, he's very tall and thin;
You would know him if you saw him, for his eyes are sunken in.
His brow is deeply lined with thought, his head is highly domed;
His coat is dusty from neglect, his whiskers are uncombed.
15 He sways his head from side to side, with movements like a snake;
And when you think he's half asleep, he's always wide awake.

Macavity, Macavity, there's no-one like Macavity,
For he's a fiend in feline shape, a monster of depravity.
You may meet him in a by-street, you may see him in the square—
20 But when a crime's discovered, then *Macavity's not there!*
He's outwardly respectable. (They say he cheats at cards.)
And his footprints are not found in any file of Scotland Yard's.
And when the larder's looted, or the jewel-case is rifled,
Or when the milk is missing, or another Peke's been stifled,
25 Or the greenhouse glass is broken, and the trellis past repair—
Ay, there's the wonder of the thing! *Macavity's not there!*

And when the Foreign Office find a Treaty's gone astray,
Or the Admiralty lose some plans and drawings by the way,
There may be a scrap of paper in the hall or on the stair—
30 But it's useless to investigate—*Macavity's not there!*
And when the loss has been disclosed, the Secret Service say:
"It *must* have been Macavity!"—but he's a mile away.
You'll be sure to find him resting, or a-licking of his thumbs,
Or engaged in doing complicated long division sums.

35 Macavity, Macavity, there's no-one like Macavity,
There never was a Cat of such deceitfulness and suavity.
He always has an alibi, and one or two to spare:
At whatever time the deed took place—MACAVITY WASN'T THERE!
And they say that all the Cats whose wicked deeds are widely known
40 (I might mention Mungojerrie, I might mention Griddlebone)
Are nothing more than agents for the Cat who all the time
Just controls their operations: the Napoleon of Crime!

Theodore Roethke   (1908—1963)
I Knew a Woman

I knew a woman, lovely in her bones,
When small birds sighed, she would sigh back at them;
Ah, when she moved, she moved more ways than one:
The shapes a bright container can contain!
5 Of her choice virtues only gods should speak,
Or English poets who grew up on Greek
(I'd have them sing in chorus, cheek to cheek).

How well her wishes went! She stroked my chin,
She taught me Turn, and Counter-turn, and Stand;
10 She taught me Touch, that undulant white skin;
I nibbled meekly from her proffered hand;
She was the sickle; I, poor I, the rake,
Coming behind her for her pretty sake
(But what prodigious mowing we did make).

15 Love likes a gander, and adores a goose:
Her full lips pursed, the errant note to seize;
She played it quick, she played it light and loose;
My eyes, they dazzled at her flowing knees;
Her several parts could keep a pure repose,
20 Or one hip quiver with a mobile nose
(She moved in circles, and those circles moved).

Let seed be grass, and grass turn into hay:
I'm martyr to a motion not my own;
What's freedom for? To know eternity.
25 I swear she cast a shadow white as stone.
But who would count eternity in days?
These old bones live to learn her wanton ways:
(I measure time by how a body sways).

W. D. Snodgrass (1926–   )
April Inventory

The green catalpa tree has turned
All white; the cherry blooms once more.
In one whole year I haven't learned
A blessed thing they pay you for.
5 The blossoms snow down in my hair;
The trees and I will soon be bare.

The trees have more than I to spare.
The sleek, expensive girls I teach,
Younger and pinker every year,
10 Bloom gradually out of reach.
The pear tree lets its petals drop
Like dandruff on a tabletop.

The girls have grown so young by now
I have to nudge myself to stare.
15 This year they smile and mind me how
My teeth are falling with my hair.
In thirty years I may not get
Younger, shrewder, or out of debt.

The tenth time, just a year ago,
20 I made myself a little list
Of all the things I'd ought to know,
Then told my parents, analyst,
And everyone who's trusted me
I'd be substantial, presently.

25 I haven't read one book about
A book or memorized one plot.
Or found a mind I did not doubt.
I learned one date. And then forgot.
And one by one the solid scholars
30 Get the degrees, the jobs, the dollars.

And smile above their starchy collars.
I taught my classes Whitehead's notions;
One lovely girl, a song of Mahler's.
Lacking a source-book or promotions,
35 I showed one child the colors of
A luna moth and how to love.

I taught myself to name my name,
To bark back, loosen love and crying;
To ease my woman so she came,
40 To ease an old man who was dying.
I have not learned how often I
Can win, can love, but choose to die.

I have not learned there is a lie
Love shall be blonder, slimmer, younger;
45 That my equivocating eye
Loves only by my body's hunger;
That I have forces, true to feel,
Or that the lovely world is real.

While scholars speak authority
50 And wear their ulcers on their sleeves,
My eyes in spectacles shall see
These trees procure and spend their leaves.
There is a value underneath
The gold and silver in my teeth.

55 Though trees turn bare and girls turn wives,
We shall afford our costly seasons;
There is a gentleness survives
That will outspeak and has its reasons.
There is a loveliness exists,
60 Preserves us, not for specialists.

The Poem of Ideas

. . . the greatness of a poet lies in
his powerful and beautiful application
of ideas to life—to the question:
How to live.

Matthew Arnold, *Essays in Criticism, Second Series*

Just about every poem ever written invites discussion in terms of what is or what seems to be its rationally clear meaning. Some poems, however, are more immediately and directly concerned with ideas or concepts than others. It is only natural for the poet as a whole human being to take on the role of thinker, to be one who defines, makes assertions, criticizes, discusses, who in general reacts with a vigorous intelligence to the world which he inhabits. There is, in fact, a whole class of poetry called *didactic* poetry—of which Pope's *Essay on Man* (p. 261) is a good example—whose intent is to teach, to convey instruction or information, to make moral observations. Pope's poem is the work of a serious moralist. The satirist, however, may also be vastly amused at the human folly and vice which he holds up to ridicule, as may be readily seen by a look at Pope's *The Rape of the Lock* (p. 242) or the selection from Byron's *Don Juan* (p. 284). In either case the satirist is normally considered a poet of ideas, for though he may range in tone from gentle to fierce he knows what his standards are and is concerned with measuring the world by them. But since poems which in the natural order of things define, assert, criticize, and discuss do not at the same time directly and necessarily intend to teach or to make satiric thrusts (gentle or fierce), it is well not to restrict ourselves to a single category. A wider perspective on the poem of ideas will be more useful and will in the end remind us of the essentially dramatic character of all poetry.

The poem of ideas is not a poem which lacks emotion, but rather a poem which combines emotion with a clear purpose of dealing with ideas. The *forms* which the expression of ideas may take are many and various. A poem of ideas typically offers explicit statement, but it may make its statement implicitly as well. The expression of ideas may be plain and direct or difficult and indirect, literal or metaphoric, concrete or abstract. A poem of ideas will normally use an appropriate combination of forms, particularly a combination of the abstract and the concrete. One might say that ideas are normally expressed abstractly, whereas poetry is normally metaphoric or symbolic, and therefore concrete. Consider the two poems which follow. They are particularly appropriate illustrations of the poem of ideas, for each is an attempt at definition. Both have, moreover, as their single, immediate, and direct concern the definition for us of what a poem is. Both deal with ideas abstractly and concretely, and both make use of metaphor.

Marianne Moore   (1887–1972)
Poetry

I, too, dislike it: there are things that are important beyond all this fiddle.
  Reading it, however, with a perfect contempt for it, one discovers in
  it after all, a place for the genuine.
    Hands that can grasp, eyes
5   that can dilate, hair that can rise
      if it must, these things are important not because a

high-sounding interpretation can be put upon them but because they are
  useful. When they become so derivative as to become unintelligible,
  the same thing may be said for all of us, that we
10   do not admire what
    we cannot understand: the bat
     holding on upside down or in quest of something to

eat, elephants pushing, a wild horse taking a roll, a tireless wolf under
  a tree, the immovable critic twitching his skin like a horse that feels a flea,
  the base-
15 ball fan, the statistician—
    nor is it valid
     to discriminate against "business documents and

school-books"; all these phenomena are important. One must make a
    distinction
  however: when dragged into prominence by half poets, the result is not
    poetry,
20 nor till the poets among us can be
    "literalists of
    the imagination"—above
     insolence and triviality and can present

for inspection, "imaginary gardens with real toads in them," shall we have
25 it. In the meantime, if you demand on the one hand,
  the raw material of poetry in
    all its rawness and
    that which is on the other hand
     genuine, you are interested in poetry.

17-18 *business documents and school-books* "Where the boundary between prose and poetry lies, I shall never be able to understand. The question is raised in manuals of style, yet the answer to it lies beyond me. Poetry is verse: prose is not verse. Or else poetry is everything with the exception of business documents and school books" (*The Diaries of Leo Tolstoy,* trans. C. J. Hogarth and A. Sirnis, New York: E. P. Dutton, 1917, p. 94).   **21-22** *literalists of the imagination* Quoted from an essay by William Butler Yeats, "William Blake and the Imagination," in *Ideas of Good and Evil* (London: A. H. Bullen, 1903), p. 182: "The limitation of his view was from the very intensity of his vision; he was a too literal realist of imagination, as others are of nature; and because he believed that the figures seen by the mind's eye, when exalted by inspiration, were 'eternal existences,' symbols of divine essences, he hated every grace of style that might obscure their lineaments."

Questions and Suggestions

1. Look up the word *poetry* in a dictionary. In what ways does Marianne Moore agree or disagree with the dictionary definition? Select one or two aspects of her definition of poetry that you think *least* likely ever to appear in a dictionary. Why did you choose as you did?
2. A key idea in this poem is that poetry is "genuine" (II. 3, 29). What in Marianne Moore's view are the key qualities that make a poem genuine?
3. Select an important phrase or statement from this poem and in a paragraph explain what you think it means.

Archibald MacLeish   (1892-   )
Ars Poetica

A poem should be palpable and mute
As a globed fruit,

Dumb
As old medallions to the thumb,

5 Silent as the sleeve-worn stone
Of casement ledges where the moss has grown—

A poem should be wordless
As the flight of birds.

A poem should be motionless in time
10 As the moon climbs,

Leaving, as the moon releases
Twig by twig the night-entangled trees,

Leaving, as the moon behind the winter leaves,
Memory by memory the mind—

15 A poem should be motionless in time
As the moon climbs.

A poem should be equal to:
Not true.

For all the history of grief
20 An empty doorway and a maple leaf.

Ars Poetica   The art of poetry, title of a work by the Roman lyric poet Horace (65-8 B.C.).

For love
The leaning grasses and the two lights above the sea—

A poem should not mean
But be.

Questions and Suggestions

1. MacLeish sums up his view of the art of poetry in his closing statement, "A poem should not mean But be." What does he mean by "mean"?—what is he against? What does he mean by "be"?—what is he for? Is the poem a convincing demonstration of what he is for? Comment on its visual appeal.
2. What in MacLeish's view are the key qualities of a poem that is a work of art? Compare and contrast his idea of what a poem is with Marianne Moore's. Which are greater, the similarities or the differences?
3. Select one of MacLeish's ideas on what a poem should be and explain in your own words what you think he means. Do you make use of metaphor in your explanation?

Though "Poetry" and "Ars Poetica" are feelingful definitions, each concentrates on something outside of the poet or of the poem's speaker. The following group of poems, by contrast, present ideas in a personal way or as an aspect of personal reaction to a situation—more largely, to the world which the speaker inhabits.

William Wordsworth   (1770—1850)
Ode to Duty

Jam non consilio bonus, sed more eo perductus, ut non tantum recte facere possim, sed nisi recte facere non possim.

Stern Daughter of the Voice of God!
O Duty! if that name thou love
Who are a light to guide, a rod
To check the erring, and reprove;
5   Thou, who art victory and law
When empty terrors overawe;
From vain temptations dost set free;
And calm'st the weary strife of frail humanity!

"**Jam non . . . possim.**"   "Now am I good not by taking counsel but brought by habit to the point that it is not so much that I can act rightly as that I cannot act except rightly." The epigraph is from the *Moral Epistles,* 120:10, of Seneca (4 B.C.- 65 A.D.), a Stoic philosopher and writer of tragedies.

There are who ask not if thine eye
10 Be on them; who, in love and truth,
Where no misgiving is, rely
Upon the genial sense of youth:
Glad Hearts! without reproach or blot;
Who do thy work, and know it not:
15 Oh! if through confidence misplaced
They fail, thy saving arms, dread Power! around them cast.

Serene will be our days and bright,
And happy will our nature be,
When love is an unerring light,
20 And joy its own security.
And they a blissful course may hold
Even now, who, not unwisely bold,
Live in the spirit of this creed;
Yet seek thy firm support, according to their need.

25 I, loving freedom, and untried,
  No sport of every random gust,
  Yet being to myself a guide,
Too blindly have reposed my trust;
And oft, when in my heart was heard
30 Thy timely mandate, I deferred
The task, in smoother walks to stray;
But thee I now would serve more strictly, if I may.

Through no disturbance of my soul,
Or strong compunction in me wrought,
35 I supplicate for thy control;
But in the quietness of thought:
Me this unchartered freedom tires;
I feel the weight of chance desires:
My hopes no more must change their name,
40 I long for a repose that ever is the same.

Stern Lawgiver! yet thou dost wear
The Godhead's most benignant grace;
Nor know we anything so fair
As is the smile upon thy face:
45 Flowers laugh before thee on their beds
And fragrance in thy footing treads;
Thou dost preserve the stars from wrong
And the most ancient heavens, through thee, are fresh and strong.

To humbler functions, awful Power!
50 I call thee: I myself commend

Unto thy guidance from this hour;
Oh, let my weakness have an end!
Give unto me, made lowly wise,
The spirit of self-sacrifice;
55 The confidence of reason give;
And in the light of truth thy Bondman let me live!

Questions and Suggestions

1. The speaker treats duty as a psychological problem. Conflicting forces tug at him. What are the main terms which he uses to describe these forces? Are his terms at a relatively high level of abstraction? Explain.
2. Comment on the speaker's use of metaphor. Is his personification of duty as a woman an effective way of dramatizing his psychological problem?
3. Write a paragraph on the ideas of this poem as they relate to our own society.

Carl Sandburg (1878–1967)
The Lawyers Know Too Much

The lawyers, Bob, know too much.
They are chums of the books of old John Marshall.
They know it all, what a dead hand wrote,
A stiff dead hand and its knuckles crumbling,
5 The bones of the fingers a thin white ash.
    The lawyers know
    a dead man's thoughts too well.

In the heels of the higgling lawyers, Bob,
Too many slippery ifs and buts and howevers,
10 Too much hereinbefore provided whereas,
Too many doors to go in and out of.

    When the lawyers are through
    What is there left, Bob?
    Can a mouse nibble at it
15   And find enough to fasten a tooth in?

    Why is there always a secret singing
    When a lawyer cashes in?
    Why does a hearse horse snicker
    Hauling a lawyer away?

2 *John Marshall*   Chief Justice of the United States Supreme Court from 1801 to 1835.

20 The work of a bricklayer goes to the blue.
    The knack of a mason outlasts a moon.
    The hands of a plasterer hold a room together.
    The land of a farmer wishes him back again.
      Singers of songs and dreamers of plays
25   Build a house no wind blows over.
    The lawyers—tell me why a hearse horse snickers hauling a lawyer's bones.
      hauling a lawyer's bones.

Questions and Suggestions

1. Imagine Sandburg writing a definition of a lawyer for a dictionary. What would his definition be?
2. What are the main uses of contrast which the poem makes?
3. What is a "hearse horse"? How is the speaker's reference to a hearse horse suggestive in a way that a reference to its contemporary equivalent would not be? Are hearse horses ever used today?

E. E. Cummings   (1894–1962)
next to of course god america i

"next to of course god america i
love you land of the pilgrims' and so forth oh
say can you see by the dawn's early my
country 'tis of centuries come and go
5 and are no more what of it we should worry
in every language even deafanddumb
thy sons acclaim your glorious name by gorry
by jingo by gee by gosh by gum
why talk of beauty what could be more beaut-
10 iful than these heroic happy dead
who rushed like lions to the roaring slaughter
they did not stop to think they died instead
then shall the voices of liberty be mute?"

He spoke. And drank rapidly a glass of water

Questions and Suggestions

1. The plain intent of this poem is to be ironic. What are the devices that make the irony apparent?
2. Give a direct statement that is equivalent in content to the poem's ironic statement.

Following is a group of poems that deals with ideas in a relatively detached or impersonal way, though each in its own way is as full of feeling as those in the preceding group.

Wallace Stevens   (1879—1955)
The Well Dressed Man with a Beard

After the final no there comes a yes
And on that yes the future world depends.
No was the night. Yes is this present sun.
If the rejected things, the things denied,
5   Slid over the western cataract, yet one,
One only, one thing that was firm, even
No greater than a cricket's horn, no more
Than a thought to be rehearsed all day, a speech
Of the self that must sustain itself on speech,
10   One thing remaining, infallible, would be
Enough. Ah! douce campagna of that thing!
Ah! douce campagna, honey in the heart,
Green in the body, out of a petty phrase,
Out of a thing believed, a thing affirmed:
15   The form on the pillow humming while one sleeps,
The aureole above the humming house . . .

It can never be satisfied, the mind, never.

11 *douce campagna*   Sweet plain.

Questions and Suggestions

1. To what does the speaker seem to refer in the phrase "the final no" (l. 1)? Why does he link "no" to "night" (l. 3)? Comment on his use of a light—dark contrast.
2. In what ways does the final assertion, "It can never be satisfied, the mind, never," appropriately climax the first sixteen lines of the poem?
3. The title seems unrelated to the poem itself. Suggest ways in which it might be related.

Vachel Lindsay   (1879—1931)
The Unpardonable Sin

This is the sin against the Holy Ghost:—
To speak of bloody power as right divine,
And call on God to guard each vile chief's house,
And for such chiefs, turn men to wolves and swine:—

5 To go forth killing in White Mercy's name,
   Making the trenches stink with spattered brains,
   Tearing the nerves and arteries apart,
   Sowing with flesh the unreaped golden plains.

   In any Church's name, to sack fair towns,
10 And turn each home into a screaming sty,
   To make the little children fugitive,
   And have their mothers for a quick death cry,—

   This is the sin against the Holy Ghost:
   This is the sin no purging can atone:—
15 To send forth rapine in the name of Christ:—
   To set the face, and make the heart a stone.

Questions and Suggestions

1. What words does the speaker use that evoke a strong response? Substitute some
    weak or neutral words for his strong words in order to illustrate the appropriateness
    of his diction to his purpose.
2. State the main idea of the poem in two or three different ways. Is it, for example,
    a comment on human hypocrisy, though the word "hypocrisy" is not used in the
    poem?

Robinson Jeffers   (1887—1962)
The Cruel Falcon

   Contemplation would make a good life, keep it strict, only
   The eyes of a desert skull drinking the sun,
   Too intense for flesh, lonely
   Exultations of white bone;
5 Pure action would make a good life, let it be sharp-
   Set between the throat and the knife.
   A man who knows death by heart
   Is the man for that life.
   In pleasant peace and security
10 How suddenly the soul in a man begins to die.
   He shall look up above the stalled oxen
   Envying the cruel falcon,
   And dig under the straw for a stone
   To bruise himself on.

Questions and Suggestions

1. What human needs, in the speaker's view, do "pleasant peace and security" not meet? Do you agree with him? Explain.
2. Is the cruel falcon an appropriate symbol for the main idea of the poem? Comment on the effectiveness of the contrast between "the stalled oxen" (l. 11) and "the cruel falcon" (l. 12).

Langston Hughes   (1902–1967)
Harlem

What happens to a dream deferred?

> Does it dry up
> like a raisin in the sun?
> Or fester like a sore—
> 5 And then run?
> Does it stink like rotten meat?
> Or crust and sugar over—
> like a syrupy sweet?

> Maybe it just sags
> 10 like a heavy load.

> *Or does it explode?*

Questions and Suggestions

1. Write a paraphrase of the poem without using questions, and then comment on the effectiveness of the interrogative mood as a device for expressing ideas.
2. Note the structure of the poem, which is like a sandwich whose center is metaphor. How do the individual metaphors in the center relate to each other? What is their total effect? Does this effect help the last line itself to explode?

C. Day Lewis   (1904–1972)
The Committee

So the committee met again, and again
Nailed themselves to the never-much-altered agenda,
Making their points as to the manner born,
Hammering them home with the skill of long practice.

5 These men and women are certainly representative
Of every interest concerned. For example, A. wears

Integrity like a sheriff's badge, while B.
Can grind an axe on either side of a question:
C. happens to have the facts, D. a vocation
10 For interpreting facts to the greater glory of Dogma:
E. is pompously charming, diffidently earnest,
F. is the acid-drop, the self-patented catalyst.
Our chairman's a prince of procedure, in temporizing
Power a Proteus, and adept in seeming to follow
15 Where actually he leads—as indeed he must be,
Or the rest would have torn him to pieces a long time ago.
Yet all, in a curious way, are public-spirited,
Groping with their *ad hoc* decisions to find
The missing, presumed omnipotent, directive.

20 Idly the sun tracing upon their papers
Doodles of plane-leaf shadows and rubbing them out:
The buzz of flies, the *gen* of the breeze, the river
Endlessly stropping its tides against the embankment:
Seasons revolving with colors like stage armies,
25 Years going west along the one-way street—
All these they ignore, whose session or obsession
Must do with means, not ends. But who called this meeting
Of irreconcileables? Will they work out some positive
Policy, something more than a *modus vivendi?*
30 Or be adjourned, *sine die,* their task half done?

So the committee, as usual, reached a compromise—
If reach is the word, denoting, as it ought to,
A destination (though why should destiny not
Favor a compromise, which is only the marriage
35 For better or worse between two or more incompatibles,
Like any marriage of minds?) and left the table,
There being no further business for today.
And the silent secretary wrote up the minutes,
Putting the leaves in order. For what? the eye
40 Of higher authority? or the seal of the dust?
Or again, to be dispersed irreparably
When the hinge turns and a brusque new life blows in?
And I regret another afternoon wasted,
And wearily think there is something to be said

14 *Proteus*   In Greek myth the prophetic "Old Man of the Sea" who had the power to assume
any shape he chose.   **18** *ad hoc*   To the particular end at hand without consideration of broader
principle.   **22** *gen*   Genus, birth, origin.   **29** *modus vivendi*   Literally, manner of living; a practical
compromise, especially one that bypasses difficulties.   **30** *sine die*   Literally, without a day; for an
indefinite period, an adjournment without setting a day for reassembling.

45 For the methods of the dictatorships—I who shall waste
Even the last drops of twilight in self-pity
That I should have to be chairman, secretary,
And all the committee, all the one-man committee.

Questions and Suggestions

1. Could the poem appropriately be called "Obsession" (l. 26)? Does the speaker offer any cause-effect explanation for the obsession of the members of the committee "with means, not ends" (l. 27)? If not, why not?
2. Why does the speaker bring in the possibility of "the methods of the dictatorships" (l. 45)? What assumptions does he seem to be making about the methods of freedom?
3. Describe some examples from your own experience or observation of events of the committee mentality as C. Day Lewis sees it.

Richard Eberhart (1904–   )
The Fury of Aerial Bombardment

You would think the fury of aerial bombardment
Would rouse God to relent; the infinite spaces
Are still silent. He looks on shock-pried faces.
History, even, does not know what is meant.

5 You would feel that after so many centuries
God would give man to repent; yet he can kill
As Cain could, but with multitudinous will,
No farther advanced than in his ancient furies.

Was man made stupid to see his own stupidity?
10 Is God by definition indifferent, beyond us all?
Is the eternal truth man's fighting soul
Wherein the Beast ravens in its own avidity?

Of Van Wettering I speak, and Averill,
Names on a list, whose faces I do not recall
15 But they are gone to early death, who late in school
Distinguished the belt feed lever from the belt holding pawl.

---

16 *belt feed lever . . . belt holding pawl* Parts of a machine gun. The belt is the ammunition belt. A *belt feed lever* is an ammunition feed mechanism component that regulates the movement of the ammunition into the gun receiver. A *belt holding pawl* is an ammunition feed mechanism component that holds the ammunition belt secure in the weapon. The terms are described and illustrated in *Department of the Army Field Manual FM 23-65* (1944, 1955), which superseded but is similar to the manual used during World War II. The Browning .50 caliber machine gun to which the terms pertain was variously used during World War II, including in the turrets of B-17 and B-24 bombers.

Questions and Suggestions

1. This poem presents a philosophical problem in direct terms. Have you seen this problem expressed in other places? See, for example, the Book of Job in the Bible. Note the speaker's allusion in line 7 to the story of Cain and Abel (Genesis 4:8-15).
2. Does the speaker regard man as responsible for his own acts?
3. What terms might serve as contemporary equivalents for "ancient furies" (l. 8)?
4. Why in the last stanza does the speaker give the names of men who have been killed in war? Similarly, what is the effect of his use of the technical terms "belt feed lever" and "belt holding pawl" in the last line of the poem?

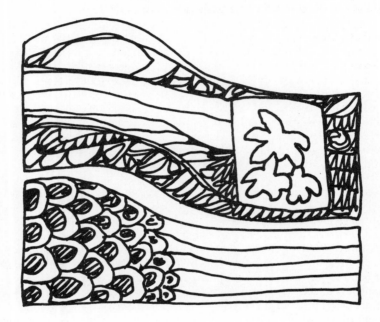

Pleasure and Judgment

. . . and if I had to live my life again
I would have made a rule to read some poetry
and listen to some music at least once every week;
for perhaps the parts of my brain now atrophied
could thus have been kept active through use.
The loss of these tastes is a loss of happiness. . . .

The Autobiography of Charles Darwin

A good poem gives pleasure, and requires judgment. The pleasure which a poem gives combines the rational and the emotional, and the judgment which it requires is not strictly intellectual but a combination of our capacity to think and to feel. Intelligence without taste, without a sense of values, without wisdom is a thing of poverty, but totality of response typically reflects the rational side of our nature, our best intelligence.

The pleasures which a good poem gives are threefold. We may designate the first *the pleasure of language,* of words as they represent our experience of life in ways that are rich and exciting, various and original, sensuous and abstract, objective and subjective, particular and universal, and in an infinite variety of rhythms and intonations. The second we may designate *the pleasure of dramatic qualities,* of characterization, situation, and dramatic moment, of the unfolding of life experience with a sense of tension and conflict. The third is *the pleasure of ideas,* of thought, of rational awareness of the world we inhabit, whether the cosmos itself or the interior dimensions of our own personality, our psychic self. Such pleasures we may healthily separate and inspect analytically for the purpose of attaining a better understanding, of living a fuller life, but in the end they are one.

The question probably most often asked with regard to judging whether a poem is good or bad, is a rich experience or a poor one, is the question of the relativity of any judgment. In poetry there are no absolutes. There is no way to prove that a poem is either a success or a failure. Why, then, can we not assert that if we respond enthusiastically to a poem it must be a good poem? Why cannot each reader of poetry assert to all other readers, "My judgment is as good as yours?" Why is intelligent judgment a must? The answer to these questions is that judgment must be recognized as a complex process. Meaningful judgment of a poem is something we win our way to. The pleasure of a poem is not pleasure in the sense of superficial titillation, a momentary thrill that dies at the end of its moment. It is rather the pleasure of truth, of *knowing* in the deepest sense of the word, a knowing that leads, directly and indirectly, to self-mastery. Our judgment of a poem should reflect our knowing, should suggest our awareness of the poem as a totality that is structure, that is form, that is art. Judgment can be judged by whether or not it reflects taste, a sense of values, an awareness of complexity, wisdom, intelligence, sensitivity. Of course the question may at once be raised, Are these things not relative too, and thus are we not going around in circles? The answer is Yes, they are relative, and we are sent around in circles. But not for long because we have the appeal to intelligence and experience to save us from philosophical absurdity. Because we are human we can some-how manage to find and affirm what is meaningful and to establish standards that belie the chaos of complete relativity, of a universe that is itself meaningless. To *discuss* a poem is part of the search and discovery that is life. There is beauty in the discussion as well as in the poem itself.

The poems which follow are offered for further study and pleasure, for response, for discussion, for judgment, for the unique experience which each may bring.

Poems for
Pleasure and Judgment

Anonymous Lyric of the Middle Ages

Western Wind

Western wind, when wilt thou blow,
The small rain down can rain?
Christ, if my love were in my arms
And I in my bed again!

Anonymous Ballads of the Middle Ages

Edward

1

"Why does your brand sae drap wi' bluid,
    Edward, Edward,
Why does your brand sae drap wi' bluid,
    And why sae sad gang ye, O?"
5 "O I ha'e killed my hawk sae guid,
    Mither, mither,
O I ha'e killed my hawk sae guid,
    And I had nae mair but he, O."

1 *brand* Sword. *sae drap wi' bluid* So drip with blood. **4** *gang ye* Do you go, do you look. **5** *ha'e* Have. *guid* Good. **6** *Mither* Mother. **8** *nae mair* No more, no other.

169

2

"Your hawke's bluid was never sae reid,
10   Edward, Edward,
Your hawke's bluid was never sae reid,
   My dear son I tell thee, O."
"O I ha'e killed my reid-roan steed,
   Mither, mither,
15 O I ha'e killed my reid-roan steed,
   That erst was sae fair and free, O."

3

"Your steed was auld, and ye ha'e gat mair,
        Edward, Edward,
Your steed was auld, and ye ha'e gat mair,
20   Some other dule ye drie, O."
"O I ha'e killed my fader dear,
   Mither, mither,
O I ha'e killed my fader dear,
   Alas, and wae is me, O!"

4

25 "And whatten penance wul ye drie for that,
        Edward, Edward?
And whatten penance wul ye drie for that,
   My dear son, now tell me O?"
"I'll set my feet in yonder boat,
30   Mither, mither,
I'll set my feet in yonder boat,
   And I'll fare over the sea, O."

5

"And what wul ye do wi' your towers and your ha',
        Edward, Edward?
35 And what wul ye do wi' your towers and your ha',
   That were sae fair to see, O?"
I'll let them stand tul they down fa',
        Mither, mither,
I'll let them stand tul they down fa',
40   For here never mair maun I be, O."

---

9 *reid* Red.   **16** *erst* Once.   **17** *auld* Old.   *ha'e gat mair* Have got more.   **20** *dule*
ye drie Grief you suffer.   **21** *fader* Father.   **24** *wae* Woe.   **25** *whatten* What sort of.   *wul*
Will.   **33** *ha'* Hall, home.   **37** *tul* Till.   *fa'* Fall.   **40** *maun* Must.

6

"And what wul ye leave to your bairns and your wife,
     Edward, Edward?
And what wul ye leave to your bairns and your wife,
    Whan ye gang over the sea, O?"
45 "The warlde's room, let them beg thrae life,
     Mither, mither,
The warlde's room, let them beg thrae life,
    For them never mair wul I see, O."

7

"And what wul ye leave to your ain mither dear,
50   Edward, Edward?
And what wul ye leave to your ain mither dear,
    My dear son, now tell me, O?"
"The curse of hell frae me sall ye bear,
     Mither, mither,
55 The curse of hell frae me sall ye bear,
    Sic counsels ye gave to me, O."

41 *wul* Will.   *bairns* Children.   **45** *warlde's room* The world's room, that is, over the
entire world.   *thrae* Through.   **49** *ain* Own.   **53** *frae me sall* From me shall.   **56** *Sic* Such.

Johnie Armstrong

1

There dwelt a man in fair Westmoreland,
   Johnie Armstrong men did him call,
He had neither lands nor rents coming in,
   Yet he kept eight score men in his hall.

2

5 He had horse and harness for them all,
   Goodly steeds were all milk-white;
O the golden bands an about their necks,
   And their weapons, they were all alike.

7 *an* And (they were).

3

News then was brought unto the king
10   That there was sic a one as he,
That livèd lyke a bold outlaw,
    And robbèd all the north country.

4

The king he writ an a letter then,
    A letter which was large and long;
15 He signèd it with his own hand,
    And he promised to do him no wrong.

5

When this letter came Johnie until,
    His heart it was as blithe as birds on the tree:
"Never was I sent for before any king,
20 My father, my grandfather, nor none but me.

6

"And if we go the king before,
    I would we went most orderly;
Every man of you shall have his scarlet cloak,
    Laced with silver laces three.

7

25 "Every one of you shall have his velvet coat,
    Laced with silver lace so white;
O the golden bands an about your necks,
    Black hats, white feathers, all alike."

8

By the morrow morning at ten of the clock,
30 Towards Edinburgh gone was he,
And with him all his eight score men;
    Good Lord, it was a goodly sight for to see!

9

When Johnie came before the king,
    He fell down on his knee;

10 *sic* Such.   **11** *lyke* Like.   **13** *an* And (it was).

35 "O pardon, my sovereign leige," he said,
   "O pardon my eight score men and me!"

10

"Thou shalt have no pardon, thou traitor strong,
   For thy eight score men nor thee;
For tomorrow morning by ten of the clock,
40   Both thou and them shall hang on the gallow-tree."

11

But Johnie looked over his left shoulder,
   Good Lord, what a grevious look looked he!
Saying, "Asking grace of a graceless face—
   Why there is none for you nor me."

12

45 But Johnie had a bright sword by his side,
   And it was made of the metal so free,
That had not the king stepped his foot aside,
   He had smitten his head from his fair body.

13

Saying, "Fight on, my merry men all,
50   And see that none of you be ta'en;
For rather than men shall say we were hanged,
   Let them report how we were slain."

14

Then, God wot, fair Edinburgh rose,
   And so beset poor Johnie round,
55 That fourscore and ten of Johnie's best men
   Lay gasping all upon the ground.

15

Then like a mad man Johnie laid about,
   And like a mad man then fought he,
Until a false Scot came Johnie behind,
60   And run him through the fair body.

16

Saying, "Fight on, my merry men all,
   And see that none of you be ta'en;

46 *free* Workable, ready, noble.   **53** *God wot* God knows.

For I will stand by and bleed but awhile,
And then will I come and fight again."

17

65 News then was brought to young Johnie Armstrong,
As he stood by his nurse's knee,
Who vowed if e'er he lived for to be a man,
O' the treacherous Scots revenged he'd be.

68 *O'* On.

Get Up and Bar the Door

1

It fell about the Martinmas time,
And a gay time it was then,
When our goodwife got puddings to make,
And she's boiled them in the pan.

2

5 The wind sae cauld blew south and north,
And blew into the floor;
Quoth our goodman to our goodwife,
"Gae out and bar the door."

3

"My hand is in my hussyfskap.
10   Goodman, as ye may see;
An it should nae be barred this hundred year,
It s' no be barred for me."

4

They made a paction 'tween them twa,
They made it firm and sure,
15 That the first word whae'er should speak,
Should rise and bar the door.

5

Then by there came two gentlemen,
At twelve o'clock at night,

1 *Martinmas time* November 11, the feast of St. Martin (Pope Martin I, died 655, the last Pope to die a martyr).   **5** *sae cauld* So cold.   **8** *Gae* Go.   **9** *hussyfskap* Housewifery.   **11** *an* If.   *nae* Not.   **12** *s'* Shall.   **13** *paction* Pact.   *twa* Two.   **15** *whae'er* Whoever.

And they could neither see house nor hall,
20   Nor coal nor candle-light.

6

"Now whether is this a rich man's house,
   Or whether is it a poor?"
But ne'er a word wad ane o' them speak,
   For barring of the door.

7

25   And first they ate the white puddings,
   And then they ate the black;
Though muckle thought the goodwife to hersel,
   Yet ne'er a word she spak.

8

Then said the one unto the other,
30   "Here, man, tak ye my knife;
Do ye tak aff the auld man's beard,
   And I'll kiss the goodwife."

9

"But there's nae water in the house,
   And what shall we do then?"
35   "What ails ye at the pudding-broo,
   That boils into the pan?"

10

O up then started our goodman,
   An angry man was he:
"Will ye kiss my wife before my een,
40   And scad me wi' pudding-bree?"

11

Then up and started our goodwife,
   Gied three skips on the floor:
"Goodman, you've spoken the foremost word,
   Get up and bar the door."

---

23 *wad ane* Would one.   **27** *muckle* Much.   *hersel* Herself.   **28** *spak* Spoke.
30 *tak ye* Take you.   **31** *aff* Off.   *auld* Old.   **35** *What ails ye at* What's the matter with.
pudding-broo Pudding-broth.   **36** *into* In.   **39** *een* Eyes.   **40** *scad* Scald.   *pudding-bree*
Pudding-broth.   **42** *Gied* Gave.

Geoffrey Chaucer   (c. 1343–1400)

From THE GENERAL PROLOGUE OF THE CANTERBURY TALES
(Translation by Nevill Coghill)

The Portrait of the Friar

A Frere ther was, a wantowne and a merye,
A lymytour, a ful solempne man.
In alle the ordres foure is noon that kan
So muche of daliaunce and fair langage.
5 He hadde maad ful many a mariage
Of yonge wommen at his owene cost.
Unto his ordre he was a noble post.
Ful wel biloved and famulier was he
With frankeleyns over al in his contree,
10 And eek with worthy wommen of the toun;
For he hadde power of confessioun,
As seyde hymself, moore than a curat,
For of his ordre he was licenciat.
Ful swetely herde he confession,
15 And plesaunt was his absolucion.
He was an esy man to yeve penaunce
Ther as he wiste to have a good pitaunce;
For unto a povre ordre for to yive
Is signe that a man is wel yshryve;
20 For if he yaf, he dorste make avaunt
He wiste that a man was repentaunt;
For many a man so hard is of his herte,
He may nat wepe althogh hym soore smerte.
Therfore, instede of wepynge and prayeres,
25 Men moote yeve silver to the povre freres.
His typet was ay farsed ful of knyves
And pynnes, for to yeven faire wyves.
And certeinly he hadde a murye note;
Wel koude he synge and pleyen on a rote;
30 Of yeddynges he baar outrely the pris.
His nekke whit was as the flour-de-lys;
Therto he strong was as a champioun.
He knew the tavernes wel in every toun,
And every hostiler and tappestere,
35 Bet than a lazar or a beggestere.
For unto swich a worthy man as he
Acorded nat, as by his facultee,
To have with sike lazars aqueyntaunce.
It is nat honeste, it may nat avaunce,
40 For to deelen with no swich poraille,
But al with riche, and selleres of vitaille.

There was a *Friar,* a wanton one and merry,
A Limiter, a very festive fellow.
In all Four Orders there was none so mellow
As he in flattery and dalliant speech.
5 He'd fixed up many a marriage, giving each
Of his young women what he could afford her.
He was a noble pillar to his Order.
Highly beloved and intimate was he
With County folk wherever he might be,
10 And worthy city women with possessions;
For he was qualified to hear confessions,
Or so he said, with more than priestly scope;
He had a special license from the Pope.
Sweetly he heard his penitents at shrift
15 With pleasant absolution, for a gift.
He was an easy man in penance-giving
Where he could hope to make a decent living;
It's a sure sign whenever gifts are given
To a poor Order that a man's well shriven,
20 And should he give enough he knew in verity
The penitent repented in sincerity.
For many a fellow is so hard of heart
He cannot weep, for all his inward smart.
Therefore instead of weeping and of prayer
25 One should give silver for a poor Friar's care.
He kept his tippet stuffed with pins for curls,
And pocket-knives, to give to pretty girls.
And certainly his voice was gay and sturdy,
For he **sang well** and played the hurdy-gurdy.
30 At sing-songs he was champion of the hour.
His neck was whiter than a lily-flower
But strong enough to butt a bruiser down.
He knew the taverns well in every town
And every innkeeper and barmaid too
35 Better than lepers, beggars and that crew,
For in so eminent a man as he
It was not fitting with the dignity
Of his position dealing with such scum.
It isn't decent, nothing good can come
40 Of having truck with slum-and-gutter dwellers,
But only with the rich and victual-sellers.

Note: These translations are not all line for line.   **2** *Limiter* A friar licensed to beg within
certain geographical limits.   **3** *Four Orders* The Dominicans, Franciscans, Carmelites, and
Augustinians.

And over al ther as profit sholde arise,
Curteis he was, and lowely of servyse;
Ther nas no man man nowher so vertuous.
45 He was the beste beggere in his hous,
For thogh a wydwe hadde noght a sho,
So plesaunt was his *In principio*
Yet wolde he have a ferthyng er he wente.
His purchas was wel bettre than his rente.
50 And rage he koude as it were right a whelpe;
In love-dayes ther koude he muchel helpe,
For ther he was nat lyk a cloysterer
With a thredbare cope, as is a povre scoler,
But he was lyk a maister or a pope.
55 Of double worstede was his semycope,
And rounded as a belle out of the presse.
Somwhat he lipsed for his wantownesse,
To make his Englissh sweete upon his tonge;
And in his harpyng, whan that he hadde songe,
60 His eyen twynkled in his heed aryght
As doon the sterres in the frosty nyght.
This worthy lymytour was cleped Huberd.

The Portrait of the Wife of Bath

A good Wif was ther of biside Bathe,
But she was somdel deef, and that was scathe.
Of clooth-makyng she hadde swich an haunt,
She passed hem of Ypres and of Gaunt.
5 In al the parisshe wif ne was ther noon
That to the offrynge bifore hire sholde goon;
And if ther dide, certeyn so wrooth was she,
That she was out of alle charitee.
Hir coverchiefs ful fyne were of ground;
10 I dorste swere they weyeden ten pound
That on a Sonday weren upon hir heed.
Hir hosen weren of fyn scarlet reed,
Ful streite yteyd, and shoes ful moyste and newe.
Boold was hir face and fair and reed of hewe.
15 She was a worthy womman al hir lyve:
Housbondes at chirche dore she hadde fyve,

But anywhere a profit might accrue
Courteous he was and lowly of service too.
Natural gifts like his were hard to match.
45 He was the finest beggar of his batch,
And, for his begging-district, payed a rent;
His brethren did no poaching where he went.
For though a widow mightn't have a shoe,
So pleasant was his holy how-d'ye-do
50 He got his farthing from her just the same
Before he left, and so his income came
To more than he laid out. And how he romped,
Just like a puppy! He was ever prompt
To arbitrate disputes on settling days
55 (For a small fee) in many helpful ways,
Not then appearing as your cloistered scholar
With threadbare habit hardly worth a dollar,
But much more like a Doctor or a Pope.
Of double-worsted was the semi-cope
60 Upon his shoulders, and the swelling fold
About him, like a bell about its mold
When it is casting, rounded out his dress.
He lisped a little out of wantonness
To make his English sweet upon his tongue.
65 When he had played his harp, or having sung,
His eyes would twinkle in his head as bright
As any star upon a frosty night.
This worthy's name was Hubert, it appeared.

A worthy *woman* from beside *Bath* city
Was with us, somewhat deaf, which was a pity.
In making cloth she showed so great a bent
She bettered those of Ypres and of Ghent.
5 In all the parish not a dame dared stir
Towards the altar steps in front of her,
And if indeed they did, so wrath was she
As to be quite put out of charity.
Her kerchiefs were of finely woven ground;
10 I dared have sworn they weighed a good ten pound,
The ones she wore on Sunday, on her head.
Her hose were of the finest scarlet red
And gartered tight; her shoes were soft and new.
Bold was her face, handsome, and red in hue.
15 A worthy woman all her life, what's more
She'd have five husbands, all at the church door,

---

4 *Ypres . . . Ghent* Centers of the Flemish wool trade.   **16** *at the church door* The celebration of marriage at the church door was a common practice in the Middle Ages.

Withouten oother compaignye in youthe—
But therof nedeth nat to speke as nowthe.
And thries hadde she been at Jerusalem;
20   She hadde passed many a straunge strem;
At Rome she hadde been, and at Boloigne,
In Galice at Seint Jame, and at Coloigne;
She koude muche of wandrynge by the weye.
Gat-tothed was she, soothly for to seye.
25   Upon an amblere esily she sat,
Ywympled wel, and on hir heed an hat
As brood as is a bokeler or a targe;
A foot-mantel aboute hir hipes large,
And on hir feet a paire of spores sharpe.
30   In felaweshipe wel koude she laughe and carpe.
Of remedies of love she knew per chaunce,
For she koude of that art the olde daunce.

The Portrait of the Pardoner

With hym ther rood a gentil Pardoner
Of Rouncival, his freend and his compeer,
That streight was comen fro the court of Rome.
Ful loude he soong, "Com hider, love, to me!"
5   This Somnour bar to hym a stif burdoun;
Was nevere trompe of half so greet a soun.
This Pardoner hadde heer as yelow as wex,
But smothe it heeng as dooth a strike of flex;
By ounces henge his lokkes that he hadde,
10   And therwith he his shuldres overspradde;
But thynne it lay, by colpons, oon and oon.
But hood for jolitee wered he noon,
For it was trussed up in his walet;
Hym thoughte he rood al of the newe jet;
15   Dischevelee save his cappe he rood al bare.
Swiche glarynge eyen hadde he as an hare,
A vernycle hadde he sowed upon his cappe.
His walet lay biforn hym in his lappe,
Bretful of pardon, comen from Rome al hoot.
20   A voys he hadde as smal as hath a goot;
No berd hadde he, ne nevere sholde have;
As smothe it was as it were late yshave;
I trowe he were a geldyng or a mare.

Apart from other company in youth;
No need just now to speak of that, forsooth.
And she had thrice been to Jerusalem,
20　Seen many strange rivers and passed over them;
She'd been to Rome and also to Boulogne,
St. James of Compostella and Cologne,
And she was skilled in wandering by the way.
She had gap-teeth, set widely, truth to say.
25　Easily on an ambling horse she sat
Well wimpled up, and on her head a hat
As broad as is a buckler or a shield;
She had a flowing mantle that concealed
Large hips, her heels spurred sharply under that.
30　In company she liked to laugh and chat
And knew the remedies for love's mischances,
An art in which she knew the oldest dances.

22 *St. James of Compostella*　St. James is the patron saint of Compostella, a city in north-
west Spain in the Galician province of Corunna. His shrine at Compostella was an important place
of pilgrimage for Christians in the Middle Ages.

He and a gentle *Pardoner* rode together,
A bird from Charing Cross of the same feather,
Just back from visiting the Court of Rome.
He loudly sang *"Come hither, love, come home!"*
5　The Summoner sang deep seconds to this song,
No trumpet ever sounded half so strong.
This Pardoner had hair as yellow as wax
Hanging down smoothly like a hank of flax.
In driblets fell his locks behind his head
10　Down to his shoulders which they overspread;
Thinly they fell, like rat-tails, one by one.
He wore no hood upon his head, for fun;
The hood inside his wallet had been stowed,
He aimed at riding in the latest mode;
15　But for a little cap his head was bare
And he had bulging eye-balls, like a hare.
He'd sowed a holy relic on his cap;
His wallet lay before him on his lap,
Brimful of pardons come from Rome all hot.
20　He had the same small voice a goat has got.
His chin no beard had harbored, nor would harbor,
Smoother than ever chin was left by barber.
I judge he was a gelding, or a mare.

5 *Summoner*　An officer who cited delinquents to appear before the ecclesiastical court.

But of his craft, fro Berwyk into Ware,
25 Ne was ther swich another pardoner.
For in his male he hadde a pilwe-beer,
Which that he seyde was Oure Lady veyl;
He seyde he hadde a gobet of the seyl
That Seint Peter hadde whan that he wente
30 Upon the see, til Jhesu Crist hym hente.
He hadde a croys of laton, ful of stones,
And in a glas he hadde pigges bones.
But with thise relikes whan that he fond
A povre person dwellynge upon lond,
35 Upon a day he gat hym moore moneye
Than that the person gat in monthes tweye;
And thus with feyned flaterye and japes,
He made the person and the peple his apes.
But trewely to tellen atte laste,
40 He was in chirche a noble ecclesiaste;
Wel koude he rede a lesson or a storie,
But alderbest he song an offertorie;
For wel he wiste whan that song was songe,
He moste preche and wel affile his tonge
45 To wynne silver, as he ful wel koude;
Therefore he song the murierly and loude.

As to his trade, from Berwick down to Ware
25 There was no pardoner of equal grace,
For in his trunk he had a pillow-case
Which he asserted was Our Lady's veil.
He said he had a gobbet of the sail
Saint Peter had the time when he made bold
30 To walk the waves, till Jesu Christ took hold.
He had a cross of metal set with stones
And, in a glass, a rubble of pigs' bones.
And with these relics, any time he found
Some poor up-country parson to astound,
35 On one short day, in money down, he drew
More than the parson in a month or two,
And by his flatteries and prevarication
Made monkeys of the priest and congregation.
But still to do him justice first and last
40 In church he was a noble ecclesiast.
How well he read a lesson or told a story!
But best of all he sang an Offertory,
For well he knew that when that song was sung
He'd have to preach and tune his honey-tongue
45 And (well he could) win silver from the crowd.
That's why he sang so merrily and loud.

24 *Berwick down to Ware*   F. N. Robinson notes that this is apparently intended to suggest
from north to south.

The Pardoner's Tale

In Flanders once there was a company
Of youngsters haunting vice and ribaldry,
Riot and gambling, stews and public-houses
Where each with harp, guitar or lute carouses,
5 Dancing and dicing day and night, and bold
To eat and drink far more than they can hold,
Doing thereby the devil sacrifice
Within that devil's temple of cursed vice,
Abominable in superfluity,
10 With oaths so damnable in blasphemy
That it's a grisly thing to hear them swear.
Our dear Lord's body they will rend and tear
As if the Jews had rent Him not enough;
And at the sin of others every tough
15 Will laugh, and presently the dancing-girls,
Small pretty ones, come in and shake their curls,
With youngsters selling fruit, and ancient bawds,
And girls with cakes and music, devil's gauds
To kindle and blow the fires of lechery
20 That are so close annexed to gluttony.
Witness the Bible, which is most express
That lust is bred of wine and drunkenness.
    Look how the drunken and unnatural Lot
Lay with his daughters, though he knew it not;
25 He was too drunk to know what he was doing.
    Take Herod too, his tale is worth pursuing.
Replete with wine and feasting, he was able
To give the order at his very table
To kill the innocent Baptist, good St. John.
30   Seneca has a thought worth pondering on;
No difference, he says, that he can find
Between a madman who has lost his mind
And one who is habitually mellow
Except that madness, when it takes a fellow,
35 Lasts longer, on the whole, than drunkenness.
O cursed gluttony, our first distress!
Cause of our first confusion, first temptation,
The very origin of our damnation,
Till Christ redeemed us with his blood again!
40 O infamous indulgence! Cursed stain
So dearly bought! And what has it been worth?
Gluttony has corrupted all the earth.

23 *Lot* See Genesis 19:30-38.   **26** *Herod* See Matthew 14:1-12.   **30** *Seneca* Roman philosopher, dramatist, and statesman (4 B.C.-65 A.D.).

Adam, our father, and his wife no less,
From Paradise to labor and distress
45 Were driven for that vice, they were indeed.
While she and Adam fasted, so I read,
They were in Paradise; when he and she
Ate of the fruit of that forbidden tree
They were at once cast forth in pain and woe.
50 O gluttony, it is to thee we owe
Our griefs! O if we knew the maladies
That follow on excess and gluttonies,
Sure we would diet, we would temper pleasure
In sitting down at table, show some measure!
55 Alas the narrow throat, the tender mouth!
Men labor east and west and north and south
In earth, in air, in water—Why, d'you think?
To get a glutton dainty meat and drink!
How well of this St. Paul's Epistle treats!
60 "Meats for the belly, belly for the meats,
But God shall yet destroy both it and them."
Alas, the filth of it! If we contemn
The name, how far more filthy is the act!
A man who swills down vintages in fact
65 Makes a mere privy of his throat, a sink
For cursed superfluities of drink!
    So the Apostle said, whom tears could soften:
"Many there are, as I have told you often,
And weep to tell, whose gluttony sufficed
70 To make them enemies of the cross of Christ,
Whose ending is destruction and whose God
Their belly!" O thou belly! stinking pod
Of dung and foul corruption, that canst send
Thy filthy music forth at either end,
75 What labor and expense it is to find
Thy sustenance! These cooks that strain and grind
And bray in mortars, transubstantiate
God's gifts into a flavor on a plate
To please a lecherous palate. How they batter
80 Hard bones to put some marrow on your platter,
Spicery, root, bark, leaf—they search and cull it
In the sweet hope of flattering a gullet!
Nothing is thrown away that could delight
Or whet anew lascivious appetite.
85 Be sure a man whom such a fare entices
Is dead indeed, though living in his vices.

60-61 *"Meats for the belly . . ."*   See I Corinthians 6:13.

Wine is a lecherous thing and drunkenness
A squalor of contention and distress.
O drunkard, how disfigured is thy face,
90 How foul thy breath, how filthy thy embrace!
And through thy drunken nose a stertorous snort
Like *"samson-samson"*—something of the sort.
Yet Samson never was a man to swig.
You totter, lurch and fall like a stuck pig,
95 Your manhood's lost, your tongue is in a burr.
Drunkenness is the very sepulcher
Of human judgment and articulation.
He that is subject to the domination
Of drink can keep no secrets, be it said.
100 Keep clear of wine, I tell you, white or red,
Especially Spanish wines which they provide
And have on sale in Fish Street and Cheapside.
That wine mysteriously finds its way
To mix itself with others—shall we say
105 Spontaneously?—that grow in neighboring regions.
Out of the mixture fumes arise in legions,
So when a man has had a drink or two,
Though he may think he is at home with you
In Cheapside, I assure you he's in Spain
110 Where it was made, at Lepé I maintain,
Not even at Bordeaux. He's soon elate
And very near the *"samson-samson"* state.
But seriously, my lords, attention, pray!
All the most notable acts, I dare to say,
115 And victories in the Old Testament,
Won under God who is omnipotent,
Were won in abstinence, were won in prayer.
Look in the Bible, you will find it there.
Or else take Attila the Conqueror;
120 Died in his sleep, a manner to abhor,
In drunken shame and bleeding at the nose.
A general should live sober, I suppose.
Moreover call to mind and ponder well
What was commanded unto Lemuel
125 —Not Samuel but Lemuel I said—
Read in the Bible, that's the fountain-head,
And see what comes of giving judges drink.
No more of that. I've said enough, I think.

93 *Samson*   A judge and hero of Israel, proverbial for his strength. See Judges 13-16.
102 *Fish Street and Cheapside*   A street and district in London.   **110** *Lepé*   Near Cadiz in Spain.
119 *Attila the Conqueror*   King of the Huns (c. 406-453).   **124** *Lemuel*   See Proverbs 31:4-5.

Having put gluttony in its proper setting
130 I wish to warn you against dice and betting.
Gambling's the very mother of robbed purses
Lies, double-dealing, perjury, and curses,
Manslaughter, blasphemy of Christ, and waste
Of time and money. Worse, you are debased
135 In public reputation, put to shame.
"A common gambler" is a nasty name.
   The more exalted such a man may be
So much the more contemptible is he.
A gambling prince would be incompetent
140 To frame a policy of government,
And he will sink in general opinion
As one unfit to exercise dominion.
   Stilbon, that wise ambassador whose mission
Took him to Corinth, was of high position;
145 Sparta had sent him with intent to frame
A treaty of alliance. When he came,
Hoping for reinforcement and advice,
It happened that he found them all at dice,
Their very nobles; so he quickly planned
150 To steal away, home to his native land.
He said, "I will not lose my reputation
Or compromise the honor of my nation
By asking dicers to negotiate.
Send other wise ambassadors of state,
155 For on my honor I would rather die
Than be a means for Corinth to ally
With gamblers; Corinth, glorious in honor,
Shall take no such alliances upon her
As dicers make, by any act of mine!"
160 He showed his sense in taking such a line.
   Again, consider King Demetrius;
The King of Parthia—history has it thus—
Sent him a pair of golden dice in scorn,
To show he reckoned him a gambler born
165 Whose honor, if unable to surmount
The vice of gambling, was of no account.
Lords can amuse themselves in other ways
Honest enough, to occupy their days.
   Now let me speak a word or two of swearing
170 And perjury; the Bible is unsparing.
It's an abominable thing to curse
And swear, it says; but perjury is worse.
Almighty God has said, "Swear not at all,"
Witness St. Matthew, and you may recall
175 The words of Jeremiah, having care

To what he says of lying: "Thou shalt swear
In truth, in judgment and in righteousness."
But idle swearing is a sin, no less.
Behold and see the tables of the Law
180 Of God's Commandments, to be held in awe;
Look at the third where it is written plain,
"Thou shalt not take the name of God in vain."
You see He has forbidden swearing first;
Not murder, no, nor other thing accurst
185 Comes before that, I say, in God's commands.
That is the order; he who understands
Knows that the third commandment is just that.
And in addition, let me tell you flat,
Vengeance on him and all his house shall fall
190 That swears outrageously, or swears at all.
"God's precious heart and passion, by God's nails
And by the blood of Christ that is at Hailes,
Seven's my luck, and yours is five and three;
God's blessed arms! If you play false with me
195 I'll stab you with my dagger!" Overthrown
By two small dice, two bitching bits of bone,
They reach rage, perjury, cheating, homicide.
O for the love of Jesu Christ who died
For us, abandon curses, small or great!
200 But, sirs, I have a story to relate.
　　It's of three rioters I have to tell
Who, long before the morning service bell,
Were sitting in a tavern for a drink.
And as they sat, they heard the hand-bell clink
205 Before a coffin being borne to church.
One called the tavern-lad and with a lurch
Said to him, "Run along and ask—look spry—
Whose corpse is in that coffin passing by;
And see you get the name correctly too."
210 "Sir," said the boy, "no need, I promise you;
Two hours before you came here I was told.
He was a friend of yours in days of old,
But suddenly killed last night in an attack,
There on the bench, dead drunk and on his back.
215 There came a privy thief, they call him Death,
Who kills us all round here, and in a breath
He speared him through the heart; he never stirred.
And then Death went his way without a word.
He's killed a thousand in the present plague,

176-77 *"Thou shalt swear . . ."* Jeremiah 4:2.　**192** *Hailes* The abbey of Hales in Gloucestershire was believed to possess some of Christ's blood.

220 And, sir, it doesn't do to be too vague
    If you should meet him; you had best be wary.
    Be on your guard with such an adversary,
    Be primed to meet him everywhere you go,
    That's what my mother said. It's all I know."
225   The publican joined in with, "By St. Mary.
    What the child says is right; you'd best be wary,
    This very year he killed, in a large village
    A mile away, man, woman, serf at tillage,
    Page in the household, children—all there were.
230 Yes, I imagine that he lives round there.
    It's well to be prepared in these alarms,
    He might do dirt on you." "What's that? God's arms!"
    The rioter said, "Is he so fierce to meet?
    I'll search for him, by Jesus, street by street.
235 God's blessed bones! I'll register a vow!
    Here, chaps! The three of us together now,
    Hold up your hands, like me, and we'll be brothers
    In this affair, and each defend the others.
    We'll kill this double-crosser Death, I say;
240 Away with him as he has made away
    With all our friends. God's dignity! To-night!"
       They made their bargain, swore with appetite,
    These three, to live and die for one another
    As brother-born might swear to his born brother.
245 And up they started in their drunken rage
    And made towards this village which the page
    And publican had spoken of before.
    Many and grisly were the oaths they swore,
    Tearing Christ's blessed body to a shred;
250 "If we can only catch him, Death is dead!"
       When they had gone not fully half a mile,
    Just as they were about to cross a stile,
    They came upon a very poor old man
    Who humbly greeted them and thus began,
255 "God look to you, my lords, and give you quiet!"
    To which the proudest of these men of riot
    Gave back the answer, "What, old fool? Give place!
    Why are you all wrapped up except your face?
    Why live so long? Isn't it time to die?"
260   The old, old fellow looked him in the eye
    And said, "Because I never yet have found,
    Though I have walked to India, searching round
    Village and city on my pilgrimage,
    One who would change his youth to have my age.
265 And so my age is mine and must be still
    Upon me, for such time as God may will.

"Not even Death, alas, will take my life;
So, like a wretched prisoner at strife
Within himself, I walk alone and wait
270 About the earth, which is my mother's gate,
Knock-knocking with my staff from night to noon
And crying, "Mother, open to me soon!
Look at me, mother, won't you let me in?
See how I wither, flesh and blood and skin!
275 Alas! When will these bones be laid to rest?
Mother, I would exchange—for that were best—
The wardrobe in my chamber, standing there
So long, for yours! Aye, for a shirt of hair
To wrap me in!" She has refused her grace,
280 Whence comes the pallor of my withered face.
     "But it dishonored you when you began
To speak so roughly, sir, to an old man,
Unless he had injured you in word or deed.
It says in holy writ, as you may read,
285 "Thou shalt rise up before the hoary head
And honor it." And therefore be it said
"Do no more harm to an old man than you,
Being now young, would have another do
When you are old"—if you should live till then.
290 And so may God be with you, gentlemen,
For I must go whither I have to go."
     "By God," the gambler said, "you shan't do so,
You don't get off so easy, by St. John!
I heard you mention, just a moment gone,
295 A certain traitor Death who singles out
And kills the fine young fellows hereabout.
And you're his spy, by God! You wait a bit.
Say where he is or you shall pay for it,
By God and by the Holy Sacrament!
300 I say you've joined together by consent
To kill us younger folk, you thieving swine!"
     "Well, sir," he said, "if it be your design
To find out Death, turn up this crooked way
Towards that grove. I left him there to-day
305 Under a tree, and there you'll find him waiting.
He isn't one to hide for all your prating.
You see that oak? He won't be far to find.
And God protect you that redeemed mankind,
Aye, and amend you!" Thus that ancient man.
310   At once the three young rioters began
To run, and reached the tree, and there they found

285-86 *"Thou shalt . . ."* See Leviticus 19:32.

A pile of golden florins on the ground,
New-coined, eight bushels of them as they thought.
No longer was it Death those fellows sought,
315 For they were all so thrilled to see the sight,
The florins were so beautiful and bright,
That down they sat beside the precious pile.
The wickedest spoke first after a while.
"Brothers," he said, "you listen to what I say.
320 I'm pretty sharp, although I joke away.
It's clear that Fortune has bestowed this treasure
So as to let us live our lives in pleasure.
Light come, light go! We'll spend it as we ought.
God's precious dignity! Who would have thought
325 This morning was to be our lucky day?
        "If one could only get the gold away,
Back to my house, or else to yours, perhaps—
For as you know, the gold is ours, chaps—
We'd all be at the top of fortune, hey?
330 But certainly it can't be done by day.
People would call us robbers—a strong gang,
So our own property would make us hang.
No; we must bring this treasure back by night
Some prudent way, and keep it out of sight.
335 And so as a solution I propose
We draw for lots and see the way it goes.
The one who draws the longest, lucky man,
Shall run to town as quickly as he can
To fetch us bread and wine—but keep things dark—
340 While two remain in hiding here to mark
Our heap of treasure. If there's no delay,
When night comes down we'll carry it away,
All three of us, wherever we have planned."
        He gathered lots and hid them in his hand
345 Bidding them draw for where the luck should fall.
It fell upon the youngest of them all,
And off he ran at once towards the town.
        As soon as he had gone the first sat down
And thus began a parley with the other:
350 "You know that you can trust me as a brother;
Let me point out the advantage to you there.
Our friend has gone, as you are well aware,
And here's a lot of gold that is to be
Divided equally amongst us three.
355 Nevertheless, if I could shape things thus
So that we shared it out—the two of us—
Wouldn't you take it as a friendly turn?"
        "How?" said the other. "Maybe I can learn,

But still he knows the gold's with me and you;
360 What can we tell him? What are we to do?"
   "Is it a bargain," said the first, "or no?
For I can tell you in a word or so
What's to be done to bring the thing about."
"Trust me," the other said, "you needn't doubt
365 My word. I won't betray you, I'll be true."
   "Well," said his friend, "you see that we are two,
And two are twice as powerful as one.
Now look; when he comes back, get up in fun
And have a wrestle with him, just a rag;
370 Then I'll jump up and slice him through the bag
While he is struggling, thinking it a game;
You draw your dagger too and do the same.
Then all this money will be ours to spend,
Divided equally of course, dear friend.
375 Then we can gratify our lusts and fill
The day with dicing at our own sweet will."
Thus these two miscreants agreed to slay
The third and youngest, as you heard me say.
   The youngest, as he ran towards the town,
380 Kept turning over, rolling up and down
Within his heart the beauty of those bright
New florins, saying, "Lord, to think I might
Have all that treasure to myself alone!
Could there be anyone beneath the throne
385 Of God so happy as I then should be?"
   And so the Fiend, our common enemy,
Was given power to put it in his thought
That there was always poison to be bought,
And that with poison he could kill his friends.
390 To men in such a state the Devil sends
Thoughts of this kind, and has a full permission
To lure them on to sorrow and perdition;
For this young man was utterly content
To kill them both and never to repent.
395   And on he ran, he had no thought to tarry,
Came to the town, found an apothecary
And said, "Sell me some poison if you will,
I have a lot of rats I want to kill
And there's a polecat too about my yard
400 That takes my chickens and it hits me hard;
But I'll get even, as is only right,
With vermin that destroy a man by night."
   The chemist answered, "I've a preparation
Which you shall have, and by my soul's salvation
405 If any living creature eat or drink

A mouthful, ere he has the time to think,
Though he took less than makes a grain of wheat,
You'll see him fall down dying at your feet;
Yes, die he must, and in so short a while
410 You'd hardly have the time to walk a mile,
The poison is so strong, you understand."
   This cursed fellow grabbed into his hand
The box of poison and away he ran
Into a neighboring street, and found a man
415 Who lent him three large bottles. He withdrew
And deftly poured the poison into two.
He kept the third one clean, as well he might,
For his own drink, meaning to work all night
Stacking the gold and carrying it away.
420 And when this rioter, this devil's clay,
Had filled his bottles up with wine, all three,
Then back to join his comrades sauntered he.
   Why make a sermon of it? Why waste breath?
Exactly in the way they'd planned his death
425 They fell on him and slew him, two to one.
Then said the first of them when this was done,
"Now for a drink. Sit down and let's be merry,
For later on there'll be the corpse to bury."
And, as it happened, reaching for a sup,
430 He took a bottle full of poison up
And drank; and his companion, nothing loth,
Drank from it also, and they perished both.
   There is, in Avicenna's long relation
Concerning poison and its operation,
435 Trust me, no ghastlier section to transcend
What these two wretches suffered at their end.
Thus these two murderers received their due,
So did the treacherous young poisoner too.
   O cursed sin! O blackguardly excess!
440 O treacherous homicide! O wickedness!
O gluttony that lusted on and diced!
O blasphemy that took the name of Christ
With habit-hardened oaths that pride began!
Alas, how comes it that a mortal man,
445 That thou, to thy Creator, Him that wrought thee,
That paid His precious blood for thee and bought thee,
Art so unnatural and false within?
   Dearly beloved, God forgive your sin
And keep you from the vice of avarice!

433 *Avicenna*   An Arabian physician and philosopher (980-1037).

450 My holy pardon frees you all of this,
     Provided that you make the right approaches,
     That is with sterling, rings, or silver brooches.
     Bow down your heads under this holy bull!
     Come on, you women, offer up your wool!
455 I'll write your name into my ledger; so!
     Into the bliss of Heaven you shall go.
     For I'll absolve you by my holy power,
     You that make offering, clean as at the hour
     When you were born. . . . That, sirs, is how I preach.
460 And Jesu Christ, soul's healer, aye, the leech
     Of every soul, grant pardon and relieve you
     Of sin, for that is best, I won't deceive you.
         One thing I should have mentioned in my tale,
     Dear people. I've some relics in my bale
465 And pardons too, as full and fine I hope
     As any in England, given me by the Pope.
     If there be one among you that is willing
     To have my absolution, for a shilling
     Devoutly given, come! and do not harden
470 Your hearts, but kneel in humbleness for pardon;
     Or else, receive my pardon as we go.
     You can renew it every town or so,
     Always provided that you still renew
     Each time, and in good money, what is due.
475 It is an honor for you to have found
     A pardoner with his credentials sound,
     Who can absolve you, as you ply the spur,
     In any accident that may occur.
     For instance—we are all at Fortune's beck—
480 Your horse may throw you down and break your neck.
     What a security it is to all
     To have me here among you and at call
     With pardon for the lowly and the great,
     When soul leaves body for the future state!
485 And I advise our Host here to begin,
     The most enveloped of you all in sin.
     Come forward, Host, you shall be first to pay,
     And kiss my holy relics right away.
     Only a groat. Come on, unbuckle your purse!"
490   "No, no," said he, "not I, and may the curse
     Of Christ descend upon me if I do!
     You'll have me kissing your old breeches too
     And swear they were the relic of a saint
     Although your fundament supplied the paint!
495 Now by St. Helen and the Holy Land
     I wish I had your cullions in my hand

Instead of relics in a reliquarium;
Have them cut off and I will help to carry 'em.
We'll have them shrined for you in a hog's turd.''
500   The Pardoner said nothing, not a word;
He was so angry that he couldn't speak.
"Well," said our Host, "if you're for showing pique,
I'll joke no more, not with an angry man."
      The worthy Knight immediately began,
505 Seeing the fun was getting rather rough,
And said, "No more, we've all had quite enough.
Now, Master Pardoner, perk up, look cheerly!
And you, Sir Host, whom I esteem so dearly,
I beg of you to kiss the Pardoner.
510   "Come, Pardoner, draw nearer, my dear sir.
Let's laugh again and keep the ball in play."
They kissed, and we continued on our way.

Sir Thomas Wyatt   (1503–1542)

They Flee from Me

They flee from me, that sometime did me seek,
With naked foot stalking in my chamber.
I have seen them, gentle, tame, and meek,
That now are wild, and do not remember
5 That sometime they put themselves in danger
To take bread at my hand; and now they range,
Busily seeking with a continual change.

Thanked be Fortune it hath been otherwise,
Twenty times better; but once in special,
10 In thin array, after a pleasant guise,
When her loose gown from her shoulders did fall,
And she me caught in her arms long and small,
And therewith all sweetly did me kiss
And softly said, "Dear heart, how like you this?"

15 It was no dream, I lay broad waking.
But all is turned, thorough my gentleness,
Into a strange fashion of forsaking;
And I have leave to go, of her goodness,
And she also to use newfangleness.
20 But since that I so kindly am served,
I fain would know what she hath deserved.

12 *small*   Slender.

Sir Walter Ralegh   (c. 1552–1618)

The Nymph's Reply to the Shepherd

If all the world and love were young,
And truth in every shepherd's tongue,
These pretty pleasures might me move
To live with thee and be thy love.

5 Time drives the flocks from field to fold
When rivers rage and rocks grow cold,
And Philomel becometh dumb;
The rest complains of cares to come.

The flowers do fade, and wanton fields
10 To wayward winter reckoning yields;
A honey tongue, a heart of gall,
Is fancy's spring, but sorrow's fall.

Thy gowns, thy shoes, thy beds of roses,
Thy cap, thy kirtle, and thy posies
15 Soon break, soon wither, soon forgotten—
In folly ripe, in reason rotten.

Thy belt of straw and ivy buds,
Thy coral clasps and amber studs,
All these in me no means can move
20 To come to thee and be thy love.

But could youth last and love still breed,
Had joys no date nor age no need,
Then these delights my mind might move
To live with thee and be thy love.

The Nymph's Reply   This poem was written in reply to Marlowe's "The Passionate Shepherd to His Love" (p. 197).   **7** *Philomel*   The nightingale. In Greek myth the gods changed the two sisters Procne and Philomela into a nightingale and a swallow as they were about to be killed by Tereus. Roman writers reversed the identities, making Philomela the nightingale.   **14** *kirtle*   A long gown or dress worn by women.

Christopher Marlowe   (1564–1593)

The Passionate Shepherd to His Love

Come live with me and be my love,
And we will all the pleasures prove,
That valleys, groves, hills, and fields,
And all the craggy mountains yields.

5 There we will sit upon the rocks,
And see the shepherds feed their flocks,
By shallow rivers to whose falls
Melodious birds sing madrigals.

And I will make thee beds of roses
10 With a thousand fragrant posies,
A cap of flowers, and a kirtle
Embroidered all with leaves of myrtle;

A gown made of the finest wool
Which from our pretty lambs we pull;
15 Fair lined slippers for the cold,
With buckles of the purest gold;

A belt of straw and ivy buds,
With coral clasps and amber studs:
And if these pleasures may thee move,
20 Come live with me and be my love.

The shepherds' swains shall dance and sing
For thy delight each May morning:
If these delights thy mind may move,
Then live with me and be my love.

The Passionate Shepherd   Sir Walter Ralegh responds to this poem in ''The Nymph's Reply to the Shepherd'' (p. 196).   **2** *prove* Try.   **11** *kirtle* A long gown or dress.   **21** *swains* Companions.

William Shakespeare   (1564–1616)

Sonnets

23

As an unperfect actor on the stage,
Who with his fear is put besides his part,

Or some fierce thing replete with too much rage,
Whose strength's abundance weakens his own heart,
5 So I, for fear of trust, forget to say
The perfect ceremony of love's rite,
And in mine own love's strength seem to decay,
O'ercharged with burden of mine own love's might.
Oh, let my books be then the eloquence
10 And dumb presagers of my speaking breast,
Who plead for love, and look for recompense,
More than that tongue that more hath more expressed.
  Oh, learn to read what silent love hath writ.
  To hear with eyes belongs to love's fine wit.

73

That time of year thou mayst in me behold
When yellow leaves, or none, or few, do hang
Upon those boughs which shake against the cold,
Bare ruined choirs, where late the sweet birds sang.
5 In me thou see'st the twilight of such day
As after sunset fadeth in the west,
Which by and by black night doth take away,
Death's second self that seals up all in rest.
In me thou see'st the glowing of such fire,
10 That on the ashes of his youth doth lie,
As the death-bed, whereon it must expire
Consumed with that which it was nourished by.
  This thou perceiv'st, which makes thy love more strong
  To love that well, which thou must leave ere long.

4 *choirs*   A *choir* is that part of a church reserved for the singers.

138

When my love swears that she is made of truth,
I do believe her, though I know she lies,
That she might think me some untutored youth,
Unlearnèd in the world's false subtleties.
5 Thus vainly thinking that she thinks me young,
Although she knows my days are past the best,
Simply I credit her false-speaking tongue;
On both sides thus is simple truth suppressed.
But wherefore says she not she is unjust?
10 And wherefore say not I that I am old?

Oh, love's best habit is in seeming trust,
And age in love loves not to have years told.
　Therefore I lie with her and she with me,
　And in our faults by lies we flattered be.

143

Lo, as a careful housewife runs to catch
One of her feather'd creatures broke away,
Sets down her babe, and makes all swift dispatch
In pursuit of the thing she would have stay,
5　Whilst her neglected child holds her in chase,
Cries to catch her whose busy care is bent
To follow that which flies before her face,
Not prizing her poor infant's discontent;
So runn'st thou after that which flies from thee,
10　Whilst I thy babe chase thee afar behind,
But if thou catch thy hope, turn back to me,
And play the mother's part, kiss me, be kind:
　So will I pray that thou mayst have thy *Will,*
　If thou turn back and my loud crying still.

146

Poor soul, the center of my sinful earth,
Thrall to these rebel powers that thee array,
Why dost thou pine within and suffer dearth,
Painting thy outward walls so costly gay?
5　Why so large cost, having so short a lease,
Dost thou upon thy fading mansion spend?
Shall worms, inheritors of this excess,
Eat up thy charge? Is this thy body's end?
Then, soul, live thou upon thy servant's loss,
10　And let that pine to aggravate thy store;
Buy terms divine in selling hours of dross;
Within be fed, without be rich no more:
　So shalt thou feed on Death, that feeds on men,
　And Death once dead, there's no more dying then.

151

Love is too young to know what conscience is;
Yet who knows not conscience is born of love?

Then, gentle cheater, urge not my amiss,
Lest guilty of my faults thy sweet self prove:
5   For thou betraying me, I do betray
My nobler part to my gross body's treason;
My soul doth tell my body that he may
Triumph in love; flesh stays no farther reason,
But, rising at thy name, doth point out thee
10   As his triumphant prize: proud of this pride,
He is contented thy poor drudge to be,
To stand in thy affairs, fall by thy side.
        No want of conscience hold it that I call
        Her "love" for whose dear love I rise and fall.

3 *urge not my amiss*   Do not stress my wrongdoing.

If I Profane with My Unworthiest Hand

From ROMEO AND JULIET (I, v, 95–108)

   Romeo. If I profane with my unworthiest hand
This holy shrine, the gentle fine is this:
My lips, two blushing pilgrims, ready stand
To smooth that rough touch with a tender kiss.
5   *Juliet.* Good pilgrim, you do wrong your hand too much,
Which mannerly devotion shows in this;
For saints have hands that pilgrims' hands do touch,
And palm to palm is holy palmers' kiss.
   Romeo. Have not saints lips, and holy palmers too?
10   *Juliet.* Ay, pilgrim, lips that they must use in pray'r.
   Romeo. O, then, dear saint, let lips do what hands do;
They pray; grant thou, lest faith turn to despair.
   Juliet. Saints do not move, though grant for prayers' sake.
   Romeo. Then move not while my prayer's effect I take.
                                        Kisses her.

Songs from the Plays

When Daisies Pied
From LOVE'S LABOUR'S LOST (V, ii, 904–939)

Spring

When daisies pied and violets blue
   And ladysmocks all silver-white

Pied   Spotted, mottled.   **2** *ladysmocks*   Cuckooflowers.

And cuckoobuds of yellow hue
  Do paint the meadows with delight,
5 The cuckoo then, on every tree,
  Mocks married men; for thus sings he,
         Cuckoo;
Cuckoo, cuckoo: Oh word of fear,
Unpleasing to a married ear!

10 When shepherds pipe on oaten straws,
  And merry larks are plowmen's clocks,
When turtles tread, and rooks, and daws,
  And maidens bleach their summer smocks,
The cuckoo then, on every tree,
15 Mocks married men; for thus sings he,
         Cuckoo;
Cuckoo, cuckoo: Oh word of fear,
Unpleasing to a married ear!

Winter

When icicles hang by the wall
20 And Dick the shepherd blows his nail
And Tom bears logs into the hall,
  And milk comes frozen home in pail.
When blood is nipped and ways be foul,
Then nightly sings the staring owl,
25   Tu-who;
Tu-whit, tu-who, a merry note,
While greasy Joan doth keel the pot.

When all aloud the wind doth blow,
  And coughing drowns the parson's saw,
30 And birds sit brooding in the snow,
  And Marian's nose looks red and raw,
When roasted crabs hiss in the bowl,
Then nightly sings the staring owl,
         Tu-who;
35 Tu-whit, tu-who, a merry note
While greasy Joan doth keel the pot.

---

3 *cuckoobuds* Buttercups.   **6** *Mocks married men.* The cuckoo's song, "cuckoo," has a sound similar to "cuckold," a husband whose wife is unfaithful to him.   **12** *turtles tread* Turtle-doves mate.   *rooks* Crowlike birds.   *daws* Jackdaws, birds resembling crows.   **20** *blows his nail* Breathes on his fingers to warm them; also, waits patiently, or impatiently.   **27** *keel* Keep from boiling over by stirring.   **29** *saw* Wise saying, maxim.   **32** *crabs* Crab apples.

It Was a Lover and His Lass
From AS YOU LIKE IT (V, iii, 17–34)

It was a lover and his lass,
    With a hey, and a ho, and a hey nonino,
That o'er the green cornfield did pass
    In springtime, the only pretty ring-time,
5 When birds do sing, hey ding a ding, ding,
Sweet lovers love the spring.

Between the acres of the rye,
    With a hey, and a ho, and a hey nonino,
These pretty country-folks would lie,
10   In springtime, &c.

This carol they began that hour,
    With a hey, and a ho, and a hey nonino,
How that a life was but a flower
    In springtime, &c.

15 And therefore take the present time,
    With a hey, and a ho, and a hey nonino;
For love is crownèd with the prime
    In springtime, &c.

4 *ring-time* The season for exchanging rings, the time of marriage or betrothal.

O Mistress Mine
From TWELFTH NIGHT (II, iii, 40–53)

O mistress mine, where are you roaming?
O, stay and hear, your truelove's coming,
    That can sing both high and low.
Trip no further, pretty sweeting,
5 Journeys end in lovers meeting,
    Every wise man's son doth know.

What is love? 'tis not hereafter;
Present mirth hath present laughter,
    What's to come is still unsure.
10 In delay there lies no plenty,
Then come kiss me, sweet and twenty,
    Youth's a stuff will not endure.

For I the Ballad Will Repeat
From ALL'S WELL THAT ENDS WELL (I, iii, 64–67)

For I the ballad will repeat,
    Which men full true shall find;
Your marriage comes by destiny,
    Your cuckoo sings by kind.

Take, O Take Those Lips Away
From MEASURE FOR MEASURE (IV, i, 1–8)

Take, O take those lips away,
  That so sweetly were forsworn,
And those eyes, the break of day,
  Lights that do mislead the morn;
5 But my kisses bring again,
      Bring again,
Seals of love, but sealed in vain,
      Sealed in vain.

Full Fathom Five
From THE TEMPEST (I, ii, 396–404)

Full fathom five thy father lies;
  Of his bones are coral made;
Those are pearls that were his eyes:
  Nothing of him that doth fade,
5 But doth suffer a sea-change
Into something rich and strange.
Sea nymphs hourly ring his knell:
  Ding-dong.
Hark! now I hear them—Ding-dong, bell.

From the Tragedies

It Is the Cause, It Is the Cause, My Soul
From OTHELLO (V, ii, 1–22)

        Desdemona [asleep] in her bed.
        Enter Othello with a light.
  Othello. It is the cause, it is the cause, my soul.
Let me not name it to you, you chaste stars!
It is the cause. Yet I'll not shed her blood,
Nor scar that whiter skin of hers than snow,

5 And smooth as monumental alabaster.
Yet she must die, else she'll betray more men.
Put out the light, and then put out the light.
If I quench thee, thou flaming minister,
I can again thy former light restore,
10 Should I repent me; but once put out thy light,
Thou cunning'st pattern of excelling nature,
I know not where is that Promethean heat
That can thy light relume. When I have plucked the rose,
I cannot give it vital growth again;
15 It needs must wither. I'll smell thee on the tree.
                    He kisses her.
O balmy breath, that dost almost persuade
Justice to break her sword! One more, one more!
Be thus when thou art dead, and I will kill thee,
And love thee after. One more, and this the last!
20 So sweet was ne'er so fatal. I must weep,
But they are cruel tears. This sorrow's heavenly;
It strikes where it doth love. She wakes.

Behold, I Have a Weapon
From OTHELLO (V, ii, 260–283)

Othello.   Behold, I have a weapon;
A better never did itself sustain
Upon a soldier's thigh. I have seen the day
That with this little arm and this good sword
I have made my way through more impediments
5 Than twenty times your stop. But O vain boast!
Who can control his fate? 'Tis not so now.
Be not afraid, though you do see me weaponed.
Here is my journey's end, here is my butt,
And very seamark of my utmost sail.
10 Do you go back dismayed? 'Tis a lost fear.
Man but a rush against Othello's breast,
And he retires. Where should Othello go?
Now, how dost thou look now? O ill-starred wench!
Pale as thy smock! When we shall meet at compt,
15 This look of thine will hurl my soul from heaven,
And fiends will snatch at it. Cold, cold, my girl?
Even like thy chastity.
O cursèd, cursèd slave! Whip me, ye devils,
From the possession of this heavenly sight!
20 Blow me about in winds! roast me in sulphur!
Wash me in steep-down gulfs of liquid fire!
O Desdemona, Desdemona! dead!
O! O! O!

The Barge She Sat in, Like a Burnished Throne
From ANTONY AND CLEOPATRA (II, ii, 196–223)

    Enobarbus. The barge she sat in, like a burnish'd throne
Burn'd on the water: the poop was beaten gold;
Purple the sails, and so perfumed that
The winds were love-sick with them; the oars were silver,
5 Which to the tune of flutes kept stroke, and made
The water which they beat to follow faster,
As amorous of their strokes. For her own person,
It beggar'd all description: she did lie
In her pavilion—cloth of gold, of tissue—
10 O'er-picturing that Venus where we see
The fancy outwork nature. On each side her,
Stood pretty dimpled boys, like smiling Cupids,
With divers-colour'd fans, whose wind did seem
To glow the delicate cheeks which they did cool,
15 And what they undid did.
    Agrippa.   O, rare for Antony!
    Enobarbus. Her gentlewomen, like the Nereides,
So many mermaids, tended her i' the eyes,
And made their bends adornings. At the helm
A seeming mermaid steers: the silken tackle
20 Swell with the touches of those flower-soft hands,
That yarely frame the office. From the barge
A strange invisible perfume hits the sense
Of the adjacent wharfs. The city cast
Her people out upon her; and Antony,
25 Enthron'd i' the market-place, did sit alone,
Whistling to the air; which, but for vacancy,
Had gone to gaze on Cleopatra too,
And made a gap in nature.

16 *Nereides* In Greek myth the Nereides, nymphs of the sea, were fifty lovely daughters of Nerus, God of the Mediterranean Sea, and his wife Doris.   **21** *yarely* Nimbly, easily.

Thomas Campion   (1567–1620)

What If a Day

What if a day, or a month, or a year
Crown thy delights with a thousand sweet contentings?
Cannot a chance of a night or an hour
Cross thy desires with as many sad tormentings?

2 *contentings* Satisfactions, contentments.

5 Fortune, honor, beauty, youth
Are but blossoms dying;
Wanton pleasure, doting love
Are but shadows flying.
All our joys are but toys,
10 Idle thoughts deceiving;
None have power of an hour
In their lives' bereaving.

Earth's but a point to the world, and a man
Is but a point to the world's comparèd centure;
15 Shall then a point of a point be so vain
As to triumph in a sely point's adventure?
All is hazard that we have,
There is nothing biding;
Days of pleasure are like streams
20 Through fair meadows gliding.
Weal and woe, time doth go,
Time is never turning;
Secret fates guide our states,
Both in mirth and mourning.

14 *centure* Center.   **16** *sely* Harmless, insignificant.

There Is a Garden in Her Face

There is a garden in her face
Where roses and white lilies grow;
A heavenly paradise is that place
Wherein all pleasant fruits do flow.
5 There cherries grow which none may buy,
Till "Cherry Ripe" themselves do cry.

Those cherries fairly do enclose
Of orient pearl a double row,
Which when her lovely laughter shows,
10 They look like rosebuds filled with snow;
Yet them nor peer nor prince can buy,
Till "Cherry Ripe" themselves do cry.

Her eyes like angels watch them still,
Her brows like bended bows do stand,
15 Threatening with piercing frowns to kill
All that attempt with eye or hand
Those sacred cherries to come nigh,
Till "Cherry Ripe" themselves do cry.

6 *"Cherry Ripe"* The cry of a London street vendor.

Beauty Is But a Painted Hell

Beauty is but a painted hell:
  Aye me, aye me,
She wounds them that admire it,
She kills them that desire it.
5 Give her pride but fuel,
  No fire is more cruel.

Pity from ev'ry heart is fled,
  Aye me, aye me;
Since false desire could borrow
10 Tears of dissembled sorrow,
  Constant vows turn truthless,
  Love cruel, Beauty ruthless.

Sorrow can laugh, and Fury sing,
  Aye me, aye me;
15 My raving griefs discover
I liv'd too true a lover:
  The first step to madness
  Is the excess of sadness.

Think'st Thou to Seduce Me Then

Think'st thou to seduce me then with words that have no meaning?
Parrots so can learn to prate, our speech by pieces gleaning;
Nurses teach their children so about the time of weaning.

Learn to speak first, then to woo; to wooing much pertaineth;
5 He that courts us, wanting art, soon falters when he feigneth,
Looks asquint on his discourse, and smiles when he complaineth.

Skilful anglers hide their hooks, fit baits for every season;
But with crooked pins fish thou, as babes do that want reason:
Gudgeons only can be caught with such poor tricks of treason.

10 Ruth forgive me, if I erred from human heart's compassion,
When I laughed sometimes too much to see thy foolish fashion;
But, alas, who less could do, that found so good occasion?

6 *asquint on his discourse* With sidelong glance at his written speech.   **9** *Gudgeons* Small freshwater fish related to carps.   **10** *Ruth* Sympathy (here not the name of a girl).

John Donne   (1572–1631)

The Good-Morrow

I wonder by my troth, what thou and I
Did, till we loved? Were we not weaned till then,
But sucked on country pleasures, childishly?
Or snorted we in the seven sleepers' den?
5   'Twas so; but this, all pleasures fancies be.
If ever any beauty I did see,
Which I desired, and got, 'twas but a dream of thee.

And now good morrow to our waking souls,
Which watch not one another out of fear;
10   For love all love of other sights controls,
And makes one little room an everywhere.
Let sea-discoverers to new worlds have gone,
Let maps to other, worlds on worlds have shown;
Let us possess one world; each hath one, and is one.

15   My face in thine eye, thine in mine appears,
And true plain hearts do in the faces rest;
Where can we find two better hemispheres
Without sharp north, without declining west?
Whatever dies was not mixed equally;
20   If our two loves be one, or thou and I
Love so alike that none do slacken, none can die.

4 *seven sleepers' den*   A cave in which, during the persecutions of Emperor Decius in 250 A.D., seven young Christian men of Ephesus were walled and slept for over two hundred years.

The Sun Rising

Busy old fool, unruly sun,
Why dost thou thus,
Through windows and through curtains call on us?
Must to thy motions lovers' seasons run?
5   Saucy pedantic wretch, go chide
Late school boys and sour prentices,
Go tell court huntsmen that the king will ride,
Call country ants to harvest offices;
Love, all alike, no season knows nor clime,
10   Nor hours, days, months, which are the rags of time.

Thy beams, so reverend and strong
Why shouldst thou think?

I could eclipse and cloud them with a wink,
But that I would not lose her sight so long;
15   If her eyes have not blinded thine,
      Look, and tomorrow late tell me,
Whether both th' Indias of spice and mine
   Be where thou leftst them, or lie here with me.
Ask for those kings whom thou saw'st yesterday,
20 And thou shalt hear, All here in one bed lay.

      She's all states, and all princes, I,
      Nothing else is.
Princes do but play us; compared to this,
All honor's mimic, all wealth alchemy.
25   Thou, sun, art half as happy as we,
      In that the world's contracted thus;
Thine age asks ease, and since thy duties be
   To warm the world, that's done in warming us.
Shine here to us, and thou art everywhere;
30 This bed thy center is, these walls, thy sphere.

17 *both th' Indias* India and the West Indies, sources of spices and gold, product of the mine.
24 *alchemy* Falseness, fraud.

The Indifferent

      I can love both fair and brown,
Her whom abundance melts, and her whom want betrays,
Her who loves loneness best, and her who masks and plays,
Her whom the country form'd, and whom the town,
5   Her who believes, and her who tries,
      Her who still weeps with spongy eyes,
   And her who is dry cork and never cries;
I can love her, and her, and you, and you;
I can love any, so she be not true.

10   Will no other vice content you?
Will it not serve your turn to do as did your mothers?
Or have you all old vices spent, and now would find out others?
      Or doth a fear that men are true torment you?
        O we are not; be not you so.
15   Let me, and do you, twenty know.
      Rob me, but bind me not, and let me go.
Must I, who came to travail through you,
Grow your fix'd subject because you are true?

Venus heard me sigh this song,
20 And by love's sweetest part, variety, she swore
She heard not this till now, and that it should be so no more.
  She went, examin'd, and return'd ere long,
    And said, "Alas, some two or three
    Poor heretics in love there be,
25   Which think to 'stablish dangerous constancy,
But I have told them, 'Since you will be true,
You shall be true to them who're false to you.'"

Sweetest Love, I Do Not Go

Sweetest love, I do not go
  For weariness of thee,
Nor in hope the world can show
  A fitter love for me:
5   But since that I
Must die at last, 'tis best
To use myself in jest
  Thus by feigned deaths to die.

Yesternight the sun went hence,
10   And yet is here today;
He hath no desire nor sense,
  Nor half so short a way:
    Then fear not me,
But believe that I shall make
15 Speedier journeys, since I take
  More wings and spurs than he.

O how feeble is man's power,
  That if good fortune fall,
Cannot add another hour,
20   Nor a lost hour recall!
    But come bad chance,
And we join to it our strength,
And we teach it art and length,
  Itself o'er us to advance.

25 When thou sigh'st, thou sigh'st not wind,
  But sigh'st my soul away;
When thou weep'st, unkindly kind,
  My life's blood doth decay.
    It cannot be
30 That thou lov'st me, as thou say'st,
If in thine my life thou waste,
  That art the best of me.

      Let not thy divining heart
         Forethink me any ill;
35 Destiny may take thy part,
         And may thy tears fulfil;
           But think that we
      Are but turned aside to sleep;
      They who one another keep
40   Alive, ne'er parted be.

The Funeral

      Whoever comes to shroud me, do not harm
           Nor question much
      That subtile wreath of hair which crowns mine arm;
      The mystery, the sign, you must not touch,
5   For 'tis my outward soul,
      Viceroy to that, which then to heav'n being gone,
           Will leave this to control
And keep these limbs, her provinces, from dissolution.

      For if the sinewy thread my brain lets fall
10   Through every part
      Can tie those parts and make me one of all,
      These hairs, which upward grew, and strength and art
          Have, from a better brain,
      Can better do't; except she meant that I
15   By this should know my pain,
As prisoners then are manacled, when they're condemn'd to die.

      Whate'er she meant by't, bury it with me,
          For since I am
      Love's martyr, it might breed idolatry
20   If into others' hands these relics came.
          As 'twas humility
      T' afford to it all which a soul can do,
          So 'tis some bravery
That since you would save none of me, I bury some of you.

From Holy Sonnets

3

O might those sighs and tears return again
Into my breast and eyes, which I have spent,
That I might in this holy discontent

Mourn with some fruit, as I have mourn'd in vain;
5 In mine Idolatry what showers of rain
Mine eyes did waste? what griefs my heart did rent?
That sufferance was my sin; now I repent;
'Cause I did suffer I must suffer pain.
Th'hydroptic drunkard, and night-scouting thief,
10 The itchy Lecher, and self tickling proud
Have the remembrance of past joys, for relief
Of coming ills. To (poor) me is allow'd
No ease; for, long, yet vehement grief hath been
Th'effect and cause, the punishment and sin.

6 *rent* Rend, tear.   **7** *sufferance* Long suffering; also, permission, consent, submission.
9 *hydroptic* Dropsical, affected with dropsy, an abnormal accumulation of fluid in cellular tissue
of the body.   **10** *proud* Proud man.

10

Death, be not proud, though some have called thee
Mighty and dreadful, for thou art not so;
For those whom thou think'st thou dost overthrow
Die not, poor Death, nor yet canst thou kill me.
5 From rest and sleep, which but thy pictures be,
Much pleasure, then from thee much more must flow,
And soonest our best men with thee do go,
Rest of their bones and soul's delivery.
Thou'rt slave to fate, chance, kings, and desperate men,
10 And dost with poison, war, and sickness dwell,
And poppy or charms can make us sleep as well,
And better than thy stroke. Why swell'st thou then?
One short sleep past, we wake eternally,
And death shall be no more. Death, thou shalt die.

14

Batter my heart, three person'd God, for you
As yet but knock, breathe, shine, and seek to mend;
That I may rise and stand, o'erthrow me 'nd bend
Your force to break, blow, burn, and make me new.
5 I, like an usurp'd town t' another due,
Labor t' admit you, but O, to no end!
Reason, your viceroy in me, me should defend,
But is captiv'd, and proves weak or untrue.
Yet dearly I love you 'nd would be loved fain,
10 But am betroth'd unto your enemy.

Divorce me, untie, or break that knot again,
Take me to you, imprison me, for I,
Except y' enthrall me, never shall be free,
Nor ever chaste except you ravish me.

A Hymn to God the Father

Wilt Thou forgive that sin where I begun,
  Which was my sin, though it were done before?
Wilt Thou forgive that sin through which I run,
  And do run still, though still I do deplore?
5   When Thou hast done, Thou hast not done,
        For I have more.

Wilt Thou forgive that sin which I have won
  Others to sin, and made my sin their door?
Wilt Thou forgive that sin which I did shun
10   A year or two, but wallowed in a score?
        When Thou hast done, Thou hast not done,
          For I have more.
I have a sin of fear, that when I have spun
  My last thread, I shall perish on the shore;
15 Swear by Thyself, that at my death Thy Son
  Shall shine as he shines now and heretofore;
    And having done that, Thou hast done;
        I fear no more.

Ben Jonson   (1573–1637)

Inviting a Friend to Supper

Tonight, grave sir, both my poor house and I
Do equally desire your company;
Not that we think us worthy such a guest,
But that your worth will dignify our feast
5 With those that come, whose grace may make that seem
Something, which else could hope for no esteem.
It is the fair acceptance, sir, creates
The entertainment perfect; not the cates.
Yet you shall have, to rectify your palate,
10 An olive, capers, or some better salad
Ush'ring the mutton; with a short-legged hen,

8 *cates* Delicate or luxurious food.

If we can get her, full of eggs, and then
Lemons and wine for sauce; to these a coney
Is not to be despaired of, for our money;
15   And though fowl now be scarce, yet there are clerks,
The sky not falling, think we may have larks.
I'll tell you of more, and lie, so you will come:
Of partridge, pheasant, woodcock, of which some
May yet be there; and godwit, if we can;
20   Knat, rail, and ruff too. Howsoe'er, my man
Shall read a piece of Virgil, Tacitus,
Livy, or of some better book to us,
Of which we'll speak our minds, amidst our meat.
And I'll profess no verses to repeat;
25   To this, if aught appear which I not know of,
That will the pastry, not my paper, show of.
Digestive cheese and fruit there sure will be;
But that which most doth take my Muse and me
Is a pure cup of rich Canary wine,
30   Which is the Mermaid's now, but shall be mine;
Of which had Horace or Anacreon tasted,
Their lives, as do their lines, till now had lasted.
Tobacco, nectar, or the Thespian spring
Are all but Luther's beer to this I sing.
35   Of this we will sup free, but moderately,
And we will have no Polly or Parrot by;
Nor shall our cups make any guilty men,
But at our parting we will be as when
We innocently met. No simple word
40   That shall be uttered at our mirthful board,
Shall make us sad next morning, or affright
The liberty that we'll enjoy tonight.

13 *coney* Rabbit.   **19** *godwit* A curlew-like shore bird and a table delicacy.   **20** *Knat* Gnat, a kind of sandpiper.   *rail* A game bird.   *ruff* Male sandpiper.   **21-22** *Virgil, Tacitus, Livy* Virgil (70-19 B.C.) was a Roman poet, author of the *Aeneid;* Tacitus (c. 55-117 A.D.) was a Roman orator, politician, and historian; *Livy* (59 B.C.-17 A.D.) was a Roman historian.   **28** *Muse* Goddess of poetry, source of inspiration.   **29** *Canary wine* A wine from the Canary Islands, similar to Madeira and usually sweet.   **30** *the Mermaid's* A well-known tavern in London and one of Jonson's favorites.   **31** *Horace or Anacreon* Horace (65-8 B.C.) was a Roman lyric poet and satirist; *Anacreon* (c. 572-488 B.C.) was a Greek lyric poet.   **33** *Tobacco* In Elizabethan England smoking was referred to as "drinking tobacco."   *Thespian spring* A spring associated with the Muses.   **34** *Luther's beer* German beer, regarded as inferior.

V. Song. To Celia

Come, my Celia, let us prove,
While we can, the sports of love.

Time will not be ours forever;
He, at length, our good will sever.
5 Spend not then his gifts in vain:
Suns that set may rise again
But if once we lose this light,
'Tis with us perpetual night.
Why should we defer our joys?
10 Fame and rumour are but toys.
Cannot we delude the eyes
Of a few poor household spies?
Or his easier ears beguile,
Thus removed by our wile?
15 'Tis no sin love's fruits to steal,
But the sweet thefts to reveal;
To be taken, to be seen,
These have crimes accounted been.

VI. To the Same

Kiss me, sweet; the wary lover
Can your favors keep, and cover,
When the common courting jay
All your bounties will betray.
5 Kiss again; no creature comes.
Kiss, and score up wealthy sums
On my lips, thus hardly sundered,
While you breath. First give a hundred,
Then a thousand, then another
10 Hundred, then unto the tother
Add a thousand, and so more:
Till you equal with the store,
All the grass that *Rumney* yields,
Or the sands in *Chelsey* fields,
15 Or the drops in silver *Thames,*
Or the stars, that guild his streams,
In the silent summer-nights,
When youths ply their stolen delights.
That the curious may not know
20 How to tell 'hem, as they flow,
And the envious, when they find
What their number is, be pin'd.

3 *jay* A chatterer, a person absurdly dressed, a greenhorn.   **13** *Rumney* A district of London.   **14** *Chelsey* A district of London.   **22** *be pin'd* Be afflicted with pain or longing.

From THE KING JAMES VERSION OF THE BIBLE

The Book of Psalms

1

Blessed *is* the man that walketh not in the counsel of the ungodly, nor standeth in the way of sinners, nor sitteth in the seat of the scornful.

2 But his delight *is* in the law of the LORD; and in his law doth he meditate day and night.

3 And he shall be like a tree planted by the rivers of water, that bringeth forth his fruit in his season; his leaf also shall not wither; and whatsoever he doeth shall prosper.

4 The ungodly *are* not so: but *are* like the chaff which the wind driveth away.

5 Therefore the ungodly shall not stand in the judgment, nor sinners in the congregation of the righteous.

6 For the LORD knoweth the way of the righteous: but the way of the ungodly shall perish.

19

The heavens declare the glory of God; and the firmament sheweth his handywork.

2 Day unto day uttereth speech, and night unto night sheweth knowledge.

3 *There is* no speech nor language, *where* their voice is not heard.

4 Their line is gone out through all the earth, and their words to the end of the world. In them hath he set a tabernacle for the sun,

5 Which *is* as a bridegroom coming out of his chamber, *and* rejoiceth as a strong man to run a race.

6 His going forth *is* from the end of the heaven, and his circuit unto the ends of it: and there is nothing hid from the heat thereof.

7 The law of the LORD *is* perfect, converting the soul: the testimony of the LORD *is* sure, making wise the simple.

8 The statutes of the LORD *are* right, rejoicing the heart: the commandment of the LORD *is* pure, enlightening the eyes.

9 The fear of the LORD *is* clean, enduring for ever: the judgments of the LORD *are* true *and* righteous altogether.

10 More to be desired *are they* than gold, yea, than much fine gold: sweeter also than honey and the honeycomb.

11 Moreover by them is thy servant warned: *and* in keeping of them *there is* great reward.

12 Who can understand *his* errors? cleanse thou me from secret *faults.*

13 Keep back thy servant also from presumptuous *sins;* let them not have dominion over me: then shall I be upright, and I shall be innocent from the great transgression.

14 Let the words of my mouth, and the meditation of my heart, be acceptable in thy sight, O LORD, my strength, and my redeemer.

23

The LORD *is* my shepherd; I shall not want.

2 He maketh me to lie down in green pastures: he leadeth me beside the still waters.

3 He restoreth my soul: he leadeth me in the paths of righteousness for his name's sake.

4 Yea, though I walk through the valley of the shadow of death, I will fear no evil: for thou *art* with me; thy rod and thy staff they comfort me.

5 Thou preparest a table before me in the presence of mine enemies: thou anointest my head with oil; my cup runneth over.

6 Surely goodness and mercy shall follow me all the days of my life: and I will dwell in the house of the LORD for ever.

102

Hear my prayer, O LORD, and let my cry come unto thee.

2 Hide not thy face from me in the day *when* I am in trouble; incline thine ear unto me: in the day *when* I call answer me speedily.

3 For my days are consumed like smoke, and my bones are burned as an hearth.

4 My heart is smitten, and withered like grass; so that I forget to eat my bread.

5 By reason of the voice of my groaning my bones cleave to my skin.

6 I am like a pelican of the wilderness: I am like an owl of the desert.

7 I watch, and am as a sparrow alone upon the house top.

8 Mine enemies reproach me all the day; *and* they that are mad against me are sworn against me.

9 For I have eaten ashes like bread, and mingled my drink with weeping,

10 Because of thine indignation and thy wrath: for thou hast lifted me up, and cast me down.

11 My days *are* like a shadow that declineth; and I am withered like grass.

12 But thou, O LORD, shalt endure for ever; and thy remembrance unto all generations.

13 Thou shalt arise, *and* have mercy upon Zion: for the time to favour her, yea, the set time, is come.

14 For thy servants take pleasure in her stones, and favour the dust thereof.

15 So the heathen shall fear the name of the LORD, and all the kings of the earth thy glory.

16 When the LORD shall build up Zion, he shall appear in his glory.

17 He will regard the prayer of the destitute, and not despise their prayer.

18 This shall be written for the generation to come: and the people which shall be created shall praise the LORD.

19 For he hath looked down from the height of his sanctuary; from heaven did the LORD behold the earth;

20 To hear the groaning of the **prisoner**; to loose those that are appointed to death;

21 To declare the name of the LORD in Zion, and his praise in Jerusalem;

22 When the people are gathered together, and the kingdoms, to serve the LORD.

23 He weakened my strength in the way; he shortened my days.

24 I said, O my God, take me not away in the midst of my days: thy years *are* throughout all generations.

25 Of old hast thou laid the foundation of the earth: and the heavens *are* the work of thy hands.

26 They shall perish, but thou shalt endure: yea, all of them shall wax old like a garment; as a vesture shalt thou change them, and they shall be changed:

27 But thou *art* the same, and thy years shall have no end.

28 The children of thy servants shall continue, and their seed shall be established before thee.

127

Except the LORD build the house, they labour in vain that build it: except the LORD keep the city, the watchman waketh *but* in vain.

2 *It is* vain for you to rise up early, to sit up late, to eat the bread of sorrows: *for* so he giveth his beloved sleep.

3 Lo, children *are* an heritage of the LORD: *and* the fruit of the womb *is his* reward.

4 As arrows *are* in the hand of a mighty man; so *are* children of the youth.

5 Happy *is* the man that hath his quiver full of them: they shall not be ashamed, but they shall speak with the enemies in the gate.

The Book of Proverbs

Chapter 15

A soft answer turneth away wrath: but grievous words stir up anger.

2 The tongue of the wise useth knowledge aright: but the mouth of fools poureth out foolishness.

3 The eyes of the LORD *are* in every place, beholding the evil and the good.

4 A wholesome tongue *is* a tree of life: but perverseness therein *is* a breach in the spirit.

5 A fool despiseth his father's instruction: but he that regardeth reproof is prudent.

6 In the house of the righteous *is* much treasure: but in the revenues of the wicked is trouble.

7 The lips of the wise disperse knowledge: but the heart of the foolish *doeth* not so.

8 The sacrifice of the wicked *is* an abomination to the LORD: but the prayer of the upright *is* his delight.

9 The way of the wicked *is* an abomination unto the LORD: but he loveth him that followeth after righteousness.

10 Correction *is* grievous unto him that forsaketh the way: *and* he that hateth reproof shall die.

11 Hell and destruction *are* before the LORD: how much more then the hearts of the children of men?

12 A scorner loveth not one that reproveth him: neither will he go unto the wise.

13 A merry heart maketh a cheerful countenance: but by sorrow of the heart the spirit is broken.

14 The heart of him that hath understanding seeketh knowledge: but the mouth of fools feedeth on foolishness.

15 All the days of the afflicted *are* evil: but he that is of a merry heart *hath* a continual feast.

16 Better *is* little with the fear of the LORD than great treasure and trouble therewith.

17 Better *is* a dinner of herbs where love is, than a stalled ox and hatred therewith.

18 A wrathful man stirreth up strife: but *he that is* slow to anger appeaseth strife.

19 The way of the slothful *man is* as an hedge of thorns: but the way of the righteous *is* made plain.

20 A wise son maketh a glad father: but a foolish man despiseth his mother.

21 Folly *is* joy to *him that is* destitute of wisdom: but a man of understanding walketh uprightly.   .

22 Without counsel purposes are disappointed: but in the multitude of counsellors they are established.

23 A man hath joy by the answer of his mouth: and a word *spoken* in due season, how good *is it!*

24 The way of life *is* above to the wise, that he may depart from hell beneath.

25 The LORD will destroy the house of the proud: but he will establish the border of the widow.

26 The thoughts of the wicked *are* an abomination to the LORD: but *the words* of the pure *are* pleasant words.

27 He that is greedy of gain troubleth his own house; but he that hateth gifts shall live.

28 The heart of the righteous studieth to answer: but the mouth of the wicked poureth out evil things.

29 The LORD *is* far from the wicked: but he heareth the prayer of the righteous.

30 The light of the eyes rejoiceth the heart: *and* a good report maketh the bones fat.

31 The ear that heareth the reproof of life abideth among the wise.

32 He that refuseth instruction despiseth his own soul: but he that heareth reproof getteth understanding.

33 The fear of the LORD *is* the instruction of wisdom; and before honour *is* humility.

Chapter 26

As snow in summer, and as rain in harvest, so honour is not seemly for a fool.

2 As the bird by wandering, as the swallow by flying, so the curse causeless shall not come.

3 A whip for the horse, a bridle for the ass, and a rod for the fool's back.

4 Answer not a fool according to his folly, lest thou also be like unto him.

5 Answer a fool according to his folly, lest he be wise in his own conceit.

6 He that sendeth a message by the hand of a fool cutteth off the feet, *and* drinketh damage.

7 The legs of the lame are not equal: so *is* a parable in the mouth of fools.

8 As he that bindeth a stone in a sling, so *is* he that giveth honour to a fool.

9 *As* a thorn goeth up into the hand of a drunkard, so *is* a parable in the mouth of fools.

10 The Great *God* that formed all *things* both rewardeth the fool, and rewardeth transgressors.

11 As a dog returneth to his vomit, *so* a fool returneth to his folly.

12 Seest thou a man wise in his own conceit? *there is* more hope of a fool than of him.

13 The slothful *man* saith, *There is* a lion in the way; a lion *is* in the streets.

14 *As* the door turneth upon his hinges, so *doth* the slothful upon his bed.

15 The slothful hideth his hand in *his* bosom; it grieveth him to bring it again to his mouth.

16 The sluggard *is* wiser in his own conceit than seven men that can render a reason.

17 He that passeth by, *and* meddleth with strife *belonging* not to him, *is like* one that taketh a dog by the ears.

18 As a mad *man* who casteth firebrands, arrows, and death,

19 So *is* the man *that* deceiveth his neighbour, and saith, Am not I in sport?

20 Where no wood is, *there* the fire goeth out: so where *there is* no talebearer, the strife ceaseth.

21 *As* coals *are* to burning coals, and wood to fire; so *is* a contentious man to kindle strife.

22 The words of a talebearer *are* as wounds, and they go down into the innermost parts of the belly.

23 Burning lips and a wicked heart *are like* a potsherd covered with silver dross.

24 He that hateth dissembleth with his lips, and layeth up deceit within him;

25 When he speaketh fair, believe him not: for *there are* seven abominations in his heart.

26 *Whose* hatred is covered by deceit, his wickedness shall be shewed before the *whole* congregation.

27 Whoso diggeth a pit shall fall therein: and he that rolleth a stone, it will return upon him.

28 A lying tongue hateth *those that are* afflicted by it; and a flattering mouth worketh ruin.

The Song of Solomon

Chapter 2

I *am* the rose of Sharon, *and* the lily of the valleys.

2 As the lily among thorns, so *is* my love among the daughters.

Verse 1 *rose of Sharon* Variously identified, perhaps the autumn crocus.

3 As the apple tree among the trees of the wood, so *is* my beloved among the sons. I sat down under his shadow with great delight, and his fruit *was* sweet to my taste.

4 He brought me to the banqueting house, and his banner over me *was* love.

5 Stay me with flagons, comfort me with apples: for I *am* sick of love.

6 His left hand *is* under my head, and his right hand doth embrace me.

7 I charge you, O ye daughters of Jerusalem, by the roes, and by the hinds of the field, that ye stir not up, nor awake *my* love, till he please.

8 The voice of my beloved! behold, he cometh leaping upon the mountains, skipping upon the hills.

9 My beloved is like a roe or a young hart: behold, he standeth behind our wall, he looketh forth at the windows, shewing himself through the lattice.

10 My beloved spake, and said unto me, Rise up, my love, my fair one, and come away.

11 For, lo, the winter is past, the rain is over *and* gone;

12 The flowers appear on the earth; the time of the singing *of birds* is come, and the voice of the turtle is heard in our land;

13 The fig tree putteth forth her green figs, and the vines *with* the tender grape give a *good* smell. Arise, my love, my fair one, and come away.

14 O my dove, *that art* in the clefts of the rock, in the secret *places* of the stairs, let me see thy countenance, let me hear thy voice; for sweet *is* thy voice, and thy countenance *is* comely.

15 Take us the foxes, the little foxes, that spoil the vines: for our vines *have* tender grapes.

16 My beloved *is* mine, and I *am* his: he feedeth among the lilies.

17 Until the day break, and the shadows flee away, turn, my beloved, and be thou like a roe or a young hart upon the mountains of Bether.

Chapter 4

Behold, thou *art* fair, my love; behold, thou *art* fair; thou *hast* doves' eyes within thy locks: thy hair *is* as a flock of goats, that appear from mount Gilead.

2 Thy teeth *are* like a flock *of sheep that are even* shorn, which came up from the washing; whereof every one bear twins, and none *is* barren among them.

3 Thy lips *are* like a thread of scarlet, and thy speech *is* comely: thy temples *are* like a piece of a pomegranate within thy locks.

4 Thy neck *is* like the tower of David builded for an armoury, whereon there hang a thousand bucklers, all shields of mighty men.

5 Thy two breasts *are* like two young roes that are twins, which feed among the lilies.

6 Until the day break, and the shadows flee away, I will get me to the mountain of myrrh, and to the hill of frankincense.

7 Thou *art* all fair, my love; *there is* no spot in thee.

Verse 1 *mount Gilead*   Highest mountain (3597 feet) in Gilead, a mountainous region in Jordan east of the Jordan River between the Sea of Galilee and the Dead Sea.

8 Come with me from Lebanon, *my* spouse, with me from Lebanon: look from the top of Amana, from the top of Shenir and Hermon, from the lions' dens, from the mountains of the leopards.

9 Thou hast ravished my heart, my sister, *my* spouse; thou hast ravished my heart with one of thine eyes, with one chain of thy neck.

10 How fair is thy love, my sister, *my* spouse! how much better is thy love than wine! and the smell of thine ointments than all spices!

11 Thy lips, O *my* spouse, drop *as* the honeycomb: honey and milk *are* under thy tongue; and the smell of thy garments *is* like the smell of Lebanon.

12 A garden inclosed *is* my sister, *my* spouse; a spring shut up, a fountain sealed.

13 Thy plants *are* an orchard of pomegranates, with pleasant fruits; camphire, with spikenard,

14 Spikenard and saffron; calamus and cinnamon, with all trees of frankincense; myrrh and aloes, with all the chief spices:

15 A fountain of gardens, a well of living waters, and streams from Lebanon.

16 Awake, O north wind; and come, thou south; blow upon my garden, *that* the spices thereof may flow out. Let my beloved come into his garden, and eat his pleasant fruits.

Verse 8 *Amana . . . Shenir and Hermon* Mountains of Anti-Lebanon, a range running north and south on the border between Syria and Lebanon. Shenir, or Senir, and Hermon, also known as Mt. Sion, are high peaks, Mt. Hermon (9232 feet) the highest of the range. **Verse 14** *Spikenard* An aromatic substance used in the preparation of a costly ointment in ancient times. *calamus* A reed, an aromatic plant.

The Gospel According to St. Matthew

Chapter 5

And seeing the multitudes, he went up into a mountain: and when he was set, his disciples came unto him:

2 And he opened his mouth, and taught them, saying,

3 Blessed *are* the poor in spirit: for their's is the kingdom of heaven.

4 Blessed *are* they that mourn: for they shall be comforted.

5 Blessed *are* the meek: for they shall inherit the earth.

6 Blessed *are* they which do hunger and thirst after righteousness: for they shall be filled.

7 Blessed *are* the merciful: for they shall obtain mercy.

8 Blessed *are* the pure in heart: for they shall see God.

9 Blessed *are* the peacemakers: for they shall be called the children of God.

10 Blessed *are* they which are persecuted for righteousness' sake: for their's is the kingdom of heaven.

11 Blessed are ye, when *men* shall revile you, and persecute *you,* and shall say all manner of evil against you falsely, for my sake.

12 Rejoice, and be exceeding glad: for great *is* your reward in heaven: for so persecuted they the prophets which were before you.

13 Ye are the salt of the earth: but if the salt have lost his savour, wherewith shall

it be salted? it is thenceforth good for nothing, but to be cast out, and to be trodden under foot of men.

14 Ye are the light of the world. A city that is set on an hill cannot be hid.

15 Neither do men light a candle, and put it under a bushel, but on a candlestick; and it giveth light unto all that are in the house.

16 Let your light so shine before men, that they may see your good works, and glorify your Father which is in heaven.

17 Think not that I am come to destroy the law, or the prophets: I am not come to destroy, but to fulfil.

18 For verily I say unto you, Till heaven and earth pass, one jot or one tittle shall in no wise pass from the law, till all be fulfilled.

19 Whosoever therefore shall break one of these least commandments, and shall teach men so, he shall be called the least in the kingdom of heaven: but whosoever shall do and teach *them,* the same shall be called great in the kingdom of heaven.

20 For I say unto you, That except your righteousness shall exceed *the righteousness* of the scribes and Pharisees, ye shall in no case enter into the kingdom of heaven.

21 Ye have heard that it was said by them of old time, Thou shalt not kill; and whosoever shall kill shall be in danger of the judgment:

22 But I say unto you, That whosoever is angry with his brother without a cause shall be in danger of the judgment: and whosoever shall say to his brother, Raca, shall be in danger of the council: but whosoever shall say, Thou fool, shall be in danger of hell fire.

23 Therefore if thou bring thy gift to the altar, and there rememberest that thy brother hath ought against thee;

24 Leave there thy gift before the altar, and go thy way; first be reconciled to thy brother, and then come and offer thy gift.

25 Agree with thine adversary quickly, whiles thou art in the way with him; lest at any time the adversary deliver thee to the judge, and the judge deliver thee to the officer, and thou be cast into prison.

26 Verily I say unto thee, Thou shalt by no means come out thence, till thou hast paid the uttermost farthing.

27 Ye have heard that it was said by them of old time, Thou shalt not commit adultery:

28 But I say unto you, That whosoever looketh on a woman to lust after her hath committed adultery with her already in his heart.

29 And if thy right eye offend thee, pluck it out, and cast *it* from thee: for it is profitable for thee that one of thy members should perish, and not *that* thy whole body should be cast into hell.

30 And if thy right hand offend thee, cut it off, and cast *it* from thee: for it is profitable for thee that one of thy members should perish, and not *that* thy whole body should be cast into hell.

31 It hath been said, Whosoever shall put away his wife, let him give her a writing of divorcement:

32 But I say unto you, That whosoever shall put away his wife, saving for the cause of fornication, causeth her to commit adultery: and whosoever shall marry her that is divorced committeth adultery.

33 Again, ye have heard that it hath been said by them of old time, Thou shalt not forswear thyself, but shalt perform unto the Lord thine oaths:

34 But I say unto you, Swear not at all; neither by heaven; for it is God's throne:

35 Nor by the earth; for it is his footstool: neither by Jerusalem; for it is the city of the great King.

36 Neither shalt thou swear by thy head, because thou canst not make one hair white or black.

37 But let your communication be, Yea, yea; Nay, nay: for whatsoever is more than these cometh of evil.

38 Ye have heard that it hath been said, An eye for an eye, and a tooth for a tooth:

39 But I say unto you, That ye resist not evil: but whosoever shall smite thee on thy right cheek, turn to him the other also.

40 And if any man will sue thee at the law, and take away thy coat, let him have *thy* cloke also.

41 And whosoever shall compel thee to go a mile, go with him twain.

42 Give to him that asketh thee, and from him that would borrow of thee turn not thou away.

43 Ye have heard that it hath been said, Thou shalt love thy neighbour, and hate thine enemy.

44 But I say unto you, Love your enemies, bless them that curse you, do good to them that hate you, and pray for them which despitefully use you, and persecute you;

45 That ye may be the children of your Father which is in heaven: for he maketh his sun to rise on the evil and on the good, and sendeth rain on the just and on the unjust.

46 For if ye love them which love you, what reward have ye? do not even the publicans the same?

47 And if ye salute your brethren only, what do ye more *than others?* do not even the publicans so?

48 Be ye therefore perfect, even as your Father which is in heaven is perfect.

Robert Herrick   (1591–1674)

Delight in Disorder

A sweet disorder in the dress
Kindles in clothes a wantonness:
A lawn about the shoulders thrown
Into a fine distraction,
5   An erring lace, which here and there
Enthralls the crimson stomacher,

---

3 *lawn* Fine linen. **6** *stomacher* An ornamental covering, often jeweled or embroidered, worn under the open front of a bodice.

A cuff neglectful, and thereby
Ribands to flow confusedly,
A winning wave, deserving note,
10　In the tempestuous petticoat,
A careless shoestring, in whose tie
I see a wild civility,
Do more bewitch me than when art
Is too precise in every part.

8 *Ribands*　Ribbons.

Corinna's Going A-Maying

Get up, get up for shame, the blooming morn
Upon her wings presents the god unshorn.
　　See how Aurora throws her fair
　　Fresh-quilted colors through the air;
5　Get up, sweet slug-a-bed, and see
　　The dew bespangling herb and tree.
Each flower has wept and bowed toward the east
Above an hour since, yet you not dressed;
　　Nay, not so much as out of bed.
10　When all the birds have matins said,
　　And sung their thankful hymns, 'tis sin,
　　Nay, profanation to keep in,
Whenas a thousand virgins on this day
Spring, sooner than the lark, to fetch in May.

15　Rise and put on your foliage, and be seen
To come forth like the springtime, fresh and green,
　　And sweet as Flora. Take no care
　　For jewels for your gown or hair;
　　Fear not, the leaves will strew
20　Gems in abundance upon you;
Besides, the childhood of the day has kept,
Against you come, some orient pearls unwept;
　　Come and receive them while the light
　　Hangs on the dew-locks of the night,
25　And Titan on the eastern hill
　　Retires himself, or else stands still

2 *the god unshorn*　Apollo, god of the sun.　3 *Aurora*　Goddess of the dawn.　17 *Flora*
Goddess of flowers.　25 *Titan*　The sun god.

Till you come forth. Wash, dress, be brief in praying:
Few beads are best when once we go a-maying.

Come, my Corinna, come; and coming, mark
30 How each field turns a street, each street a park
  Made green and trimmed with trees; see how
  Devotion gives each house a bough
  Or branch; each porch, each door, ere this,
  An ark, a tabernacle is,
35 Made up of white-thorn neatly interwove,
As if here were those cooler shades of love.
  Can such delights be in the street
  And open fields, and we not see't?
  Come, we'll abroad, and let's obey
40   The proclamation made for May,
And sin no more, as we have done, by staying;
But, my Corinna, come, let's go a-maying.

There's not a budding boy or girl this day
But is got up, and gone to bring in May.
45   A deal of youth, ere this, is come
  Back, and with white-thorn laden, home.
  Some have despatched their cakes and cream
  Before that we have left to dream;
And some have wept, and wooed, and plighted troth,
50 And chose their priest, ere we can cast off sloth;
  Many a green-gown has been given,
  Many a kiss, both odd and even,
  Many a glance too has been sent
  From out the eye, love's firmament,
55 Many a jest told of the keys betraying
This night, and locks picked, yet we're not a-maying.
Come, let us go while we are in our prime,
And take the harmless folly of the time.
  We shall grow old apace, and die
60   Before we know our liberty.
  Our life is short, and our days run
  As fast away as does the sun;
And as a vapor, or a drop of rain
Once lost, can ne'er be found again,
65   So when or you or I are made
  A fable, song, or fleeting shade,
  All love, all liking, all delight
  Lies drowned with us in endless night.
Then while time serves, and we are but decaying,
70 Come, my Corinna, come, let's go a-maying.

George Herbert   (1593–1633)

The Collar

     I struck the board and cried, No more!
          I will abroad.
     What? Shall I ever sigh and pine?
     My lines and life are free, free as the road,
5   Loose as the wind, as large as store.
         Shall I be still in suit?
     Have I no harvest but a thorn
     To let me blood, and not restore
     What I have lost with cordial fruit?
10   Sure there was wine
     Before my sighs did dry it; there was corn
         Before my tears did drown it.
     Is the year only lost to me?
         Have I no bays to crown it?
15   No flowers, no garlands gay? All blasted?
         All wasted?
     Not so, my heart! But there is fruit,
         And thou hast hands.
     Recover all thy sigh-blown age
20   On double pleasures. Leave thy cold dispute
     Of what is fit and not. Forsake thy cage,
         Thy rope of sands,
     Which petty thoughts have made, and made to thee
     Good cable, to enforce and draw,
25   And be thy law,
     While thou didst wink and wouldst not see.
         Away! Take heed!
         I will abroad.
     Call in thy death's head there. Tie up thy fears.
30   He that forbears
         To suit and serve his need
         Deserves his load.
     But as I raved and grew more fierce and wild
         At every word,
35   Methought I heard one calling, *Child!*
         And I replied, *My Lord.*

Collar Herbert, a clergyman, puns on "clerical collar," "caller," one who calls (see line 35), and "choler," anger. **1** *board* Table. **5** *store* A quantity of supplies, abundance. **9** *cordial* Invigorating the heart, reviving. **14** *bays* A garland of laurel and a symbol of honor or renown. **29** *death's head* A human skull or a representation of one intended as a reminder that all men must someday die.

John Milton   (1608–1674)

Lycidas

Yet once more, O ye laurels, and once more,
Ye myrtles brown, with ivy never sere,
I come to pluck your berries harsh and crude,
And with forced fingers rude
5 Shatter your leaves before the mellowing year.
Bitter constraint and sad occasion dear
Compels me to disturb your season due:
For Lycidas is dead, dead ere his prime.
Young Lycidas, and hath not left his peer.
10 Who would not sing for Lycidas? he knew
Himself to sing, and build the lofty rhyme.
He must not float upon his watery bier
Unwept, and welter to the parching wind,
Without the meed of some melodious tear.
15   Begin then, Sisters of the sacred well
That from beneath the seat of Jove doth spring;
Begin, and somewhat loudly sweep the string;
Hence with denial vain and coy excuse;
So may some gentle Muse
20 With lucky words favor my destined urn;
And as he passes, turn
And bid fair peace be to my sable shroud.
    For we were nursed upon the self-same hill,
Fed the same flock by fountain, shade, and rill.
25 Together both, ere the high lawns appeared
Under the opening eye-lids of the Morn.
We drove a-field, and both together heard
What time the gray-fly winds her sultry horn,
Battening our flocks with the fresh dews of night,
30 Oft till the star, that rose at evening bright,
Toward heaven's descent had sloped his westering wheel.
Meanwhile the rural ditties were not mute;
Tempered to the oaten flute,
Rough Satyrs danced, and Fauns with cloven heel

Lycidas A pastoral name for Edward King, a fellow student of Milton's at Cambridge. King
was drowned in the Irish Sea in 1637.   **1** *laurels* Trees or shrubs whose foliage was used by the
ancient Greeks for garlands signifying honor or victory. *Myrtle* and *ivy* (l. 2) were put to similar use.
6 *dear* Esteemed, precious.   **13** *welter to* Be tossed about by.   **14** *meed* Tribute.   **15** *Sisters*
The Muses, goddesses of song and poetry and of the arts and sciences, to whom the poet traditionally
turns for inspiration. The well sacred to them was Aganippe, at the foot of Mt. Helicon in east central
Greece.   **19** *Muse* Poet inspired by a Muse.   **25** *lawns* Pastures.   **30** *the star* The planet
Venus.   **31** *westering* Directed toward the west.

35 From the glad sound would not be absent long;
And old Damoetas loved to hear our song.
　　But, O! the heavy change, now thou art gone,
Now thou art gone, and never must return!
Thee, Shepherd, thee the woods and desert caves,
40 With wild thyme and the gadding vine o'ergrown,
And all their echoes, mourn:
The willows and the hazel copses green
Shall now no more be seen
Fanning their joyous leaves to thy soft lays.
45 As killing as the canker to the rose,
Or taint-worm to the weanling herds that graze,
Or frost to flowers, that their gay wardrobe wear
When first the white thorn blows:
Such, Lycidas, thy loss to shepherd's ear.
50 　　Where were ye, Nymphs, when the remorseless deep
Closed o'er the head of your loved Lycidas?
For neither were ye playing on the steep
Where your old bards, the famous Druids, lie,
Nor on the shaggy top of Mona high,
55 Nor yet where Deva spreads her wizard stream.
Aye me! I fondly dream
"Had ye been there,"—for what could that have done?
What could the Muse herself that Orpheus bore,
The Muse herself, for her enchanting son,
60 Whom universal nature did lament,
When by the route that made the hideous roar,
His gory visage down the stream was sent,
Down the swift Hebrus to the Lesbian shore?
　　Alas! what boots it with uncessant care
65 To tend the homely, slighted, shepherd's trade,
And strictly meditate the thankless Muse?
Were it not better done, as others use,
To sport with Amaryllis in the shade,
Or with the tangles of Neaera's hair?
70 Fame is the spur that the clear spirit doth raise
(That last infirmity of noble mind)
To scorn delights, and live laborious days;
But the fair guerdon when we hope to find,

---

36 *Damoetas* A shepherd, here probably referring to a Cambridge tutor.   **52** *steep* Mountain slope.   **53** *Druids* Celtic priests and poets.   **54** *Mona* Island off Wales.   **55** *Deva* The river Dee, which empties into the Irish Sea and is referred to as "wizard" because its changes of course were said to foretell the country's fortune.   **58** *Orpheus* Son of the Muse Calliope. He was torn to pieces by Thracian women, who threw his head into the river Hebrus, from which it drifted across the Aegean to the island of Lesbos.   **68-69** *Amaryllis . . . Neaera* Maidens of pastoral tradition.

And think to burst out into sudden blaze,
75 Comes the blind Fury with the abhorred shears
And slits the thin-spun life. "But not the praise,"
Phoebus replied, and touched my trembling ears:
"Fame is no plant that grows on mortal soil,
Nor in the glistering foil
80 Set off to the world, nor in broad rumor lies:
But lives and spreads aloft by those pure eyes
And perfect witness of all-judging Jove;
As he pronounces lastly on each deed,
Of so much fame in heaven expect thy meed."
85   O fountain Arethuse, and thou honored flood,
Smooth-sliding Mincius, crowned with vocal reeds,
That strain I heard was of a higher mood.
But now my oat proceeds,
And listens to the herald of the sea
90 That came in Neptune's plea;
He asked the waves, and asked the felon winds,
What hard mishap hath doomed this gentle swain?
And questioned every gust of rugged wings
That blows from off each beaked promontory:
95 They knew not of his story;
And sage Hippotades their answer brings,
That not a blast was from his dungeon strayed;
The air was calm, and on the level brine
Sleek Panope with all her sisters played.
100 It was that fatal and perfidious bark,
Built in the eclipse, and rigged with curses dark,
That sunk so low that sacred head of thine.
    Next Camus, reverend sire, went footing slow,
His mantle hairy, and his bonnet sedge,
105 Inwrought with figures dim, and on the edge
Like to that sanguine flower inscribed with woe.
"Ah! who hath reft," quoth he, "my dearest pledge?"
Last came, and last did go
The Pilot of the Galilean lake;
110 Two massy keys he bore of metals twain
(The golden opes, the iron shuts amain);

---

75 *Fury* Atropos, the Fate who cuts the thread of life.   **77** *Phoebus* Apollo, god of poetry.
85 *Arethuse* A fountain in Sicily.   **86** *Mincius* A river in northern Italy associated with pastoral
poetry and mentioned by Virgil.   **89** *herald* Triton, Neptune's son.   **96** *Hippotades* Aeolus, god
of the winds.   **99** *Panope* A sea nymph.   **103** *Camus* God of the river Cam, here wearing tradi-
tional academic robe of Cambridge University.   **106** *sanguine flower* The hyacinth.   **109** *Pilot of*
the Galilean lake St. Peter, the fisherman of Galilee. As the first bishop he wears a miter and bears
the keys of Heaven given him by Jesus.

He shook his mitred locks, and stern bespake:
"How well could I have spared for thee, young swain,
Enow of such, as for their bellies' sake
115 Creep and intrude and climb into the fold!
Of other care they little reckoning make
Than how to scramble at the shearers' feast,
And shove away the worthy bidden guest.
Blind mouths! that scarce themselves know how to hold
120 A sheep-hook, or have learned aught else the least
That to the faithful herdman's art belongs!
What recks it them? What need they? They are sped;
And when they list, their lean and flashy songs
Grate on their scrannel pipes of wretched straw;
125 The hungry sheep look up, and are not fed,
But, swol'n with wind and the rank mist they draw,
Rot inwardly, and foul contagion spread:
Besides what the grim wolf with privy paw
Daily devours apace, and nothing said:
130 —But that two-handed engine at the door
Stands ready to smite once, and smite no more."
    Return, Alpheus; the dread voice is past
That shrunk thy streams; return, Sicilian Muse,
And call the vales, and bid them hither cast
135 Their bells and flowerets of a thousand hues.
Ye valleys low, where the mild whispers use
Of shades, and wanton winds, and gushing brooks
On whose fresh lap the swart star sparely looks;
Throw hither all your quaint enameled eyes
140 That on the green turf suck the honeyed showers,
And purple all the ground with vernal flowers.
Bring the rathe primrose that forsaken dies,
The tufted crow-toe, and pale jessamine,
The white pink, and the pansy freaked with jet,
145 The glowing violet,
The musk-rose, and the well-attired woodbine,
With cowslips wan that hang the pensive head,
And every flower that sad embroidery wears;
Bid amaranthus all his beauty shed,
150 And daffodillies fill their cups with tears
To strew the laureate hearse where Lycid lies.
For so to interpose a little ease,
Let our frail thoughts dally with false surmise.

---

114 *Enow* Enough.   **122** *What recks it them* What does it matter to them?   **132** *Alpheus*
Sicilian river god who loved Arethusa.   **138** *swart star* Sirius.   **142** *rathe* Early.   **144** *freaked*
with jet Mottled with deep black.   **149** *amaranthus* An imaginary flower that never fades.

Ay me! whilst thee the shores and sounding seas
155 Wash far away, where'er thy bones are hurled;
Whether beyond the stormy Hebrides
Where thou, perhaps, under the whelming tide,
Visit'st the bottom of the monstrous world;
Or whether thou, to our moist vows denied,
160 Sleep'st by the fable of Bellerus old,
Where the great Vision of the guarded mount
Looks toward Namancos and Bayona's hold.
Look homeward, Angel, now, and melt with ruth:
And, O ye dolphins, waft the hapless youth!
165 　Weep no more, woeful shepherds, weep no more,
For Lycidas, your sorrow, is not dead,
Sunk though he be beneath the watery floor;
So sinks the day-star in the ocean bed,
And yet anon repairs his drooping head,
170 And tricks his beams, and with new-spangled ore
Flames in the forehead of the morning sky:
So Lycidas sunk low, but mounted high
Through the dear might of Him that walked the waves;
Where, other groves and other streams along,
175 With nectar pure his oozy locks he laves,
And hears the unexpressive nuptial song
In the blest kingdoms meek of joy and love.
There entertain him all the saints above
In solemn troops, and sweet societies,
180 That sing, and singing in their glory move,
And wipe the tears for ever from his eyes.
Now, Lycidas, the shepherds weep no more;
Henceforth thou art the Genius of the shore
In thy large recompense, and shalt be good
185 To all that wander in that perilous flood.
　Thus sang the uncouth swain to the oaks and rills,
While the still morn went out with sandals gray;
He touched the tender stops of various quills,
With eager thought warbling his Doric lay:
190 And now the sun had stretched out all the hills,
And now was dropt into the western bay.
At last he rose, and twitched his mantle blue:
Tomorrow to fresh woods, and pastures new.

---

156 *Hebrides* Islands west of Scotland. **160** *Bellerus* A giant of fable for whom Land's End, the tip of Cornwall, was supposedly given its Roman name. **161** *guarded mount* St. Michael's Mount, off Cornwall, looking toward Spain. **168** *day-star* The sun. **170** *tricks* Dresses, decks, adorns. *ore* Gold. **176** *unexpressive* Inexpressible. **183** *Genius* Guardian spirit. **186** *uncouth* Awkward in his bearing. **189** *Doric* Pastoral, referring to a Greek dialect.

Satan's Address to the Sun
From PARADISE LOST (IV, 23—113)

               Now conscience wakes despair
That slumbered, wakes the bitter memory
Of what he was, what is, and what must be
Worse; of worse deeds worse sufferings must ensue.
5 Sometimes towards Eden which now in his view
Lay pleasant, his grieved look he fixes sad,
Sometimes towards Heaven and the full-blazing sun,
Which now sat high in his meridian tower
Then much revolving, thus in sighs began.
10 "O thou that with surpassing glory crowned,
Lookest from thy sole dominion like the god
Of this new world; at whose sight all the stars
Hide their diminished heads; to thee I call,
But with no friendly voice, and add thy name,
15 O Sun, to tell thee how I hate thy beams
That bring to my remembrance from what state
I fell, how glorious once above thy sphere,
Till pride and worse ambition threw me down
Warring in Heaven against Heaven's matchless king.
20 Ah wherefore! he deserved no such return
From me, whom he created what I was
In that bright eminence, and with his good
Upbraided none, nor was his service hard.
What could be less than to afford him praise,
25 The easiest recompense, and pay him thanks,
How due! yet all his good proved ill in me,
And wrought but malice; lifted up so high
I'sdained subjection, and thought one step higher
Would set me highest, and in a moment quit
30 The debt immense of endless gratitude,
So burdensome still paying, still to owe;
Forgetful what from him I still received,
And understood not that a grateful mind
By owing owes not, but still pays, at once
35 Indebted and discharged; what burden then?
O had his powerful destiny ordained
Me some inferior angel, I had stood
Then happy; no unbounded hope had raised
Ambition. Yet why not? some other power
40 As great might have aspired, and me, though mean,
Drawn to his part; but other powers as great
Fell not, but stand unshaken, from within
Or from without, to all temptations armed.

Hadst thou the same free will and power to stand?
45 Thou hadst: whom hast thou then or what to accuse,
But heaven's free love dealt equally to all?
Be then his love accursed, since love or hate,
To me alike, it deals eternal woe.
Nay cursed be thou; since against his thy will
50 Chose freely what it now so justly rues.
Me miserable! which way shall I fly
Infinite wrath, and infinite despair?
Which way I fly is Hell; myself am Hell;
And in the lowest deep a lower deep
55 Still threatening to devour me opens wide,
To which the Hell I suffer seems a Heaven.
O then at last relent: is there no place
Left for repentance, none for pardon left?
None left but by submission; and that word
60 Disdain forbids me, and my dread of shame
Among the spirits beneath, whom I seduced
With other promises and other vaunts
Than to submit, boasting I could subdue
The omnipotent. Ay me, they little know
65 How dearly I abide that boast so vain,
Under what torments inwardly I groan;
While they adore me on the throne of Hell,
With diadem and scepter high advanced
The lower still I fall, only supreme
70 In misery; such joy ambition finds.
But say I could repent and could obtain
By act of grace my former state; how soon
Would height recall high thoughts, how soon unsay
What feigned submission swore: ease would recant
75 Vows made in pain, as violent and void.
For never can true reconcilement grow
Where wounds of deadly hate have pierced so deep:
Which would but lead me to a worse relapse
And heavier fall: so should I purchase dear
80 Short intermission bought with double smart.
This knows my punisher; therefore as far
From granting he, as I from begging peace:
All hope excluded thus, behold instead
Of us outcast, exiled, his new delight,
85 Mankind created, and for him this world.
So farewell hope, and with hope farewell fear,
Farewell remorse: all good to me is lost;
Evil be thou my good; by thee at least
Divided empire with Heaven's king I hold,
90 By thee, and more than half perhaps will reign;
As man erelong, and this new world shall know.''

Epithalamion: Hail Wedded Love
From PARADISE LOST (IV, 750–75)

Hail, wedded Love, mysterious law, true source
Of human offspring, sole propriety
In Paradise of all things common else!
By thee adulterous lust was driven from men
5 Among the bestial herds to range; by thee,
Founded in reason, loyal, just, and pure,
Relations dear, and all the charities
Of father, son, and brother, first were known.
Far be it that I should write thee sin or blame,
10 Or think thee unbefitting holiest place,
Perpetual fountain of domestic sweets,
Whose bed is undefiled and chaste pronounced,
Present, or past, as saints and patriarchs used.
Here Love his golden shafts employs, here lights
15 His constant lamp, and waves his purple wings,
Reigns here and revels; not in the bought smile
Of harlots—loveless, joyless, unendeared,
Casual fruition; nor in court amours,
Mixed dance, or wanton mask, or midnight ball,
20 Or serenate, which the starved lover sings
To his proud fair, best quitted with disdain.
These, lulled by nightingales, embracing slept,
And on their naked limbs the flowery roof
Showered roses, which the morn repaired. Sleep on,
25 Blest pair! and, O! yet happiest, if ye seek
No happier state, and know to know no more!

Sir John Suckling   (1609–1642)

Song: Why So Pale and Wan, Fond Lover?

Why so pale and wan, fond lover?
  Prithee, why so pale?
Will, when looking well can't move her,
  Looking ill prevail?
5 Prithee, why so pale?

Why so dull and mute, young sinner?
  Prithee, why so mute?
Will, when speaking well can't win her,
  Saying nothing do 't?
10 Prithee, why so mute?

Quit, quit, for shame; this will not move,
   This cannot take her.
If of herself she will not love,
   Nothing can make her:
15   The devil take her!

Richard Lovelace (1618–1658)

To Althea, from Prison

When Love with unconfinèd wings
Hovers within my gates,
And my divine Althea brings
To whisper at the grates;
5 When I lie tangled in her hair
And fettered to her eye,
The birds that wanton in the air
Know no such liberty.

When flowing cups run swiftly round,
10 With no allaying Thames,
Our careless heads with roses bound,
Our hearts with loyal flames;
When thirsty grief in wine we steep,
When healths and draughts go free,
15 Fishes, that tipple in the deep,
Know no such liberty.

When, like committed linnets, I
With shriller throat shall sing
The sweetness, mercy, majesty,
20 And glories of my King;
When I shall voice aloud how good
He is, how great should be,
Enlargèd winds, that curl the flood,
Know no such liberty.

25 Stone walls do not a prison make,
Nor iron bars a cage;
Minds innocent and quiet take
That for an hermitage.

---

10 *no allaying Thames* Not diluted by the water of the Thames River. **15** *tipple* Drink constantly. **17** *committed* Caged. **20** *my King* Charles I (1600-1649). **23** *curl the flood* Make the ocean waves.

If I have freedom in my love,
30 And in my soul am free,
    Angels alone, that soar above,
    Enjoy such liberty.

Andrew Marvell (1621–1678)

To His Coy Mistress

    Had we but world enough, and time,
    This coyness, lady, were no crime.
    We would sit down, and think which way
    To walk, and pass our long love's day.
  5 Thou by the Indian Ganges' side
    Should'st rubies find: I by the tide
    Of Humber would complain. I would
    Love you ten years before the Flood,
    And you should, if you please, refuse
10 Till the conversion of the Jews.
    My vegetable love should grow
    Vaster than empires, and more slow.
    An hundred years should go to praise
    Thine eyes, and on thy forehead gaze:
15 Two hundred to adore each breast:
    But thirty thousand to the rest;
    An age at least to every part,
    And the last age should show your heart.
    For, lady, you deserve this state,
20 Nor would I love at lower rate.
      But at my back I always hear
    Time's wingèd chariot hurrying near:
    And yonder all before us lie
    Deserts of vast eternity.
25 Thy beauty shall no more be found;
    Nor, in thy marble vault, shall sound
    My echoing song: then worms shall try
    That long-preserved virginity,
    And your quaint honor turn to dust,

---

5 *Indian Ganges'* The Ganges River in India, which flows from the Himalayas to the Bay of Bengal. **7** *Humber* The Humber River, which flows through Marvell's birthplace of Hull. **8** *the Flood* The universal deluge recorded in the Bible as having taken place during the life of Noah. See Genesis 7. **10** *Till the conversion of the Jews* At the end of recorded history. **11** *vegetable* Like plants, having the power of growth but not of consciousness. **29** *quaint* Cunning, ingenious, clever.

30   And into ashes all my lust.
      The grave's a fine and private place,
      But none, I think, do there embrace.
          Now, therefore, while the youthful hue
      Sits on thy skin like morning dew,
35   And while thy willing soul transpires
      At every pore with instant fires,
      Now let us sport us while we may;
      And now, like amorous birds of prey,
      Rather at once our Time devour,
40   Than languish in his slow-chapt power.
      Let us roll all our strength and all
      Our sweetness up into one ball,
      And tear our pleasures with rough strife
      Thorough the iron gates of life.
45   Thus, though we cannot make our sun
      Stand still, yet we will make him run.

35 *transpires* Breathes out.   **40** *slow-chapt* Slow-jawed.

The Garden

          How vainly men themselves amaze
      To win the palm, the oak, or bays,
      And their incessant labors see
      Crowned from some single herb, or tree,
5   Whose short and narrow-vergèd shade
      Does prudently their toils upbraid;
      While all flowers and all trees do close
      To weave the garlands of repose!

          Fair Quiet, have I found thee here,
10   And Innocence, thy sister dear?
      Mistaken long, I sought you then
      In busy companies of men.
      Your sacred plants, if here below,
      Only among the plants will grow;
15   Society is all but rude
      To this delicious solitude.

          No white nor red was ever seen
      So amorous as this lovely green.
      Fond lovers, cruel as their flame,

2 *the palm, the oak, or bays* The wreaths used in ancient Greece to symbolize athletic, civic, and poetic achievement respectively.   **5** *narrow-vergèd* Confined, limited.   **7** *close* Join.

20 Cut in these trees their mistress' name:
Little, alas, they know or heed
How far these beauties hers exceed!
Fair trees, wheresoe'er your barks I wound,
No name shall but your own be found.

25   When we have run our passion's heat,
Love hither makes his best retreat.
The gods, that mortal beauty chase,
Still in a tree did end their race:
Apollo hunted Daphne so,
30 Only that she might laurel grow;
And Pan did after Syrinx speed,
Not as a nymph, but for a reed.

What wondrous life is this I lead!
Ripe apples drop about my head;
35 The luscious clusters of the vine
Upon my mouth do crush their wine;
The nectarine and curious peach
Into my hands themselves do reach;
Stumbling on melons, as I pass,
40 Insnared with flowers, I fall on grass.

Meanwhile the mind, from pleasure less,
Withdraws into its happiness;
The mind, that ocean where each kind
Does straight its own resemblance find;
45 Yet it creates, transcending these,
Far other worlds and other seas,
Annihilating all that's made
To a green thought in a green shade.

Here at the fountain's sliding foot,
50 Or at some fruit tree's mossy root,
Casting the body's vest aside,
My soul into the boughs does glide:
There, like a bird, it sits and sings,
Then whets and combs its silver wings,

29 *Apollo hunted Daphne* The sun god Apollo fell in love with the huntress Daphne and pursued her through the woods. As she reached the river she called to her father, the river god, for help, and was changed into a laurel tree. Apollo mourned her and chose the leaves of the laurel tree for the wreaths that go to victors.   **31** *Pan did after Syrinx speed* The God Pan pursued the nymph Syrinx, who was turned into a tuft of reeds just as he was about to seize her. From the reeds Pan made a shepherd's pipe or flutelike instrument.   **37** *curious* Exquisite, choice.   **43-44** *that ocean . . . find* An allusion to the belief that each land creature had a sea creature counterpart.   **51** *vest* Garment.   **54** *whets* Whets or sharpens its beak.

55 And, till prepared for longer flight,
Waves in its plumes the various light.

Such was that happy garden-state,
While man there walked without a mate:
After a place so pure and sweet,
60 What other help could yet be meet!
But 'twas beyond a mortal's share
To wander solitary there:
Two paradises 'twere in one
To live in paradise alone.

65 How well the skillful gardener drew
Of flowers and herbs this dial new,
Where, from above, the milder sun
Does through a fragrant zodiac run;
And as it works, th' industrious bee
70 Computes its time as well as we!
How could such sweet and wholesome hours
Be reckoned but with herbs and flowers?

56 *various* Varicolored.　　**66** *dial* Sundial.

John Dryden　(1631–1700)

A Song for Saint Cecilia's Day, November 22, 1687

From harmony, from heavenly harmony
　This universal frame began;
　When Nature underneath a heap
　Of jarring atoms lay,
5　And could not heave her head,
The tuneful voice was heard from high,
　Arise, ye more than dead.
The cold and hot and moist and dry
　In order to their stations leap,
10　And Music's power obey.
From harmony, from heavenly harmony
　This universal frame began;
　From harmony to harmony

Saint Cecilia The patron saint of music, to whom the invention of the organ was attributed.
8 *The cold and hot and moist and dry* Attributes of earth, fire, water, and air, identified in the old science as the four elements.

Through all the compass of the notes it ran,
15 The diapason closing full in Man.

What passion cannot Music raise and quell?
    When Jubal struck the corded shell,
  His listening brethren stood around,
    And, wondering, on their faces fell
20 To worship that celestial sound.
Less than a god they thought there could not dwell
  Within the hollow of that shell,
  That spoke so sweetly, and so well.
What passion cannot Music raise and quell?

25   The trumpet's loud clangor
      Excites us to arms
   With shrill notes of anger
    And mortal alarms.
   The double, double, double beat
30   Of the thundering drum
   Cries, "Hark! the foes come;
Charge, charge, 'tis too late to retreat!"

   The soft complaining flute
   In dying notes discovers
35   The woes of hopeless lovers,
Whose dirge is whispered by the warbling lute.

    Sharp violins proclaim
Their jealous pangs and desperation,
Fury, frantic indignation,
40 Depth of pains and height of passion,
    For the fair, disdainful dame.

  But, oh! what art can teach,
  What human voice can reach
    The sacred organ's praise?
45   Notes inspiring holy love,
  Notes that wing their heavenly ways
    To mend the choirs above.

  Orpheus could lead the savage race,
  And trees unrooted left their place,

---

15 *diapason* A burst of harmonious sound.   **17** *Jubal* "The father of all such as handle the harp and organ" (Genesis 4:21).   *the corded shell* The lyre, which was originally made from a tortoise shell.   **48** *Orpheus* In Greek myth, a musician of very great power. Playing his lyre, he led the beasts of the wilderness; even the trees followed him.

50   Sequacious of the lyre,
      But bright Cecilia raised the wonder higher;
      When to her organ vocal breath was given,
      An angel heard, and straight appeared,
          Mistaking earth for heaven.

55   As from the power of sacred lays
          The spheres began to move,
      And sung the great Creator's praise
          To all the blest above;
      So when the last and dreadful hour
60   This crumbling pageant shall devour,
      The trumpet shall be heard on high,
      The dead shall live, the living die,
      And Music shall untune the sky.

50 *Sequacious* Inclined to follow.

Alexander Pope   (1688–1744)

The Rape of the Lock

CANTO I

      What dire offense from am'rous causes springs,
      What mighty contests rise from trivial things,
      I sing—This verse to CARYL, Muse! is due:
      This, even Belinda may vouchsafe to view:
5   Slight is the subject, but not so the praise,
      If She inspire, and He approve my lays.
          Say what strange motive, Goddess! could compel
      A well-bred Lord t' assault a gentle Belle?
      O say what stranger cause, yet unexplored,
10   Could make a gentle Belle reject a Lord?
      In tasks so bold, can little men engage,
      And in soft bosoms dwells such mighty Rage?
          Sol through white curtains shot a tim'rous ray,
      And oped those eyes that must eclipse the day:
15   Now lap-dogs give themselves the rousing shake,
      And sleepless lovers, just at twelve, awake:
      Thrice rung the bell, the slipper knocked the ground,

3 *CARYL*   The poem was written at the suggestion of John Caryll to help end a quarrel be-
tween the families of Arabella Fermor and Lord Petre, who literally cut off a lock of the lady's hair.

And the pressed watch returned a silver sound.
Belinda still her downy pillow prest,
20 Her guardian Sylph prolonged the balmy rest:
'Twas He had summoned to her silent bed
The morning-dream that hovered o'er her head;
A Youth more glitt'ring than a Birth-night Beau,
(That even in slumber caused her cheek to glow)
25 Seemed to her ear his winning lips to lay,
And thus in whispers said, or seemed to say:
   "Fairest of mortals, thou distinguished care
Of thousand bright Inhabitants of Air!
If e'er one vision touched thy infant thought,
30 Of all the Nurse and all the Priest have taught;
Of airy Elves by moonlight shadows seen,
The silver token, and the circled green,
Or virgins visited by Angel-powers,
With golden crowns and wreaths of heav'nly flowers;
35 Hear and believe! thy own importance know,
Nor bound thy narrow views to things below.
Some secret truths, from learnèd pride concealed,
To Maids alone and Children are revealed:
What though no credit doubting Wits may give?
40 The Fair and Innocent shall still believe.
Know, then, unnumbered Spirits round thee fly,
The light Militia of the lower sky:
These, though unseen, are ever on the wing,
Hang o'er the Box, and hover round the Ring.
45 Think what an equipage thou hast in Air,
And view with scorn two Pages and a Chair.
As now your own, our beings were of old,
And once inclosed in Woman's beauteous mould;
Thence, by a soft transition, we repair
50 From earthly Vehicles to these of air.
Think not, when Woman's transient breath is fled,
That all her vanities at once are dead;
Succeeding vanities she still regards,
And though she plays no more, o'erlooks the cards.
55 Her joy in gilded Chariots, when alive,
And love of Ombre, after death survive.
For when the Fair in all their pride expire,
To their first Elements their Souls retire:
The Sprites of fiery Termagants in Flame
60 Mount up, and take a Salamander's name.

23 *Birth-night* Dressed in finery for a royal birthday ball.   **32** *silver token* A coin left by fairies in the shoe of maids whom they approve.   **44** *Box . . . Ring* A theatre box and a riding circle in Hyde Park.   **56** *Ombre* A card game. See Canto III, 27 ff.

Soft yielding minds to Water glide away,
And sip, with Nymphs, their elemental Tea.
The graver Prude sinks downward to a Gnome,
In search of mischief still on Earth to roam.
65 The light Coquettes in Sylphs aloft repair,
And sport and flutter in the fields of Air.
   "Know further yet; whoever fair and chaste
Rejects mankind, is by some Sylph embraced:
For Spirits, freed from mortal laws, with ease
70 Assume what sexes and what shapes they please.
What guards the purity of melting Maids,
In courtly balls, and midnight masquerades,
Safe from the treach'rous friend, the daring spark,
The glance by day, the whisper in the dark,
75 When kind occasion prompts their warm desires,
When music softens, and when dancing fires?
'Tis but their Sylph, the wise Celestials know,
Though Honor is the word with Men below.`
   "Some nymphs there are, too conscious of their face,
80 For life predestined to the Gnomes' embrace.
These swell their prospects and exalt their pride,
When offers are disdained, and love denied:
Then gay Ideas crowd the vacant brain,
While Peers, and Dukes, and all their sweeping train,
85 And Garters, Stars, and Coronets appear,
And in soft sounds, 'Your Grace' salutes their ear.
'Tis these that early taint the female soul,
Instruct the eyes of young Coquettes to roll,
Teach Infant-cheeks a bidden blush to know,
90 And little hearts to flutter at a Beau.
   "Oft, when the world imagine women stray,
The Sylphs through mystic mazes guide their way,
Through all the giddy circle they pursue,
And old impertinence expel by new.
95 What tender maid but must a victim fall
To one man's treat, but for another's ball?
When Florio speaks what virgin could withstand,
If gentle Damon did not squeeze her hand?
With varying vanities, from every part,
100 They shift the moving Toyshop of their heart;
Where wigs with wigs, with sword-knots sword-knots strive,
Beaux banish beaux, and coaches coaches drive.
This erring mortals Levity may call;
Oh blind to truth! the Sylphs contrive it all.

97-98 *Florio . . . Damon* Characters from pastoral poetry.   **101** *sword-knots* Ribbons or
tassels on sword hilts.

105 "Of these am I, who thy protection claim,
A watchful sprite, and Ariel is my name.
Late, as I ranged the crystal wilds of air,
In the clear Mirror of thy ruling Star
I saw, alas! some dread event impend,
110 Ere to the main this morning sun descend,
But heaven reveals not what, or how, or where:
Warned by the Sylph, oh pious maid, beware!
This to disclose is all thy guardian can:
Beware of all, but most beware of Man!"
115 He said; when Shock, who thought she slept too long,
Leaped up, and waked his mistress with his tongue.
'Twas then, Belinda, if report say true,
Thy eyes first opened on a Billet-doux;
Wounds, Charms, and Ardors were no sooner read,
120 But all the Vision vanished from thy head.
  And now, unveiled, the Toilet stands displayed,
Each silver Vase in mystic order laid.
First, robed in white, the Nymph intent adores,
With head uncovered, the Cosmetic powers.
125 A heav'nly image in the glass appears,
To that she bends, to that her eyes she rears;
Th' inferior Priestess, at her altar's side,
Trembling begins the sacred rites of Pride.
Unnumbered treasures ope at once, and here
130 The various off'rings of the world appear;
From each she nicely culls with curious toil,
And decks the Goddess with the glitt'ring spoil.
This casket India's glowing gems unlocks,
And all Arabia breathes from yonder box.
135 The Tortoise here and Elephant unite,
Transformed to combs, the speckled, and the white.
Here files of pins extend their shining rows,
Puffs, Powders, Patches, Bibles, Billet-doux.
Now awful Beauty puts on all its arms;
140 The fair each moment rises in her charms,
Repairs her smiles, awakens every grace,
And calls forth all the wonders of her face;
Sees by degrees a purer blush arise,
And keener lightnings quicken in her eyes.
145 The busy Sylphs surround their darling care,
These set the head, and those divide the hair,
Some fold the sleeve, whilst others plait the gown;
And Betty's praised for labors not her own.

115 *Shock* Belinda's lap dog.   **148** *Betty* The maid.

CANTO II

Not with more glories, in th' etherial plain,
The Sun first rises o'er the purpled main,
Than, issuing forth, the rival of his beams
Launched on the bosom of the silver Thames.
5 Fair Nymphs, and well-drest Youths around her shone,
But every eye was fixed on her alone.
On her white breast a sparkling Cross she wore,
Which Jews might kiss, and Infidels adore.
Her lively looks a sprightly mind disclose,
10 Quick as her eyes, and as unfixed as those:
Favors to none, to all she smiles extends;
Oft she rejects, but never once offends.
Bright as the sun, her eyes the gazers strike,
And, like the sun, they shine on all alike.
15 Yet graceful ease, and sweetness void of pride,
Might hide her faults, if Belles had faults to hide:
If to her share some female errors fall,
Look on her face, and you'll forget 'em all.
   This Nymph, to the destruction of mankind,
20 Nourished two Locks, which graceful hung behind
In equal curls, and well conspired to deck
With shining ringlets the smooth iv'ry neck.
Love in these labyrinths his slaves detains,
And mighty hearts are held in slender chains.
25 With hairy springes we the birds betray,
Slight lines of hair surprise the finny prey,
Fair tresses man's imperial race ensnare,
And beauty draws us with a single hair.
   Th' advent'rous Baron the bright locks admired;
30 He saw, he wished, and to the prize aspired.
Resolved to win, he meditates the way,
By force to ravish, or by fraud betray;
For when success a Lover's toil attends,
Few ask, if fraud or force attained his ends.
35   For this, ere Phoebus rose, he had implored
Propitious heaven, and every power adored,
But chiefly Love—to Love an Altar built,
Of twelve vast French Romances, neatly gilt.
There lay three garters, half a pair of gloves;
40 And all the trophies of his former loves;
With tender Billet-doux he lights the pyre,
And breathes three am'rous sighs to raise the fire.

35 *Phoebus*   The sun.

Then prostrate falls, and begs with ardent eyes
Soon to obtain, and long possess the prize:
45 The powers gave ear, and granted half his prayer,
The rest, the winds dispersed in empty air.
　　But now secure the painted vessel glides,
The sun-beams trembling on the floating tides:
While melting music steals upon the sky,
50 And softened sounds along the waters die;
Smooth flow the waves, the Zephyrs gently play,
Belinda smiled, and all the world was gay.
All but the Sylph—with careful thoughts opprest,
Th' impending woe sat heavy on his breast.
55 He summons strait his Denizens of air;
The lucid squadrons round the sails repair:
Soft o'er the shrouds aërial whispers breathe,
That seemed but Zephyrs to the train beneath.
Some to the sun their insect-wings unfold,
60 Waft on the breeze, or sink in clouds of gold;
Transparent forms, too fine for mortal sight,
Their fluid bodies half dissolved in light,
Loose to the wind their airy garments flew,
Thin glitt'ring textures of the filmy dew,
65 Dipt in the richest tincture of the skies,
Where light disports in ever-mingling dyes,
While every beam new transient colors flings,
Colors that change whene'er they wave their wings.
Amid the circle, on the gilded mast,
70 Superior by the head, was Ariel placed;
His purple pinions opening to the sun,
He raised his azure wand, and thus begun:
　　"Ye Sylphs and Sylphids, to your chief give ear!
Fays, Fairies, Genii, Elves, and Dæmons, hear!
75 Ye know the spheres and various tasks assigned
By laws eternal to th' aërial kind.
Some in the fields of purest Æther play,
And bask and whiten in the blaze of day.
Some guide the course of wand'ring orbs on high,
80 Or roll the planets through the boundless sky.
Some less refined, beneath the moon's pale light
Pursue the stars that shoot athwart the night,
Or suck the mists in grosser air below,
Or dip their pinions in the painted bow,
85 Or brew fierce tempests on the wintry main,
Or o'er the glebe distil the kindly rain.

84 *the painted bow*   The rainbow.   **86** *glebe*   Farmland.

Others on earth o'er human race preside,
Watch all their ways, and all their actions guide:
Of these the chief the care of Nations own,
90   And guard with Arms divine the British Throne.
      "Our humbler province is to tend the Fair,
Not a less pleasing, though less glorious care;
To save the powder from too rude a gale,
Nor let th' imprisoned essences exhale;
95   To draw fresh colors from the vernal flowers;
To steal from rainbows e'er they drop in showers
A brighter wash; to curl their waving hairs,
Assist their blushes, and inspire their airs;
Nay oft, in dreams, invention we bestow,
100   To change a Flounce, or add a Furbelow.
      "This day, black Omens threat the brightest Fair,
That e'er deserved a watchful spirit's care;
Some dire disaster, or by force, or slight;
But what, or where, the fates have wrapt in night.
105   Whether the nymph shall break Diana's law,
Or some frail China jar receive a flaw;
Or stain her honor or her new brocade;
Forget her prayers, or miss a masquerade;
Or lose her heart, or necklace, at a ball;
110   Or whether Heaven has doomed that Shock must fall.
Haste, then, ye spirits! to your charge repair:
The flutt'ring fan be Zephyretta's care;
The drops to thee, Brillante, we consign;
And, Momentilla, let the watch be thine;
115   Do thou, Crispissa, tend her fav'rite Lock;
Ariel himself shall be the guard of Shock.
      "To fifty chosen Sylphs, of special note,
We trust th' important charge, the Petticoat:
Oft have we known that seven-fold fence to fail,
120   Though stiff with hoops, and armed with ribs of whale;
Form a strong line about the silver bound,
And guard the wide circumference around.
      "Whatever spirit, careless of his charge,
His post neglects, or leaves the fair at large,
125   Shall feel sharp vengeance soon o'ertake his sins,
Be stopped in vials, or transfixed with pins;
Or plunged in lakes of bitter washes lie,
Or wedged whole ages in a bodkin's eye:
Gums and Pomatums shall his flight restrain,

---

105 *Diana's law* Chastity.   **113** *drops* Earrings.   **115** *Crispissa* To crisp hair means
to curl it.

130 While clogged he beats his silken wings in vain;
Or Alum styptics with contracting power
Shrink his thin essence like a riveled flower:
Or, as Ixion fixed, the wretch shall feel
The giddy motion of the whirling Mill,
135 In fumes of burning Chocolate shall glow,
And tremble at the sea that froths below!"
   He spoke; the spirits from the sails descend;
Some, orb in orb, around the nymph extend;
Some thrid the mazy ringlets of her hair;
140 Some hang upon the pendants of her ear:
With beating hearts the dire event they wait,
Anxious, and trembling for the birth of Fate.

CANTO III

Close by those meads, forever crowned with flowers,
Where Thames with pride surveys his rising towers,
There stands a structure of majestic frame,
Which from the neighb'ring Hampton takes its name.
5 Here Britain's statesmen oft the fall foredoom
Of foreign Tyrants and of Nymphs at home;
Here thou, great ANNA! whom three realms obey,
Dost sometimes counsel take—and sometimes Tea.
   Hither the heroes and the nymphs resort,
10 To taste awhile the pleasures of a Court;
In various talk th' instructive hours they past,
Who gave the ball, or paid the visit last;
One speaks the glory of the British Queen,
And one describes a charming Indian screen;
15 A third interprets motions, looks, and eyes;
At every word a reputation dies.
Snuff, or the fan, supply each pause of chat,
With singing, laughing, ogling, and all that.
   Meanwhile, declining from the noon of day,
20 The sun obliquely shoots his burning ray;
The hungry Judges soon the sentence sign,
And wretches hang that jury-men may dine;
The merchant from th' Exchange returns in peace,
And the long labors of the Toilet cease.
25 Belinda now, whom thirst of fame invites,
Burns to encounter two advent'rous Knights,

---

132 *riveled* Shriveled.   **133** *Ixion* Legendary king who was bound on an eternally revolving wheel as punishment for loving Hera, queen of the gods.   **134** *Mill* Cocoa mill, used to grind cocoa beans.   **3** *a structure* Hampton Court, one of the royal residences.   **7** *ANNA* Queen Anne (1702–1714).

At Ombre singly to decide their doom;
And swells her breast with conquests yet to come.
Straight the three bands prepare in arms to join,
30 Each band the number of the sacred nine.
Soon as she spreads her hand, th' aërial guard
Descend, and sit on each important card:
First Ariel perched upon a Matadore,
Then each, according to the rank they bore;
35 For Sylphs, yet mindful of their ancient race,
Are, as when women, wondrous fond of place.
   Behold, four Kings in majesty revered,
With hoary whiskers and a forky beard;
And four fair Queens whose hands sustain a flower,
40 Th' expressive emblem of their softer power;
Four Knaves in garbs succinct, a trusty band,
Caps on their heads, and halberts in their hand;
And particolored troops, a shining train,
Draw forth to combat on the velvet plain.
45   The skilful Nymph reviews her force with care:
"Let Spades be trumps!" she said, and trumps they were.
   Now move to war her sable Matadores,
In show like leaders of the swarthy Moors.
Spadillio first, unconquerable Lord!
50 Led off two captive trumps, and swept the board.
As many more Manillio forced to yield,
And marched a victor from the verdant field.
Him Basto followed, but his fate more hard
Gained but one trump and one Plebeian card.
55 With his broad sabre next, a chief in years,
The hoary Majesty of Spades appears,
Puts forth one manly leg, to sight revealed,
The rest, his many-colored robe concealed.
The rebel Knave, who dares his prince engage,
60 Proves the just victim of his royal rage.
Even mighty Pam, that Kings and Queens o'erthrew
And mowed down armies in the fights of Lu,
Sad chance of war! now destitute of aid,
Falls undistinguished by the victor spade!
65   Thus far both armies to Belinda yield;
Now to the Baron fate inclines the field.
His warlike Amazon her host invades,
Th' imperial consort of the crown of Spades.

---

30 *the sacred nine* The Muses.   **47** *Matadores* The three highest trumps in Ombre; *Spadillio* is the ace of spades, *Manillio* is the low card of the trump suit, and *Basto* is the ace of clubs. Spades are Belinda's trumps, so her Matadores are all black. She takes four successive tricks.   **61** *Pam* Jack of clubs, high trump in the game of Loo.

The Club's black Tyrant first her victim died,
70 Spite of his haughty mien, and barb'rous pride:
What boots the regal circle on his head,
His giant limbs, in state unwieldy spread;
That long behind he trails his pompous robe,
And, of all monarchs, only grasps the globe?
75   The Baron now his Diamonds pours apace;
Th' embroidered King who shows but half his face,
And his refulgent Queen, with powers combined
Of broken troops an easy conquest find.
Clubs, Diamonds, Hearts, in wild disorder seen,
80 With throngs promiscuous strow the level green.
Thus when dispersed a routed army runs,
Of Asia's troops, and Afric's sable sons,
With like confusion different nations fly,
Of various habit, and of various dye,
85 The pierced battalions disunited fall,
In heaps on heaps; one fate o'erwhelms them all.
    The knave of diamonds tries his wily arts,
And wins (oh, shameful chance!) the Queen of Hearts.
At this, the blood the virgin's cheek forsook,
90 A livid paleness spreads o'er all her look;
She sees, and trembles at th' approaching ill,
Just in the jaws of ruin, and Codille.
And now (as oft in some distempered State)
On one nice Trick depends the general fate.
95 An Ace of Hearts steps forth: The King unseen
    Lurked in her hand, and mourned his captive Queen:
He springs to Vengeance with an eager pace,
And falls like thunder on the prostrate Ace.
The nymph exulting fills with shouts the sky;
100 The walls, the wood, and long canals reply.
    Oh thoughtless mortals! ever blind to fate,
Too soon dejected, and too soon elate.
Sudden, these honors shall be snatched away,
And cursed for ever this victorious day.
105   For lo! the board with cups and spoons is crowned,
The berries crackle, and the mill turns round;
On shining Altars of Japan they raise
The silver lamp; the fiery spirits blaze:
From silver spouts the grateful liquors glide,
110 While China's earth receives the smoking tide:
At once they gratify their scent and taste,
And frequent cups prolong the rich repast.

92 *Codille* Defeat of the challenger.

Straight hover round the Fair her airy band;
Some, as she sipped, the fuming liquor fanned,
115 Some o'er her lap their careful plumes displayed,
Trembling, and conscious of the rich brocade.
Coffee (which makes the politician wise,
And see through all things with his half-shut eyes)
Sent up in vapors to the Baron's brain
120 New Stratagems, the radiant Lock to gain.
Ah cease, rash youth! desist ere 'tis too late,
Fear the just Gods, and think of Scylla's Fate!
Changed to a bird, and sent to flit in air,
She dearly pays for Nisus' injured hair!
125   But when to mischief mortals bend their will,
How soon they find fit instruments of ill!
Just then, Clarissa drew with tempting grace
A two-edged weapon from her shining case:
So Ladies in Romance assist their Knight,
130 Present the spear, and arm him for the fight.
He takes the gift with rev'rence, and extends
The little engine on his fingers' ends;
This just behind Belinda's neck he spread,
As o'er the fragrant steams she bends her head.
135 Swift to the Lock a thousand Sprites repair,
A thousand wings, by turns, blow back the hair;
And thrice they twitched the diamond in her ear;
Thrice she looked back and thrice the foe drew near.
Just in that instant, anxious Ariel sought
140 The close recesses of the Virgin's thought;
As on the nosegay in her breast reclined,
He watched th' Ideas rising in her mind,
Suddenly he viewed, in spite of all her art,
An earthly Lover lurking at her heart.
145 Amazed, confused, he found his power expired,
Resigned to fate, and with a sigh retired.
The Peer now spreads the glitt'ring Forfex wide,
T' inclose the Lock; now joins it, to divide.
Even then, before the fatal engine closed,
150 A wretched Sylph too fondly interposed;
Fate urged the shears, and cut the Sylph in twain,
(But airy substance soon unites again)
The meeting points the sacred hair dissever
From the fair head, forever, and forever!
155   Then flashed the living lightning from her eyes,

122 *Scylla's Fate* Scylla, daughter of Nisus, plucked from her father's head a purple hair
on which the prosperity of his kingdom depended and gave it to his enemy Minos, with whom she
was in love. But Minos repudiated her act and the two were changed into birds.

And screams of horror rend th' affrighted skies.
Not louder shrieks to pitying heaven are cast,
When husbands, or when lap-dogs breathe their last;
Or when rich China vessels fall'n from high,
160 In glitt'ring dust and painted fragments lie!
    "Let wreaths of triumph now my temples twine,"
(The victor cried) "the glorious Prize is mine!
While fish in streams, or birds delight in air,
Or in a coach and six the British Fair,
165 As long as *Atalantis* shall be read,
Or the small pillow grace a Lady's bed,
While visits shall be paid on solemn days,
When num'rous wax-lights in bright order blaze,
While nymphs take treats, or assignations give,
170 So long my honor, name, and praise shall live!
What Time would spare, from Steel receives its date,
And monuments, like men, submit to fate!
Steel could the labor of the Gods destroy,
And strike to dust th' imperial towers of Troy;
175 Steel could the works of mortal pride confound,
And hew triumphal arches to the ground.
What wonder then, fair nymph! thy hairs should feel,
The conq'ring force of unresisted steel?"

CANTO IV

But anxious cares the pensive nymph oppressed,
And secret passions labored in her breast.
Not youthful kings in battle seized alive,
Not scornful virgins who their charms survive,
5 Not ardent lovers robbed of all their bliss,
Not ancient ladies when refused a kiss,
Not tyrants fierce that unrepenting die,
Not Cynthia when her manteau's pinned awry,
E'er felt such rage, resentment, and despair,
10 As thou, sad Virgin! for thy ravished Hair.
    For, that sad moment, when the Sylphs withdrew
And Ariel weeping from Belinda flew,
Umbriel, a dusky, melancholy sprite,
As ever sullied the fair face of light,
15 Down to the central earth, his proper scene,
Repaired to search the gloomy Cave of Spleen.
    Swift on his sooty pinions flits the Gnome,
And in a vapour reached the dismal dome.

165 *Atalantis* A contemporary book of scandal.   **16** *Spleen* Place of low spirits, or nervous upset.   **17** *Gnome* A spirit of a prudish woman.

No cheerful breeze this sullen region knows,
20 The dreaded East is all the wind that blows.
Here in a grotto, sheltered close from air,
And screened in shades from day's detested glare,
She sighs forever on her pensive bed,
Pain at her side, and Megrim at her head.
25   Two handmaids wait the throne: alike in place,
But diff'ring far in figure and in face.
Here stood Ill-nature like an ancient maid,
Her wrinkled form in black and white arrayed;
With store of prayers, for mornings, nights, and noons,
30 Her hand is filled; her bosom with lampoons.
   There Affectation, with a sickly mien,
Shows in her cheek the roses of eighteen,
Practised to lisp, and hang the head aside,
Faints into airs, and languishes with pride,
35 On the rich quilt sinks with becoming woe,
Wrapt in a gown, for sickness, and for show.
The fair ones feel such maladies as these,
When each new night-dress gives a new disease.
   A constant Vapor o'er the palace flies;
40 Strange phantoms rising as the mists arise;
Dreadful, as hermit's dreams in haunted shades,
Or bright, as visions of expiring maids.
Now glaring fiends, and snakes on rolling spires,
Pale specters, gaping tombs, and purple fires:
45 Now lakes of liquid gold, Elysian scenes,
And crystal domes, and angels in machines.
   Unnumbered throngs on every side are seen,
Of bodies changed to various forms by Spleen.
Here living Tea-pots stand, one arm held out,
50 One bent; the handle this, and that the spout:
A Pipkin there, like Homer's Tripod walks;
Here sighs a Jar, and there a Goose-pie talks;
Men prove with child, as powerful fancy works,
And maids turned bottles, call aloud for corks.
55   Safe past the Gnome through this fantastic band,
A branch of healing Spleenwort in his hand.
Then thus addressed the power: "Hail, wayward Queen!
Who rule the sex to fifty from fifteen:
Parent of vapors and of female wit,
60 Who give th' hysteric or poetic fit,
On various tempers act by various ways,

---

24 *Megrim* Migraine headache.   **51** *Homer's tripod* In the *Iliad* Vulcan's tripods were placed on golden wheels that rolled in obedience to the wishes of the gods.

Make some take physic, others scribble plays;
Who cause the proud their visits to delay,
And send the godly in a pet to pray.
65   A nymph there is, that all thy power disdains,
And thousands more in equal mirth maintains.
But oh! if e'er thy Gnome could spoil a grace,
Or raise a pimple on a beauteous face,
Like Citron-waters matrons' cheeks inflame,
70   Or change complexions at a losing game;
If e'er with airy horns I planted heads,
Or rumpled petticoats, or tumbled beds,
Or caus'd suspicion when no soul was rude,
Or discomposed the head-dress of a Prude,
75   Or e'er to costive lap-dog gave disease,
Which not the tears of brightest eyes could ease:
Hear me, and touch Belinda with chagrin,
That single act gives half the world the spleen."
      The Goddess with a discontented air
80   Seems to reject him, though she grants his prayer.
A wondrous Bag with both her hands she binds,
Like that where once Ulysses held the winds;
There she collects the force of female lungs,
Sighs, sobs, and passions, and the war of tongues.
85   A Vial next she fills with fainting fears,
Soft sorrows, melting griefs, and flowing tears.
The Gnome rejoicing bears her gifts away,
Spreads his black wings, and slowly mounts to day.
      Sunk in Thalestris' arms the nymph he found,
90   Her eyes dejected and her hair unbound.
Full o'er their heads the swelling bag he rent,
And all the Furies issued at the vent.
Belinda burns with more than mortal ire,
And fierce Thalestris fans the rising fire.
95   "Oh wretched maid!" she spread her hands, and cried,
(While Hampton's echoes, "Wretched maid!" replied)
"Was it for this you took such constant care
The bodkin, comb, and essence to prepare?
For this your locks in paper durance bound,
100 For this with torturing irons wreathed around?
For this with fillets strained your tender head,
And bravely bore the double loads of lead?
Gods! shall the ravisher display your hair,
While the Fops envy, and the Ladies stare!
105 Honor forbid! at whose unrivaled shrine

69 *Citron-waters*   Orange brandy.

Ease, pleasure, virtue, all our sex resign.
Methinks already I your tears survey,
Already hear the horrid things they say,
Already see you a degraded toast,
110 And all your honor in a whisper lost!
How shall I, then, your helpless fame defend?
'Twill then be infamy to seem your friend!
And shall this prize, th' inestimable prize,
Exposed through crystal to the gazing eyes,
115 And heightened by the diamond's circling rays,
On that rapacious hand forever blaze?
Sooner shall grass in Hyde-park Circus grow,
And wits take lodgings in the sound of Bow;
Sooner let earth, air, sea, to Chaos fall,
120 Men, monkeys, lap-dogs, parrots, perish all!"
　　She said; then raging to Sir Plume repairs,
And bids her Beau demand the precious hairs:
(Sir Plume of amber snuff-box justly vain,
And the nice conduct of a clouded cane)
125 With earnest eyes, and round unthinking face,
He first the snuff-box opened, then the case,
And thus broke out—"My Lord, why, what the devil?
Z—ds! damn the lock! 'fore Gad, you must be civil!
Plague on't! 'tis past a jest—nay prithee, pox!
130 Give her the hair"—he spoke, and rapped his box.
　　"It grieves me much" (replied the Peer again)
"Who speaks so well should ever speak in vain.
But by this Lock, this sacred Lock I swear,
(Which never more shall join its parted hair;
135 Which never more its honors shall renew,
Clipped from the lovely head where late it grew)
That while my nostrils draw the vital air,
This hand, which won it, shall for ever wear."
He spoke, and speaking, in proud triumph spread
140 The long-contended honours of her head.
　　But Umbriel, hateful Gnome! forbears not so;
He breaks the Vial whence the sorrows flow.
Then see! the nymph in beauteous grief appears,
Her eyes half-languishing, half-drowned in tears;
145 On her heaved bosom hung her drooping head,
Which, with a sigh, she raised; and thus she said:
　　"Forever cursed be this detested day,
Which snatched my best, my fav'rite curl away!
Happy! ah ten times happy had I been,

118 *Bow*　The bells of St. Mary le Bow, a church in an unfashionable section of town.

150 If Hampton-Court these eyes had never seen!
Yet am not I the first mistaken maid,
By love of Courts to numerous ills betrayed.
Oh had I rather un-admired remained
In some lone isle, or distant Northern land;
155 Where the gilt Chariot never marks the way,
Where none learn Ombre, none e'er taste Bohea!
There kept my charms concealed from mortal eye,
Like roses, that in deserts bloom and die.
What moved my mind with youthful Lords to roam?
160 Oh had I stayed, and said my prayers at home!
'Twas this, the morning omens seemed to tell,
Thrice from my trembling hand the patch-box fell;
The tott'ring China shook without a wind,
Nay, Poll sat mute, and Shock was most unkind!
165 A Sylph too warned me of the threats of fate,
In mystic visions, now believed too late!
See the poor remnants of these slighted hairs!
My hands shall rend what even thy rapine spares:
These in two sable ringlets taught to break,
170 Once gave new beauties to the snowy neck;
The sister-lock now sits uncouth, alone,
And in its fellow's fate foresees its own;
Uncurled it hangs, the fatal shears demands,
And tempts once more, thy sacrilegious hands.
175 Oh hadst thou, cruel! been content to seize
Hairs less in sight, or any hairs but these!"

CANTO V

She said: the pitying audience melt in tears.
But Fate and Jove had stopped the Baron's ears.
In vain Thalestris with reproach assails,
For who can move when fair Belinda fails?
5 Not half so fixed the Trojan could remain,
While Anna begged and Dido raged in vain.
Then grave Clarissa graceful waved her fan;
Silence ensued, and thus the nymph began.
   "Say why are Beauties praised and honored most,
10 The wise man's passion, and the vain man's toast?
Why decked with all that land and sea afford,
Why Angels called, and Angel-like adored?

156 *Bohea* Black tea.   **6** *Anna . . . Dido* Dido and her sister *Anna* begged Aeneas to stay
in Carthage.

Why round our coaches crowd the white-gloved Beaux,
Why bows the side-box from its inmost rows;
15 How vain are all these glories, all our pains,
Unless good sense preserve what beauty gains:
That men may say, when we the front box grace:
'Behold the first in virtue as in face!'
Oh! if to dance all night, and dress all day,
20 Charmed the small-pox, or chased old-age away;
Who would not scorn what housewife's cares produce,
Or who would learn one earthly thing of use?
To patch, nay ogle, might become a Saint,
Nor could it sure be such a sin to paint.
25 But since, alas! frail beauty must decay,
Curled or uncurled, since Locks will turn to grey;
Since painted, or not painted, all shall fade,
And she who scorns a man, must die a maid;
What then remains but well our power to use,
30 And keep good-humor still whate'er we lose?
And trust me, dear! good-humor can prevail,
When airs, and flights, and screams, and scolding fail.
Beauties in vain their pretty eyes may roll;
Charms strike the sight, but merit wins the soul."
35   So spoke the Dame, but no applause ensued;
Belinda frowned, Thalestris called her Prude.
"To arms, to arms!" the fierce Virago cries,
And swift as lightning to the combat flies.
All side in parties, and begin th' attack;
40 Fans clap, silks rustle, and tough whalebones crack;
Heroes' and Heroines' shouts confus'dly rise,
And bass and treble voices strike the skies.
No common weapons in their hands are found,
Like Gods they fight, nor dread a mortal wound.
45   So when bold Homer makes the Gods engage,
And heavenly breasts with human passions rage;
'Gainst Pallas, Mars; Latona, Hermes arms;
And all Olympus rings with loud alarms:
Jove's thunder roars, heaven trembles all around,
50 Blue Neptune storms, the bellowing deeps resound:
Earth shakes her nodding towers, the ground gives way,
And the pale ghosts start at the flash of day!
   Triumphant Umbriel on a sconce's height
Clapped his glad wings, and sat to view the fight:
55 Propped on their bodkin spears, the Sprites survey
The growing combat, or assist the fray.
   While through the press enraged Thalestris flies,
And scatters death around from both her eyes,
A Beau and Witling perished in the throng,

60 One died in metaphor, and one in song.
   "O cruel nymph! a living death I bear,"
   Cried Dapperwit, and sunk beside his chair.
   A mournful glance Sir Fopling upwards cast,
   "Those eyes are made so killing"—was his last.
65 Thus on Mæander's flowery margin lies
   Th' expiring Swan, and as he sings he dies.
      When bold Sir Plume had drawn Clarissa down,
   Chloe stepped in, and killed him with a frown;
   She smiled to see the doughty hero slain,
70 But, at her smile, the Beau revived again.
      Now Jove suspends his golden scales in air,
   Weighs the Men's wits against the Lady's hair;
   The doubtful beam long nods from side to side;
   At length the wits mount up, the hairs subside.
75   See, fierce Belinda on the Baron flies,
   With more than usual lightning in her eyes:
   Nor feared the Chief th' unequal fight to try,
   Who sought no more than on his foe to die.
   But this bold Lord with manly strength endued,
80 She with one finger and a thumb subdued:
   Just where the breath of life his nostrils drew,
   A charge of Snuff the wily virgin threw;
   The Gnomes direct, to every atom just,
   The pungent grains of titillating dust.
85 Sudden, with starting tears each eye o'erflows,
   And the high dome re-echoes to his nose.
      "Now meet thy fate," incensed Belinda cried,
   And drew a deadly bodkin from her side.
   (The same, his ancient personage to deck,
90 Her great great grandsire wore about his neck,
   In three seal-rings; which after, melted down,
   Formed a vast buckle for his widow's gown:
   Her infant grandame's whistle next it grew,
   The bells she jingled, and the whistle blew;
95 Then in a bodkin graced her mother's hairs,
   Which long she wore, and now Belinda wears.)
      "Boast not my fall" (he cried) "insulting foe!
   Thou by some other shalt be laid as low,
   Nor think, to die dejects my lofty mind:
100 All that I dread is leaving you behind!
   Rather than so, ah let me still survive,
   And burn in Cupid's flames—but burn alive."

62 *Dapperwit*   Character in Wycherley's *Love in a Wood.*   **63** *Sir Fopling*   Character in Etherege's *The Man of Mode; or Sir Fopling Flutter.*   **65** *Mæander*   A winding river in Phrygia.

"Restore the Lock!" she cries; and all around
"Restore the Lock!" the vaulted roofs rebound.
105 Not fierce Othello in so loud a strain
Roared for the handkerchief that caused his pain.
But see how oft ambitious aims are crossed,
And chiefs contend till all the prize is lost!
The Lock, obtained with guilt, and kept with pain,
110 In every place is sought, but sought in vain:
With such a prize no mortal must be blest,
So heaven decrees! with heaven who can contest?
     Some thought it mounted to the Lunar sphere,
Since all things lost on earth are treasured there.
115 There Hero's wits are kept in pond'rous vases,
And beau's in snuff-boxes and tweezer-cases.
There broken vows and death-bed alms are found,
And lover's hearts with ends of riband bound,
The courtier's promises, and sick man's prayers,
120 The smiles of harlots, and the tears of heirs,
Cages for gnats, and chains to yoke a flea,
Dried butterflies, and tomes of casuistry.
     But trust the Muse—she saw it upward rise,
Though marked by none but quick, poetic eyes:
125 (So Rome's great founder to the heavens withdrew,
To Proculus alone confessed in view)
A sudden Star, it shot through liquid air,
And drew behind a radiant trail of hair.
Not Berenice's Locks first rose so bright,
130 The heavens bespangling with disheveled light.
The Sylphs behold it kindling as it flies,
And pleased pursue its progress through the skies.
     This the Beau monde shall from the Mall survey,
And hail with music its propitious ray.
135 This the blest Lover shall for Venus take,
And send up vows from Rosamonda's lake.
This Partridge soon shall view in cloudless skies,
When next he looks through Galileo's eyes;
And hence th' egregious wizard shall foredoom
140 The fate of Louis, and the fall of Rome.
     Then cease, bright Nymph! to mourn thy ravished hair,

---

125 *Rome's great founder* Romulus.   **126** *Proculus* A Roman senator who saw Romulus,
founder of Rome, taken to heaven.   **129** *Berenice's locks* Ptolemy III's wife Berenice dedicated her
hair to Venus to insure his safe return from battle, but the hair disappeared and was said to have be-
come the constellation Coma Berenices.   **133** *Beau monde* Fashionable society; literally, beautiful
world.   *Mall* Promenade in St. James's Park.   **136** *Rosamonda's lake* In St. James's Park; asso-
ciated with unhappiness in love.   **137** *Partridge* John Partridge (1644-1715), quack almanac maker
and astrologer.   **138** *Galileo's eyes* A telescope.   **140** *Louis* Louis XIV of France.

Which adds new glory to the shining sphere!
Not all the tresses that fair head can boast,
Shall draw such envy as the Lock you lost.
145 For, after all the murders of your eye,
When, after millions slain, yourself shall die:
When those fair suns shall set, as set they must,
And all those tresses shall be laid in dust,
This Lock, the Muse shall consecrate to fame,
150 And 'midst the stars inscribe Belinda's name.

From An Essay on Man   (I, 35-61)

Presumptuous man! the reason wouldst thou find,
Why formed so weak, so little, and so blind?
First, if thou canst, the harder reason guess,
Why formed no weaker, blinder, and no less!
5 Ask of thy mother earth, why oaks are made
Taller or stronger than the weeds they shade?
Or ask of yonder argent fields above,
Why Jove's satellites are less than Jove?
Of systems possible, if 'tis confessed
10 That Wisdom Infinite must form the best,
Where all must full or not coherent be,
And all that rises, rise in due degree;
Then, in the scale of reasoning life, 'tis plain,
There must be, somewhere, such a rank as man:
15 And all the question (wrangle e'er so long)
Is only this, if God has placed him wrong?
Respecting man, whatever wrong we call,
May, must be right, as relative to all.
In human works, though labored on with pain,
20 A thousand movements scarce one purpose gain;
In God's, one single can its end produce;
Yet serves to second too some other use.
So man, who here seems principal alone,
Perhaps acts second to some sphere unknown,
25 Touches some wheel, or verges to some goal;
'Tis but a part we see, and not a whole.

---

7 *argent* Silver, white.   **8** *Jove's satellites* The apparent surface of the heavens, of which half forms the dome of the visible sky.   **24** *sphere* In the Ptolemaic astronomy a revolving shell in which the stars, sun, planets, and moon are set.

Thomas Gray   (1716–1784)

Elegy Written in a Country Churchyard

The curfew tolls the knell of parting day,
  The lowing herd wind slowly o'er the lea,
The ploughman homeward plods his weary way,
  And leaves the world to darkness and to me.

5 Now fades the glimmering landscape on the sight,
  And all the air a solemn stillness holds,
Save where the beetle wheels his droning flight,
  And drowsy tinklings lull the distant folds;

Save that from yonder ivy-mantled tower
10 The moping owl does to the moon complain
Of such as, wandering near her secret bower,
  Molest her ancient solitary reign.

Beneath those rugged elms, that yew-tree's shade,
  Where heaves the turf in many a moldering heap,
15 Each in his narrow cell forever laid,
  The rude forefathers of the hamlet sleep.

The breezy call of incense-breathing morn,
  The swallow twittering from the straw-built shed,
The cock's shrill clarion, or the echoing horn,
20 No more shall rouse them from their lowly bed.

For them no more the blazing hearth shall burn,
  Or busy housewife ply her evening care:
No children run to lisp their sire's return,
  Or climb his knees the envied kiss to share.

25 Oft did the harvest to their sickle yield;
  Their furrow oft the stubborn glebe has broke;
How jocund did they drive their team afield!
  How bowed the woods beneath their sturdy stroke!

Let not Ambition mock their useful toil,
30 Their homely joys, and destiny obscure;
Nor Grandeur hear with a disdainful smile
  The short and simple annals of the poor.

26 *glebe*   Farmland.

The boast of heraldry, the pomp of power,
   And all that beauty, all that wealth e'er gave,
35 Awaits alike the inevitable hour:
   The paths of glory lead but to the grave.

   Nor you, ye proud, impute to these the fault,
      If Memory o'er their tomb no trophies raise,
   Where through the long-drawn aisle and fretted vault
40   The pealing anthem swells the note of praise.

   Can storied urn or animated bust
      Back to its mansion call the fleeting breath?
   Can Honor's voice provoke the silent dust,
      Or Flattery soothe the dull, cold ear of Death?

45 Perhaps in this neglected spot is laid
      Some heart once pregnant with celestial fire;
   Hands that the rod of empire might have swayed,
      Or waked to ecstasy the living lyre.

   But Knowledge to their eyes her ample page,
50   Rich with the spoils of time, did ne'er unroll;
   Chill Penury repressed their noble rage,
      And froze the genial current of the soul.

   Full many a gem of purest ray serene,
      The dark unfathomed caves of ocean bear:
55 Full many a flower is born to blush unseen,
      And waste its sweetness on the desert air.

   Some village Hampden, that with dauntless breast
      The little tyrant of his fields withstood;
   Some mute, inglorious Milton here may rest,
60   Some Cromwell, guiltless of his country's blood.

   The applause of listening senates to command,
      The threats of pain and ruin to despise,
   To scatter plenty o'er a smiling land,
      And read their history in a nation's eyes,

65 Their lot forbade: nor circumscribed alone
      Their growing virtues, but their crimes confined;

---

41 *storied urn* A funeral vase with an epitaph.   **57** *Hampden* John Hampden (1594-1643), who led opposition to Charles I and was killed in action during the English Civil Wars.   **59** *Milton* John Milton (1608-1674), English poet.   **60** *Cromwell* Oliver Cromwell (1599-1658), Puritan military and political leader during the English Civil Wars.

Forbade to wade through slaughter to a throne,
And shut the gates of mercy on mankind;

The struggling pangs of conscious truth to hide,
70   To quench the blushes of ingenuous shame,
Or heap the shrine of Luxury and Pride
With incense kindled at the Muse's flame.

Far from the madding crowd's ignoble strife,
Their sober wishes never learned to stray;
75 Along the cool, sequestered vale of life
They kept the noiseless tenor of their way.

Yet even these bones from insult to protect,
Some frail memorial still erected nigh,
With uncouth rhymes and shapeless sculpture decked,
80   Implores the passing tribute of a sigh.

Their name, their years, spelt by the unlettered Muse,
The place of fame and elegy supply;
And many a holy text around she strews,
That teach the rustic moralist to die.

85 For who, to dumb forgetfulness a prey,
This pleasing anxious being e'er resigned,
Left the warm precincts of the cheerful day,
Nor cast one longing lingering look behind?

On some fond breast the parting soul relies,
90   Some pious drops the closing eye requires;
E'en from the tomb the voice of Nature cries,
E'en in our ashes live their wonted fires.

For thee who, mindful of the unhonored dead,
Dost in these lines their artless tale relate;
95 If chance, by lonely contemplation led,
Some kindred spirit shall inquire thy fate,—

Haply some hoary-headed swain may say,
"Oft have we seen him at the peep of dawn
Brushing with hasty steps the dews away,
100   To meet the sun upon the upland lawn.

72 *the Muse's flame* In Greek myth the Muses were nine sister goddesses of song and poetry, and of the arts and sciences. Poets traditionally turned to the Muse for poetic inspiration. **73** *madding* Frenzied.   **97** *Haply* By chance.

"There at the foot of yonder nodding beech
  That wreathes its old fantastic roots so high,
His listless length at noontide would he stretch,
  And pore upon the brook that babbles by.

105 "Hard by yon wood, now smiling as in scorn,
  Muttering his wayward fancies he would rove;
Now drooping, woeful-wan, like one forlorn,
  Or crazed with care, or crossed in hopeless love.

"One morn I missed him on the customed hill,
110   Along the heath, and near his favorite tree;
Another came; nor yet beside the rill,
  Nor up the lawn, nor at the wood was he;

"The next, with dirges due, in sad array,
  Slow through the church-way path we saw him borne.
115 Approach and read (for thou canst read) the lay,
  Graved on the stone beneath yon aged thorn."

THE EPITAPH

Here rests his head upon the lap of earth,
  A youth to Fortune and to Fame unknown;
Fair Science frowned not on his humble birth,
120   *And Melancholy marked him for her own.*

Large was his bounty, and his soul sincere;
  Heaven did a recompense as largely send:
He gave to Misery (all he had), a tear;
  He gained from Heaven ('twas all he wished) a friend.

125 *No farther seek his merits to disclose,*
  Or draw his frailties from their dread abode,
(There they alike in trembling hope repose,)
  The bosom of his Father and his God.

William Blake (1757–1827)

The Little Black Boy

My mother bore me in the southern wild,
And I am black, but O! my soul is white;
White as an angel is the English child,
But I am black, as if bereav'd of light.

5 My mother taught me underneath a tree,
And sitting down before the heat of day,
She took me on her lap and kissed me,
And pointing to the East, began to say:

"Look on the rising sun: there God does live,
10 And gives his light, and gives his heat away,
And flowers and trees and beasts and men receive
Comfort in morning, joy in the noonday.

"And we are put on earth a little space,
That we may learn to bear the beams of love;
15 And these black bodies and this sunburnt face
Is but a cloud, and like a shady grove.

"For when our souls have learn'd the heat to bear,
The cloud will vanish, we shall hear his voice,
Saying, 'Come out from the grove, my love & care,
20 And round my golden tent like lambs rejoice.'"

Thus did my mother say, and kissed me,
And thus I say to little English boy:
When I from black, and he from white cloud free,
And round the tent of God like lambs we joy,

25 I'll shade him from the heat till he can bear
To lean in joy upon our Father's knee;
And then I'll stand and stroke his silver hair,
And be like him, and he will then love me.

The Human Abstract

Pity would be no more
If we did not make somebody poor;
And Mercy no more could be
If all were as happy as we.

5 And mutual fear brings peace,
Till the selfish loves increase:
Then Cruelty knits a snare,
And spreads his baits with care.

He sits down with holy fears,
10 And waters the ground with tears;
Then Humility takes its root
Underneath his foot.

Soon spreads the dismal shade
Of Mystery over his head;
15 And the caterpillar and fly
Feed on the Mystery.

And it bears the fruit of Deceit,
Ruddy and sweet to eat;
And the raven his nest has made
20 In its thickest shade.

The Gods of the earth and sea
Sought through Nature to find this tree;
But their search was all in vain:
There grows one in the Human brain.

Auguries of Innocence

To see a World in a grain of sand
And a Heaven in a wild flower,
Hold Infinity in the palm of your hand
And Eternity in an hour.

5 A robin redbreast in a cage
Puts all Heaven in a rage.
A dove-house filled with doves and pigeons
Shudders Hell through all its regions.
A dog starved at his master's gate
10 Predicts the ruin of the State.
A horse misused upon the road
Calls to Heaven for human blood.
Each outcry of the hunted hare
A fiber from the brain does tear.
15 A skylark wounded in the wing,
A cherubim does cease to sing.
The game-cock clipped and armed for fight
Does the rising sun affright.
Every wolf's and lion's howl
20 Raises from Hell a Human soul.
The wild deer, wandering here and there,
Keeps the Human soul from care.
The lamb misused breeds public strife
And yet forgives the butcher's knife.
25 The bat that flits at close of eve
Has left the brain that won't believe.
The owl that calls upon the night
Speaks the unbeliever's fright.

He who shall hurt the little wren
30 Shall never be beloved by men.
He who the ox to wrath has moved
Shall never be by woman loved.
The wanton boy that kills the fly
Shall feel the spider's enmity.
35 He who torments the chafer's sprite
Weaves a bower in endless night.
The caterpillar on the leaf
Repeats to thee thy mother's grief.
Kill not the moth nor butterfly.
40 For the Last Judgment draweth nigh.
He who shall train the horse to war
Shall never pass the polar bar.
The beggar's dog and widow's cat,
Feed them, and thou wilt grow fat.
45 The gnat that sings his summer's song
Poison gets from Slander's tongue.
The poison of the snake and newt
Is the sweat of Envy's foot.
The poison of the honey-bee
50 Is the artist's jealousy.
The prince's robes and beggar's rags
Are toadstools on the miser's bags.
A truth that's told with bad intent
Beats all the lies you can invent.
55 It is right it should be so;
Man was made for joy and woe;
And when this we rightly know
Through the world we safely go.
Joy and woe are woven fine,
60 A clothing for the soul divine;
Under every grief and pine
Runs a joy with silken twine.
The babe is more than swaddling-bands;
Throughout all these human lands
65 Tools were made, and born were hands,
Every farmer understands.
Every tear from every eye
Becomes a babe in Eternity;
This is caught by Females bright
70 And returned to its own delight.
The bleat, the bark, bellow, and roar
Are waves that beat on Heaven's shore.

35 *chafer's sprite* Beetle's spirit.   47 *newt* A small salamander.

The babe that weeps the rod beneath
Writes revenge in realms of death.
75 The beggar's rags, fluttering in air,
Does to rags the heavens tear.
The soldier, armed with sword and gun,
Palsied strikes the summer's sun.
The poor man's farthing is worth more
80 Than all the gold on Afric's shore.
One mite wrung from the labourer's hands
Shall buy and sell the miser's lands:
Or, if protected from on high,
Does that whole nation sell and buy.
85 He who mocks the infant's faith
Shall be mocked in Age and Death.
He who shall teach the child to doubt
The rotting grave shall ne'er get out.
He who respects the infant's faith
90 Triumphs over Hell and Death.
The child's toys and the old man's reasons
Are the fruits of the two seasons.
The questioner, who sits so sly,
Shall never know how to reply.
95 He who replies to words of Doubt
Doth put the light of knowledge out.
The strongest poison ever known
Came from Caesar's laurel crown.
Naught can deform the human race
100 Like to the armour's iron brace.
When gold and gems adorn the plough
To peaceful arts shall Envy bow.
A riddle, or the cricket's cry,
Is to Doubt a fit reply.
105 The emmet's inch and eagle's mile
Make lame Philosophy to smile.
He who doubts from what he sees
Will ne'er believe, do what you please.
If the Sun and Moon should doubt,
110 They'd immediately go out.
To be in a passion you good may do,
But no good if a passion is in you.
The whore and gambler, by the state
Licensed, build that nation's fate.
115 The harlot's cry from street to street
Shall weave Old England's winding-sheet.

98 *Caesar's laurel crown*   The victory wreath of Julius Caesar (100-44 B.C.), who became
dictator of Rome in 49 B.C.   **105** *emmet*   Ant.

The winner's shout, the loser's curse,
Dance before dead England's hearse.
Every night and every morn
120 Some to misery are born.
Every morn and every night
Some are born to sweet delight.
Some are born to sweet delight,
Some are born to endless night.
125 We are led to believe a lie
When we see not through the eye,
Which was born in a night, to perish in a night,
When the Soul slept in beams of light.
God appears and God is Light
130 To those poor souls who dwell in Night,
But does a Human Form display
To those who dwell in realms of Day.

Mock On, Mock On, Voltaire, Rousseau

Mock on, mock on, Voltaire, Rousseau,
Mock on, mock on, 'tis all in vain!
You throw the sand against the wind,
And the wind blows it back again.

5 And every sand becomes a gem
Reflected in the beams divine;
Blown back they blind the mocking eye,
But still in Israel's paths they shine.

The atoms of Democritus
10 And Newton's particles of light
Are sands upon the Red Sea shore,
Where Israel's tents do shine so bright.

Voltaire, Rousseau François Marie Arouet de Voltaire (1694–1778) and Jean Jacques
Rousseau (1712-1778), philosophers of the Enlightenment who criticized religion and the established
order.   **9** *Democritus* Greek philosopher of the fifth century B.C. who postulated the atomic
structure of the world.   **10** *Newton* Sir Isaac Newton (1642-1727), English scientist who held the
theory that light consists of particles, that is, is a material substance.   **11** *Red Sea shore* God
delivered the Israelites from the Egyptians by parting the waters of the Red Sea (Exodus 14).

Robert Burns   (1759–1796)

To a Mouse
On Turning Her Up in Her Nest
with the Plough, November, 1785

Wee, sleekit, cow'rin, tim'rous beastie,
O, what a panic's in thy breastie!
Thou need na start awa sae hasty,
           Wi' bickering brattle!
5 I wad be laith to rin an' chase thee,
           Wi' murd'ring pattle!

I'm truly sorry man's dominion
Has broken Nature's social union,
An' justifies that ill opinion
10   Which makes thee startle
At me, thy poor earth-born companion,
           An' fellow-mortal!

I doubt na, whiles, but thou may thieve;
What then? poor beastie, thou maun live!
15 A daimen icker in a thrave
           'S a sma' request
I'll get a blessin wi' the lave,
           And never miss't!

Thy wee bit housie, too, in ruin!
20 Its silly wa's the win's are strewin!
An' naething, now, to big a new ane,
           O' foggage green!
An' bleak December's winds ensuin,
           Baith snell an' keen!

25 Thou saw the fields laid bare and waste,
An' weary winter comin fast,
An' cozie here, beneath the blast,
           Thou thought to dwell,
Till crash! the cruel coulter past
30   Out thro' thy cell.

---

1 *sleekit* Sleek.   **3** *na* Not.   *awa* Away.   *sae* So.   **4** *bickering brattle* Hurrying scamper.   **5** *wad be laith* Would be loath.   *rin* Run.   **6** *pattle* Plowstaff.   **13** *whiles* Sometimes.   **14** *maun* Must.   **15** *A daimen icker in a thrave* An occasional ear in twenty-four sheaves of grain.   **16** *'S a sma'* It's a small.   **17** *lave* The rest, the others.   **19** *housie* House.
20 *silly wa's* Frail walls.   *win's* Winds.   **21** *naething* Nothing.   *big* Build.   *ane* One.
22 *foggage* Moss.   **24** *Baith snell* Both bitter.   **29** *coulter* Colter, a cutter on a plow to cut the turf.

That wee bit heap o' leaves an' stibble
Has cost thee mony a weary nibble!
Now thou's turn'd out, for a' thy trouble,
      But house or hald,
35 To thole the winter's sleety dribble,
        An' cranreuch cauld!

But, Mousie, thou art no thy lane,
In proving foresight may be vain:
The best laid schemes o' mice an' men
40   Gang aft a-gley.
An' lea'e us nought but grief an' pain
      For promised joy.

Still thou art blest, compared wi' me!
The present only toucheth thee:
45 But och! I backward cast my e'e
      On prospects drear!
An' forward, tho' I canna see,
      I guess an' fear!

31 *stibble* Stubble. **32** *mony* Many. **34** *But house or hald* Without house or possession. **35** *thole* Bear, endure. *dribble* Drizzle. **36** *cranreuch* Hoarfrost. **37** *no thy lane* Not alone. **40** *Gang aft a-gley* Often go amiss. **45** *och* Ach (an exclamation). *e'e* Eye. **46** *drear* Dreary, depressing.

I Love My Jean

Of a' the airts the wind can blaw,
    I dearly like the west,
For there the bonnie lassie lives,
    The lassie I lo'e best:
5 There's wild woods grow, and rivers row,
    And mony a hill between;
But day and night my fancy's flight
    Is ever wi' my Jean.

I see her in the dewy flowers,
10   I see her sweet and fair;
I hear her in the tunefu' birds,
    I hear her charm the air:
There's not a bonnie flower that springs
    By fountain, shaw, or green,
15 There's not a bonnie bird that sings,
    But minds me o' my Jean.

1 *a'* All. *airts* Directions. *blaw* Blow. **3** *bonnie lassie* Attractive girl. **5** *row* Flow. **6** *mony* Many. **11** *tunefu'* Tuneful. **14** *shaw* Wood.

A Red, Red Rose

O, my luve is like a red, red rose
That's newly sprung in June.
O, my luve is like the melodie
That's sweetly played in tune.

5 As fair art thou, my bonnie lass,
So deep in luve am I,
And I will luve thee still, my dear,
Till a' the seas gang dry.

Till a' the seas gang dry, my dear,
10 And the rocks melt wi' the sun:
And I will luve thee still, my dear,
While the sands o' life shall run.

1 *luve* Love.   **8** *a'* All.   *gang* Go.

William Wordsworth   (1770– 1850)

Lines Composed a Few Miles Above Tintern Abbey

Five years have past; five summers, with the length
Of five long winters! and again I hear
These waters, rolling from their mountain-springs
With a soft inland murmur.—Once again
5 Do I behold these steep and lofty cliffs,
That on a wild secluded scene impress
Thoughts of more deep seclusion; and connect
The landscape with the quiet of the sky.
The day is come when I again repose
10 Here, under this dark sycamore, and view
These plots of cottage-ground, these orchard-tufts,
Which at this season, with their unripe fruits,
Are clad in one green hue, and lose themselves
'Mid groves and copses. Once again I see
15 These hedge-rows, hardly hedge-rows, little lines
Of sportive wood run wild: these pastoral farms,
Green to the very door; and wreaths of smoke

Tintern Abbey   The ruins of a medieval abbey located in the valley of the west bank of the River Wye, in Monmouthshire, about five miles north of Chepstow.

Sent up, in silence from among the trees!
With some uncertain notice, as might seem
20 Of vagrant dwellers in the houseless woods,
Or of some Hermit's cave, where by his fire
The Hermit sits alone.
                                    These beauteous forms
Through a long absence, have not been to me
As is a landscape to a blind man's eye:
25 But oft, in lonely rooms, and 'mid the din
Of towns and cities, I have owed to them
In hours of weariness, sensations sweet,
Felt in the blood, and felt along the heart;
And passing even into my purer mind,
30 With tranquil restoration:—feelings too
Of unremembered pleasure: such, perhaps,
As have no slight or trivial influence
On that best portion of a good man's life.
His little, nameless, unremembered acts
35 Of kindness and of love. Nor less, I trust,
To them I may have owed another gift,
Of aspect more sublime; that blessed mood,
In which the burthen of the mystery,
In which the heavy and the weary weight
40 Of all this unintelligible world,
Is lightened:—that serene and blessed mood,
In which the affections gently lead us on,—
Until, the breath of this corporeal frame
And even the motion of our human blood
45 Almost suspended, we are laid asleep
In body, and become a living soul:
While with an eye made quiet by the power
Of harmony, and the deep power of joy,
We see into the life of things.
                                        If this
50 Be but a vain belief, yet, oh! how oft—
In darkness and amid the many shapes
Of joyless daylight; when the fretful stir
Unprofitable, and the fever of the world,
Have hung upon the beatings of my heart—
55 How oft, in spirit, have I turned to thee,
O sylvan Wye! thou wanderer thro' the woods,
How often has my spirit turned to thee!
    And now, with gleams of half-extinguished thought,
With many recognitions dim and faint,
60 And somewhat of a sad perplexity,
The picture of the mind revives again:
While here I stand, not only with the sense

Of present pleasure, but with pleasing thoughts
That in this moment there is life and food
65 For future years. And so I dare to hope,
Though changed, no doubt, from what I was when first
I came among these hills; when like a roe
I bounded o'er the mountains, by the sides
Of the deep rivers, and the lonely streams,
70 Wherever nature led: more like a man
Flying from something that he dreads, than one
Who sought the thing he loved. For nature then
(The coarser pleasures of my boyish days,
And their glad animal movements all gone by)
75 To me was all in all.—I cannot paint
What then I was. The sounding cataract
Haunted me like a passion: the tall rock,
The mountain, and the deep and gloomy wood,
Their colors and their forms, were then to me
80 An appetite; a feeling and a love,
That had no need of a remoter charm,
By thought supplied, nor any interest
Unborrowed from the eye.—That time is past,
And all its aching joys are now no more,
85 And all its dizzy raptures. Not for this
Faint I, nor mourn nor murmur; other gifts
Have followed; for such loss, I would believe,
Abundant recompense. For I have learned
To look on nature, not as in the hour
90 Of thoughtless youth; but hearing oftentimes
The still, sad music of humanity,
Nor harsh nor grating, though of ample power
To chasten and subdue. And I have felt
A presence that disturbs me with the joy
95 Of elevated thoughts; a sense sublime
Of something far more deeply interfused,
Whose dwelling is the light of setting suns,
And the round ocean and the living air,
And the blue sky, and in the mind of man;
100 A motion and a spirit, that impels
All thinking things, all objects of all thought,
And rolls through all things. Therefore am I still
A lover of the meadows and the woods,
And mountains; and of all that we behold
105 From this green earth; of all the mighty world
Of eye, and ear,—both what they half create,
And what perceive; well pleased to recognise
In nature and the language of the sense,
The anchor of my purest thoughts, the nurse,

110 The guide, the guardian of my heart, and soul
    Of all my moral being.
                            Nor perchance,
    If I were not thus taught, should I the more
    Suffer my genial spirits to decay:
    For thou art with me here upon the banks
115 Of this fair river; thou my dearest Friend,
    My dear, dear Friend; and in thy voice I catch
    The language of my former heart, and read
    My former pleasures in the shooting lights
    Of thy wild eyes. Oh! yet a little while
120 May I behold in thee what I was once,
    My dear, dear Sister! and this prayer I make
    Knowing that Nature never did betray
    The heart that loved her; 'tis her privilege,
    Through all the years of this our life, to lead
125 From joy to joy: for she can so inform
    The mind that is within us, so impress
    With quietness and beauty, and so feed
    With lofty thoughts, that neither evil tongues,
    Rash judgments, nor the sneers of selfish men,
130 Nor greetings where no kindness is, nor all
    The dreary intercourse of daily life,
    Shall e'er prevail against us, or disturb
    Our cheerful faith, that all which we behold
    Is full of blessings. Therefore let the moon
135 Shine on thee in thy solitary walk;
    And let the misty mountain-winds be free
    To blow against thee: and, in after years,
    When these wild ecstasies shall be matured
    Into a sober pleasure; when thy mind
140 Shall be a mansion for all lovely forms,
    Thy memory be as a dwelling-place
    For all sweet sounds and harmonies; oh! then,
    If solitude, or fear, or pain, or grief,
    Should be thy portion, with what healing thoughts
145 Of tender joy wilt thou remember me,
    And these my exhortations! Nor, perchance—
    If I should be where I no more can hear
    Thy voice, nor catch from thy wild eyes these gleams
    Of past existence—wilt thou then forget
150 That on the banks of this delightful stream
    We stood together, and that I, so long
    A worshipper of Nature, hither came

115 *Friend* Wordsworth's sister Dorothy, who accompanied him on his tour.

Unwearied in that service: rather say
With warmer love—oh! with far deeper zeal
155 Of holier love. Nor wilt thou then forget,
That after many wanderings, many years
Of absence, these steep woods and lofty cliffs,
And this green pastoral landscape, were to me
More dear, both for themselves and for thy sake!

A Slumber Did My Spirit Seal

A slumber did my spirit seal;
  I had no human fears:
She seemed a thing that could not feel
  The touch of earthly years.

5 No motion has she now, no force;
  She neither hears nor sees;
Rolled round in earth's diurnal course,
  With rocks, and stones, and trees.

London, 1802

Milton! thou shouldst be living at this hour:
England hath need of thee: she is a fen
Of stagnant waters: altar, sword, and pen,
Fireside, the heroic wealth of hall and bower,
5 Have forfeited their ancient English dower
Of inward happiness. We are selfish men;
Oh! raise us up, return to us again;
And give us manners, virtue, freedom, power.
Thy soul was like a star, and dwelt apart;
10 Thou hadst a voice whose sound was like the sea.
Pure as the naked heavens, majestic, free,
So didst thou travel on life's common way,
In cheerful godliness; and yet thy heart
The lowliest duties on herself did lay.

1 *Milton*   John Milton (1608-1674), Wordsworth's idol as a poet.   2 *fen*   Low, flat, swampy land.   4 *hall*   Large public room in a mansion or palace.   *bower*   Inner apartment (in contrast to a hall).   5 *dower*   Inheritance, natural endowment.   14 *lowliest duties*   Milton served, for example, as foreign secretary to Oliver Cromwell.

My Heart Leaps Up

My heart leaps up when I behold
  A rainbow in the sky:
So was it when my life began;
So is it now I am a man;
5 So be it when I shall grow old,
  Or let me die!
The Child is father of the Man;
And I could wish my days to be
Bound each to each by natural piety.

Ode: Intimations of Immortality from Recollections of Early Childhood

1

There was a time when meadow, grove, and stream,
The earth, and every common sight,
    To me did seem
    Apparelled in celestial light,
5 The glory and the freshness of a dream.
It is not now as it hath been of yore;—
    Turn wheresoe'er I may,
      By night or day,
The things which I have seen I now can see no more.

2

10   The rainbow comes and goes,
    And lovely is the rose,
    The moon doth with delight
Look round her when the heavens are bare;
    Waters on a starry night
15   Are beautiful and fair;
  The sunshine is a glorious birth;
  But yet I know, where'er I go,
That there hath past away a glory from the earth.

3

Now, while the birds thus sing a joyous song,
20   And while the young lambs bound
    As to the tabor's sound,

21 *tabor* A small drum, often used to beat time to dancing.

To me alone there came a thought of grief:
A timely utterance gave that thought relief,
  And I again am strong:
25 The cataracts blow their trumpets from the steep;
No more shall grief of mine the season wrong;
I hear the echoes through the mountains throng,
The winds come to me from the fields of sleep,
  And all the earth is gay;
30   Land and sea
  Give themselves up to jollity,
    And with the heart of May
  Doth every beast keep holiday;—
    Thou child of joy,
35 Shout round me, let me hear thy shouts, thou happy shepherd-boy!

4

Ye blessèd creatures, I have heard the call
  Ye to each other make; I see
The heavens laugh with you in your jubilee;
  My heart is at your festival,
40   My head hath its coronal,
The fulness of your bliss, I feel—I feel it all.
  Oh evil day! if I were sullen
  While earth herself is adorning,
    This sweet May-morning,
45 And the children are culling
    On every side,
  In a thousand valleys far and wide,
  Fresh flowers; while the sun shines warm,
And the babe leaps up on his mother's arm:—
50 I hear, I hear, with joy I hear!
  —But there's a tree, of many, one,
A single field which I have looked upon,
Both of them speak of something that is gone:
  The pansy at my feet
55 Doth the same tale repeat:
Whither is fled the visionary gleam?
Where is it now, the glory and the dream?

5

Our birth is but a sleep and a forgetting:
The soul that rises with us, our life's star,

---

25 *cataracts* Waterfalls.   *steep* Mountainside.   **38** *jubilee* A season of celebration.
40 *coronal* Crown, wreath.

60   Hath had elsewhere its setting,
        And cometh from afar:
        Not in entire forgetfulness,
        And not in utter nakedness,
        But trailing clouds of glory do we come
65   From God, who is our home:
        Heaven lies about us in our infancy!
        Shades of the prison-house begin to close
            Upon the growing boy,
        But he beholds the light, and whence it flows,
70   He sees it in his joy;
        The youth, who daily farther from the east
            Must travel, still is Nature's priest,
            And by the vision splendid
            Is on his way attended;
75   At length the man perceives it die away,
        And fade into the light of common day.

            6

        Earth fills her lap with pleasures of her own;
        Yearnings she hath in her own natural kind,
        And, even with something of a mother's mind,
80   And no unworthy aim,
            The homely nurse doth all she can
        To make her foster-child, her inmate man,
            Forget the glories he hath known,
        And that imperial palace whence he came.

            7

85   Behold the child among his new-born blisses,
        A six year's darling of a pigmy size!
        See, where 'mid work of his own hand he lies,
        Fretted by sallies of his mother's kisses,
        With light upon him from his father's eyes!
90   See, at his feet, some little plan or chart,
        Some fragment from his dream of human life,
        Shaped by himself with newly-learnèd art;
            A wedding or a festival,
            A mourning or a funeral;
95   And this hath now his heart,
            And unto this he frames his song:

        81 *homely* Simple, kindly.   **88** *Fretted* Vexed, but perhaps intended in the root sense of
"devoured."

      Then will he fit his tongue
To dialogues of business, love, or strife;
    But it will not be long
100   Ere this be thrown aside,
     And with new joy and pride
The little actor cons another part;
Filling from time to time his "humorous stage"
With all the persons, down to palsied age,
105 That life brings with her in her equipage;
    As if his whole vocation
    Were endless imitation.

    8

    Thou, whose exterior semblance doth belie
     Thy soul's immensity;
110 Thou best philosopher, who yet dost keep
Thy heritage, thou eye among the blind,
That, deaf and silent, read'st the eternal deep,
Haunted for ever by the eternal mind,—
    Mighty prophet! Seer blest!
115 On whom those truths do rest,
Which we are toiling all our lives to find,
In darkness lost, the darkness of the grave;
Thou, over whom thy immortality
Broods like the day, a master o'er a slave,
120 A presence which is not to be put by;
Thou little child, yet glorious in the might
Of heaven-born freedom on thy being's height,
Why with such earnest pains dost thou provoke
The years to bring the inevitable yoke,
125 Thus blindly with thy blessedness at strife?
Full soon thy soul shall have her earthly freight,
And custom lie upon thee with a weight,
Heavy as frost, and deep almost as life!

    9

    O joy! that in our embers
130 Is something that doth live,
    That nature yet remembers
    What was so fugitive!
The thought of our past years in me doth breed

---

102 *cons* Studies, learns.   **103** *"humorous stage"* In Elizabethan England characters in
plays were often designated according to various temperaments called "humors," such as melancholy.
105 *equipage* Coach, horse-drawn carriage.   **132** *fugitive* Brief, fleeting.

Perpetual benediction: not indeed
135 For that which is most worthy to be blest;
Delight and liberty, the simple creed
Of childhood, whether busy or at rest,
With new-fledged hope still fluttering in his breast:—
        Not for these I raise
140   The song of thanks and praise;
    But for those obstinate questionings
    Of sense and outward things,
    Fallings from us, vanishings;
    Blank misgivings of a creature
145 Moving about in worlds not realized,
High instincts before which our mortal nature
Did tremble like a guilty thing surprised:
        But for those first affections,
        Those shadowy recollections,
150   Which, be they what they may,
Are yet the fountain light of all our day,
Are yet a master light of all our seeing;
    Uphold us, cherish, and have power to make
Our noisy years seem moments in the being
155 Of the eternal silence: truths that wake,
        To perish never;
Which neither listlessness, nor mad endeavor,
        Nor man nor boy,
Nor all that is at enmity with joy,
160 Can utterly abolish or destroy!
        Hence in a season of calm weather
        Though inland far we be,
Our souls have sight of that immortal sea
        Which brought us hither,
165   Can in a moment travel thither,
And see the children sport upon the shore,
And hear the mighty waters rolling evermore.

        10

Then sing, ye birds, sing, sing a joyous song!
        And let the young lambs bound
170   As to the tabor's sound!
We in thought will join your throng,
        Ye that pipe and ye that play,
        Ye that through your hearts today
        Feel the gladness of the May!
175 What though the radiance which was once so bright
Be now forever taken from my sight,
        Though nothing can bring back the hour

Of splendor in the grass, of glory in the flower;
    We will grieve not, rather find
180   Strength in what remains behind;
    In the primal sympathy
    Which having been must ever be;
    In the soothing thoughts that spring
    Out of human suffering;
185   In the faith that looks through death,
In years that bring the philosophic mind.

11

And O, ye fountains, meadows, hills, and groves,
Forebode not any severing of our loves!
Yet in my heart of hearts I feel your might;
190 I only have relinquished one delight
To live beneath your more habitual sway.
I love the brooks which down their channels fret,
Even more than when I tripped lightly as they;
The innocent brightness of a new-born day
195   Is lovely yet;
The clouds that gather round the setting sun
Do take a sober coloring from an eye
That hath kept watch o'er man's mortality;
Another race hath been, and other palms are won.
200 Thanks to the human heart by which we live,
Thanks to its tenderness, its joys, and fears,
To me the meanest flower that blows can give
Thoughts that do often lie too deep for tears.

188 *Forebode not* Do not fear, do not anticipate.   192 *fret* Ripple.

Scorn Not the Sonnet

Scorn not the Sonnet; Critic, you have frowned,
Mindless of its just honours; with this key
Shakespeare unlocked his heart; the melody
Of this small lute gave ease to Petrarch's wound;
5 A thousand times this pipe did Tasso sound;
With it Camöens soothed an exile's grief;
The Sonnet glittered a gay myrtle leaf

4 *Petrarch* Italian poet and sonneteer (1304-1374).   5 *Tasso* Italian poet (1544-1595).
6 *Camöens* Portuguese poet (1524-1580).

Amid the cypress with which Dante crowned
His visionary brow: a glow-worm lamp,
10   It cheered mild Spenser, called from Faery-land
To struggle through dark ways; and when a damp
Fell round the path of Milton, in his hand
The Thing became a trumpet; whence he blew
Soul-animating strains—alas, too few!

Samuel Taylor Coleridge   (1772–1834)

Work Without Hope

All nature seems at work. Slugs leave their lair—
The bees are stirring—birds are on the wing—
And Winter slumbering in the open air,
Wears on his smiling face a dream of Spring!
5   And I the while, the sole unbusy thing,
Nor honey make, nor pair, nor build, nor sing.

Yet well I ken the banks where amaranths blow,
Have traced the fount whence streams of nectar flow.
Bloom, O ye amaranths! bloom for whom ye may,
10   For me ye bloom not! Glide, rich streams, away!
With lips unbrightened, wreathless brow, I stroll:
And would you learn the spells that drowse my soul?
Work without Hope draws nectar in a sieve,
And Hope without an object cannot live.

7 *ken* Know.   *amaranths* An imaginary flower that never fades.

George Gorden, Lord Byron   (1788–1824)

From Canto I of Don Juan

136

'Twas midnight—Donna Julia was in bed,
Sleeping, most probably,—when at her door
Arose a clatter might awake the dead,
If they had never been awoke before,
5   And that they have been so we all have read,
And are to be so, at the least, once more;—
The door was fasten'd, but with voice and fist
First knocks were heard, then "Madam—Madam—hist!

137

    "For God's sake, Madam—Madam—here's my master,
10   With more than half the city at his back—
    Was ever heard of such a curst disaster!
      'Tis not my fault—I kept good watch—Alack!
    Do pray undo the bolt a little faster—
      They're on the stair just now, and in a crack
15 Will all be here; perhaps he yet may fly—
    Surely the window's not so *very* high!"

138

    By this time Don Alfonso was arrived,
      With torches, friends, and servants in great number;
    The major part of them had long been wived,
20   And therefore paused not to disturb the slumber
    Of any wicked woman, who contrived
      By stealth her husband's temples to encumber:
    Examples of this kind are so contagious,
    Were *one* not punish'd, *all* would be outrageous.

139

25 I can't tell how, or why, or what suspicion
      Could enter into Don Alfonso's head;
    But for a cavalier of his condition
      It surely was exceedingly ill-bred,
    Without a word of previous admonition,
30   To hold a levee round his lady's bed,
    And summon lackeys, arm'd with fire and sword,
    To prove himself the thing he most abhorr'd.

140

    Poor Donna Julia! starting as from sleep
      (Mind—that I do not say—she had not slept),
35 Began at once to scream, and yawn, and weep;
      Her maid, Antonia, who was an adept,
    Contrived to fling the bed-clothes in a heap,
      As if she had just now from out them crept:
    I can't tell why she should take all this trouble
40 To prove her mistress had been sleeping double.

    22 *her husband's temples to encumber* Horns on the forehead were the traditional symbol of the cuckold, a husband whose wife had betrayed him by having a love affair with another man. **27** *condition* Rank.   **30** *levee* A reception of visitors held upon arising from bed.

141

But Julia mistress, and Antonia maid,
   Appear'd like two poor harmless women, who
Of goblins, but still more of men afraid,
   Had thought one man might be deterr'd by two,
45 And therefore side by side were gently laid,
   Until the hours of absence should run through,
And truant husband should return, and say,
"My dear, I was the first who came away."

142

Now Julia found at length a voice, and cried,
50   "In heaven's name, Don Alfonso, what d'ye mean?
Has madness seized you? Would that I had died
   Ere such a monster's victim I had been!
What may this midnight violence betide,
   A sudden fit of drunkenness or spleen?
55 Dare you suspect me, whom the thought would kill?
Search, then, the room!"—Alfonso said, "I will."

143

He search'd, *they* search'd, and rummaged everywhere,
   Closet and clothes-press, chest and window-seat,
And found much linen, lace, and several pair
60   Of stockings, slippers, brushes, combs, complete,
With other articles of ladies fair,
   To keep them beautiful, or leave them neat:
Arras they prick'd and curtains with their swords,
And wounded several shutters, and some boards.

144

65 Under the bed they search'd, and there they found—
   No matter what—it was not that they sought;
They open'd windows, gazing if the ground
   Had signs or footmarks, but the earth said nought;
And then they stared each other's faces round:
70   'Tis odd, not one of all these seekers thought,
And seems to me almost a sort of blunder,
Of looking *in* the bed as well as under.

63 *Arras* Wall tapestry.

145

During this inquisition Julia's tongue
   Was not asleep—"Yes, search and search," she cried,
75 "Insult on insult heap, and wrong on wrong!
   It was for this that I became a bride!
For this in silence I have suffer'd long
   A husband like Alfonso at my side;
But now I'll bear no more, nor here remain,
80 If there be law or lawyers in all Spain.

146

"Yes, Don Alfonso! husband now no more,
   If ever you indeed deserved the name,
Is't worthy of your years?—you have three-score—
   Fifty, or sixty, it is all the same—
85 Is't wise or fitting, causeless to explore
   For facts against a virtuous woman's fame?
Ungrateful, perjured, barbarous Don Alfonso,
How dare you think your lady would go on so?

147

"Is it for this I have disdain'd to hold
90   The common privileges of my sex?
That I have chosen a confessor so old
   And deaf, that any other it would vex,
And never once he has had cause to scold,
   But found my very innocence perplex
95 So much, he always doubted I was married—
How sorry you will be when I've miscarried!

148

"Was it for this that no Cortejo e'er
   I yet have chosen from out the youth of Seville?
Is it for this I scarce went anywhere,
100   Except to bull-fights, mass, play, rout, and revel?
Is it for this, whate'er my suitors were,
   I favour'd none—nay, was almost uncivil?
Is it for this that General Count O'Reilly,
Who took Algiers, declares I used him vilely?

97 *Cortejo* Spanish term for the acknowledged lover of a married woman.   **104** *took Algiers*
Byron says in a note on this, "Donna Julia here made a mistake. Count O'Reilly did not take Algiers—
but Algiers very nearly took him; he and his army and fleet retreated with great loss, and not much
credit, from before that city, in the year 1775."

149

105 "Did not the Italian *Musico* Cazzani
      Sing at my heart six months at least in vain?
    Did not his countryman, Count Corniani,
      Call me the only virtuous wife in Spain?
    Were there not also Russians, English, many?
110   The Count Strongstroganoff I put in pain,
    And Lord Mount Coffeehouse, the Irish peer,
    Who kill'd himself for love (with wine) last year.

150

    "Have I not had two bishops at my feet?
      The Duke of Ichar, and Don Fernan Nunez?
115 And is it thus a faithful wife you treat?
      I wonder in what quarter now the moon is:
    I praise your vast forbearance not to beat
      Me also, since the time so opportune is—
    Oh, valiant man! with sword drawn and cock'd trigger,
120 Now, tell me, don't you cut a pretty figure?

151

    "Was it for this you took your sudden journey,
      Under pretence of business indispensable,
    With that sublime of rascals your attorney,
      Whom I see standing there, and looking sensible
125 Of having play'd the fool? though both I spurn, he
      Deserves the worst, his conduct's less defensible,
    Because, no doubt, 'twas for his dirty fee,
    And not from any love to you nor me.

152

    "If he comes here to take a deposition,
130   By all means let the gentleman proceed;
    You've made the apartment in a fit condition:—
      There's pen and ink for you, sir, when you need—
    Let everything be noted with precision,
      I would not you for nothing should be fee'd—
135 But as my maid's undrest, pray turn your spies out."
    "Oh!" sobb'd Antonia, "I could tear their eyes out."

153

    "There is the closet, there the toilet, there
      The antechamber—search them under, over;

There is the sofa, there the great arm-chair,
140   The chimney—which would really hold a lover.
I wish to sleep, and beg you will take care
    And make no further noise, till you discover
The secret cavern of this lurking treasure—
And when 'tis found, let me, too, have that pleasure.

154

145 "And now, Hidalgo! now that you have thrown
    Doubt upon me, confusion over all,
Pray have the courtesy to make it known
    Who is the man you search for? how d'ye call
Him? what's his lineage? let him but be shown—
150   I hope he's young and handsome—is he tall?
Tell me—and be assured, that since you stain
Mine honour thus, it shall not be in vain.

155

"At least, perhaps, he has not sixty years,
    At that age he would be too old for slaughter,
155 Or for so young a husband's jealous fears—
    (Antonia! let me have a glass of water.)
I am ashamed of having shed these tears,
    They are unworthy of my father's daughter;
My mother dream'd not in my natal hour,
160 That I should fall into a monster's power.

156

"Perhaps 'tis of Antonia you are jealous,
    You saw that she was sleeping by my side,
When you broke in upon us with your fellows;
    Look where you please—we've nothing, sir, to hide;
165 Only another time, I trust, you'll tell us,
    Or for the sake of decency abide
A moment at the door, that we may be
Drest to receive so much good company.

157

"And now, sir, I have done, and say no more;
170   The little I have said may serve to show
The guileless heart in silence may grieve o'er
    The wrongs to whose exposure it is slow:—
I leave you to your conscience as before,

'Twill one day ask you, *why* you used me so?
175 God grant you feel not then the bitterest grief!
Antonia! where's my pocket-handkerchief?''

158

She ceased, and turn'd upon her pillow; pale
   She lay, her dark eyes flashing through their tears,
Like skies that rain and lighten; as a veil,
180   Waved and o'ershading her wan cheek, appears
Her streaming hair; the black curls strive, but fail,
   To hide the glossy shoulder, which uprears
Its snow through all;—her soft lips lie apart,
And louder than her breathing beats her heart.

159

185 The Senhor Don Alfonso stood confused;
   Antonia bustled round the ransack'd room,
And, turning up her nose, with looks abused
   Her master, and his myrmidons, of whom
Not one, except the attorney, was amused;
190   He, like Achates, faithful to the tomb,
So there were quarrels, cared not for the cause,
Knowing they must be settled by the laws.

160

With prying snub-nose, and small eyes, he stood,
   Following Antonia's motions here and there,
195 With much suspicion in his attitude;
   For reputations he had little care;
So that a suit or action were made good,
   Small pity had he for the young and fair,
And ne'er believed in negatives, till these
200 Were proved by competent false witnesses.

161

But Don Alfonso stood with downcast looks,
   And, truth to say, he made a foolish figure;
When, after searching in five hundred nooks,
   And treating a young wife with so much rigour,
205 He gain'd no point, except some self-rebukes,

188 *myrmidons* Faithful servants.   **190** *Achates* Fidus Achates (faithful Achates), the loyal companion of Aeneas in Virgil's *Aeneid*.

Added to those his lady with such vigour
Had pour'd upon him for the last half hour,
Quick, thick, and heavy—as a thunder-shower.

162

At first he tried to hammer an excuse,
210   To which the sole reply was tears and sobs,
And indications of hysterics, whose
    Prologue is always certain throes, and throbs,
Gasps, and whatever else the owners choose:
    Alfonso saw his wife, and thought of Job's;
215 He saw too, in perspective, her relations,
And then he tried to muster all his patience.

163

He stood in act to speak, or rather stammer,
    But sage Antonia cut him short before
The anvil of his speech received the hammer,
220   With "Pray, sir, leave the room, and say no more,
Or madam dies."—Alfonso mutter'd, "D—n her."
    But nothing else, the time of words was o'er;
He cast a rueful look or two, and did,
He knew not wherefore, that which he was bid.

164

225 With him retired his *"posse comitatus,"*
    The attorney last, who linger'd near the door
Reluctantly, still tarrying there as late as
    Antonia let him—not a little sore
At this strange and unexplain'd *"hiatus"*
230   In Don Alfonso's facts, which just now wore
An awkward look; as he revolved the case,
The door was fasten'd in his legal face.

165

No sooner was it bolted, than—Oh shame!
    Oh sin! Oh sorrow! and Oh womankind!
235 How can you do such things and keep your fame,

214 *Job's*   "Then said his wife unto him, Dost thou still retain thine integrity? curse God, and die" (Job 2:9).   **225** *"posse comitatus"* A body of men summoned by a sheriff in order to maintain peace in a county; literally, power of the county; complete form of the modern word "posse."
229 *"hiatus"* Gap in a series.

Unless this world, and t'other too, be blind?
Nothing so dear as an unfilch'd good name!
But to proceed—for there is more behind:
With much heartfelt reluctance be it said,
240 Young Juan slipp'd, half-smother'd, from the bed.

166

He had been hid—I don't pretend to say
    How, nor can I indeed describe the where—
Young, slender, and pack'd easily, he lay,
    No doubt, in little compass, round or square;
245 But pity him I neither must nor may
    His suffocation by that pretty pair;
'Twere better, sure, to die so, than be shut
With maudlin Clarence in his Malmsey butt.

167

And, secondly, I pity not, because
250   He had no business to commit a sin,
Forbid by heavenly, fined by human laws,
    At least 'twas rather early to begin;
But at sixteen the conscience rarely gnaws
    So much as when we call our old debts in
255 At sixty years, and draw the accompts of evil,
And find a deuced balance with the devil.

168

Of his position I can give no notion:
    'Tis written in the Hebrew Chronicle,
How the physicians, leaving pill and potion,
260   Prescribed, by way of blister, a young belle,
When old King David's blood grew dull in motion,
    And that the medicine answer'd very well;
Perhaps 'twas in a different way applied,
For David lived, but Juan nearly died.

169

265 What's to be done? Alfonso will be back
    The moment he has sent his fools away.

248 *maudlin Clarence in his Malmsey butt*   The Duke of Clarence (1449-1478), a brother of Richard III, was said to have been murdered by being drowned in a butt or cask of malmsey, a strong sweet wine. Shakespeare alludes to the malmsey butt in *Richard III,* I, iv, 277.   **255** *accompts* Accounts.   **258** *Hebrew Chronicle*   See Kings 1.

Antonia's skill was put upon the rack,
   But no device could be brought into play—
And how to parry the renew'd attack?
270   Besides, it wanted but few hours of day:
Antonia puzzled; Julia did not speak,
But press'd her bloodless lip to Juan's cheek.

170

He turn'd his lip to hers, and with his hand
   Call'd back the tangles of her wandering hair;
275 Even then their love they could not all command,
   And half forgot their danger and despair:
Antonia's patience now was at a stand—
   "Come, come, 'tis no time now for fooling there,"
She whisper'd, in great wrath—"I must deposit
280 This pretty gentleman within the closet:

171

"Pray, keep your nonsense for some luckier night—
   Who can have put my master in this mood?
What will become on't—I'm in such a fright,
   The devil's in the urchin, and no good—
285 Is this a time for giggling? this a plight?
   Why, don't you know that it may end in blood?
You'll lose your life, and I shall lose my place,
My mistress all, for that half-girlish face.

172

"Had it but been for a stout cavalier
290   Of twenty-five or thirty—(come, make haste)
But for a child, what piece of work is here!
   I really, madam, wonder at your taste—
(Come, sir, get in)—my master must be near:
   There, for the present, at the least, he's fast,
295 And if we can but till the morning keep
Our counsel—(Juan, mind, you must not sleep)."

173

Now, Don Alfonso entering, but alone,
   Closed the oration of the trusty maid:
She loiter'd, and he told her to be gone,
300   An order somewhat sullenly obey'd;
However, present remedy was none,

And no great good seem'd answer'd if she staid;
Regarding both with slow and sidelong view,
She snuff'd the candle, curtsied, and withdrew.

174

305 Alfonso paused a minute—then began
    Some strange excuses for his late proceeding:
He would not justify what he had done,
    To say the best, it was extreme ill-breeding
But there were ample reasons for it, none
310   Of which he specified in this his pleading:
    His speech was a fine sample, on the whole,
    Of rhetoric, which the learn'd call *"rigmarole."*

175

Julia said nought; though all the while there rose
    A ready answer, which at once enables
315 A matron, who her husband's foible knows,
    By a few timely words to turn the tables,
Which, if it does not silence, still must pose,—
    Even if it should comprise a pack of fables;
'Tis to retort with firmness, and when he
320 Suspects with *one,* do you reproach with *three.*

176

Julia, in fact, had tolerable grounds,—
    Alfonso's loves with Inez were well known;
But whether 'twas that one's own guilt confounds—
    But that can't be, as has been often shown,
325 A lady with apologies abounds;—
    It might be that her silence sprang alone
From delicacy to Don Juan's ear,
To whom she knew his mother's fame was dear.

177

There might be one more motive, which makes two,
330   Alfonso ne'er to Juan had alluded,—
Mentioned his jealousy, but never who
    Had been the happy lover, he concluded,
Conceal'd amongst his premises; 'tis true,
    His mind the more o'er this its mystery brooded

312 *"rigmarole"* A succession of incoherent statements.   **317** *pose* Confuse.

335 To speak of Inez now were, one may say,
     Like throwing Juan in Alfonso's way.

178

  A hint, in tender cases, is enough;
    Silence is best: besides there is a *tact*—
  (That modern phrase appears to me sad stuff,
340   But it will serve to keep my verse compact)—
  Which keeps, when push'd by questions rather rough,
    A lady always distant from the fact:
  The charming creatures lie with such a grace,
  There's nothing so becoming to the face.

179

345 They blush, and we believe them, at least I
    Have always done so; 'tis of no great use,
  In any case, attempting a reply,
    For then their eloquence grows quite profuse;
  And when at length they're out of breath, they sigh,
350   And cast their languid eyes down, and let loose
  A tear or two, and then we make it up;
  And then—and then—and then—sit down and sup.

180

  Alfonso closed his speech, and begg'd her pardon,
    Which Julia half withheld, and then half granted,
355 And laid conditions, he thought very hard, on,
    Denying several little things he wanted:
  He stood like Adam lingering near his garden,
    With useless penitence perplex'd and haunted
  Beseeching she no further would refuse,
360 When, lo! he stumbled o'er a pair of shoes.

181

  A pair of shoes!—what then? not much, if they
    Are such as fit with ladies' feet, but these
  (No one can tell how much I grieve to say)
    Were masculine; to see them, and to seize,
365 Was but a moment's act.—Ah! well-a-day!
    My teeth begin to chatter, my veins freeze—
  Alfonso first examined well their fashion,
  And then flew out into another passion.

182

He left the room for his relinquish'd sword,
370   And Julia instant to the closet flew,
"Fly, Juan, fly! for heaven's sake—not a word—
The door is open—you may yet slip through
The passage you so often have explored—
Here is the garden-key—Fly—fly—Adieu!
375 Haste—haste! I hear Alfonso's hurrying feet—
Day has not broke—there's no one in the street."

183

None can say that this was not good advice,
    The only mischief was, it came too late;
Of all experience 'tis the usual price,
380   A sort of income-tax laid on by fate:
Juan had reach'd the room-door in a trice,
    And might have done so by the garden-gate,
But met Alfonso in his dressing-gown,
Who threaten'd death—so Juan knock'd him down.

184

385 Dire was the scuffle, and out went the light;
    Antonia cried out "Rape!" and Julia "Fire!"
But not a servant stirr'd to aid the fight.
    Alfonso, pommell'd to his heart's desire,
Swore lustily he'd be revenged this night;
390   And Juan, too, blasphemed an octave higher;
His blood was up: though young, he was a Tartar,
And not at all disposed to prove a martyr.

185

Alfonso's sword had dropp'd ere he could draw it,
    And they continued battling hand to hand,
395 For Juan very luckily ne'er saw it;
    His temper not being under great command,
If at that moment he had chanced to claw it,
    Alfonso's days had not been in the land
Much longer—Think of husbands', lovers' lives!
400 And how ye may be doubly widows—wives!

391 *Tartar*   A violent or ferocious person; originally a native inhabitant of Central Asia.

186

Alfonso grappled to detain the foe,
  And Juan throttled him to get away,
And blood ('twas from the nose) began to flow;
  At last, as they more faintly wrestling lay,
405 Juan contrived to give an awkward blow,
   And then his only garment quite gave way;
He fled, like Joseph, leaving it; but there,
I doubt, all likeness ends between the pair.

187

Lights came at length, and man, and maids, who found
410   An awkward spectacle their eyes before;
Antonia in hysterics, Julia swoon'd,
  Alfonso leaning, breathless, by the door;
Some half-torn drapery scatter'd on the ground
  Some blood, and several footsteps, but no more:
415 Juan the gate gain'd, turn'd the key about,
And liking not the inside, lock'd the out.

188

Here ends this canto.—Need I sing, or say,
  How Juan, naked, favour'd by the night,
Who favours what she should not, found his way,
420   And reach'd his home in an unseemly plight?
The pleasant scandal which arose next day,
  The nine days' wonder which was brought to light,
And how Alfonso sued for a divorce,
Were in the English newspapers, of course.

407 *Joseph* In Genesis 39:12 the chaste Joseph rejects the advances of Potiphar's wife: "And she caught him by his garment, saying, Lie with me; and he left his garment in her hand, and fled, and got him out."

Percy Bysshe Shelley (1792–1822)

Hymn to Intellectual Beauty

1

The awful shadow of some unseen power
  Floats though unseen among us,—visiting

Intellectual Conceived by the intellect or the spirit rather than experienced by the senses.
1 *awful* Awe-inspiring.

This various world with as inconstant wing
As summer winds that creep from flower to flower,—
5 Like moonbeams that behind some piny mountain shower,
    It visits with inconstant glance
    Each human heart and countenance;
Like hues and harmonies of evening,—
    Like clouds in starlight widely spread,—
10   Like memory of music fled,—
    Like aught that for its grace may be
Dear, and yet dearer for its mystery.

2

Spirit of Beauty, that dost consecrate
    With thine own hues all thou dost shine upon
15 Of human thought or form,—where art thou gone?
Why dost thou pass away and leave our state,
This dim vast vale of tears, vacant and desolate?
    Ask why the sunlight not for ever
    Weaves rainbows o'er yon mountain river,
20 Why aught should fail and fade that once is shown,
    Why fear and dream and death and birth
    Cast on the daylight of this earth
    Such gloom,—why man has such a scope
For love and hate, despondency and hope?

3

25 No voice from some sublimer world hath ever
    To sage or poet these responses given—
    Therefore the names of Demon, Ghost, and Heaven,
Remain the records of their vain endeavor,
Frail spells—whose uttered charm might not avail to sever,
30   From all we hear and all we see,
    Doubt, chance, and mutability.
Thy light alone—like mist o'er mountains driven,
    Or music by the night wind sent
    Through strings of some still instrument,
35   Or moonlight on a midnight stream,
Gives grace and truth to life's unquiet dream.

4

Love, hope, and self-esteem, like clouds depart
    And come, for some uncertain moments lent.

11 *aught* Anything.

Man were immortal, and omnipotent,
40 Didst thou, unknown and awful as thou art,
Keep with thy glorious train firm state within his heart.
    Thou messenger of sympathies,
    That wax and wane in lovers' eyes—
Thou—that to human thought art nourishment,
45   Like darkness to a dying flame!
    Depart not as thy shadow came,
    Depart not—lest the grave should be,
Like life and fear, a dark reality.

5

While yet a boy I sought for ghosts, and sped
50 Through many a listening chamber, cave, and ruin,
    And starlight wood, with fearful steps pursuing
Hopes of high talk with the departed dead.
I called on poisonous names with which our youth is fed;
    I was not heard—I saw them not—
55   When musing deeply on the lot
Of life, at that sweet time when winds are wooing
    All vital things that wake to bring
    News of birds and blossoming,—
    Sudden, thy shadow fell on me;
60 I shrieked, and clasped my hands in ecstasy!

6

I vowed that I would dedicate my powers
    To thee and thine—have I not kept the vow?
    With beating heart and streaming eyes, even now
I call the phantoms of a thousand hours
65 Each from his voiceless grave: they have in visioned bowers
    Of studious zeal or love's delight
    Outwatched with me the envious night—
They know that never joy illumed my brow
    Unlinked with hope that thou wouldst free
70   This world from its dark slavery,
    That thou—O awful Loveliness,
Wouldst give whate'er these words cannot express.

7

The day becomes more solemn and serene
    When noon is past—there is a harmony

53 *poisonous names* Names of ghosts or spirits in the practice of magic.

75   In autumn, and a luster in its sky,
        Which through the summer is not heard or seen,
        As if it could not be, as if it had not been!
            Thus let thy power, which like the truth
            Of nature on my passive youth
80   Descended, to my onward life supply
            Its calm—to one who worships thee,
            And every form containing thee,
            Whom, Spirit fair, thy spells did bind
        To fear himself, and love all human kind.

William Cullen Bryant   (1794–1878)

Inscription for the Entrance to a Wood

Stranger, if thou hast learned a truth which needs
No school of long experience, that the world
Is full of guilt and misery, and hast seen
Enough of all its sorrows, crimes, and cares,
5   To tire thee of it, enter this wild wood
And view the haunts of Nature. The calm shade
Shall bring a kindred calm, and the sweet breeze
That makes the green leaves dance, shall waft a balm
To thy sick heart. Thou wilt find nothing here
10   Of all that pained thee in the haunts of men
And made thee loathe thy life. The primal curse
Fell, it is true, upon the unsinning earth,
But not in vengeance. God hath yoked to guilt
Her pale tormentor, misery. Hence these shades
15   Are still the abodes of gladness; the thick roof
Of green and stirring branches is alive
And musical with birds, that sing and sport
In wantonness of spirit; while below
The squirrel, with raised paws and form erect,
20   Chirps merrily. Throngs of insects in the shade
Try their thin wings and dance in the warm beam
That waked them into life. Even the green trees
Partake the deep contentment; as they bend
To the soft winds, the sun from the blue sky
25   Looks in and sheds a blessing on the scene.
Scarce less the cleft-born wild-flower seems to enjoy
Existence, than the winged plunderer
That sucks its sweets. The mossy rocks themselves,
And the old and ponderous trunks of prostrate trees
30   That lead from knoll to knoll a causey rude,

30 *causey rude*   A rough paved way.

Or bridge the sunken brook, and their dark roots,
With all their earth upon them, twisting high,
Breathe fixed tranquillity. The rivulet
Sends forth glad sounds, and tripping o'er its bed
35 Of pebbly sands, or leaping down the rocks,
Seems, with continuous laughter, to rejoice
In its own being. Softly tread the marge,
Lest from her midway perch thou scare the wren
That dips her bill in water. The cool wind,
40 That stirs the stream in play, shall come to thee,
Like one that loves thee nor will let thee pass
Ungreeted, and shall give its light embrace.

John Keats   (1795–1821)

On First Looking into Chapman's Homer

Much have I travelled in the realms of gold,
  And many goodly states and kingdoms seen;
  Round many western islands have I been
Which bards in fealty to Apollo hold.
5 Oft of one wide expanse had I been told
  That deep-browed Homer ruled as his demesne;
  Yet did I never breathe its pure serene
Till I heard Chapman speak out loud and bold:
Then felt I like some watcher of the skies
10   When a new planet swims into his ken;
Or like stout Cortez when with eagle eyes
  He stared at the Pacific—and all his men
Looked at each other with a wild surmise—
  Silent, upon a peak in Darien.

Chapman's Homer   George Chapman (c. 1559-1634) was an English poet and dramatist who in rhymed verse translated Homer's *Iliad, Odyssey,* and *Hymns.*   **4** *fealty* Allegiance.   *Apollo* God of light, truth, music, and poetry.   **6** *demesne* Realm, domain.   **7** *serene* Air.   **11** *Cortez* Hernando Cortez (1485-1547) was the Spanish conqueror of Mexico. Balboa (1475-1517), not Cortez, was the first European to see the Pacific Ocean from Darien (l. 14) in Panama.

On the Grasshopper and the Cricket

The poetry of earth is never dead:
When all the birds are faint with the hot sun,
And hide in cooling trees, a voice will run
From hedge to hedge about the new-mown mead;

4 *mead* Meadow.

5 That is the Grasshopper's—he takes the lead
In summer luxury,—he has never done
With his delights; for when tired out with fun
He rests at ease beneath some pleasant weed.
The poetry of earth is ceasing never:
10 On a lone winter evening, when the frost
Has wrought a silence, from the stove there shrills
The Cricket's song, in warmth increasing ever,
And seems to one in drowsiness half lost,
The Grasshopper's among some grassy hills.

When I Have Fears That I May Cease to Be

When I have fears that I may cease to be
  Before my pen has gleaned my teeming brain,
Before high-pilèd books, in charact'ry,
  Hold like rich garners the full-ripened grain;
5 When I behold, upon the night's starred face,
  Huge cloudy symbols of a high romance,
And think that I may never live to trace
  Their shadows, with the magic hand of chance;
And when I feel, fair creature of an hour,
10   That I shall never look upon thee more,
Never have relish in the faery power
  Of unreflecting love!—then on the shore
Of the wide world I stand alone, and think
Till Love and Fame to nothingness do sink.

2 *gleaned* Gathered the products of, bit by bit. To *glean* literally means to gather grain or other produce left by reapers.   3 *charact'ry* Written symbols.   4 *garners* Grain bins.   11 *faery* Magical.

Ode to a Nightingale

My heart aches, and a drowsy numbness pains
  My sense, as though of hemlock I had drunk,
Or emptied some dull opiate to the drains
  One minute past, and Lethe-wards had sunk:
5 'Tis not through envy of thy happy lot,
  But being too happy in thine happiness—
    That thou, light wingèd Dryad of the trees,

2 *hemlock* A poisonous drink made from the fruit of the herb hemlock.   3 *opiate* A derivative of opium or, more broadly, a narcotic.   4 *Lethe* River of forgetfulness in Hades.
7 *Dryad* Wood nymph.

In some melodious plot
Of beechen green, and shadows numberless,
10   Singest of summer in full-throated ease.

O, for a draught of vintage! that hath been
Cool'd a long age in the deep-delvèd earth,
Tasting of Flora and the country green,
Dance, and Provençal song, and sunburnt mirth!
15 O for a beaker full of the warm South,
Full of the true, the blushful Hippocrene,
With beaded bubbles winking at the brim,
And purple-stainèd mouth;
That I might drink, and leave the world unseen,
20   And with thee fade away into the forest dim:

Fade far away, dissolve, and quite forget
What thou among the leaves hast never known,
The weariness, the fever, and the fret
Here, where men sit and hear each other groan;
25 Where palsy shakes a few, sad, last gray hairs,
Where youth grows pale, and spectre-thin, and dies;
Where but to think is to be full of sorrow
And leaden-eyed despairs,
Where Beauty cannot keep her lustrous eyes,
30   Or new Love pine at them beyond to-morrow.

Away! away! for I will fly to thee,
Not charioted by Bacchus and his pards,
But on the viewless wings of Poesy,
Though the dull brain perplexes and retards:
35 Already with thee! tender is the night,
And haply the Queen-Moon is on her throne,
Cluster'd around by all her starry Fays;
But here there is no light,
Save what from heaven is with the breezes blown
40   Through verdurous glooms and winding mossy ways.

I cannot see what flowers are at my feet,
Nor what soft incense hangs upon the boughs,
But, in embalmèd darkness, guess each sweet

---

13 *Flora* Goddess of flowers.   14 *Provençal* Provence, France, was a medieval poetry and music center.   16 *Hippocrene* A fountain whose waters inspire the poet who drinks from it; on Mount Helicon in southern Greece.   33 *viewless* Invisible.   37 *Fays* Fairies.   43 *embalmèd* Perfumed.

Wherewith the seasonable month endows
45 The grass, the thicket, and the fruit-tree wild;
White hawthorn, and the pastoral eglantine;
Fast fading violets cover'd up in leaves;
And mid-May's eldest child,
The coming musk-rose, full of dewy wine,
50 The murmurous haunt of flies on summer eves.

Darkling I listen; and, for many a time
I have been half in love with easeful Death,
Call'd him soft names in many a musèd rhyme,
To take into the air my quiet breath;
55 Now more than ever seems it rich to die,
To cease upon the midnight with no pain,
While thou art pouring forth thy soul abroad
In such an ecstasy!
Still wouldst thou sing, and I have ears in vain—
60 To thy high requiem become a sod.

Thou wast not born for death, immortal Bird!
No hungry generations tread thee down;
The voice I hear this passing night was heard
In ancient days by emperor and clown:
65 Perhaps the self-same song that found a path
Through the sad heart of Ruth, when, sick for home,
She stood in tears amid the alien corn;
The same that oft-times hath
Charm'd magic casements, opening on the foam
70 Of perilous seas, in faery lands forlorn.

Forlorn! the very word is like a bell
To toll me back from thee to my sole self!
Adieu! the fancy cannot cheat so well
As she is fam'd to do, deceiving elf.
75 Adieu! adieu! thy plaintive anthem fades
Past the near meadows, over the still stream,
Up the hill-side; and now 'tis buried deep
In the next valley-glades:
Was it a vision, or a waking dream?
80 Fled is that music:—Do I wake or sleep?

53 *musèd rhyme* Contemplative verse.   **69** *casements* Window sashes opening on side hinges.

Ode on a Grecian Urn

1

Thou still unravished bride of quietness,
  Thou foster-child of silence and slow time,
Sylvan historian, who canst thus express
  A flowery tale more sweetly than our rhyme:
5 What leaf-fringed legend haunts about thy shape
  Of deities or mortals, or of both,
    In Tempe or the dales of Arcady?
What men or gods are these? What maidens loath?
  What mad pursuit? What struggle to escape?
10   What pipes and timbrels? What wild ecstasy?

2

Heard melodies are sweet, but those unheard
  Are sweeter; therefore, ye soft pipes, play on;
Not to the sensual ear, but, more endeared,
  Pipe to the spirit ditties of no tone:
15 Fair youth, beneath the trees, thou canst not leave
  Thy song, nor ever can those trees be bare;
    Bold Lover, never, never canst thou kiss,
Though winning near the goal—yet, do not grieve;
  She cannot fade, though thou hast not thy bliss,
20   Forever wilt thou love, and she be fair!

3

Ah, happy, happy boughs! that cannot shed
  Your leaves, nor ever bid the spring adieu;
And, happy melodist, unwearièd,
  Forever piping songs forever new;
25 More happy love! more happy, happy love!
  Forever warm and still to be enjoyed,
    Forever panting, and forever young;
All breathing human passion far above,
  That leaves a heart high-sorrowful and cloyed,
30   A burning forehead, and a parching tongue.

a Grecian Urn An urn or vase with sculptured reliefs; ancient urns were used especially as receptacles for the ashes of the dead.   **3** *Sylvan* Woodland.   **7** *Tempe . . . Arcady* Idyllic pastoral landscapes in Greece.   **10** *timbrels* Tambourines.   **29** *cloyed* Surfeited.

4

Who are these coming to the sacrifice?
  To what green altar, O mysterious priest,
Lead'st thou that heifer lowing at the skies,
  And all her silken flanks with garlands dressed?
35 What little town by river or sea shore,
  Or mountain-built with peaceful citadel,
    Is emptied of this folk, this pious morn?
And, little town, thy streets forevermore
  Will silent be; and not a soul to tell
40   Why thou art desolate, can e'er return.

5

O Attic shape! Fair attitude! with brede
  Of marble men and maidens overwrought,
With forest branches and the trodden weed;
  Thou, silent form, dost tease us out of thought
45 As doth eternity: Cold Pastoral!
  When old age shall this generation waste,
    Thou shalt remain, in midst of other woe
Than ours, a friend to man, to whom thou say'st,
  "Beauty is truth, truth beauty,—that is all
50   Ye know on earth, and all ye need to know."

41 *Attic* Athenian or, more generally, Greek.   *brede* Pattern.   **42** *overwrought* That is, in bas-relief, or sculpture in which the figures project only slightly from the background.

Ralph Waldo Emerson   (1803–1882)

Fable

The mountain and the squirrel
Had a quarrel,
And the former called the latter "Little Prig;"
Bun replied,
5 "You are doubtless very big;
But all sorts of things and weather
Must be taken in together,
To make up a year
And a sphere.

4 *Bun* A dialect word for a rabbit's tail and hence a rabbit or a squirrel.

10　And I think it no disgrace
　　　To occupy my place.
　　　If I'm not so large as you,
　　　You are not so small as I,
　　　And not half so spry.
15　I'll not deny you make
　　　A very pretty squirrel track;
　　　Talents differ; all is well and wisely put;
　　　If I cannot carry forests on my back,
　　　Neither can you crack a nut."

Brahma

　　　If the red slayer think he slays,
　　　　Or if the slain think he is slain,
　　　They know not well the subtle ways
　　　　I keep, and pass, and turn again.

5　Far or forgot to me is near;
　　　　Shadow and sunlight are the same;
　　　The vanished gods to me appear;
　　　　And one to me are shame and fame.

　　　They reckon ill who leave me out;
10　　When me they fly, I am the wings;
　　　I am the doubter and the doubt,
　　　　And I the hymn the Brahmin sings.

　　　The strong gods pine for my abode,
　　　　And pine in vain the sacred Seven;
15　But thou, meek lover of the good!
　　　　Find me, and turn thy back on heaven.

Brahma   In the Hindu religion God, the creator and the ultimate reality of the universe.
1 *red slayer* Death.   **10** *fly* Flee from.   **12** *Brahmin* Hindu of the highest caste and worshipper of Brahma.   **14** *Seven* Highest ranking saints in the Hindu religion.

Edward Fitzgerald   (1809–1883)

From The Rubáiyát of Omar Khayyám

1

Wake! for the Sun, who scattered into flight
The Stars before him from the Field of Night,
   Drives Night along with them from Heav'n, and strikes
The Sultán's Turret with a Shaft of Light.

2

5 Before the phantom of False morning died,
Methought a Voice within the Tavern cried,
   "When all the Temple is prepared within,
Why nods the drowsy Worshipper outside?"

3

And, as the cock crew, those who stood before
10 The Tavern shouted—"Open then the Door!
   You know how little while we have to stay,
And, once departed, may return no more."

4

Now the New Year reviving old Desires,
The thoughtful Soul to Solitude retires,
15   Where the White Hand of Moses on the Bough
Puts out, and Jesus from the Ground suspires.

5

Iram indeed is gone with all his Rose,
And Jamshyd's Sev'n-ring'd Cup where no one knows;
   But still a Ruby kindles in the Vine,
20 And many a Garden by the Water blows.

Omar Khayyám   Persian poet and astronomer (c. 1050-1123).   **15** *the White Hand of Moses on the Bough*   Moses "put his hand into his bosom: and when he took it out, behold, his hand was leprous as snow" (Exodus 4:6).   **17** *Iram*   A Persian royal garden, now lost.   **18** *Jamshyd*   In Persian myth a god who boasted of his immortality and was compelled to live on earth for 700 years, becoming a Persian king. His cup, invented by Kaikhosrú (l. 38), great grandson of Kaikobád (l. 36), was decorated with signs whereby its owner could foretell the future.

6

And David's lips are lockt; but in divine
High-piping Pehleví, with "Wine! Wine! Wine!
   Red Wine!"—the Nightingale cries to the Rose
That sallow cheek of hers to incarnadine.

7

25 Come, fill the Cup, and in the fire of Spring
Your Winter-garment of Repentance fling:
   The Bird of Time has but a little way
To flutter—and the Bird is on the Wing.

8

   Whether at Naishápúr or Babylon,
30 Whether the Cup with sweet or bitter run,
   The Wine of Life keeps oozing drop by drop,
The Leaves of Life keep falling one by one.

9

Each morn a thousand Roses brings, you say;
Yes, but where leaves the Rose of Yesterday?
35   And this first Summer month that brings the Rose
Shall take Jamshyd and Kaikobád away.

10

Well, let it take them! What have we to do
With Kaikobád the Great, or Kaikhosrú?
   Let Zál and Rustum bluster as they will,
40 Or Hátim call to Supper—heed not you.

11

With me along the strip of Herbage strown
That just divides the desert from the sown,
   Where name of Slave and Sultán is forgot—
And Peace to Mahmúd on his golden Throne!

---

   22 *Pehleví* Ancient literary language of Persia.   **29** *Naishápúr* City in Persia and birthplace of Omar Khayyám.   *Babylon* Large Persian city, reknowned for its luxury and wickedness. **36** *Jamshyd, Kaikobád* See note to line 18.   **39** *Zál, Rustum* In Persian myth *Rustum* was a mighty warrior. *Zál* was his father.   **40** *Hátim* Persian chieftan known for his hospitality. **44** *Mahmúd* Sultan of Ghazni, in Afghanistan (971-1031).

12

45 A Book of Verses underneath the Bough,
A Jug of Wine, a Loaf of Bread—and Thou
   Beside me singing in the Wilderness—
Oh, Wilderness were Paradise enow!

13

Some for the Glories of This World; and some
50 Sigh for the Prophet's Paradise to come;
   Ah, take the Cash, and let the Credit go,
Nor heed the rumble of a distant Drum!

14

Look to the blowing Rose about us—"Lo,
"Laughing," she says, "into the world I blow,
55   "At once the silken tassel of my Purse
"Tear, and its Treasure on the Garden throw."

15

And those who husbanded the Golden grain,
And those who flung it to the winds like Rain,
   Alike to no such aureate Earth are turned
60 As, buried once, Men want dug up again.

16

The Worldly Hope men set their Hearts upon
Turns ashes—or it prospers; and anon,
   Like Snow upon the Desert's dusty Face,
Lighting a little hour or two—is gone.

19

65 I sometimes think that never blows so red
The Rose as where some buried Caesar bled;
   That every Hyacinth the Garden wears
Dropt in her Lap from some once lovely Head.

50 *the Prophet* Mohammed.

29

Into this Universe, and *Why* not knowing
70   Nor *Whence,* like Water willy-nilly flowing;
      And out of it, as Wind along the Waste,
      I know not *Whither,* willy-nilly blowing.

49

Would you that spangle of Existence spend
About THE SECRET—quick about it, Friend!
75   A Hair perhaps divides the False and True—
      And upon what, prithee, may life depend?

64

Strange, is it not? that of the myriads who
Before us passed the door of Darkness through,
      Not one returns to tell us of the Road,
80 Which to discover we must travel too.

66

I sent my Soul through the Invisible,
Some letter of that Afterlife to spell:
      And by and by my Soul returned to me,
      And answered "I Myself am Heav'n and Hell:"

67

85 Heav'n but the Vision of fulfilled Desire,
      And Hell the Shadow from a Soul on fire,
      Cast on the Darkness into which Ourselves,
      So late emerged from, shall so soon expire.

71

The Moving Finger writes; and, having writ,
90 Moves on: nor all your Piety nor Wit
      Shall lure it back to cancel half a Line,
      Nor all your Tears wash out a Word of it.

96

Yet Ah, that Spring should vanish with the Rose!
That Youth's sweet-scented manuscript should close!

95   The Nightingale that in the branches sang,
Ah whence, and whither flown again, who knows!

99

Ah Love! could you and I with Him conspire
To grasp this sorry Scheme of Things entire,
    Would not we shatter it to bits—and then
100 Remold it nearer to the Heart's Desire!

Alfred, Lord Tennyson   (1809–1892)

Mariana

> "Mariana in the moated grange."
> *Measure for Measure*

With blackest moss the flower-plots
    Were thickly crusted, one and all:
The rusted nails fell from the knots
    That held the pear to the gable-wall.
5 The broken sheds look'd sad and strange:
    Unlifted was the clinking latch;
    Weeded and worn the ancient thatch
Upon the lonely moated grange.
        She only said, "My life is dreary,
10   He cometh not," she said;
        She said, "I am aweary, aweary,
            I would that I were dead!"

Her tears fell with the dews at even;
    Her tears fell ere the dews were dried:
15 She could not look on the sweet heaven,
    Either at morn or eventide.
After the flitting of the bats,
    When thickest dark did trance the sky,
    She drew her casement-curtain by,
20 And glanced athwart the glooming flats.
        She only said, "The night is dreary,
            He cometh not," she said;
        She said, "I am aweary, aweary,
            I would that I were dead!"

19 *casement-curtain* Window curtain.   20 *athwart* Across.   *glooming* Looking dark or threatening.

25 Upon the middle of the night,
        Waking she heard the night-fowl crow:
    The cock sung out an hour ere light:
        From the dark fen the oxen's low
    Came to her: without hope of change,
30   In sleep she seem'd to walk forlorn,
        Till cold winds woke the gray-eyed morn
    About the lonely moated grange.
            She only said, "The day is dreary,
                He cometh not," she said;
35   She said, "I am aweary, aweary,
                I would that I were dead!"

    About a stone-cast from the wall
        A sluice with blacken'd waters slept,
    And o'er it many, round and small,
40   The cluster'd marish-mosses crept.
    Hard by a poplar shook alway,
        All silver-green with gnarled bark:
    For leagues no other tree did mark
    The level waste, the rounding gray.
45   She only said, "My life is dreary,
                He cometh not," she said;
            She said, "I am aweary, aweary,
                I would that I were dead!"

    And ever when the moon was low,
50   And the shrill winds were up and away,
    In the white curtain, to and fro,
        She saw the gusty shadow sway.
    But when the moon was very low,
        And wild winds bound within their cell,
55   The shadow of the poplar fell
    Upon her bed, across her brow.
            She only said, "The night is dreary,
                He cometh not," she said;
            She said, "I am aweary, aweary,
60   I would that I were dead!"

    All day within the dreamy house,
        The doors upon their hinges creak'd;
    The blue fly sung in the pane; the mouse
        Behind the mouldering wainscot shriek'd,
65 Or from the crevice peer'd about.

40 *marish-mosses* Marshy mosses.

Old faces glimmer'd thro' the doors,
Old footsteps trod the upper floors,
Old voices called her from without.
    She only said, "My life is dreary,
70   He cometh not," she said;
    She said, "I am aweary, aweary,
      I would that I were dead!"

The sparrow's chirrup on the roof,
    The slow clock ticking, and the sound
75 Which to the wooing wind aloof
    The poplar made, did all confound
Her sense; but most she loathed the hour
    When the thick-moted sunbeam lay
Athwart the chambers, and the day
80 Was sloping toward his western bower.
    Then, said she, "I am very dreary,
      He will not come," she said;
    She wept, "I am aweary, aweary,
      Oh God, that I were dead!"

Break, Break, Break

Break, break, break,
  On thy cold gray stones, O Sea!
And I would that my tongue could utter
  The thoughts that arise in me.

5 O well for the fisherman's boy,
  That he shouts with his sister at play!
O well for the sailor lad,
  That he sings in his boat on the bay!

And the stately ships go on
10   To their haven under the hill;
But O for the touch of a vanish'd hand,
  And the sound of a voice that is still!

Break, break, break,
  At the foot of thy crags, O Sea!
15 But the tender grace of a day that is dead
  Will never come back to me.

From IN MEMORIAM A. H. H.

15

Tonight the winds begin to rise
  And roar from yonder dropping day;
  The last red leaf is whirled away,
The rooks are blown about the skies;

5 The forest cracked, the waters curled,
    The cattle huddled on the lea;
    And wildly dashed on tower and tree
The sunbeam strikes along the world:

And but for fancies, which aver
10   That all thy motions gently pass
    Athwart a plane of molten glass,
I scarce could brook the strain and stir

That makes the barren branches loud;
  And but for fear it is not so,
15   The wild unrest that lives in woe
Would dote and pore on yonder cloud

That rises upward always higher,
  And onward drags a laboring breast,
  And topples round the dreary west,
20 A looming bastion fringed with fire.

4 *rooks* Birds, crows. **6** *lea* Pasture. **11** *Athwart* Across. **16** *pore* Gaze intently.

54

O, yet we trust that somehow good
  Will be the final goal of ill,
  To pangs of nature, sins of will,
Defects of doubt, and taints of blood;

5 That nothing walks with aimless feet;
    That not one life shall be destroyed,
    Or cast as rubbish to the void,
When God hath made the pile complete;

That not a worm is cloven in vain;
10   That not a moth with vain desire

Is shrivelled in a fruitless fire,
Or but subserves another's gain.

Behold, we know not anything;
  I can but trust that good shall fall
15 At last—far off—at last, to all,
And every winter change to spring.

So runs my dream; but what am I?
  An infant crying in the night;
  An infant crying for the light,
20 And with no language but a cry.

Northern Farmer
New Style

I

Dosn't thou 'ear my 'erse's legs, as they canters awaäy?
Proputty, proputty, proputty—that's what I 'ears 'em saäy.
Proputty, proputty, proputty—Sam, thou 's an ass for thy paaïns;
Theer's moor sense i' one o' 'is legs, nor in all thy braaïns.

II

5 Woä—theer 's a craw to pluck wi' tha, Sam: yon's Parson's 'ouse—
Dosn't thou knaw that a man mun be eäther a man or a mouse?
Time to think on it then; for thou'll be twenty to weeäk.
Proputty, proputty—woä then, woä—let ma 'ear mysén speäk.

III

Me an' thy muther, Sammy, 'as beän a-talkin' o' thee;
10 Thou's beän talkin' to muther, an' she beän a-tellin' it me.
Thou'll not marry for munny—thou's sweet upo' Parson's lass—
Noä—thou'll marry for luvv—an' we boäth on us thinks tha an ass.

IV

Seeä'd her to-daäy goä by—Saäint's-daäy—they was ringing the bells.
She's a beauty, thou thinks—an' soä is scoors o' gells,

1 *'ear* Hear. *'erse's* Horse's. 2 *Proputty* Property. 4 *moor* More. *nor in* Than in. 5 *craw to pluck* Crow to pluck, matter to dispute. *'ouse* House. 6 *knaw* Know. *mun* May. *eäther* Either. 7 *twenty to weeäk* Twenty in a week. 8 *mysén* Myself. 9 *'as beän* Have been. 11 *munny* Money. 12 *tha* Thou (you). 14 *scoors o' gells* Scores of girls.

15   Them as 'as munny an' all—wot's a beauty?—the flower as blaws.
     But proputty, proputty sticks, an' proputty, proputty graws.

V

     Do'ant be stunt; taäke time. I knaws what maäkes tha sa mad.
     Warn't I craäzed fur the lasses mysén when I wur a lad?
     But I knaw'd a Quaäker feller as often 'as towd ma this:
20   "Doänt thou marry for munny, but goä wheer munny is!"

VI

     An' I went wheer munny war; an' thy muther coom to 'and,
     Wi' lots o' munny laaïd by, an' a nicetish bit o' land.
     Maäybe she warn't a beauty—I niver giv it a thowt—
     But warn't she as good to cuddle an' kiss as a lass as 'ant nowt?

VII

25   Parson's lass 'ant nowt, an' she weant 'a nowt when 'e's deäd,
     Mun be a guvness, lad, or summut, and addle her breäd.
     Why? fur 'e's nobbut a curate, an' weänt niver get hissén clear,
     An' 'e maäde the bed as 'e ligs on afoor 'e coom'd to the shere.

VIII

     An' thin 'e coom'd to the parish wi' lots o' Varsity debt,
30   Stook to his taaïl they did, an' 'e 'ant got shut on 'em yet.
     An' 'e ligs on 'is back i' the grip, wi' noän to lend 'im a shuvv,
     Woorse nor a far-welter'd yowe; fur, Sammy, 'e married fur luvv.

IX

     Luvv? what's luvv? thou can luvv thy lass an' 'er munny too,
     Maäkin' 'em goä togither, as they've good right to do.
35   Couldn I luvv thy muther by cause o' 'er munny laaïd by?
     Naäy—fur I luvv'd 'er a vast sight moor fur it; reäson why.

---

15 *wot's* What's.   *blaws* Blows.   **16** *graws* Grows.   **17** *Do'ant be stunt* Don't be obstinate.   **19** *towd ma* Told me.   **21** *war* Was.   *coom to 'and* Came to land, inherited land. **23** *niver* Never.   *thowt* Thought.   **24** *'ant nowt* Has nothing.   **25** *weant 'a nowt* Won't have anything.   *'e's* He's.   **26** *guvness* Governess.   *summut* Something.   *addle* Earn. **27** *nobbut* Nothing but.   *weänt niver get hissén clear* Will never get himself clear, will never be out of debt.   **28** *ligs on* Lies on.   *afoor 'e coom'd* Before he came.   *shere* Shire.   **29** *thin* Then.   *Varsity* University.   **30** *Stook to his taaïl* Stuck to his tail.   *'ant got shut on 'em* Hasn't gotten clear of them.   **31** *ligs* Lies.   *grip* An open furrow or ditch.   *noän* No one. **32** *far-welter'd yowe* A prostrate ewe, or female sheep.

X

Ay, an' thy muther says thou wants to marry the lass,
Cooms of a gentleman burn; an' we boäth on us thinks tha an ass.
Woä then, proputty, wiltha?—an ass as near as mays nowt—
40 Woä then, wiltha? dangtha!—the bees is as fell as owt.

XI

Breäk me a bit o' the esh for his 'eäd, lad, out o' the fence!
Gentleman burn! what's gentleman burn? is it shillins an' pence?
Proputty, proputty's ivrything 'ere, an', Sammy, I'm blest
If it isn't the saäme oop yonder, fur them as 'as it's the best.

XII

45 Tis 'n them as 'as munny as breäks into 'ouses an' steäls,
Them as 'as coäts to their backs an' taäkes their regular meäls.
Noä, but it's them as niver knaws wheer a meäl's to be 'ad.
Taäke my word for it, Sammy, the poor in a loomp is bad.

XIII

Them or thir feythers, tha sees, mun 'a beän a laäzy lot,
50 Fur work mun 'a gone to the gittin' whiniver munny was got.
Feyther 'ad ammost nowt; leästways 'is munny was 'id.
But 'e tued an' moil'd issén deäd, an' 'e died a good un, 'e did.

XIV

Looök thou theer wheer Wrigglesby beck cooms out by the 'ill!
Feyther run oop to the farm, an' I runs oop to the mill;
55 An' I'll run oop to the brig, an' that thou'll live to see;
And if thou marries a good un I'll leäve the land to thee.

XV

Thim's my noätions, Sammy, wheerby I meäns to stick;
But if thou marries a bad un, I'll leäve the land to Dick.—
Coom oop, proputty, proputty—that's what I 'ears 'im saäy—
60 Proputty, proputty, proputty—canter an' canter awaäy.

38 *burn* Born. **39** *wiltha* Will you. *Mays nowt* Makes nothing. **40** *the bees is as fell as owt* The flies are as fierce as anything. **41** *esh* Ash tree. *'eäd* Head. **45** *Tis 'n* It's not. **48** *loomp* Lump. **49** *thir feythers* Their fathers. *mun 'a beän* Might have been. **52** *'e tued an' moil'd issén* He stewed and worked himself. **53** *beck* Brook. *'ill* Hill. **54** *run oop* (His land) ran up. **55** *brig* Bridge. **57** *Thim's* Them's (those are). *noätions* Notions.

Crossing the Bar

Sunset and evening star,
  And one clear call for me!
And may there be no moaning of the bar,
  When I put out to sea,

5 But such a tide as moving seems asleep,
  Too full for sound and foam,
When that which drew from out the boundless deep
  Turns again home.

Twilight and evening bell,
10 And after that the dark!
And may there be no sadness of farewell,
  When I embark;

For though from out our bourne of Time and Place
  The flood may bear me far,
15 I hope to see my Pilot face to face
  When I have crossed the bar.

Robert Browning   (1812–1899)

The Pied Piper of Hamelin
A Child's Story

1

  Hamelin town's in Brunswick,
By famous Hanover city;
  The river Weser, deep and wide,
  Washes its wall on the southern side;
5 A pleasanter spot you never spied;
But, when begins my ditty,
  Almost five hundred years ago,
  To see the townsfolk suffer so
    From vermin, was a pity.

---

1 *Hamelin town's in Brunswick*   The German town of Hamelin lies on the Weser River about twenty-eight miles southwest of Hanover. Brunswick was a German duchy from medieval times to 1918 and is today part of Lower Saxony.

2

10 Rats!
   They fought the dogs and killed the cats,
     And bit the babies in the cradles,
   And ate the cheeses out of the vats,
     And licked the soup from the cooks' own ladles,
15 Split open the kegs of salted sprats,
   Made nests inside men's Sunday hats,
   And even spoiled the women's chats
     By drowning their speaking
     With shrieking and squeaking
20 In fifty different sharps and flats.

3

   At last the people in a body
     To the Town Hall came flocking:
   " 'Tis clear," cried they, "our Mayor's a noddy;
     And as for our Corporation—shocking
25 To think we buy gowns lined with ermine
   For dolts that can't or won't determine
   What's best to rid us of our vermin!
   You hope, because you're old and obese,
   To find in the furry civic robe ease?
30 Rouse up, sirs! Give your brains a racking
   To find the remedy we're lacking,
   Or, sure as fate, we'll send you packing!"
   At this the Mayor and Corporation
   Quaked with a mighty consternation.

4

35 An hour they sat in council;
     At length the Mayor broke silence:
   "For a guilder I'd my ermine gown sell,
     I wish I were a mile hence!
   It's easy to bid one rack one's brain—
40 I'm sure my poor head aches again,
   I've scratched it so, and all in vain.
   Oh for a trap, a trap, a trap!"
   Just as he said this, what should hap
   At the chamber door but a gentle tap?
45 "Bless us," cried the Mayor, "what's that?

15 *sprats* Herring.   **37** *guilder* Gold coin.

(With the Corporation as he sat,
Looking little though wondrous fat;
Nor brighter was his eye, nor moister
Than a too-long-opened oyster,
50 Save when at noon his paunch grew mutinous
For a plate of turtle green and glutinous)
"Only a scraping of shoes on the mat?
Anything like the sound of a rat
Makes my heart go pit-a-pat!"

5

55 "Come in!"—the Mayor cried, looking bigger;
And in did come the strangest figure!
His queer long coat from heel to head
Was half of yellow and half of red,
And he himself was tall and thin,
60 With sharp blue eyes, each like a pin,
And light loose hair, yet swarthy skin,
No tuft on cheek nor beard on chin,
But lips where smiles went out and in;
There was no guessing his kith and kin;
65 And nobody could enough admire
The tall man and his quaint attire.
Quoth one: "It's as my great-grandsire,
Starting up at the Trump of Doom's tone,
Had walked this way from his painted tombstone!"

6

70 He advanced to the council table:
And, "Please your honors," said he, "I'm able,
By means of a secret charm, to draw
All creatures living beneath the sun,
That creep or swim or fly or run,
75 After me so as you never saw!
And I chiefly use my charm
On creatures that do people harm,
The mole and toad and newt and viper;
And people call me the Pied Piper."
80 (And here they noticed round his neck
A scarf of red and yellow stripe,
To match with his coat of the selfsame check;
And at the scarf's end hung a pipe;

51 *glutinous* Sticky, gummy.   **64** *kith* Friends, neighbors, or relatives.

And his fingers, they noticed, were ever straying
85 As if impatient to be playing
Upon this pipe, as low it dangled
Over his vesture so oldfangled.)
"Yet," said he, "poor piper as I am,
In Tartary I freed the Cham,
90 Last June, from his huge swarms of gnats;
I eased in Asia the Nizam
Of a monstrous brood of vampire bats;
And as for what your brain bewilders,
If I can rid your town of rats
95 Will you give me a thousand guilders?"
"One? fifty thousand!"—was the exclamation
Of the astonished Mayor and Corporation.

7

Into the street the Piper stepped,
    Smiling first a little smile,
100 As if he knew what magic slept
    In his quiet pipe the while;
Then, like a musical adept,
To blow the pipe his lips he wrinkled,
And green and blue his sharp eyes twinkled,
105 Like a candle flame where salt is sprinkled;
And ere three shrill notes the pipe uttered,
You heard as if an army muttered;
And the muttering grew to a grumbling;
And the grumbling grew to a mighty rumbling;
110 And out of the houses the rats came tumbling.
Great rats, small rats, lean rats, brawny rats,
Brown rats, black rats, gray rats, tawny rats,
Grave old plodders, gay young friskers,
    Fathers, mothers, uncles, cousins,
115 Cocking tails and pricking whiskers,
    Families by tens and dozens,
Brothers, sisters, husbands, wives—
Followed the Piper for their lives.
From street to street he piped advancing,
120 And step for step they followed dancing,
Until they came to the river Weser,
Wherein all plunged and perished!
    —Save one who, stout as Julius Caesar,

---

89 *Cham*   Khan, ruler of the Tartar empire.   **91** *Nizam*   Hereditary title of the rulers
of Hyderabad, in India.

Swam across and lived to carry
125 (As he, the manuscript he cherished)
To Rat-land home his commentary:
Which was, "At the first shrill notes of the pipe,
I heard a sound as of scraping tripe,
And putting apples, wondrous ripe,
130 Into a cider press's gripe;
And a moving away of pickle-tub boards,
And a leaving ajar of conserve cupboards,
And a drawing the corks of train-oil flasks,
And a breaking the hoops of butter casks;
135 And it seemed as if a voice
(Sweeter far than by harp or by psaltery
Is breathed) called out, 'Oh rats, rejoice!
The world is grown to one vast drysaltery!
So munch on, crunch on, take your nuncheon,
140 Breakfast, supper, dinner, luncheon!'
And just as a bulky sugar puncheon,
All ready staved, like a great sun shone
Glorious scarce an inch before me,
Just as methought it said, 'Come, bore me!'
145 —I found thee Weser rolling o'er me."

8

You should have heard the Hamelin people
Ringing the bells till they rocked the steeple.
"Go," cried the Mayor, "and get long poles,
Poke out the nests and block up the holes!
150 Consult with carpenters and builders,
And leave in our town not even a trace
Of the rats!"—when suddenly, up the face
Of the Piper perked in the market place,
With a, "First, if you please, my thousand guilders!"

9

155 A thousand guilders! The Mayor looked blue;
So did the Corporation too.
For council dinners made rare havoc
With Claret, Moselle, Vin-de-Grave, Hock;
And half the money would replenish

---

138 *drysaltery*   The store of one who deals in dry and salted meats, pickles, and the like.
139 *nuncheon*   Snack.   **141** *puncheon*   A large cask.   **158** *Claret, Moselle, Vin-de-Grave, Hock*
Varieties of wine.

160   Their cellar's biggest butt with Rhenish.
      To pay this sum to a wandering fellow
      With a gypsy coat of red and yellow!
      "Beside," quoth the Mayor with a knowing wink,
      "Our business was done at the river's brink;
165   We saw with our eyes the vermin sink,
      And what's dead can't come to life, I think.
      So, friend, we're not the folks to shrink
      From the duty of giving you something for drink,
      And a matter of money to put in your poke;
170   But as for the guilders, what we spoke
      Of them, as you very well know, was in joke.
      Beside, our losses have made us thrifty.
      A thousand guilders! Come, take fifty!"

      10

      The Piper's face fell, and he cried,
175   "No trifling! I can't wait, beside!
      I've promised to visit by dinner time
      Bagdat, and accept the prime
      Of the Head Cook's pottage, all he's rich in,
      For having left, in the Caliph's kitchen,
180   Of a nest of scorpions no survivor;
      With him I proved no bargain-driver,
      With you, don't think I'll bate a stiver!
      And folks who put me in a passion
      May find me pipe after another fashion."

      11

185   "How?" cried the Mayor, "d'ye think I brook
      Being worse treated than a Cook?
      Insulted by a lazy ribald
      With idle pipe and vesture piebald?
      You threaten us, fellow? Do your worst,
190   Blow your pipe there till you burst!"

      12

      Once more he stepped into the street,
          And to his lips again
      Laid his long pipe of smooth straight cane;

---

160 *Rhenish* Rhine wine.   **177** *Bagdat.* Baghdad.   **178** *pottage* A thick soup.
179 *Caliph* Chief Mohammedan civil and religious ruler.   **182** *bate* Deduct.   *stiver* A small
coin of the Low Countries.   **188** *piebald* Of different colors.

And ere he blew three notes (such sweet
195 Soft notes as yet musician's cunning
    Never gave the enraptured air)
There was a rustling that seemed like a bustling
Of merry crowds justling at pitching and hustling;
Small feet were pattering, wooden shoes clattering,
200 Little hands clapping and little tongues chattering
And, like fowls in a farmyard when barley is scattering,
Out came the children running.
All the little boys and girls,
With rosy cheeks and flaxen curls,
205 And sparkling eyes and teeth like pearls,
Tripping and skipping, ran merrily after
The wonderful music with shouting and laughter.

13

The Mayor was dumb, and the Council stood
As if they were changed into blocks of wood,
210 Unable to move a step, or cry
To the children merrily skipping by
—Could only follow with the eye
That joyous crowd at the piper's back.
But how the Mayor was on the rack,
215 And the wretched Council's bosoms beat,
As the Piper turned from the High Street
To where the Weser rolled its waters
Right in the way of their sons and daughters!
However, he turned from south to west,
220 And to Koppelberg Hill his steps addressed,
And after him the children pressed;
Great was the joy in every breast.
"He never can cross that mighty top!
He's forced to let the piping drop,
225 And we shall see our children stop!"
When, lo, as they reached the mountainside,
A wondrous portal opened wide,
As if a cavern was suddenly hollowed;
And the Piper advanced and the children followed,
230 And when all were in to the very last,
The door in the mountainside shut fast.
Did I say, all? No! One was lame,
And could not dance the whole of the way;
And in after years, if you would blame
235 His sadness, he was used to say—
"It's dull in our town since my playmates left!
I can't forget that I'm bereft

Of all the pleasant sights they see,
Which the Piper also promised me.
240 For he led us, he said, to a joyous land,
Joining the town and just at hand,
Where waters gushed and fruit trees grew
And flowers put forth a fairer hue,
And everything was strange and new;
245 The sparrows were brighter than peacocks here,
And their dogs outran our fallow deer,
And honeybees had lost their stings,
And horses were born with eagles' wings;
And just as I became assured
250 My lame foot would be speedily cured,
The music stopped and I stood still,
And found myself outside the hill,
Left alone against my will,
To go now limping as before,
255 And never hear of that country more!''

14

Alas, alas for Hamelin!
There came into many a burgher's pate
A text which says that heaven's gate
Opes to the rich at as easy rate
260 As the needle's eye takes a camel in!
The Mayor sent east, west, north, and south,
To offer the Piper, by word of mouth,
Wherever it was men's lot to find him,
Silver and gold to his heart's content,
265 If he'd only return the way he went,
And bring the children behind him.
But when they saw 'twas a lost endeavor,
And Piper and dancers were gone forever,
They made a decree that lawyers never
270 Should think their records dated duly
If, after the day of the month and year,
These words did not as well appear,
"And so long after what happened here
On the Twenty-second of July,
275 Thirteen hundred and seventy-six'';
And the better in memory to fix
The place of the children's last retreat,

257 *burgher* Inhabitant of a town.   **258** *a text* ''Again I tell you, it is easier for a camel
to go through the eye of a needle than for a rich man to enter the kingdom of God'' (Matthew 19:24).

They called it, the Pied Pipers Street—
Where anyone playing on pipe or tabor
280 Was sure for the future to lose his labor.
Nor suffered they hostelry or tavern
   To shock with mirth a street so solemn;
But opposite the place of the cavern
   They wrote the story on a column.
285 And on the great church window painted
The same, to make the world acquainted
How their children were stolen away,
And there it stands to this very day.
And I must not omit to say
290 That in Transylvania there's a tribe
Of alien people who ascribe
The outlandish ways and dress
On which their neighbors lay such stress,
To their fathers and mothers having risen
295 Out of some subterraneous prison
Into which they were trepanned
Long time ago in a mighty band
Out of Hamelin town in Brunswick land,
But how or why, they don't understand.

15

300 So, Willy, let me and you be wipers
Of scores out with all men—especially pipers!
And, whether they pipe us free from rats or from mice,
If we've promised them aught, let us keep our promise!

279 *tabor* A small drum.   **290** *Transylvania* A region in central Rumania.   **296** *trepanned*
Tricked, ensnared.

Fra Lippo Lippi

I am poor brother Lippo, by your leave!
You need not clap your torches to my face.
Zooks, what's to blame? you think you see a monk!
What, it's past midnight, and you go the rounds,
5 And here you catch me at an alley's end
Where sportive ladies leave their doors ajar?
The Carmine's my cloister: hunt it up,

Fra Lippo Lippi A Florentine painter (1406-1469).   **3** *Zooks* An exclamation or oath
expressing surprise or vexation.   **7** *Carmine* Maria del Carmine in Florence.

Do,—harry out, if you must show your zeal,
Whatever rat, there, haps on his wrong hole,
10 And nip each softling of wee white mouse,
Weke, weke, that's crept to keep him company!
Aha, you know your betters! Then, you'll take
Your hand away that's fiddling on my throat,
And please to know me likewise. Who am I?
15 Why, one, sir, who is lodging with a friend
Three streets off—he's a certain . . . how d'ye call?
Master—a . . . Cosimo of the Medici,
In the house that caps the corner. Boh! you were best!
Remember and tell me, the day you're hanged,
20 How you affected such a gullet's-gripe!
But you, sir, it concerns you that your knaves
Pick up a manner nor discredit you:
Zooks, are we pilchards, that they sweep the streets
And count fair prize what comes into their net?
25 He's Judas to a tittle, that man is!
Just such a face! why, sir, you make amends.
Lord, I'm not angry! Bid your hang-dogs go
Drink out this quarter-florin to the health
Of the munificent House that harbours me
30 (And many more beside, lads! more beside!)
And all's come square again. I'd like his face—
His, elbowing on his comrade in the door
With the pike and lantern,—for the slave that holds
John Baptist's head a-dangle by the hair
35 With one hand ("Look you, now," as who should say)
And his weapon in the other, yet unwiped!
It's not your chance to have a bit of chalk,
A wood-coal or the like? or you should see!
Yes, I'm the painter, since you style me so.
40 What, brother Lippo's doings, up and down,
You know them and they take you? like enough!
I saw the proper twinkle in your eye—
'Tell you, I liked your looks at very first.
Let's sit and set things straight now, hip to haunch.
45 Here's spring come, and the nights one makes up bands
To roam the town and sing out carnival,
And I've been three weeks shut within my mew,
A-painting for the great man, saints and saints
And saints again. I could not paint all night—

---

17 *Cosimo of the Medici* Cosimo de Medici (1389-1464), Fra Lippo's patron in Florence and a man of great political power.   **20** *gullet's-gripe* Grip on my throat.   **23** *pilchards* Fish. **25** *that man* One of the watchmen who have arrested Fra Lippo.   **47** *mew* A cage for hawks, that is, his quarters at the Medici palace.

50 Ouf! I leaned out of window for fresh air.
    There came a hurry of feet and little feet,
    A sweep of lute-strings, laughs, and whifts of song,—
    Flower o' the broom,
    Take away love, and our earth is a tomb!
55 *Flower o' the quince,*
    I let Lisa go, and what good in life since?
    Flower o' the thyme—and so on. Round they went.
    Scarce had they turned the corner when a titter
    Like the skipping of rabbits by moonlight,—three slim shapes—
60 And a face that looked up . . . zooks, sir, flesh and blood,
    That's all I'm made of! Into shreds it went,
    Curtain and counterpane and coverlet,
    All the bed-furniture—dozen knots,
    There was a ladder! Down I let myself,
65 Hands and feet, scrambling somehow, and so dropped,
    And after them. I came up with the fun
    Hard by Saint Laurence, hail fellow, well met,—
    Flower o' the rose,
    If I've been merry, what matter who knows?
70 And so as I was stealing back again
    To get to bed and have a bit of sleep
    Ere I rise up to-morrow and go work
    On Jerome knocking at his poor old breast
    With his great round stone to subdue the flesh,
75 You snap me of the sudden. Ah I see!
    Though your eye twinkles still, you shake your head—
    Mine's shaved,—a monk, you say—the sting's in that!
    If Master Cosimo announced himself,
    Mum's the word naturally; but a monk!
80 Come, what am I a beast for? tell us, now!
    I was a baby when my mother died
    And father died and left me in the street.
    I starved there, God knows how, a year or two
    On fig-skins, melon-parings, rinds and shucks,
85 Refuse and rubbish. One fine frosty day
    My stomach being empty as your hat,
    The wind doubled me up and down I went.
    Old Aunt Lapaccia trussed me with one hand,
    (Its fellow was a stinger as I knew)
90 And so along the wall, over the bridge,
    By the straight cut to the convent. Six words there,
    While I stood munching my first bread that month:

67 *Saint Laurence* The church of San Lorenzo, located a short distance from the Medici
palace. **73** *Jerome* St. Jerome (340-420), one of the four Doctors of the Church.

"So, boy, you're minded," quoth the good fat father
Wiping his own mouth, 'twas refection-time,—
95 "To quit this very miserable world?
Will you renounce" . . . The mouthful of bread? thought I;
By no means! Brief, they made a monk of me;
I did renounce the world, its pride and greed,
Palace, farm, villa, shop and banking-house,
100 Trash, such as these poor devils of Medici
Have given their hearts to—all at eight years old.
Well, sir, I found in time, you may be sure,
'Twas not for nothing—the good bellyful,
The warm serge and the rope that goes all round,
105 And day-long blessed idleness beside!
"Let's see what the urchin's fit for"—that came next.
Not overmuch their way, I must confess.
Such a to-do! they tried me with their books:
Lord, they'd have taught me Latin in pure waste!
110 *Flower o' the clove,*
All the Latin I construe is, "amo" I love!
But, mind you, when a boy starves in the streets
Eight years together, as my fortune was,
Watching folk's faces to know who will fling
115 The bit of half-stripped grape-bunch he desires,
And who will curse or kick him for his pains,—
Which gentleman processional and fine,
Holding a candle to the Sacrament
Will wink and let him lift a plate and catch
120 The droppings of the wax to sell again,
Or holla for the Eight and have him whipped,—
How say I?—nay, which dog bites, which lets drop
His bone from the heap of offal in the street,—
Why, soul and sense of him grow sharp alike,
125 He learns the look of things, and none the less
For admonition from the hunger-pinch.
I had a store of such remarks, be sure,
Which, after I found leisure, turned to use.
I drew men's faces on my copy-books,
130 Scrawled them within the antiphonary's marge,
Joined legs and arms to the long music-notes,
Found eyes and nose and chin for A's and B's,
And made a string of pictures of the world
Betwixt the ins and outs of verb and noun,
135 On the wall, the bench, the door. The monks looked black.

104 *serge* Fabric.   **121** *the Eight* Magistrates of Florence.   **130** *antiphonary's marge*
Margin of a book containing the choral parts of a divine office.

"Nay," quoth the Prior, "turn him out, d'ye say?
In no wise. Lose a crow and catch a lark.
What if at last we get our man of parts,
We Carmelites, like those Camaldolese
140 And Preaching Friars, to do our church up fine
And put the front on it that ought to be!"
And hereupon they bade me daub away.
Thank you! my head being crammed, the walls a blank,
Never was such prompt disemburdening.
145 First, every sort of monk, the black and white,
I drew them, fat and lean: then, folk at church,
From good old gossips waiting to confess
Their cribs of barrel-droppings, candle-ends,—
To the breathless fellow at the altar-foot,
150 Fresh from his murder, safe and sitting there
With the little children round him in a row
Of admiration, half for his beard and half
For that white anger of his victim's son
Shaking a fist at him with one fierce arm,
155 Signing himself with the other because of Christ
(Whose sad face on the cross sees only this
After the passion of a thousand years)
Till some poor girl, her apron o'er her head,
(Which the intense eyes looked through) came at eve
160 On tiptoe, said a word, dropped in a loaf,
Her pair of earrings and a bunch of flowers
(The brute took growling), prayed, and so was gone.
I painted all, then cried " 'tis ask and have;
Choose, for more's ready!"—laid the ladder flat,
165 And showed my covered bit of cloister-wall.
The monks closed in a circle and praised loud
Till checked, taught what to see and not to see,
Being simple bodies,—"That's the very man!
Look at the boy who stoops to pat the dog!
170 That woman's like the Prior's niece who comes
To care about his asthma: it's the life!"
But there my triumph's straw-fire flared and funked;
Their betters took their turn to see and say:
The Prior and the learned pulled a face
175 And stopped all that in no time. "How? what's here?
Quite from the mark of painting, bless us all!
Faces, arms, legs and bodies like the true

---

139 *Camaldolese*   Members of a religious order at Camaldoli, an upland valley in the Abruzzi, a region of central Italy that includes the Appenines.   **140** *Preaching Friars*   Dominicans.
155 *Signing himself*   Making the sign of the cross.

As much as pea and pea! it's devil's-game!
Your business is not to catch men with show,
180 With homage to the perishable clay,
But lift them over it, ignore it all,
Make them forget there's such a thing as flesh.
Your business is to paint the souls of men—
Man's soul, and it's a fire, smoke . . . no, it's not . . .
185 It's vapour done up like a new-born babe—
(In that shape when you die it leaves your mouth)
It's . . . well, what matters talking, it's the soul!
Give us no more of body than shows soul!
Here's Giotto, with his Saint a-praising God,
190 That sets us praising,—why not stop with him?
Why put all thoughts of praise out of our heads
With wonder at lines, colours, and what not?
Paint the soul, never mind the legs and arms!
Rub all out, try at it a second time.
195 Oh, that white smallish female with the breasts,
She's just my niece . . . Herodias, I would say,—
Who went and danced and got men's heads cut off!
Have it all out!'' Now, is this sense, I ask?
A fine way to paint soul, by painting body
200 So ill, the eye can't stop there, must go further
And can't fare worse! Thus, yellow does for white
When what you put for yellow's simply black,
And any sort of meaning looks intense
When all beside itself means and looks nought.
205 Why can't a painter lift each foot in turn,
Left foot and right foot, go a double step,
Make his flesh liker and his soul more like,
Both in their order? Take the prettiest face,
The Prior's niece . . . patron-saint—is it so pretty
210 You can't discover if it means hope, fear,
Sorrow or joy? won't beauty go with these?
Suppose I've made her eyes all right and blue,
Can't I take breath and try to add life's flash,
And then add soul and heighten them threefold?
215 Or say there's beauty with no soul at all—
(I never saw it—put the case the same—)
If you get simple beauty and nought else,
You get about the best thing God invents:
That's somewhat: and you'll find the soul you have missed,
220 Within yourself, when you return him thanks.

189 *Giotto* A famous Italian painter (1276-1337).   **196** *Herodias* Mother of Salome, who danced before Herod and so pleased him that he promised her anything she asked. Herodias told her to ask for the head of John the Baptist on a platter. See Matthew 14:1-12.

"Rub all out!" Well, well, there's my life, in short,
And so the thing has gone on ever since.
I'm grown a man no doubt, I've broken bounds:
You should not take a fellow eight years old
225 And make him swear to never kiss the girls.
I'm my own master, paint now as I please—
Having a friend, you see, in the Corner-house!
Lord, it's fast holding by the rings in front—
Those great rings serve more purposes than just
230 To plant a flag in, or tie up a horse!
And yet the old schooling sticks, the old grave eyes
Are peeping o'er my shoulder as I work,
The heads shake still—"It's art's decline, my son!
You're not of the true painters, great and old;
235 Brother Angelico's the man, you'll find;
Brother Lorenzo stands his single peer:
Fag on at flesh, you'll never make the third!"
Flower o' the pine,
You keep your mistr . . . manners, and I'll stick to mine!
240 I'm not the third, then: bless us, they must know!
Don't you think they're the likeliest to know,
They with their Latin? So, I swallow my rage,
Clench my teeth, suck my lips in tight, and paint
To please them—sometimes do, and sometimes don't;
245 For, doing most, there's pretty sure to come
A turn, some warm eve finds me at my saints—
A laugh, a cry, the business of the world—
(Flower o' the peach,
Death for us all, and his own life for each!)
250 And my whole soul revolves, the cup runs over,
The world and life's too big to pass for a dream,
And I do these wild things in sheer despite,
And play the fooleries you catch me at,
In pure rage! the old mill-horse, out at grass
255 After hard years, throws up his stiff heels so,
Although the miller does not preach to him
The only good of grass is to make chaff.
What would men have? Do they like grass or no—
May they or mayn't they? all I want's the thing
260 Settled for ever one way. As it is,
You tell too many lies and hurt yourself:
You don't like what you only like too much,
You do like what, if given you at your word,

235-36 *Brother Angelico . . . Brother Lorenzo*   Two painters of the traditional school Lippi
opposes: Angelico (1387-1455), Lorenzo (c. 1370-c. 1425).

You find abundantly detestable.
265 For me, I think I speak as I was taught;
I always see the garden and God there
A-making man's wife: and, my lesson learned,
The value and significance of flesh,
I can't unlearn ten minutes afterwards.

270   You understand me: I'm a beast, I know.
But see, now—why, I see as certainly
As that the morning-star's about to shine,
What will hap some day. We've a youngster here
Comes to our convent, studies what I do,
275 Slouches and stares and lets no atom drop—
His name is Guidi—he'll not mind the monks—
They call him Hulking Tom, he lets them talk—
He picks my practice up—he'll paint apace,
I hope so—though I never live so long,
280 I know what's sure to follow. You be judge!
You speak no Latin more than I, belike;
However, you're my man, you've seen the world
—The beauty and the wonder and the power,
The shapes of things, their colours, lights and shades,
285 Changes, surprises,—and God made it all!
—For what? do you feel thankful, ay or no,
For this fair town's face, yonder river's line,
The mountain round it and the sky above,
Much more the figures of man, woman, child,
290 These are the frame to? What's it all about?
To be passed over, despised? or dwelt upon,
Wondered at? oh, this last of course!—you say.
But why not do as well as say,—paint these
Just as they are, careless what comes of it?
295 God's works—paint anyone, and count it crime
To let a truth slip. Don't object, "His works
Are here already; nature is complete:
Suppose you reproduce her—(which you can't)
There's no advantage! you must beat her, then."
300 For, don't you mark? we're made so that we love
First when we see them painted, things we have passed
Perhaps a hundred times nor cared to see;
And so they are better, painted—better to us,
Which is the same thing. Art was given for that;
305 God uses us to help each other so,
Lending our minds out. Have you noticed, now,

277 *Hulking Tom*   Masaccio (1401-1428), not in fact Lippi's pupil but like Lippi a realist.

Your cullion's hanging face? A bit of chalk,
And trust me but you should, though! How much more,
If I drew higher things with the same truth!
310 That were to take the Prior's pulpit-place,
Interpret God to all of you! Oh, oh,
It makes me mad to see what men shall do
And we in our graves! This world's no blot for us,
Nor blank; it means intensely, and means good:
315 To find its meaning is my meat and drink.
"Ay, but you don't so instigate to prayer!"
Strikes in the Prior: "when your meaning's plain
It does not say to folk—remember matins,
Or, mind you fast next Friday!" Why, for this
320 What need of art at all? A skull and bones,
Two bits of stick nailed crosswise, or, what's best,
A bell to chime the hour with, does as well.
I painted a Saint Laurence six months since
At Prato, splashed the fresco in fine style:
325 "How looks my painting, now the scaffold's down?"
I ask a brother: "Hugely," he returns—
"Already not one phiz of your three slaves
Who turn the Deacon off his toasted side,
But's scratched and prodded to our heart's content,
330 The pious people have so eased their own
When coming to say prayers there in a rage:
We get on fast to see the bricks beneath.
Expect another job this time next year,
For pity and religion grow i' the crowd—
335 Your painting serves its purpose!" Hang the fools!

        —That is—you'll not mistake an idle word
Spoke in a huff by a poor monk, God wot,
Tasting the air this spicy night which turns
The unaccustomed head like Chianti wine!
340 Oh, the church knows! don't misreport me, now!
It's natural a poor monk out of bounds
Should have his apt word to excuse himself:
And hearken how I plot to make amends.
I have bethought me: I shall paint a piece
345 . . . There's for you! Give me six months, then go, see
Something in Sant' Ambrogio's! Bless the nuns!

---

324 *Prato* A town near Florence.   **327** *phiz* Face (a shortened and altered form of physiognomy).   **328** *his toasted side* According to legend St. Laurence, martyred by being roasted on a gridiron, told his executioners to turn him over because he was done on one side. **337** *God wot* God knows.   **346** *Something in Sant' Ambrogio's* Fra Lippo painted the "Coronation of the Virgin" for the high altar of Sant' Ambrogio between 1441 and 1447.

They want a cast o' my office. I shall paint
God in the midst, Madonna and her babe,
Ringed by a bowery flowery angel-brood,
350 Lilies and vestments and white faces, sweet
As puff on puff of grated orris-root
When ladies crowd to church at midsummer.
And then i' the front, of course a saint or two—
Saint John, because he saves the Florentines,
355 Saint Ambrose, who puts down in black and white
The convent's friends and gives them a long day,
And Job, I must have him there past mistake,
The man of Uz (and Us without the z,
Painters who need his patience). Well, all these
360 Secured at their devotions, up shall come
Out of a corner when you least expect,
As one by a dark stair into a great light,
Music and talking, who but Lippo! I!—
Mazed, motionless and moon-struck—I'm the man!
365 Back I shrink—what is this I see and hear?
I, caught up with my monk's-things by mistake,
My old serge gown and rope that goes all round,
I, in this presence, this pure company!
Where's a hole, where's a corner for escape?
370 Then steps a sweet angelic slip of a thing
Forward, puts out a soft palm—"Not so fast!"
—Addresses the celestial presence, "nay—
He made you and devised you, after all,
Though he's none of you! Could Saint John there draw—
375 His camel-hair make up a painting-brush?
We come to brother Lippo for all that,
Iste perfecit opus!" So, all smile—
I shuffle sideways with my blushing face
Under the cover of a hundred wings
380 Thrown like a spread of kirtles when you're gay
And play hot cockles, all the doors being shut,
Till, wholly unexpected, in there pops
The hothead husband! Thus I scuttle off
To some safe bench behind, not letting go
385 The palm of her, the little lily thing
That spoke the good word for me in the nick,
Like the Prior's niece . . . Saint Lucy, I would say.

351 *orris-root* The fragrant root of the iris, used in perfume.   **354** *Saint John* Patron
saint of Florence.   **375** *His camel-hair* "And John was clothed with camel's hair" (Mark 1:6).
377 *Iste perfecit opus* This man accomplished the work.   **380** *kirtles* Women's gowns.
381 *hot cockles* A rustic game in which a blindfolded player guesses who has struck him.
387 *Saint Lucy* A martyr at Syracuse in Sicily. According to legend she was martyred for refusing
to marry because she had taken a vow of virginity.

And so all's saved for me, and for the church
A pretty picture gained. Go, six months hence!
390 Your hand, sir, and good-bye: no lights, no lights!
The street's hushed, and I know my own way back,
Don't fear me! There's the grey beginning. Zooks!

Prospice

Fear death?—to feel the fog in my throat,
    The mist in my face,
When the snows begin, and the blasts denote
    I am nearing the place,
5 The power of the night, the press of the storm,
    The post of the foe;
Where he stands, the Arch Fear in a visible form,
    Yet the strong man must go:
For the journey is done and the summit attained,
10   And the barriers fall,
Though a battle's to fight ere the guerdon be gained,
    The reward of it all.
I was ever a fighter, so—one fight more,
    The best and the last!
15 I would hate that death bandaged my eyes and forbore,
    And bade me creep past.
No! let me taste the whole of it, fare like my peers
    The heroes of old,
Bear the brunt, in a minute pay glad life's arrears
20   Of pain, darkness, and cold.
For sudden the worst turns the best to the brave,
    The black minute's at end,
And the elements' rage, the fiend-voices that rave,
    Shall dwindle, shall blend,
25 Shall change, shall become first a peace out of pain,
    Then a light, then thy breast,
O thou soul of my soul! I shall clasp thee again,
    And with God be the rest!

Prospice Look ahead. **11** *guerdon* Prize. **26** *thy breast* Elizabeth Barrett Browning died in 1861, her husband Robert in 1889.

Walt Whitman   (1819–1892)

From SONG OF MYSELF

1

I celebrate myself, and sing myself,
And what I assume you shall assume,
For every atom belonging to me as good belongs to you.

I loafe and invite my soul,
5   I lean and loafe at my ease observing a spear of summer grass.

My tongue, every atom of my blood, form'd from this soil, this air,
Born here of parents born here from parents the same, and their parents the same,
I, now thirty-seven years old in perfect health begin,
Hoping to cease not till death.

10   Creeds and schools in abeyance,
Retiring back a while sufficed at what they are, but never forgotten,
I harbor for good or bad, I permit to speak at every hazard,
Nature without check with original energy.

5

I believe in you my soul, the other I am must not abase itself to you,
And you must not be abased to the other.

Loafe with me on the grass, loose the stop from your throat,
Not words, not music or rhyme I want, not custom or lecture, not even the best,
5   Only the lull I like, the hum of your valvèd voice.

I mind how once we lay such a transparent summer morning,
How you settled your head athwart my hips and gently turn'd over upon me,
And parted the shirt from my bosom-bone, and plunged your tongue to my bare-
    stript heart,
And reach'd till you felt my beard, and reach'd till you held my feet.

10   Swiftly arose and spread around me the peace and knowledge that pass all the
    argument of the earth,
And I know that the hand of God is the promise of my own,
And I know that the spirit of God is the brother of my own,
And that all the men ever born are also my brothers, and the women my sisters
    and lovers,

And that a kelson of the creation is love,
15 And limitless are leaves stiff or drooping in the fields,
And brown ants in the little wells beneath them,
And mossy scabs of the worm fence, heap'd stones, elder, mullein and poke-weed.

---

14 *kelson* A timber or girder placed parallel and bolted to a ship's keel for strength.
17 *mullein* A woolly-leaved herb.   *poke-weed* A coarse American perennial herb.

17

These are really the thoughts of all men in all ages and lands, they are not original
    with me,
If they are not yours as much as mine they are nothing, or next to nothing,
If they are not the riddle and the untying of the riddle they are nothing,
If they are not just as close as they are distant they are nothing.

5 This is the **grass** that grows wherever the land is and the water is,
This the common air that bathes the globe.

46

I know I have the best of time and space, and was never measured and never will be
    measured.

I tramp a perpetual journey, (come listen all!)
My signs are a rain-proof coat, good shoes, and a staff cut from the woods,
No friend of mine takes his ease in my chair,
5 I have no chair, no church, no philosophy,
I lead no man to a dinner-table, library, exchange,
But each man and each woman of you I lead upon a knoll,
My left hand hooking you round the waist,
My right hand pointing to landscapes of continents and the public road.

10 Not I, not any one else can travel that road for you,
You must travel it for yourself.

It is not far, it is within reach,
Perhaps you have been on it since you were born and did not know,
Perhaps it is everywhere on water and on land.

15 Shoulder your duds dear son, and I will mine, and let us hasten forth,
Wonderful cities and free nations we shall fetch as we go.

If you tire, give me both burdens, and rest the chuff of your hand on my hip,
And in due time you shall repay the same service to me,
For after we start we never lie by again.

20 This day before dawn I ascended a hill and look'd at the crowded heaven,
And I said to my spirit *When we become the enfolders of those orbs, and the*
   pleasure and knowledge of every thing in them, shall we be fill'd and satisfied
   then?
And my spirit said *No, we but level that lift to pass and continue beyond.*

You are also asking me questions and I hear you,
I answer that I cannot answer, you must find out for yourself.
25 Sit a while dear son,
Here are biscuits to eat and here is milk to drink,
But as soon as you sleep and renew yourself in sweet clothes, I kiss you with a
   good-by kiss and open the gate for your egress hence.

Long enough have you dream'd contemptible dreams,
Now I wash the gum from your eyes,
30 You must habit yourself to the dazzle of the light and of every moment of your
   life.

Long have you timidly waded holding a plank by the shore,
Now I will you to be a bold swimmer,
To jump off in the midst of the sea, rise again, nod to me, shout, and laughingly
   dash with your hair.

17 *chuff* Heel.   **21** *orbs* Celestial spheres.

52

The spotted hawk swoops by and accuses me, he complains of my gab and my
   loitering.

I too am not a bit tamed, I too am untranslatable,
I sound my barbaric yawp over the roofs of the world.

The last scud of day holds back for me,
5 It flings my likeness after the rest and true as any on the shadow'd wilds,
It coaxes me to the vapor and the dusk.

I depart as air, I shake my white locks at the runaway sun,
I effuse my flesh in eddies, and drift it in lacy jags.

3 *yawp* A raucous noise, rough vigorous language.   **8** *eddies* Contrary or circular currents.
jags Sharp projecting parts.

I bequeath myself to the dirt to grow from the grass I love,
10 If you want me again look for me under your **boot-soles**.

You will hardly know who I am or what I mean,
But I shall be good health to you nevertheless,
And filter and fibre your blood.

Failing to fetch me at first keep encouraged,
15 Missing me one place search another,
I stop somewhere waiting for you.

The World Below the Brine

The world below the brine,
Forests at the bottom of the sea, the branches and leaves,
Sea-lettuce, vast lichens, strange flowers and seeds, the thick tangle, openings, and
   pink turf,
Different colors, pale gray and green, purple, white, and gold, the play of light
   through the water,
5 Dumb swimmers there among the rocks, coral, gluten, grass, rushes, and the
   aliment of the swimmers,
Sluggish existences grazing there suspended, or slowly crawling close to the bottom,
The sperm-whale at the surface blowing air and spray, or disporting with his flukes,
The leaden-eyed shark, the walrus, the turtle, the hairy sea-leopard, and the sting-
   ray,
Passions there, wars, pursuits, tribes, sight in those ocean-depths, breathing that
   thick-breathing air, as so many do,
10 The change thence to the sight here, and to the subtle air breathed by beings like us
   who walk this sphere,
The change onward from ours to that of beings who walk other spheres.

3 *lichens* Flowerless plants.   **5** *gluten* A tough, sticky substance.   *aliment* Food.
7 *disporting* Frolicking.   *flukes* Rounded projections on the whale's tail.

Beat! Beat! Drums!

Beat! beat! drums! blow! bugles! blow!
Through the windows—through doors—burst like a ruthless force,
Into the solemn church, and scatter the congregation,
Into the school where the scholar is studying;
5 Leave not the bridegroom quiet—no happiness must he have now with his bride,

Nor the peaceful farmer any peace, ploughing his field or gathering his grain,
So fierce you whirr and pound you drums—so shrill you bugles blow.

Beat! beat! drums!—blow! bugles! blow!
Over the traffic of cities—over the rumble of wheels in the streets;
10 Are beds prepared for sleepers at night in the houses? no sleepers must sleep in
those beds,
No bargainers' bargains by day—no brokers or speculators—would they continue?
Would the talkers be talking? would the singer attempt to sing?
Would the lawyer rise in the court to state his case before the judge?
Then rattle quicker, heavier drums—you bugles wilder blow.
15 Beat! beat! drums!—blow! bugles! blow!
Make no parley—stop for no expostulation,
Mind not the timid—mind not the weeper or prayer,
Mind not the old man beseeching the young man,
Let not the child's voice be heard, nor the mother's entreaties,
20 Make even the trestles to shake the dead where they lie awaiting the hearses,
So strong you thump O terrible drums—so loud you bugles blow.

A Sight in Camp in the Daybreak Gray and Dim

A sight in camp in the daybreak gray and dim,
As from my tent I emerge so early sleepless,
As slow I walk in the cool fresh air the path near by the hospital tent,
Three forms I see on stretchers lying, brought out there untended lying,
5 Over each the blanket spread, ample brownish woolen blanket,
Gray and heavy blanket, folding, covering all.

Curious I halt and silent stand,
Then with light fingers I from the face of the nearest the first just lift the blanket;
Who are you elderly man so gaunt and grim, with well-gray'd hair, and flesh all
sunken about thy eyes?
10 Who are you my dear comrade?

Then to the second I step—and who are you my child and darling?
Who are you sweet boy with cheeks yet blooming?

Then to the third—a face nor child nor old, very calm, as of beautiful yellow-white
ivory;
Young man I think I know you—I think this face is the face of the dead Christ
himself,
15 Dead and divine and brother of all, and here again he lies.

When Lilacs Last in the Dooryard Bloom'd

1

When lilacs last in the dooryard bloom'd,
And the great star early droop'd in the western sky in the night,
I mourn'd, and yet shall mourn with ever-returning spring.

Ever-returning spring, trinity sure to me you bring,
5 Lilac blooming perennial and drooping star in the west,
And thought of him I love.

2

O powerful western fallen star!
O shades of night—O moody, tearful night!
O great star disappear'd—O the black murk that hides the star!
10 O cruel hands that hold me powerless—O helpless soul of me!
O harsh surrounding cloud that will not free my soul.

3

In the dooryard fronting an old farm-house near the whitewash'd palings,
Stands the lilac-bush tall-growing with heart-shaped leaves of rich green,
With many a pointed blossom rising delicate, with the perfume strong I love,
15 With every leaf a miracle—and from this bush in the dooryard,
With delicate-color'd blossoms and heart-shaped leaves of rich green,
A sprig with its flower I break.

4

In the swamp in secluded recesses,
A shy and hidden bird is warbling a song.

20 Solitary the thrush,
The hermit withdrawn to himself, avoiding the settlements,
Sings by himself a song.

Song of the bleeding throat,
Death's outlet song of life, (for well dear brother I know,
25 If thou wast not granted to sing thou would'st surely die.)

2 *great star* The planet Venus.   **6** *him I love* Abraham Lincoln, who was shot by John
Wilkes Booth in Ford's Theatre, Washington, D.C., on April 14, 1865, and died the next day.

5

Over the breast of the spring, the land, amid cities,
Amid lanes and through old woods, where lately the violets peep'd from the
    ground, spotting the gray débris,
Amid the grass in the fields each side of the lanes, passing the endless grass,
Passing the yellow-spear'd wheat, every grain from its shroud in the dark-brown
    fields uprisen,
30 Passing the apple-tree blows of white and pink in the orchards,
Carrying a corpse to where it shall rest in the grave,
Night and day journeys a coffin.

6

Coffin that passes through lanes and streets,
Through day and night with the great cloud darkening the land,
35 With the pomp of the inloop'd flags with the cities draped in black,
With the show of the States themselves as of crape-veil'd women standing,
With processions long and winding and the flambeaus of the night,
With the countless torches lit, with the silent sea of faces and the unbared heads,
With the waiting depot, the arriving coffin, and the somber faces,
40 With dirges through the night, with the thousand voices rising strong and solemn,
With all the mournful voices of the dirges pour'd around the coffin,
The dim-lit churches and the shuddering organs—where amid these you journey,
With the tolling tolling bells' perpetual clang,
Here, coffin that slowly passes,
45 I give you my sprig of lilac.

7

(Nor for you, for one alone,
Blossoms and branches green to coffins all I bring,
For fresh as the morning, thus would I chant a song for you O sane and sacred
    death.

All over bouquets of roses,
50 O death, I cover you over with roses and early lilies,
But mostly and now the lilac that blooms the first,
Copious I break, I break the sprigs from the bushes,
With loaded arms I come, pouring for you,
For you and the coffins all of you O death.)

33 *through lanes and streets*   On the way from Washington to Springfield, Illinois
37 *flambeaus*   Torches.

8

55 O western orb sailing the heaven,
Now I know what you must have meant as a month since I walk'd,
As I walk'd in silence the transparent shadowy night,
As I saw you had something to tell as you bent to me night after night,
As you droop'd from the sky low down as if to my side, (while the other stars
all look'd on,)
60 As we wander'd together the solemn night, (for something I know not what kept
me from sleep,)
As the night advanced, and I saw on the rim of the west how full you were of woe,
As I stood on the rising ground in the breeze in the cool transparent night,
As I watch'd where you pass'd and was lost in the netherward black of the night,
As my soul in its trouble dissatisfied sank, as where you sad orb,
65 Concluded, dropt in the night, and was gone.

9

Sing on there in the swamp,
O singer bashful and tender, I hear your notes, I hear your call,
I hear, I come presently, I understand you,
But a moment I linger, for the lustrous star has detain'd me,
70 The star my departing comrade holds and detains me.

10

O how shall I warble myself for the dead one there I loved?
And how shall I deck my song for the large sweet soul that has gone?
And what shall my perfume be for the grave of him I love?

Sea-winds blown from east and west,
75 Blown from the Eastern sea and blown from the Western sea, till there on the
prairies meeting,
These and with these and the breath of my chant,
I'll perfume the grave of him I love.

11

O what shall I hang on the chamber walls?
And what shall the pictures be that I hang on the walls,
80 To adorn the burial-house of him I love?

Pictures of growing spring and farms and homes,
With the Fourth-month eve at sundown, and the gray smoke lucid and bright,

55 *western orb* Venus.   **63** *netherward* Downward.

With floods of the yellow gold of the gorgeous, indolent, sinking sun, burning,
   expanding the air,
With the fresh sweet herbage under foot, and the pale green leaves of the trees
   prolific,
85 In the distance the flowing glaze, the breast of the river, with a wind-dapple here
   and there,
With ranging hills on the banks, with many a line against the sky, and shadows,
And the city at hand, with dwellings so dense, and stacks of chimneys,
And all the scenes of life and the workshops, and the workmen homeward
   returning.

12

Lo, body and soul—this land,
90 My own Manhattan with spires, and the sparkling and hurrying tides, and the ships,
The varied and ample land, the South and the North in the light, Ohio's shores and
   flashing Missouri,
And ever the far-spreading prairies cover'd with grass and corn.

Lo, the most excellent sun so calm and haughty,
The violet and purple morn with just-felt breezes,
95 The gentle soft-born measureless light,
The miracle spreading bathing all, the fulfill'd noon,
The coming eve delicious, the welcome night and the stars,
Over my cities shining all, enveloping man and land.

13

Sing on, sing on you gray-brown bird,
100 Sing from the swamps, the recesses, pour your chant from the bushes,
Limitless out of the dusk, out of the cedars and pines.

Sing on dearest brother, warble your reedy song,
Loud human song, with voice of uttermost woe.

O liquid and free and tender!
105 O wild and loose to my soul—O wondrous singer!
You only I hear—yet the star holds me (but will soon depart,)
Yet the lilac with mastering odor holds me.

14

Now while I sat in the day and look'd forth,
In the close of the day with its light and the fields of spring, and the farmers
   preparing their crops,

110 In the large unconscious scenery of my land with its lakes and forests,
In the heavenly aerial beauty, (after the perturb'd winds and the storms,)
Under the arching heavens of the afternoon swift passing, and the voices of
children and women,
The many-moving sea-tides, and I saw the ships how they sail'd,
And the summer approaching with richness, and the fields all busy with labor,
115 And the infinite separate houses, how they all went on, each with its meals and
minutia of daily usages,
And the streets how their throbbings throbb'd, and the cities pent—lo, then and
there,
Falling upon them all and among them all, enveloping me with the rest,
Appear'd the cloud, appear'd the long black trail,
And I knew death, its thought, and the sacred knowledge of death.

120 Then with the knowledge of death as walking one side of me,
And the thought of death close-walking the other side of me,
And I in the middle as with companions, and as holding the hands of companions,
I fled forth to the hiding receiving night that talks not,
Down to the shores of the water, the path by the swamp in the dimness,
125 To the solemn shadowy cedars and ghostly pines so still.

And the singer so shy to the rest receiv'd me,
The gray-brown bird I know receiv'd us comrades three,
And he sang the carol of death, and a verse for him I love.

From deep secluded recesses,
130 From the fragrant cedars and the ghostly pines so still,
Came the carol of the bird.

And the charm of the carol rapt me
As I held as if by their hands my comrades in the night,
And the voice of my spirit tallied the song of the bird.

135 *Come lovely and soothing death,*
Undulate round the world, serenely arriving, arriving,
In the day, in the night, to all, to each,
Sooner or later delicate death.

Prais'd be the fathomless universe,
140 *For life and joy, and for objects and knowledge curious,*
And for love, sweet love—but praise! praise! praise!
For the sure-enwinding arms of cool-enfolding death.

Dark mother always gliding near with soft feet,
Have none chanted for thee a chant of fullest welcome?
145 *Then I chant it for thee, I glorify thee above all,*
I bring thee a song that when thou must indeed come, come unfalteringly.

Approach strong deliveress,
When it is so, when thou hast taken them I joyously sing the dead,
Lost in the loving floating ocean of thee,
150 *Laved in the flood of thy bliss O death.*

From me to thee glad serenades,
Dances for thee I propose saluting thee, adornments and feastings for thee,
And the sights of the open landscape and the high-spread sky are fitting,
And life and the fields, and the huge and thoughtful night.

155 *The night in silence under many a star,*
The ocean shore and the husky whispering wave whose voice I know,
And the soul turning to thee O vast and well-veil'd death,
And the body gratefully nestling close to thee.

Over the tree-tops I float thee a song,
160 *Over the rising and sinking waves, over the myriad fields and the prairies wide,*
Over the dense-pack'd cities all and the teeming wharves and ways,
I float this carol with joy, with joy to thee O death.

15

To the tally of my soul,
Loud and strong kept up the gray-brown bird,
165 With pure deliberate notes spreading filling the night.

Loud in the pines and cedars dim,
Clear in the freshness moist and the swamp-perfume,
And I with my comrades there in the night.

While my sight that was bound in my eyes unclosed,
170 As to long panoramas of visions.

And I saw askant the armies,
I saw as in noiseless dreams hundreds of battle-flags,
Borne through the smoke of the battles and pierc'd with missiles I saw them,
And carried hither and yon through the smoke, and torn and bloody,
175 And at last but a few shreds left on the staffs, (and all in silence,)
And the staffs all splinter'd and broken.

I saw battle-corpses, myriads of them,
And the white skeletons of young men, I saw them,
I saw the débris and débris of all the slain soldiers of the war,
180 But I saw they were not as was thought,
They themselves were fully at rest, they suffer'd not,
The living remain'd and suffer'd, the mother suffer'd,

And the wife and the child and the musing comrade suffer'd,
And the armies that remain'd suffer'd.

16

185 Passing the visions, passing the night,
Passing, unloosing the hold of my comrades' hands,
Passing the song of the hermit bird and the tallying song of my soul,
Victorious song, death's outlet song, yet varying ever-altering song,
As low and wailing, yet clear the notes, rising and falling, flooding the night,
190 Sadly sinking and fainting, as warning and warning, and yet again bursting with joy,
Covering the earth and filling the spread of the heaven,
As that powerful psalm in the night I heard from recesses,
Passing, I leave thee lilac with heart-shaped leaves,
I leave thee there in the dooryard, blooming, returning with spring.

195 I cease from my song for thee,
From my gaze on thee in the west, fronting the west, communing with thee,
O comrade lustrous with silver face in the night

Yet each to keep and all, retrievements out of the night,
The song, the wondrous chant of the gray-brown bird,
200 And the tallying chant, the echo arous'd in my soul,
With the lustrous and drooping star with the countenance full of woe,
With the holders holding my hand nearing the call of the bird,
Comrades mine and I in the midst, and their memory ever to keep, for the dead
    I loved so well,
For the sweetest, wisest soul of all my days and lands—and this for his dear sake,
205 Lilac and star and bird twined with the chant of my soul,
There in the fragrant pines and the cedars dusk and dim.

There Was a Child Went Forth

There was a child went forth every day,
And the first object he look'd upon, that object he became,
And that object became part of him for the day or certain part of the day,
Or for many years or stretching cycles of years.
5 The early lilacs became part of this child,
And grass and white and red morning-glories, and white and red clover, and the
    song of the phœbe-bird,
And the Third-month lambs and the sow's pink-faint litter, and the mare's foal
    and the cow's calf,
And the noisy brood of the barnyard or by the mire of the pond-side,

And the fish suspending themselves so curiously below there, and the beautiful curious liquid,

10   And the water-plants with their graceful flat heads, all became part of him.

The field-sprouts of Fourth-month and Fifth-month became part of him,
Winter-grain sprouts and those of the light-yellow corn, and the esculent roots of the garden,
And the apple-trees cover'd with blossoms and the fruit afterward, and wood-berries, and the commonest weeds by the road,
And the old drunkard staggering home from the outhouse of the tavern whence he had lately risen,

15   And the schoolmistress that pass'd on her way to the school,
And the friendly boys that pass'd, and the quarrelsome boys,
And the tidy and fresh-cheek'd girls, and the barefoot negro boy and girl,
And all the changes of city and country wherever he went.

His own parents, he that had father'd him and she that had conceiv'd him in her womb and birth'd him,

20   They gave this child more of themselves than that,
They gave him afterward every day, they became part of him.
The mother at home quietly placing the dishes on the supper-table,
The mother with mild words, clean her cap and gown, a wholesome odor falling off her person and clothes as she walks by,
The father, strong, self-sufficient, manly, mean, anger'd, unjust,

25   The blow, the quick loud word, the tight bargain, the crafty lure,
The family usages, the language, the company, the furniture, the yearning and swelling heart,
Affection that will not be gainsay'd, the sense of what is real, the thought if after all it should prove unreal,
The doubts of day-time and the doubts of night-time, the curious whether and how,
Whether that which appears so is so, or is it all flashes and specks?

30   Men and women crowding fast in the streets, if they are not flashes and specks what are they?
The streets themselves and the façades of houses, and goods in the windows,
Vehicles, teams, the heavy-plank'd wharves, the huge crossing at the ferries,
The village on the highland seen from afar at sunset, the river between,
Shadows, aureola and mist, the light falling on roofs and gables of white or brown two miles off,

35   The schooner near by sleepily dropping down the tide, the little boat slack-tow'd astern,
The hurrying tumbling waves, quick-broken crests, slapping,
The strata of color'd clouds, the long bar of maroon-tint away solitary by itself, the spread of purity it lies motionless in,
The horizon's edge, the flying sea-crow, the fragrance of salt marsh and shore mud,
These became part of that child who went forth every day, and who now goes, and will always go forth every day.

Sparkles from the Wheel

Where the city's ceaseless crowd moves on the livelong day,
Withdrawn I join a group of children watching, I pause aside with them.
By the curb toward the edge of the flagging,
A knife-grinder works at his wheel sharpening a great knife,
5 Bending over he carefully holds it to the stone, by foot and knee,
With measur'd tread he turns rapidly, as he presses with light but firm hand,
Forth issue then in copious golden jets,
Sparkles from the wheel.

The scene and all its belongings, how they seize and affect me,
10 The sad sharp-chinn'd old man with worn clothes and broad shoulder-band of
leather,
Myself effusing and fluid, a phantom curiously floating, now here absorb'd and
arrested,
The group, (an unminded point set in a vast surrounding,)
The attentive, quiet children, the loud, proud, restive base of the streets,
The low hoarse purr of the whirling stone, the light-press'd blade,
15 Diffusing, dropping, sideways-darting, in tiny showers of gold,
Sparkles from the wheel.

A Noiseless Patient Spider

A noiseless patient spider,
I mark'd where on a little promontory it stood isolated,
Mark'd how to explore the vacant vast surrounding,
It launched forth filament, filament, filament, out of itself,
5 Ever unreeling them, ever tirelessly speeding them.

And you O my soul where you stand,
Surrounded, detached, in measureless oceans of space,
Ceaselessly musing, venturing, throwing, seeking the spheres to connect them,
Till the bridge you will need be form'd, till the ductile anchor hold,
10 Till the gossamer thread you fling catch somewhere, O my soul.

Matthew Arnold   (1822–1888)

Shakespeare

Others abide our question. Thou art free.
We ask and ask—Thou smilest and art still,
Out-topping knowledge. For the loftiest hill,
Who to the stars uncrowns his majesty,

5 Planting his steadfast footsteps in the sea,
   Making the heaven of heavens his dwelling-place,
   Spares but the cloudy border of his base
   To the foiled searching of mortality;
   And thou, who didst the stars and sunbeams know,
10 Self-schooled, self-scanned, self-honored, self-secure,
   Didst tread on earth unguessed at—better so!
   All pains the immortal spirit must endure,
   All weakness which impairs, all griefs which bow,
   Find their sole speech in that victorious brow.

Dover Beach

   The sea is calm tonight.
   The tide is full, the moon lies fair
   Upon the straits; on the French coast the light
   Gleams and is gone; the cliffs of England stand,
5 Glimmering and vast, out in the tranquil bay.
   Come to the window, sweet is the night air!

   Only, from the long line of spray
   Where the sea meets the moon-blanched land,
   Listen! you hear the grating roar
10 Of pebbles which the waves draw back, and fling,
   At their return, up the high strand,
   Begin, and cease, and then again begin,
   With tremulous cadence slow, and bring
   The eternal note of sadness in.

15 Sophocles long ago
   Heard it on the Ægean, and it brought
   Into his mind the turbid ebb and flow
   Of human misery; we
   Find also in the sound a thought,
20 Hearing it by this distant northern sea.

   The Sea of Faith
   Was once, too, at the full, and round earth's shore
   Lay like the folds of a bright girdle furled.
   But now I only hear
25 Its melancholy, long, withdrawing roar,
   Retreating, to the breath

15-16 *Sophocles . . . Ægean* In his play *Antigone* Sophocles compares the curse on the house of Oedipus with the force of the sea. The Ægean Sea is on the east coast of Greece. **23** *girdle* An article of dress encircling the body.

Of the night wind, down the vast edges drear
And naked shingles of the world.

Ah, love, let us be true
30 To one another! for the world, which seems
To lie before us like a land of dreams,
So various, so beautiful, so new,
Hath really neither joy, nor love, nor light,
Nor certitude, nor peace, nor help for pain;
35 And we are here as on a darkling plain,
Swept with confused alarms of struggle and flight,
Where ignorant armies clash by night.

28 *shingles* Pebble-covered beaches.

Emily Dickinson   (1830–1886)

I Meant to Have But Modest Needs

I meant to have but modest needs—
Such as Content—and Heaven—
Within my income—these could lie
And Life and I—keep even—

5 But since the last—included both—
It would suffice my Prayer
But just for One—to stipulate—
And Grace would grant the Pair—

And so—upon this wise—I prayed—
10 Great Spirit—Give to me
A Heaven not so large as Yours,
But large enough—for me—

A Smile suffused Jehovah's face—
The Cherubim—withdrew—
15 Grave Saints stole out to look at me—
And showed their dimples—too—

I left the Place, with all my might—
I threw my Prayer away—
The Quiet Ages picked it up—
20 And Judgment—twinkled—too—

That one so honest—be extant—
It take the Tale for true—
That "Whatsoever Ye shall ask—
Itself be given You"—

25 But I, grown shrewder—scan the Skies
With a suspicious Air—
As Children—swindled for the first
All Swindlers—be—infer—

A Bird Came Down the Walk

A Bird came down the Walk—
He did not know I saw—
He bit an Angleworm in halves
And ate the fellow, raw,

5 And then he drank a Dew
From a convenient Grass—
And then hopped sidewise to the Wall
To let a Beetle pass—

He glanced with rapid eyes
10 That hurried all around—
They looked like frightened Beads, I thought—
He stirred his Velvet Head

Like one in danger, Cautious,
I offered him a Crumb
15 And he unrolled his feathers
And rowed him softer home—
Than Oars divide the Ocean,
Too silver for a seam—
Or Butterflies, off Banks of Noon
20 Leap, plashless as they swim.

20 *plashless*   Splashless.

It Was Not Death

It was not Death, for I stood up,
And all the Dead, lie down—
It was not Night, for all the Bells
Put out their Tongues, for Noon.

5 It was not Frost, for on my Flesh
  I felt Siroccos—crawl—
  Nor Fire—for just my Marble feet
  Could keep a Chancel, cool—

  And yet, it tasted, like them all,
10 The Figures I have seen
  Set orderly, for Burial,
  Reminded me, of mine—

  As if my life were shaven,
  And fitted to a frame,
15 And could not breathe without a key,
  And 'twas like Midnight, some—

  When everything that ticked—has stopped—
  And Space stares all around—
  Or Grisly frosts—first Autumn morns,
20 Repeal the Beating Ground—

  But, most, like Chaos—Stopless—cool—
  Without a Chance, or Spar—
  Or even a Report of Land—
  To justify—Despair.

6 *Siroccos* Hot dust-laden winds from the Libyan desert; hot, moist, oppressive southeasterly winds that blow in the Mediterranean region.   **8** *Chancel* That part of a church reserved for the clergy and choir.

In Winter in My Room

  In Winter in my Room
  I came upon a Worm—
  Pink, lank and warm—
  But as he was a worm
5 And worms presume
  Not quite with him at home—
  Secured him by a string
  To something neighboring
  And went along.

10 A Trifle afterward
  A thing occurred
  I'd not believe it if I heard
  But state with creeping blood—
  A snake with mottles rare
15 Surveyed my chamber floor

In feature as the worm before
But ringed with power—
The very string with which
I tied him—too
20   When he was mean and new
That string was there—

I shrank—"How fair you are"!
Propitiation's claw—
"Afraid," he hissed
25   "Of me"?
"No cordiality"—
He fathomed me—
Then to a Rhythm *Slim*
Secreted in his Form
30   As Patterns swim
Projected him.

That time I flew
Both eyes his way
Lest he pursue
35   Nor ever ceased to run
Till in a distant Town
Towns on from mine
I set me down
This was a dream.

Christina Rossetti   (1830–1894)

Ferry Me Across the Water

"Ferry me across the water,
    Do, boatman, do."
"If you've a penny in your purse
    I'll ferry you."

5   "I have a penny in my purse,
    And my eyes are blue;
So ferry me across the water,
    Do, boatman, do!"

"Step into my ferry-boat,
10   Be they black or blue,
And for the penny in your purse
    I'll ferry you."

Lewis Carroll (Charles Lutwidge Dodgson)   (1832–1898)

Father William

"You are old, Father William," the young man said,
  "And your hair has become very white,
And yet you incessantly stand on your head—
  Do you think, at your age, it is right?"

5 "In my youth," Father William replied to his son,
  "I feared it might injure the brain;
But now that I'm perfectly sure I have none,
  Why, I do it again and again."

"You are old," said the youth, "as I mentioned before,
10   And have grown uncommonly fat;
Yet you turned a back-somersault in at the door—
  Pray, what is the reason of that?"

"In my youth," said the sage, as he shook his gray locks,
  "I kept all my limbs very supple
15 By the use of this ointment—one shilling the box—
  Allow me to sell you a couple."

"You are old," said the youth, "and your jaws are too weak
  For anything tougher than suet;
Yet you finished the goose, with the bones and the beak;
20   Pray, how did you manage to do it?"

"In my youth," said his father, "I took to the law,
  And argued each case with my wife;
And the muscular strength which it gave to my jaw
  Has lasted the rest of my life."

25 "You are old," said the youth, "one would hardly suppose
  That your eye was as steady as ever;
Yet you balanced an eel on the end of your nose—
  What made you so awfully clever?"

"I have answered three questions, and that is enough,"
30   Said his father; "don't give yourself airs!
Do you think I can listen all day to such stuff?
  Be off, or I'll kick you downstairs!"

Father William   This poem is a parody of Robert Southey's poem "The Old Man's Comforts and How He Gained Them."

Thomas Hardy   (1840–1928)

A Broken Appointment

You did not come,
And marching Time drew on, and wore me numb.
Yet less for loss of your dear presence there
Than that I thus found lacking in your make
5 That high compassion which can overbear
Reluctance for pure lovingkindness' sake
Grieved I, when, as the hope-hour stroked its sum,
You did not come.

You love not me,
10 And love alone can lend you loyalty;
—I know and knew it. But, unto the store
Of human deeds divine in all but name,
Was it not worth a little hour or more
To add yet this: Once you, a woman, came
15 To soothe a time-torn man; even though it be
You love not me?

The Convergence of the Twain
Lines on the Loss of the Titanic

1

In a solitude of the sea
Deep from human vanity,
And the Pride of Life that planned her, stilly couches she.

2

Steel chambers, late the pyres
5 Of her salamandrine fires,
Cold currents thrid, and turn to rhythmic tidal lyres.

3

Over the mirrors meant
To glass the opulent
The sea-worm crawls—grotesque, slimed, dumb, indifferent.

Titanic The White Star liner sunk on the night of April 14-15, 1912, after hitting an iceberg in the North Atlantic on its maiden voyage from Southampton to New York; loss of life, 1517.
4 *Steel chambers* The ship's furnaces. **5** *salamandrine fires* The salamander, a lizardlike creature, according to legend could live in or withstand fire. **6** *thrid* Thread. **8** *glass* Reflect.

4

10   Jewels in joy designed
          To ravish the sensuous mind
       Lie lightless, all their sparkles bleared and black and blind.

5

          Dim moon-eyed fishes near
          Gaze at the gilded gear
15   And query: "What does this vaingloriousness down here?"

6

          Well: while was fashioning
          This creature of cleaving wing,
       The Immanent Will that stirs and urges everything

7

          Prepared a sinister mate
20   For her—so gaily great—
       A Shape of Ice, for the time far and dissociate.

8

          And as the smart ship grew,
          In stature, grace, and hue,
       In shadowy silent distance grew the Iceberg too.

9

25   Alien they seemed to be:
          No mortal eye could see
       The intimate welding of their later history,

10

          Or sign that they were bent
          By paths coincident
30   On being anon twin halves of one august event

11

          Till the Spinner of the Years
          Said "Now!" And each one hears,
       And consummation comes, and jars two hemispheres.

31 *Spinner of the Years*   In Greek myth three goddesses controlled the lives of men;
Clotho spun the web of life, Lachesis measured its length, and Atropos cut it off.

The Blinded Bird

So zestfully canst thou sing?
And all this indignity,
With God's consent, on thee!
Blinded ere yet a-wing
5   By the red-hot needle thou,
I stand and wonder how
So zestfully thou canst sing!

Resenting not such wrong,
Thy grievous pain forgot,
10 Eternal dark thy lot,
Groping thy whole life long,
After that stab of fire,
Enjailed in pitiless wire;
Resenting not such wrong!

15 Who hath charity? This bird.
Who suffereth long and is kind,
Is not provoked, though blind
And alive ensepulchred?
Who hopeth, endureth all things?
20 Who thinketh no evil, but sings?
Who is divine? This bird.

The Oxen

Christmas Eve, and twelve of the clock.
    "Now they are all on their knees,"
An elder said as we sat in a flock
    By the embers in hearthside ease.

5   We pictured the meek mild creatures where
    They dwelt in their strawy pen,
Nor did it occur to one of us there
    To doubt they were kneeling then.

So fair a fancy few would weave
10   In these years! Yet, I feel,
If someone said on Christmas Eve,
    "Come; see the oxen kneel,

"In the lonely barton by yonder coomb
    Our childhood used to know,"
15 I should go with him in the gloom,
    Hoping it might be so.

13 *barton* A farmyard; estate land not let out to tenants.   *coomb* A deep hollow or valley.

Nobody Comes

Tree-leaves labour up and down,
    And through them the fainting light
    Succumbs to the crawl of night.
Outside in the road the telegraph wire
5   To the town from the darkening land
Intones to travellers like a spectral lyre
    Swept by a spectral hand.

A car comes up, with lamps full-glare,
    That flash upon a tree:
10   It has nothing to do with me,
And whangs along in a world of its own,
    Leaving a blacker air;
And mute by the gate I stand again alone,
    And nobody pulls up there.

Gerard Manley Hopkins (1844–1889)

Spring and Fall
To a Young Child

Márgarét, are you gríeving
Over Goldengrove unleaving?
Leáves, líke the things of man, you
With your fresh thoughts care for, can you?
5 Áh! ás the heart grows older
It will come to such sights colder
By and by, nor spare a sigh
Though worlds of wanwood leafmeal lie;
And yet you wíll weep and know why.
10 Now no matter, child, the name:
Sórrow's spríngs áre the same.
Nor mouth had, no nor mind, expressed
What heart heard of, ghost guessed:
It ís the blight man was born for,
15 It is Margaret you mourn for.

2 *Goldengrove unleaving* Trees losing their leaves.   **8** *wanwood leafmeal* Pale leaves that have fallen and are becoming leaf mold.   **13** *ghost* Spirit, soul.

Hurrahing in Harvest

Summer ends now; now, barbarous in beauty, the stooks arise
  Around; up above, what wind-walks! what lovely behaviour
  Of silk-sack clouds! has wilder, wilful-wavier
Meal-drift moulded ever and melted across skies?

5   I walk, I lift up, I lift up heart, eyes,
  Down all that glory in the heavens to glean our Saviour;
  And, éyes, heárt, what looks, what lips yet gave you a
Rapturous love's greeting of realer, of rounder replies?

And the azurous hung hills are his world-wielding shoulder
10   Majestic—as a stallion stalwart, very-violet-sweet!—
These things, these things were here and but the beholder
  Wanting; which two when they once meet,
The heart rears wings bold and bolder
  And hurls for him, O half hurls earth for him off under his feet.

1 *stooks* Bundles of straw.

God's Grandeur

The world is charged with the grandeur of God.
  It will flame out, like shining from shook foil;
  It gathers to a greatness, like the ooze of oil
Crushed. Why do men then now not reck his rod?
5   Generations have trod, have trod, have trod;
  And all is seared with trade; bleared, smeared with toil;
  And wears man's smudge and shares man's smell: the soil
Is bare now, nor can foot feel, being shod.

And for all this, nature is never spent;
10   There lives the dearest freshness deep down things;
And though the last lights off the black West went
  Oh, morning, at the brown brink eastward, springs—
Because the Holy Ghost over the bent
  World broods with warm breast and with ah! bright wings.

That Nature Is a Heraclitean Fire and of the Comfort of the Resurrection

Cloud-puffball, torn tufts, tossed pillows flaunt forth, then chevy on an air-
built thoroughfare: heaven-roysterers, in gay-gangs they throng; they glitter in
   marches.
Down roughcast, down dazzling whitewash, wherever an elm arches,
Shivelights and shadowtackle in long lashes lace, lance, and pair.
5 Delightfully the bright wind boisterous ropes, wrestles, beats earth bare
Of yestertempest's creases; in pool and rutpeel parches
Squandering ooze to squeezed dough, crust, dust; stanches, starches
Squadroned masks and manmarks treadmire toil there
Footfretted in it. Million-fuelèd, nature's bonfire burns on.
10 But quench her bonniest, dearest to her, her clearest-selvèd spark
Man, how fast his firedint, his mark on mind, is gone!
Both are in an unfathomable, all is in an enormous dark
Drowned. O pity and indignation! Manshape, that shone
Sheer off, disseveral, a star, death blots black out; nor mark
15   Is any of him at all so stark
But vastness blurs and time beats level. Enough! the Resurrection,
A heart's-clarion! Away grief's gasping, joyless days, dejection.
     Across my foundering deck shone
A beacon, an eternal beam. Flesh fade, and mortal trash
20 Fall to the residuary worm; world's wildfire, leave but ash:
     In a flash, at a trumpet crash,
I am at once what Christ is, since he was what I am, and
This Jack, joke, poor potsherd, patch, matchwood, immortal diamond,
     Is immortal diamond.

Heraclitean Heraclitus was a Greek philosopher of the sixth century B.C. He thought that the world had its origin in fire and would end in fire.   **1** *chevy* Race, scamper.   **2** *roysterers* Revelers, carousers.   **4** *Shivelights* Light in splinters.   *shadowtackle* Shadows as from a ship's tackle.   **11** *firedint* The blow or power of man's spirit.   **14** *disseveral* Separate, apart. **23** *This Jack* Common person.   *potsherd* A pottery fragment.

A. E. Housman   (1859–1936)

Loveliest of Trees

Loveliest of trees, the cherry now
Is hung with bloom along the bough,
And stands about the woodland ride
Wearing white for Eastertide.

5 Now, of my threescore years and ten,
Twenty will not come again,
And take from seventy springs a score,
It only leaves me fifty more.

And since to look at things in bloom
10 Fifty springs are little room,
About the woodlands I will go
To see the cherry hung with snow.

When I Was One-and-Twenty

When I was one-and-twenty
   I heard a wise man say,
"Give crowns and pounds and guineas
   But not your heart away;
5 Give pearls away and rubies
   But keep your fancy free."
But I was one-and-twenty,
   No use to talk to me.

When I was one-and-twenty
10   I heard him say again,
"The heart out of the bosom
   Was never given in vain;
'Tis paid with sighs a-plenty
   And sold for endless rue."
15 And I am two-and-twenty,
   And oh, 'tis true, 'tis true.

To an Athlete Dying Young

The time you won your town the race
We chaired you through the market-place;
Man and boy stood cheering by,
And home we brought you shoulder-high.

5 Today, the road all runners come,
Shoulder-high we bring you home,
And set you at your threshold down,
Townsman of a stiller town.

Smart lad, to slip betimes away
10 From fields where glory does not stay,

And early though the laurel grows
It withers quicker than the rose.

Eyes the shady night has shut
Cannot see the record cut,
15 And silence sounds no worse than cheers
After earth has stopped the ears:

Now you will not swell the rout
Of lads that wore their honors out,
Runners whom renown outran
20 And the name died before the man.

So set, before its echoes fade,
The fleet foot on the sill of shade,
And hold to the low lintel up
The still-defended challenge-cup.

25 And round that early-laureled head
Will flock to gaze the strengthless dead,
And find unwithered on its curls
The garland briefer than a girl's.

11 *laurel* A tree or shrub whose foliage was used by the ancient Greeks to crown victors;
hence a symbol of victory or honor.   **23** *lintel* A horizontal top piece of a doorway.

Terence, This Is Stupid Stuff

"Terence, this is stupid stuff;
You eat your victuals fast enough;
There can't be much amiss, 'tis clear,
To see the rate you drink your beer.
5 But oh, good Lord, the verse you make,
It gives a chap the belly-ache.
The cow, the old cow, she is dead;
It sleeps well, the horned head:
We poor lads, 'tis our turn now
10 To hear such tunes as killed the cow.
Pretty friendship 'tis to rhyme
Your friends to death before their time
Moping melancholy mad:
Come, pipe a tune to dance to, lad."

Terence Roman writer of comedies (c. 190–c. 159 B.C.).

15 Why, if 'tis dancing you would be,
   There's brisker pipes than poetry.
   Say, for what were hop-yards meant,
   Or why was Burton built on Trent?
   Oh, many a peer of England brews
20 Livelier liquor than the Muse,
   And malt does more than Milton can
   To justify God's ways to man.
   Ale, man, ale's the stuff to drink
   For fellows whom it hurts to think:
25 Look into the pewter pot
   To see the world as the world's not.
   And faith, 'tis pleasant till 'tis past:
   The mischief is that 'twill not last.
   Oh, I have been to Ludlow fair
30 And left my necktie God knows where,
   And carried half way home, or near,
   Pints and quarts of Ludlow beer:
   Then the world seemed none so bad,
   And I myself a sterling lad;
35 And down in lovely muck I've lain,
   Happy till I woke again.
   Then I saw the morning sky:
   Heigho, the tale was all a lie;
   The world, it was the old world yet,
40 I was I, my things were wet,
   And nothing now remained to do
   But begin the game anew.

   Therefore, since the world has still
   Much good, but much less good than ill,
45 And while the sun and moon endure
   Luck's a chance, but trouble's sure,
   I'd face it as a wise man would,
   And train for ill and not for good.
   'Tis true, the stuff I bring for sale
50 Is not so brisk a brew as ale:
   Out of a stem that scored the hand
   I wrung it in a weary land.
   But take it: if the smack is sour,
   The better for the embittered hour;
55 It should do good to heart and head
   When your soul is in my soul's stead;

---

18 *Burton*   English brewery city. Trent is a river.   **21** *Milton*   John Milton (1608-1674), whose epic poem *Paradise Lost* had as its purpose to "justify the ways of God to men."   **25** *pewter pot*   A beer mug.   **29** *Ludlow*   A town in Shropshire.

And I will friend you, if I may,
In the dark and cloudy day.

There was a king reigned in the East:
60 There, when kings will sit to feast,
They get their fill before they think
With poisoned meat and poisoned drink.
He gathered all that springs to birth
From the many-venomed earth;
65 First a little, thence to more,
He sampled all her killing store;
And easy, smiling, seasoned sound,
Sate the king when healths went round.
They put arsenic in his meat
70 And stared aghast to watch him eat;
They poured strychnine in his cup
And shook to see him drink it up:
They shook, they stared as white's their shirt:
Them it was their poison hurt.
75 —I tell the tale that I heard told.
Mithridates, he died old.

68 *Sate* Sat.   **76** *Mithridates* Mithridates VI (c. 132-63 B.C.), king of Pontus in Asia Minor.

William Butler Yeats   (1865–1939)

To a Friend Whose Work Has Come to Nothing

Now all the truth is out,
Be secret and take defeat
From any brazen throat,
For how can you compete,
5 Being honour bred, with one
Who, were it proved he lies,
Were neither shamed in his own
Nor in his neighbours' eyes?
Bred to a harder thing
10 Than Triumph, turn away
And like a laughing string
Whereon mad fingers play
Amid a place of stone,
Be secret and exult,
15 Because of all things known
That is most difficult.

On Woman

May God be praised for woman
That gives up all her mind,
A man may find in no man
A friendship of her kind
5   That covers all he has brought
As with her flesh and bone,
Nor quarrels with a thought
Because it is not her own.

Though pedantry denies,
10   It's plain the Bible means
That Solomon grew wise
While talking with his queens,
Yet never could, although
They say he counted grass,
15   Count all the praises due
When Sheba was his lass,
When she the iron wrought, or
When from the smithy fire
It shuddered in the water:
20   Harshness of their desire
That made them stretch and yawn,
Pleasure that comes with sleep,
Shudder that made them one.
What else He give or keep
25   God grant me—no, not here,
For I am not so bold
To hope a thing so dear
Now I am growing old,
But when, if the tale's true,
30   The Pestle of the moon
That pounds up all anew
Brings me to birth again—
To find what once I had
And know what once I have known,
35   Until I am driven mad,
Sleep driven from my bed,
By tenderness and care,
Pity, an aching head,
Gnashing of teeth, despair;
40   And all because of some one
Perverse creature of chance,
And live like Solomon
That Sheba led a dance.

The Fisherman

Although I can see him still,
The freckled man who goes
To a grey place on a hill
In grey Connemara clothes
5 At dawn to cast his flies,
It's long since I began
To call up to the eyes
This wise and simple man.
All day I'd looked in the face
10 What I had hoped 'twould be
To write for my own race
And the reality;
The living men that I hate,
The dead man that I loved,
15 The craven man in his seat,
The insolent unreproved,
And no knave brought to book
Who has won a drunken cheer,
The witty man and his joke
20 Aimed at the commonest ear,
The clever man who cries
The catch-cries of the clown,
The beating down of the wise
And great Art beaten down.

25 Maybe a twelvemonth since
Suddenly I began,
In scorn of this audience,
Imagining a man,
And his sun-freckled face,
30 And grey Connemara cloth,
Climbing up to a place
Where stone is dark under froth,
And the down-turn of his wrist
When the flies drop in the stream;
35 A man who does not exist,
A man who is but a dream;
And cried, "Before I am old
I shall have written him one
Poem maybe as cold
40 And passionate as the dawn."

The Circus Animals' Desertion

1

I sought a theme and sought for it in vain,
I sought it daily for six weeks or so.
Maybe at last, being but a broken man,
I must be satisfied with my heart, although
5 Winter and summer till old age began
My circus animals were all on show,
Those stilted boys, that burnished chariot,
Lion and woman and the Lord knows what.

2

What can I but enumerate old themes?
10 First that sea-rider Oisin led by the nose
Through three enchanted islands, allegorical dreams,
Vain gaiety, vain battle, vain repose,
Themes of the embittered heart, or so it seems,
That might adorn old songs or courtly shows;
15 But what cared I that set him on to ride,
I, starved for the bosom of his faery bride?

And then a counter-truth filled out its play,
The Countess Cathleen was the name I gave it;
She, pity-crazed, had given her soul away,
20 But masterful Heaven had intervened to save it.
I thought my dear must her own soul destroy,
So did fanaticism and hate enslave it,
And this brought forth a dream and soon enough
This dream itself had all my thought and love.

25 And when the Fool and Blind Man stole the bread
Cuchulain fought the ungovernable sea;
Heart-mysteries there, and yet when all is said
It was the dream itself enchanted me:
Character isolated by a deed
30 To engross the present and dominate memory.
Players and painted stage took all my love,
And not those things that they were emblems of.

3

Those masterful images because complete
Grew in pure mind, but out of what began?
35 A mound of refuse or the sweepings of a street,

Old kettles, old bottles, and a broken can,
Old iron, old bones, old rags, that raving slut
Who keeps the till. Now that my ladder's gone,
I must lie down where all the ladders start,
40 In the foul rag-and-bone shop of the heart.

Stephen Crane   (1871–1900)

Should the Wide World Roll Away

Should the wide world roll away,
Leaving black terror,
Limitless night,
Nor God, nor man, nor place to stand
5 Would be to me essential,
If thou and thy white arms were there,
And the fall to doom a long way.

Do Not Weep, Maiden, for War Is Kind

Do not weep, maiden, for war is kind.
Because your lover threw wild hands toward the sky
And the affrighted steed ran on alone,
Do not weep.
5 War is kind.

Hoarse, booming drums of the regiment,
Little souls who thirst for fight,
These men were born to drill and die.
The unexplained glory flies above them,
10 Great is the battle-god, great, and his kingdom—
A field where a thousand corpses lie.

Do not weep, babe, for war is kind.
Because your father tumbled in the yellow trenches,
Raged at his breast, gulped and died,
15 Do not weep.
War is kind.

Swift blazing flag of the regiment,
Eagle with crest of red and gold,
These men were born to drill and die.
20 Point for them the virtue of slaughter,

Make plain to them the excellence of killing
And a field where a thousand corpses lie.

Mother whose heart hung humble as a button
On the bright splendid shroud of your son,
25   Do not weep.
War is kind.

Robert Frost (1874 – 1963)

Christmas Trees
A Christmas Circular Letter

The city had withdrawn into itself
And left at last the country to the country;
When between whirls of snow not come to lie
And whirls of foliage not yet laid, there drove
5   A stranger to our yard, who looked the city,
Yet did in country fashion in that there
He sat and waited till he drew us out,
A-buttoning coats, to ask him who he was.
He proved to be the city come again
10   To look for something it had left behind
And could not do without and keep its Christmas.
He asked if I would sell my Christmas trees;
My woods—the young fir balsams like a place
Where houses all are churches and have spires.
15   I hadn't thought of them as Christmas trees.
I doubt if I was tempted for a moment
To sell them off their feet to go in cars
And leave the slope behind the house all bare,
Where the sun shines now no warmer than the moon.
20   I'd hate to have them know it if I was.
Yet more I'd hate to hold my trees, except
As others hold theirs or refuse for them,
Beyond the time of profitable growth—
The trial by market everything must come to.
25   I dallied so much with the thought of selling.
Then whether from mistaken courtesy
And fear of seeming short of speech, or whether
From hope of hearing good of what was mine,
I said, "There aren't enough to be worth while."

30 "I could soon tell how many they would cut,
  You let me look them over."
         "You could look.
  But don't expect I'm going to let you have them."
  Pasture they spring in, some in clumps too close
  That lop each other of boughs, but not a few
35 Quite solitary and having equal boughs
  All round and round. The latter he nodded "Yes" to,
  Or paused to say beneath some lovelier one,
  With a buyer's moderation, "That would do."
  I thought so too, but wasn't there to say so.
40 We climbed the pasture on the south, crossed over,
  And came down on the north.
         He said, "A thousand."

"A thousand Christmas trees!—at what apiece?"

He felt some need of softening that to me:
"A thousand trees would come to thirty dollars."

45 Then I was certain I had never meant
  To let him have them. Never show surprise!
  But thirty dollars seemed so small beside
  The extent of pasture I should strip, three cents
  (For that was all they figured out apiece)—
50 Three cents so small beside the dollar friends
  I should be writing to within the hour
  Would pay in cities for good trees like those,
  Regular vestry-trees whole Sunday Schools
  Could hang enough on to pick off enough.

55 A thousand Christmas trees I didn't know I had!
  Worth three cents more to give away than sell
  As may be shown by a simple calculation.
  Too bad I couldn't lay one in a letter.
  I can't help wishing I could send you one,
60 In wishing you herewith a Merry Christmas.

Birches

  When I see birches bend to left and right
  Across the lines of straighter darker trees,
  I like to think some boy's been swinging them.
  But swinging doesn't bend them down to stay
5 As ice storms do. Often you must have seen them
  Loaded with ice a sunny winter morning

After a rain. They click upon themselves
As the breeze rises, and turn many-colored
As the stir cracks and crazes their enamel.
10 Soon the sun's warmth makes them shed crystal shells
Shattering and avalanching on the snow crust—
Such heaps of broken glass to sweep away
You'd think the inner dome of heaven had fallen.
They are dragged to the withered bracken by the load,
15 And they seem not to break; though once they are bowed
So low for long, they never right themselves:
You may see their trunks arching in the woods
Years afterwards, trailing their leaves on the ground
Like girls on hands and knees that throw their hair
20 Before them over their heads to dry in the sun.
But I was going to say when Truth broke in
With all her matter of fact about the ice storm,
I should prefer to have some boy bend them
As he went out and in to fetch the cows—
25 Some boy too far from town to learn baseball,
Whose only play was what he found himself,
Summer or winter, and could play alone.
One by one he subdued his father's trees
By riding them down over and over again
30 Until he took the stiffness out of them,
And not one but hung limp, not one was left
For him to conquer. He learned all there was
To learn about not launching out too soon
And so not carrying the tree away
35 Clear to the ground. He always kept his poise
To the top branches, climbing carefully
With the same pains you use to fill a cup
Up to the brim, and even above the brim.
Then he flung outward, feet first, with a swish,
40 Kicking his way down through the air to the ground.
So was I once myself a swinger of birches.
And so I dream of going back to be.
It's when I'm weary of considerations,
And life is too much like a pathless wood
45 Where your face burns and tickles with the cobwebs
Broken across it, and one eye is weeping
From a twig's having lashed across it open.
I'd like to get away from earth awhile
And then come back to it and begin over.
50 May no fate willfully misunderstand me
And half grant what I wish and snatch me away
Not to return. Earth's the right place for love:
I don't know where it's likely to go better.

I'd like to go by climbing a birch tree,
55 And climb black branches up a snow-white trunk
Toward heaven, till the tree could bear no more,
But dipped its top and set me down again.
That would be good both going and coming back.
One could do worse than be a swinger of birches.

To Earthward

Love at the lips was touch
As sweet as I could bear;
And once that seemed too much;
I lived on air

5   That crossed me from sweet things,
The flow of—was it musk
From hidden grapevine springs
Down hill at dusk?

I had the swirl and ache
10 From sprays of honeysuckle
That when they're gathered shake
Dew on the knuckle.

I craved strong sweets, but those
Seemed strong when I was young;
15 The petal of the rose
It was that stung.

Now no joy but lacks salt
That is not dashed with pain
And weariness and fault;
20 I crave the stain

Of tears, the aftermark
Of almost too much love,
The sweet of bitter bark
And burning clove.

25 When stiff and sore and scarred
I take away my hand
From leaning on it hard
In grass and sand,

The hurt is not enough:
30 I long for weight and strength
To feel the earth as rough
To all my length.

Desert Places

Snow falling and night falling fast, oh, fast
In a field I looked into going past,
And the ground almost covered smooth in snow,
But a few weeds and stubble showing last.

5 The woods around it have it—it is theirs.
All animals are smothered in their lairs.
I am too absent-spirited to count;
The loneliness includes me unawares.

And lonely as it is, that loneliness
10 Will be more lonely ere it will be less—
A blander whiteness of benighted snow
With no expression, nothing to express.

They cannot scare me with their empty spaces
Between stars—on stars where no human race is.
15 I have it in me so much nearer home
To scare myself with my own desert places.

The Most of It

He thought he kept the universe alone;
For all the voice in answer he could wake
Was but the mocking echo of his own
From some tree-hidden cliff across the lake.
5 Some morning from the boulder-broken beach
He would cry out on life, that what it wants
Is not its own love back in copy speech,
But counter-love, original response.
And nothing ever came of what he cried
10 Unless it was the embodiment that crashed
In the cliff's talus on the other side,
And then in the far-distant water splashed,

---

11 *talus* A slope, especially one formed by accumulation of rock debris; rock debris at the base of a cliff.

But after a time allowed for it to swim,
Instead of proving human when it neared
15 And someone else additional to him,
As a great buck it powerfully appeared,
Pushing the crumpled water up ahead,
And landed pouring like a waterfall,
And stumbled through the rocks with horny tread,
20 And forced the underbrush—and that was all.

Wallace Stevens   (1879–1955)

Sunday Morning

1

Complacencies of the peignoir, and late
Coffee and oranges in a sunny chair,
And the green freedom of a cockatoo
Upon a rug mingle to dissipate
5 The holy hush of ancient sacrifice.
She dreams a little, and she feels the dark
Encroachment of that old catastrophe,
As a calm darkens among water-lights.
The pungent oranges and bright, green wings
10 Seem things in some procession of the dead,
Winding across wide water, without sound.
The day is like wide water, without sound,
Stilled for the passing of her dreaming feet
Over the seas, to silent Palestine,
15 Dominion of the blood and sepulchre.

2

Why should she give her bounty to the dead?
What is divinity if it can come
Only in silent shadows and in dreams?
Shall she not find in comforts of the sun,
20 In pungent fruit and bright, green wings, or else
In any balm or beauty of the earth,
Things to be cherished like the thought of heaven?
Divinity must live within herself:

---

1 *peignoir* A woman's loose negligee or dressing gown; literally, a garment worn while comb-
ing the hair.   **3** *cockatoo* A bright colored, crested parrot.

Passions of rain, or moods in falling snow;
25 Grievings in loneliness, or unsubdued
Elations when the forest blooms; gusty
Emotions on wet roads on autumn nights;
All pleasures and all pains, remembering
The bough of summer and the winter branch.
30 These are the measures destined for her soul.

3

Jove in the clouds had his inhuman birth.
No mother suckled him, no sweet land gave
Large-mannered motions to his mythy mind.
He moved among us, as a muttering king,
35 Magnificent, would move among his hinds,
Until our blood, commingling, virginal,
With heaven, brought such requital to desire
The very hinds discerned it, in a star.
Shall our blood fail? Or shall it come to be
40 The blood of paradise? And shall the earth
Seem all of paradise that we shall know?
The sky will be much friendlier then than now,
A part of labor and a part of pain,
And next in glory to enduring love,
45 Not this dividing and indifferent blue.

4

She says, "I am content when wakened birds,
Before they fly, test the reality
Of misty fields, by their sweet questionings;
But when the birds are gone, and their warm fields
50 Return no more, where, then, is paradise?
There is not any haunt of prophecy,
Nor any old chimera of the grave,
Neither the golden underground, nor isle
Melodious, where spirits gat them home,
55 Nor visionary south, nor cloudy palm
Remote on heaven's hill, that has endured
As April's green endures; or will endure
Like her remembrance of awakened birds,
Or her desire for June and evening, tipped
60 By the consummation of the swallow's wings.

38 *hinds* Female deer.   **52** *chimera* A horrible fancy, a groundless conception.
54 *gat* Got.

5

She says, "But in contentment I still feel
The need of some imperishable bliss."
Death is the mother of beauty; hence from her,
Alone, shall come fulfilment to our dreams
65 And our desires. Although she strews the leaves
Of sure obliteration on our paths,
The path sick sorrow took, the many paths
Where triumph rang its brassy phrase, or love
Whispered a little out of tenderness,
70 She makes the willow shiver in the sun
For maidens who were wont to sit and gaze
Upon the grass, relinquished to their feet.
She causes boys to pile new plums and pears
On disregarded plate. The maidens taste
75 And stray impassioned in the littering leaves.

6

Is there no change of death in paradise?
Does ripe fruit never fall? Or do the boughs
Hang always heavy in that perfect sky,
Unchanging, yet so like our perishing earth,
80 With rivers like our own that seek for seas
They never find, the same receding shores
That never touch with inarticulate pang?
Why set the pear upon those river-banks
Or spice the shores with odors of the plum?
85 Alas, that they should wear our colors there,
The silken weavings of our afternoons,
And pick the strings of our insipid lutes!
Death is the mother of beauty, mystical,
Within whose burning bosom we devise
90 Our earthly mothers waiting, sleeplessly.

7

Supple and turbulent, a ring of men
Shall chant in orgy on a summer morn
Their boisterous devotion to the sun,
Not as a god, but as a god might be,
95 Naked among them, like a savage source.
Their chant shall be a chant of paradise,
Out of their blood, returning to the sky;
And in their chant shall enter, voice by voice,
The windy lake wherein their lord delights,

100 The trees, like serafin, and echoing hills,
    That choir among themselves long afterward.
    They shall know well the heavenly fellowship
    Of men that perish and of summer morn.
    And whence they came and whither they shall go
105 The dew upon their feet shall manifest.

8

    She hears, upon that water without sound,
    A voice that cries, "The tomb in Palestine
    Is not the porch of spirits lingering.
    It is the grave of Jesus, where he lay."
110 We live in an old chaos of the sun,
    Or old dependency of day and night,
    Or island solitude, unsponsored, free,
    Of that wide water, inescapable.
    Deer walk upon our mountains, and the quail
115 Whistle about us their spontaneous cries;
    Sweet berries ripen in the wilderness;
    And, in the isolation of the sky,
    At evening, casual flocks of pigeons make
    Ambiguous undulations as they sink,
120 Downward to darkness, on extended wings.

    100 *serafin*   Angels of the highest rank and guardians of God's throne.

Anatomy of Monotony

1

    If from the earth we came, it was an earth
    That bore us as a part of all the things
    It breeds and that was lewder than it is.
    Our nature is her nature. Hence it comes,
5   Since by our nature we grow old, earth grows
    The same. We parallel the mother's death.
    She walks an autumn ampler than the wind
    Cries up for us and colder than the frost
    Pricks in our spirits at the summer's end,
10 And over the bare spaces of our skies
    She sees a barer sky that does not bend.

2

The body walks forth naked in the sun
And, out of tenderness or grief, the sun
Gives comfort, so that other bodies come,
15 Twinning our phantasy and our device,
And apt in versatile motion, touch and sound
To make the body covetous in desire
Of the still finer, more implacable chords.
So be it. Yet the spaciousness and light
20 In which the body walks and is deceived,
Falls from that fatal and that barer sky,
And this the spirit sees and is aggrieved.

Lions in Sweden

No more phrases, Swenson: I was once
A hunter of those sovereigns of the soul
And savings banks, Fides, the sculptor's prize,
All eyes and size, and galled Justitia,
5   Trained to poise the tables of the law,
Patientia, forever soothing wounds,
And mighty Fortitudo, frantic bass.
But these shall not adorn my souvenirs,
These lions, these majestic images.
10 If the fault is with the soul, the sovereigns
Of the soul must likewise be at fault, and first.
If the fault is with the souvenirs, yet these
Are the soul itself. And the whole of the soul, Swenson,
As every man in Sweden will concede,
15 Still hankers after lions, or, to shift,
Still hankers after sovereign images.
If the fault is with the lions, send them back
To Monsieur Dufy's Hamburg whence they came.
The vegetation still abounds with forms.

3 *Fides* Roman goddess of good faith, often on coins. Note also association with Fidei Defensor, Defender of the Faith, a title of English sovereigns (rulers).   4 *Justitia* Goddess of justice.   6-7 *Patientia . . . Fortitudo* Stevens seems to be spoofing in an obvious way. Patientia and Fortitudo are not among the gods. Fortitudo is not a musical term.   18 *Monsieur Dufy's Hamburg* Raoul Dufy (1877-1953), French painter and designer, is *not* particularly associated with Hamburg.

The Woman in Sunshine

It is only that this warmth and movement are like
The warmth and movement of a woman.

It is not that there is any image in the air
Nor the beginning nor end of a form:

5   It is empty. But a woman in threadless gold
Burns us with brushings of her dress

And a dissociated abundance of being,
More definite for what she is—

Because she is disembodied,
10   Bearing the odors of the summer fields,

Confessing the taciturn and yet indifferent,
Invisibly clear, the only love.

William Carlos Williams   (1883–1963)

Tract

I will teach you my townspeople
how to perform a funeral
for you have it over a troop
of artists—
5   unless one should scour the world—
you have the ground sense necessary.

See! the hearse leads.
I begin with a design for a hearse.
For Christ's sake not black—
10   nor white either—and not polished!
Let it be weathered—like a farm wagon—
with gilt wheels (this could be
applied fresh at small expense)
or no wheels at all:
15   a rough dray to drag over the ground.
Knock the glass out!
My God!—glass, my townspeople!
For what purpose? Is it for the dead
to look out or for us to see
20   how well he is housed or to see

the flowers or the lack of them—
or what?
To keep the rain and snow from him?

He will have a heavier rain soon:
25 pebbles and dirt and what not.
Let there be no glass—
and no upholstery, phew!
and no little brass rollers
and small easy wheels on the bottom—
30 my townspeople what are you thinking of?

A rough plain hearse then
with gilt wheels and no top at all.
On this the coffin lies
by its own weight.

                No wreaths please—
35 especially no hot house flowers.
Some common memento is better,
something he prized and is known by:
his old clothes—a few books perhaps—
God knows what! You realize
40 how we are about these things
my townspeople—
something will be found—anything
even flowers if he had come to that.
So much for the hearse.

45 For heaven's sake though see to the driver!
Take off the silk hat! In fact
that's no place at all for him—
up there unceremoniously
dragging our friend out to his own dignity!
50 Bring him down—bring him down!
Low and inconspicuous! I'd not have him ride
on the wagon at all—damn him—
the undertaker's understrapper!
Let him hold the reins
55 and walk at the side
and inconspicuously too!

Then briefly as to yourselves:
Walk behind—as they do in France,
seventh class, or if you ride
60 Hell take curtains! Go with some show
of inconvenience; sit openly—

to the weather as to grief.
Or do you think you can shut grief in?
What—from us? We who have perhaps
65 nothing to lose? Share with us
share with us—it will be money
in your pockets.
                        Go now
I think you are ready.

A Sort of a Song

Let the snake wait under
his weed
and the writing
be of words, slow and quick, sharp
5 to strike, quiet to wait,
sleepless.

—through metaphor to reconcile
the people and the stones.
Compose. (No ideas
10 but in things) Invent!
Saxifrage is my flower that splits
the rocks.

All That Is Perfect in Woman

The symbol of war, a war
fast accomplished
flares in all our faces
an alcoholic flame—

5 Miami sunlight:
the pattern of waves
mottled with foam
against a blond day!

The fish scream
10 in soundless agony
trapped by its
sulphuric acid—

a blow-torch flame
at exorbitant cost

15 virginity
    longing for snow and

    a quiet life
    that will (rightly)
    blossom as
20 a mangled corpse:

    Our own Joppolo Schmidt
    the G. I. Joe
    acted by himself,
    a pathetic scene laid

25 upon thin slices
    of sympathy, a snack
    between halves
    to rouse a smile.

    And in our mouths!
30 a foot minus three toes—
    In our embraces

    a head partly scorched,
    hairless and with
    no nose! Between

35 the thighs a delicious
    lung with entrails
    and a tongue or gorget!

    Blithe spirit! Monody
    with feces—you
40 must sing of her and

    behold the overpowering
    foetor of her
    girlish breasts and breath:

    tumbled seas,
45 washing waves, the grave's
    grandfather.

    Let us praise! praise
    the dreadful symbol of
    carnivorous sex—

50 The gods live!
    severally amongst us—
    This is their familiar!

—whose blue eyes
and laughing mouth affirm
55 the habeas corpus
of our resignation

Oh Lorca, Lorca—
shining singer if you
could have been
60 alive for this!

At five in the afternoon.

—fecund and jocund
are familiar to the sea
and what dangles, lacerant,

65 under the belly of
the Portuguese Man O'War is also
familiar to the sea, familiar
to the sea, the sea.

55 *habeas corpus*   A writ requiring the body of a person to be brought before a judge or into court; literally, you shall have the body.   **57** *Lorca*   Federico García Lorca (1899-1936), Spanish lyric poet and dramatist, murdered at the time of the Spanish civil war.

The Words, the Words, the Words

The perfume of the iris, sweet citron,
is enhanced by money, the
odor of buckwheat, the woman's odor.
Sand does not chafe, with money.
5 Sheep fold, horse neigh but money
mollifies it.
Leap or swim
sleep or be drunk in whatever arms
or none
10 money is the crown

Your eyes, thighs, breasts—rose pointed,
money is their couch, their room,
the light from between lattices . . .

Lady behind the hedge, behind the
15 wall:
silken limbs, white brow,

money filters in through the shelving
leaves over you

Rise and shake your skirts
20 to the buttercups, yellow as polished
gold

T. S. Eliot   (1888–1965)

The Hollow Men

Mistah Kurtz—he dead.
                    A penny for the Old Guy

I

We are the hollow men
We are the stuffed men
Leaning together
Headpiece filled with straw. Alas!
5   Our dried voices, when
We whisper together
Are quiet and meaningless
As wind in dry grass
Or rats' feet over broken glass
10 In our dry cellar

  Shape without form, shade without colour,
Paralysed force, gesture without motion;

  Those who have crossed
With direct eyes, to death's other Kingdom
15 Remember us—if at all—not as lost
Violent souls, but only
As the hollow men
The stuffed men.

Mistah Kurtz—he dead.   The first epigraph is from Joseph Conrad's long short story *Heart of Darkness* (1899), the announcement of the death of the lost and violent central figure of the story. **A penny for the Old Guy**   The second epigraph is a phrase used by English children to beg pennies for fireworks on Guy Fawkes Day (November 5). Fawkes (1570-1606) was one of the principal figures in the Gunpowder Plot, a conspiracy to kill King James I and blow up Parliament on November 5, 1605; the plot was discovered and its leaders executed. While begging for pennies the English children carry stuffed effigies of Fawkes.

II

Eyes I dare not meet in dreams
20 In death's dream kingdom
These do not appear:
There, the eyes are
Sunlight on a broken column
There, is a tree swinging
25 And voices are
In the wind's singing
More distant and more solemn
Than a fading star.

Let me be no nearer
30 In death's dream kingdom
Let me also wear
Such deliberate disguises
Rat's coat, crowskin, crossed staves
In a field
35 Behaving as the wind behaves
No nearer—

Not that final meeting
In the twilight kingdom

III

This is the dead land
40 This is cactus land
Here the stone images
Are raised, here they receive
The supplication of a dead man's hand
Under the twinkle of a fading star.

45   Is it like this
In death's other kingdom
Waking alone
At the hour when we are
Trembling with tenderness
50 Lips that would kiss
Form prayers to broken stone.

IV

The eyes are not here
There are no eyes here
In this valley of dying stars
55 In this hollow valley
This broken jaw of our lost kingdoms

In this last of meeting places
We grope together
And avoid speech
60 Gathered on this beach of the tumid river

Sightless, unless
The eyes reappear
As the perpetual star
Multifoliate rose
65 Of death's twilight kingdom
The hope only
Of empty men.

V

Here we go round the prickly pear
Prickly pear prickly pear
70 *Here we go round the prickly pear*
At five o'clock in the morning.

Between the idea
And the reality
Between the motion
75 And the act
Falls the Shadow
                        For Thine is the Kingdom

Between the conception
And the creation
80 Between the emotion
And the response
Falls the Shadow
                        Life is very long

Between the desire
85 And the spasm
Between the potency
And the existence
Between the essence
And the descent
90 Falls the Shadow
                    For Thine is the Kingdom

52-67 *The eyes . . . empty men*   See Dante's *Inferno,* 3, and *Paradiso,* 31-32. The *Multifoliate rose* (l. 64) is a complex symbol whose suggestion includes the light of God.   **68** *Here we go round . . .*   Variant of the nursery rhyme "Here we go round the mulberry bush." The *prickly pear* is a cactus (cf. l. 40).   **77** *For Thine is the Kingdom*   From the doxology or praise to God of the Lord's Prayer, "For Thine is the Kingdom, and the Power, and the Glory," used by most Protestants.

       For Thine is
    Life is
    For Thine is the

95   *This is the way the world ends*
       This is the way the world ends
       This is the way the world ends
       Not with a bang but a whimper.

From LANDSCAPES

I. New Hampshire

    Children's voices in the orchard
    Between the blossom- and the fruit-time:
    Golden head, crimson head,
    Between the green tip and the root.
5   Black wing, brown wing, hover over;
    Twenty years and the spring is over;
    To-day grieves, to-morrow grieves,
    Cover me over, light-in-leaves;
    Golden head, black wing,
10 Cling, swing,
    Spring, sing,
    Swing up into the apple-tree.

II. Virginia

    Red river, red river,
    Slow flow heat is silence
    No will is still as a river
    Still. Will heat move
5   Only through the mocking-bird
    Heard once? Still hills
    Wait. Gates wait. Purple trees,
    White trees, wait, wait,
    Delay, decay. Living, living,
10 Never moving. Ever moving
    Iron thoughts came with me
    And go with me:
    Red river, river, river.

Seek only there
10 Where the grey light meets the green air
The hermit's chapel, the pilgrim's prayer.

III.   Usk

Do not suddenly break the branch, or
Hope to find
The white hart behind the white well.
Glance aside, not for lance, do not spell
5 Old enchantments. Let them sleep.
"Gently dip, but not too deep,"
Lift your eyes
Where the roads dip and where the roads rise

Usk   A river of southeastern Wales noted for its beauty and associations with King Arthur. The river flows through the Usk Valley.   **6** *"Gently dip . . . deep"*   From the play *The Old Wives Tale* (l. 734), by George Peele (c. 1557-1596).

IV.   Rannoch, by Glencoe

Here the crow starves, here the patient stag
Breeds for the rifle. Between the soft moor
And the soft sky, scarcely room
To leap or soar. Substance crumbles, in the thin air
5 Moon cold or moon hot. The road winds in
Listlessness of ancient war
Languor of broken steel,
Clamour of confused wrong, apt
In silence. Memory is strong
10 Beyond the bone. Pride snapped,
Shadow of pride is long, in the long pass
No concurrence of bone.

Rannoch, by Glencoe   *Glencoe* is a glen in the north of Argyll, Scotland. It contains the river Coe and is associated with the Gaelic warrior and poet Ossian. A Celtic cross commemorates the 1692 massacre of the MacDonalds of Glencoe, perhaps an association of "confused wrong" (l. 8). Rannoch is a lake.

Wilfred Owen   (1893–1918)

Anthem for Doomed Youth

What passing-bells for these who die as cattle?
Only the monstrous anger of the guns.
Only the stuttering rifles' rapid rattle
Can patter out their hasty orisons.
5   No mockeries for them from prayers or bells,
Nor any voice of mourning save the choirs,—
The shrill, demented choirs of wailing shells;
And bugles calling for them from sad shires.
What candles may be held to speed them all?
10   Not in the hands of boys, but in their eyes
Shall shine the holy glimmers of good-byes.
The pallor of girls' brows shall be their pall;
Their flowers the tenderness of silent minds,
And each slow dusk a drawing-down of blinds.

E. E. Cummings   (1894–1962)

since feeling is first

since feeling is first
who pays any attention
to the syntax of things
will never wholly kiss you;
5   wholly to be a fool
while Spring is in the world

my blood approves,
and kisses are a better fate
than wisdom
10   lady i swear by all flowers. Don't cry
—the best gesture of my brain is less than
your eyelids' flutter which says

we are for each other: then
laugh, leaning back in my arms
15   for life's not a paragraph

And death i think is no parenthesis

i thank You God for most this amazing

i thank You God for most this amazing
day:for the leaping greenly spirits of trees
and a blue true dream of sky;and for everything
which is natural which is infinite which is yes

5 (i who have died am alive again today,
and this is the sun's birthday;this is the birth
day of life and of love and wings:and of the gay
great happening illimitably earth)

how should tasting touching hearing seeing
10 breathing any—lifted from the no
of all nothing—human merely being
doubt unimaginable You?

(now the ears of my ears awake and
now the eyes of my eyes are opened)

anyone lived in a pretty how town

anyone lived in a pretty how town
(with up so floating many bells down)
spring summer autumn winter
he sang his didn't he danced his did.

5 Women and men(both little and small)
cared for anyone not at all
they sowed their isn't they reaped their same
sun moon stars rain

children guessed(but only a few
10 and down they forgot as up they grew
autumn winter spring summer)
that noone loved him more by more

when by now and tree by leaf
she laughed his joy she cried his grief
15 bird by snow and stir by still
anyone's any was all to her

someones married their everyones
laughed their cryings and did their dance
(sleep wake hope and then)they
20 said their nevers they slept their dream

stars rain sun moon
(and only the snow can begin to explain
how children are apt to forget to remember
with up so floating many bells down)

25 one day anyone died i guess
(and noone stooped to kiss his face)
busy folk buried them side by side
little by little and was by was

all by all and deep by deep
30 and more by more they dream their sleep
noone and anyone earth by april
wish by spirit and if by yes.

Women and men(both dong and ding)
summer autumn winter spring
35 reaped their sowing and went their came
sun moon stars rain

Louise Bogan   (1897 – 1970)

The Crossed Apple

I've come to give you fruit from out of my orchard,
Of wide report.
I have trees there that bear me many apples
Of every sort:

5 Clear, streakèd; red and russet; green and golden;
Sour and sweet.
This apple's from a tree yet unbeholden,
Where two kinds meet,—

So that this side is red without a dapple,
10 And this side's hue
Is clear and snowy. It's a lovely apple.
It is for you.

Within are five black pips as big as peas,
As you will find,
15 Potent to breed you five great apple trees
Of varying kind:

To breed you wood for fire, leaves for shade,
Apples for sauce.
Oh, this is a good apple for a maid,
20 It is a cross,

Fine on the finer, so the flesh is tight,
And grained like silk.
Sweet Burning gave the red side, and the white
Is Meadow Milk.

25 Eat it; and you will taste more than the fruit:
The blossom, too,
The sun, the air, the darkness at the root,
The rain, the dew,

The earth we came to, and the time we flee,
30 The fire and the breast.
I claim the white part, maiden, that's for me.
You take the rest.

Langston Hughes   (1902–1967)

Bound No'th Blues

Goin' down the road, Lawd,
Goin' down the road.
Down the road, Lawd,
Way, way down the road.
5 Got to find somebody
To help me carry this load.

Road's in front o' me,
Nothin' to do but walk.
Road's in front o' me,
10 Walk . . . an' walk . . . an' walk.
I'd like to meet a good friend
To come along an' talk.

Hates to be lonely,
Lawd, I hates to be sad.
15 Says I hates to be lonely,
Hates to be lonely an' sad,
But ever' friend you finds seems
Like they try to do you bad.

Road, road, road, O!
20 Road, road . . . road . . . road, road!
Road, road, road, O!
On the no'thern road.
These Mississippi towns ain't
Fit fer a hoppin' toad.

Passing Love

Because you are to me a song
I must not sing you over-long.

Because you are to me a prayer
I cannot say you everywhere.

5   Because you are to me a rose—
You will not stay when summer goes.

Countee Cullen   (1903–1946)

A Song of Praise

You have not heard my love's dark throat,
    Slow-fluting like a reed,
Release the perfect golden note
    She caged there for my need.

5   Her walk is like the replica
    Of some barbaric dance
Wherein the soul of Africa
    Is winged with arrogance.

And yet so light she steps across
10   The ways her sure feet pass,
She does not dent the smoothest moss
    Or bend the thinnest grass.

My love is dark as yours is fair,
    Yet lovelier I hold her
15 Than listless maids with pallid hair,
    And blood that's thin and colder.

You-proud-and-to-be-pitied one,
    Gaze on her and despair;

Then seal your lips until the sun
20   Discovers one as fair.

A Thorn Forever in the Breast

A hungry cancer will not let him rest
Whose heart is loyal to the least of dreams;
There is a thorn forever in his breast
Who cannot take his world for what it seems;
5   Aloof and lonely must he ever walk,
Plying a strange and unaccustomed tongue,
An alien to the daily round of talk,
Mute when the sordid songs of earth are sung.

This is the certain end his dream achieves:
10 He sweats his blood and prayers while others sleep,
And shoulders his own coffin up a steep
Immortal mountain, there to meet his doom
Between two wretched dying men, of whom
One doubts, and one for pity's sake believes.

C. Day Lewis   (1904–1972)

Let Us Now Praise Famous Men

Let us now praise famous men,
Not your earth-shakers, not the dynamiters,
But who in the Home Counties or the Khyber,
Trimming their nails to meet an ill wind,
5   Facing the Adversary with a clean collar,
Justified the system.
Admire the venerable pile that bred them,
Bones are its foundations,
The pinnacles are stone abstractions,
10 Whose halls are whispering-galleries designed
To echo voices of the past, dead tongues.
White hopes of England here
Are taught to rule by learning to obey,
Bend over before vested interests,
15 Kiss the rod, salute the quarter-deck;

3 *Khyber*   Khyber Pass, a mountain pass on the India-Pakistan border and one of the main
gateways to India from the west.

Here is no savage discipline
Of peregrine swooping, of fire destroying,
But a civil code; no capital offender
But the cool cad, the man who goes too far.
20 Ours the curriculum
Neither of building birds nor wasteful waters,
Bound in book not violent in vein:
Here we inoculate with dead ideas
Against blood-epidemics, against
25 The infection of faith and the excess of life.
Our methods are up to date; we teach
Through head and not by heart,
Language with gramophones and sex with charts,
Prophecy by deduction, prayer by numbers.
30 For honors see prospectus: those who leave us
Will get a post and pity the poor;
Their eyes glaze at strangeness;
They are never embarrassed, have a word for everything,
Living on credit, dying when the heart stops;
35 Will wear black armlets and stand a moment in silence
For the passing of an era, at their own funeral.

17 *peregrine* A kind of falcon.   **30** *prospectus* A preliminary printed statement that describes an enterprise, such as a business, and is distributed to potential buyers or investors.

W. H. Auden   (1907–   )

Musée des Beaux Arts

About suffering they were never wrong,
The Old Masters: how well they understood
Its human position; how it takes place
While someone else is eating or opening a window or just walking dully along;
5 How, when the aged are reverently, passionately waiting
For the miraculous birth, there always must be

Musée des Beaux Arts Auden's fictional variant for the "Palais des Musées Royaux de Peinture et de Sculpture" in Brussels, Belgium. The poem first appeared under the title "Palais des Beaux Arts," which is a popular form of the museum's name. The poem refers to paintings by Pieter Brueghel the Elder (1525-1569). "Landscape with the Fall of Icarus" (ll. 14-21) hangs in the Palais. The other two, probably, are "The Census in Bethlehem" (ll. 5-8), also in the Palais, and "The Massacre of the Innocents" (ll. 9-12), in the Kunsthistorisches Museum in Vienna. Color reproductions of the three may be found in Gustav Glueck's *Peter Brueghel the Elder* (New York: George Braziller, 1936).

Children who did not specially want it to happen, skating
On a pond at the edge of the wood:
They never forgot
10 That even the dreadful martyrdom must run its course
Anyhow in a corner, some untidy spot
Where the dogs go on with their doggy life and the torturer's horse
Scratches its innocent behind on a tree.

In Brueghel's *Icarus,* for instance: how everything turns away
15 Quite leisurely from the disaster; the ploughman may
Have heard the splash, the forsaken cry,
But for him it was not an important failure; the sun shone
As it had to on the white legs disappearing into the green
Water; and the expensive delicate ship that must have seen
20 Something amazing, a boy falling out of the sky,
Had somewhere to get to and sailed calmly on.

---

14 *Icarus* In Greek myth *Icarus* was the son of Daedalus, the architect who contrived the labyrinth in Crete in which the Minotaur (a monster half human and half bull) was kept, but Daedalus was himself imprisoned in the labyrinth with his son. They escaped on wings of feathers and wax, but when Icarus flew too near the sun the wax melted and he fell into the sea.

Louis MacNeice   (1907 – 1963)

Snow

The room was suddenly rich and the great bay-window was
Spawning snow and pink roses against it
Soundlessly collateral and incompatible:
World is suddener than we fancy it.

5 World is crazier and more of it than we think,
Incorrigibly plural. I peel and portion
A tangerine and spit the pips and feel
The drunkenness of things being various.

And the fire flames with a bubbling sound for world
10 Is more spiteful and gay than one supposes—
On the tongues on the eyes on the ears in the palms of your hands—
There is more than glass between the snow and the huge roses.

The Sunlight on the Garden

The sunlight on the garden
Hardens and grows cold,
We cannot cage the minute
Within its nets of gold,
5 When all is told
We cannot beg for pardon.

Our freedom as free lances
Advances towards its end;
The earth compels, upon it
10 Sonnets and birds descend;
And soon, my friend,
We shall have no time for dances.

The sky was good for flying
Defying the church bells
15 And every evil iron
Siren and what it tells:
The earth compels,
We are dying, Egypt, dying

And not expecting pardon,
20 Hardened in heart anew,
But glad to have sat under
Thunder and rain with you,
And grateful too
For sunlight on the garden.

18 *We are dying, Egypt, dying* Echo of a line spoken by Antony to Cleopatra in Shakespeare's *Antony and Cleopatra* (IV, xv, 41), "I am dying, Egypt, dying."

Theodore Roethke (1908–1963)

Dolor

I have known the inexorable sadness of pencils,
Neat in their boxes, dolor of pad and paper-weight,
All the misery of manilla folders and mucilage,
Desolation in immaculate public places,
5 Lonely reception room, lavatory, switchboard,
The unalterable pathos of basin and pitcher,
Ritual of multigraph, paper-clip, comma,
Endless duplication of lives and objects.

And I have seen dust from the walls of institutions,
10 Finer than flour, alive, more dangerous than silica,
Sift, almost invisible, through long afternoons of tedium,
Dropping a fine film on nails and delicate eyebrows,
Glazing the pale hair, the duplicate gray standard faces.

The Waking

I wake to sleep, and take my waking slow.
I feel my fate in what I cannot fear.
I learn by going where I have to go.

We think by feeling. What is there to know?
5 I hear my being dance from ear to ear.
I wake to sleep, and take my waking slow.

Of those so close beside me, which are you?
God bless the Ground! I shall walk softly there,
And learn by going where I have to go.

10 Light takes the Tree; but who can tell us how?
The lowly worm climbs up a winding stair;
I wake to sleep, and take my waking slow.

Great Nature has another thing to do
To you and me; so take the lively air,
15 And, lovely, learn by going where to go.

This shaking keeps me steady. I should know.
What falls away is always. And is near.
I wake to sleep, and take my waking slow.
I learn by going where I have to go.

The Minimal

I study the lives on a leaf: the little
Sleepers, numb nudgers in cold dimensions,
Beetles in caves, newts, stone-deaf fishes,
Lice tethered to long limp subterranean weeds,
5 Squirmers in bogs,
And bacterial creepers
Wriggling through wounds
Like elvers in ponds,
Their wan mouths kissing the warm sutures,
10 Cleaning and caressing,
Creeping and healing.

The Rose

1

There are those to whom place is unimportant,
But this place, where sea and fresh water meet,
Is important—
Where the hawks sway out into the wind,
5   Without a single wingbeat,
And the eagles sail low over the fir trees,
And the gulls cry against the crows
In the curved harbors,
And the tide rises up against the grass
10   Nibbled by sheep and rabbits.

A time for watching the tide,
For the heron's hieratic fishing,
For the sleepy cries of the towhee,
The morning birds gone, the twittering finches,
15   But still the flash of the kingfisher, the wingbeat of the scoter,
The sun a ball of fire coming down over the water,
The last geese crossing against the reflected afterlight,
The moon retreating into a vague cloud-shape
To the cries of the owl, the eerie whooper.
20   The old log subsides with the lessening waves,
And there is silence.

I sway outside myself
Into the darkening currents,
Into the small spillage of driftwood,
25   The waters swirling past the tiny headlands.
Was it here I wore a crown of birds for a moment
While on a far point of the rocks
The light heightened,
And below, in a mist out of nowhere,
30   The first rain gathered?

2

As when a ship sails with a light wind—
The waves less than the ripples made by rising fish,
The lacelike wrinkles of the wake widening, thinning out,
Sliding away from the traveler's eye,
35   The prow pitching easily up and down,
The whole ship rolling slightly sideways,
The stern high, dipping like a child's boat in a pond—
Our motion continues.

But this rose, this rose in the sea-wind,
40 Stays,
Stays in its true place,
Flowering out of the dark,
Widening at high noon, face upward,
A single wild rose, struggling out of the white embrace of the morning-glory,
45 Out of the briary hedge, the tangle of matted underbrush,
Beyond the clover, the ragged hay,
Beyond the sea pine, the oak, the wind-tipped madrona,
Moving with the waves, the undulating driftwood,
Where the slow creek winds down to the black sand of the shore
50 With its thick grassy scum and crabs scuttling back into their glistening craters.

And I think of roses, roses,
White and red, in the wide six-hundred-foot greenhouses,
And my father standing astride the cement benches,
Lifting me high over the four-foot stems, the Mrs. Russells, and his own elaborate
    hybrids,
55 And how those flowerheads seemed to flow toward me, to beckon me, only a child,
    out of myself.

What need for heaven, then,
With that man, and those roses?

3

What do they tell us, sound and silence?
I think of American sounds in this silence:
60 On the banks of the Tombstone, the wind-harps having their say,
The thrush singing alone, that easy bird,
The killdeer whistling away from me,
The mimetic chortling of the catbird
Down in the corner of the garden, among the raggedy lilacs,
65 The bobolink skirring from a broken fencepost,
The bluebird, lover of holes in old wood, lilting its light song,
And that thin cry, like a needle piercing the ear, the insistent cicada,
And the ticking of snow around oil drums in the Dakotas,
The thin whine of telephone wires in the wind of a Michigan winter,
70 The shriek of nails as old shingles are ripped from the top of a roof,
The bulldozer backing away, the hiss of the sandblaster,
And the deep chorus of horns coming up from the streets in early morning.
I return to the twittering of swallows above water,
And that sound, that single sound,
75 When the mind remembers all,
And gently the light enters the sleeping soul,
A sound so thin it could not woo a bird,

Beautiful my desire, and the place of my desire.

I think of the rock singing, and light making its own silence,
80 At the edge of a ripening meadow, in early summer,
The moon lolling in the close elm, a shimmer of silver,
Or that lonely time before the breaking of morning
When the slow freight winds along the edge of the ravaged hillside,
And the wind tries the shape of a tree,
85 While the moon lingers,
And a drop of rain water hangs at the tip of a leaf
Shifting in the wakening sunlight
Like the eye of a new-caught fish.

4

I live with the rocks, their weeds,
90 Their filmy fringes of green, their harsh
Edges, their holes
Cut by the sea-slime, far from the crash
Of the long swell,
The oily, tar-laden walls
95 Of the toppling waves,
Where the salmon ease their way into the kelp beds,
And the sea rearranges itself among the small islands.

Near this rose, in this grove of sun-parched, wind-warped madronas,
Among the half-dead trees, I came upon the true ease of myself,
100 As if another man appeared out of the depths of my being,
And I stood outside myself,
Beyond becoming and perishing,
A something wholly other,
As if I swayed out on the wildest wave alive,
105 And yet was still.
And I rejoiced in being what I was:
In the lilac change, the white reptilian calm,
In the bird beyond the bough, the single one
With all the air to greet him as he flies,
110 The dolphin rising from the darkening waves;

And in this rose, this rose in the sea-wind,
Rooted in stone, keeping the whole of light,
Gathering to itself sound and silence—
Mine and the sea-wind's.

Light Listened

O what could be more nice
Than her ways with a man?
She kissed me more than twice
Once we were left alone.
5   Who'd look when he could feel?
She'd more sides than a seal.

The close air faintly stirred.
Light deepened to a bell,
The love-beat of a bird.
10   She kept her body still
And watched the weather flow.
We live by what we do.

All's known, all, all around:
The shape of things to be;
15   A green thing loves the green
And loves the living ground.
The deep shade gathers night;
She changed with changing light.

We met to leave again
20   The time we broke from time;
A cold air brought its rain,
The singing of a stem.
She sang a final song;
Light listened when she sang.

Hyam Plutzik   (1911–1962)

The Geese

A miscellaneous screaming that comes from nowhere
Raises the eyes at last to the moonward-flying
Squadron of wild-geese arcing the spatial cold.

Beyond the hunter's gun or the will's range
5   They press southward, toward the secret marshes
Where the appointed gunmen mark the crossing

Of flight and moment. There is no force stronger
(In the sweep of the monomaniac passion, time)
Than the will toward destiny, which is death.

10   Value the intermediate splendor of birds.

Karl Shapiro   (1913–   )

Buick

As a sloop with a sweep of immaculate wing on her delicate spine
And a keel as steel as a root that holds in the sea as she leans,
Leaning and laughing, my warm-hearted beauty, you ride, you ride,
You tack on the curves with parabola speed and a kiss of goodbye,
5   Like a thoroughbred sloop, my new high-spirited spirit, my kiss.

As my foot suggests that you leap in the air with your hips of a girl,
My finger that praises your wheel and announces your voices of song,
Flouncing your skirts, you blueness of joy, you flirt of politeness,
You leap, you intelligence, essence of wheelness with silvery nose,
10   And your platinum clocks of excitement stir like the hairs of a fern.

But how alien you are from the booming belts of your birth and the smoke
Where you turned on the stinging lathes of Detroit and Lansing at night
And shrieked at the torch in your secret parts and the amorous tests,
But now with your eyes that enter the future of roads you forget;
15   You are all instinct with your phosphorous glow and your streaking hair.

And now when we stop it is not as the bird from the shell that I leave
Or the leathery pilot who steps from his bird with a sneer of delight,
And not as the ignorant beast do you squat and watch me depart,
But with exquisite breathing you smile, with satisfaction of love,
20   And I touch you again as you tick in the silence and settle in sleep.

1 *sloop*   A single-masted fore-and-aft rigged sailing vessel used principally for racing.   **4** *tack*
Change direction by shifting the sails.   *parabola*   The most efficient.

Robert Hayden   (1913–   )

O Daedalus, Fly Away Home

Drifting night in the Georgia pines,
coonskin drum and jubilee banjo.
    Pretty Malinda, dance with me.

Daedalus   In Greek myth the architect who contrived the labyrinth in Crete in which the
Minotaur (a monster half human and half bull) was kept. Daedalus was himself imprisoned in the
labyrinth with his son Icarus, but devised wings of feathers and wax as a means of escape. When
Icarus flew too near the sun, the wax melted and he fell into the sea. Daedalus flew safely to Sicily.

Night is juba, night is conjo.
5   Pretty Malinda, dance with me.

Night is an African juju man
weaving a wish and a weariness together
     to make two wings.

     O fly away home fly away

10 Do you remember Africa?

     O cleave the air fly away home

My gran, he flew back to Africa,
just spread his arms and
     flew away home.

15 Drifting night in the windy pines;
night is a laughing, night is a longing.
     Pretty Malinda, come to me.

Night is a mourning juju man
weaving a wish and a weariness together
20   to make two wings.

     O fly away home fly away

4 *juba* A characteristic Negro dance or its music; also, in black folklore a ghost or mythical character, perhaps of African origin. *conjo* Perhaps a reference to a conjure bag, which was used by slaves to charm away evil spirits and do miraculous things for its wearer. 6 *juju man* A magician or conjurer who uses jujus, or charms and fetishes.

William Stafford (1914–)

Parentage

My father didn't really belong in history.
He kept looking over his shoulder at some mistake.
He was a stranger to me, for I belong.

There never was a particular he couldn't understand,
5 but there were too many in too long a row,
and like many another he was overwhelmed.

Today drinking coffee I look over the cup
and want to have the right amount of fear,
preferring to be saved and not, like him, heroic.

10   I want to be as afraid as the teeth are big,
I want to be as dumb as the wise are wrong:
I'd just as soon be pushed by events to where I belong.

Lake Chelan

They call it regional, this relevance—
the deepest place we have: in this pool forms
the model of our land, a lonely one,
responsive to the wind. Everything we own
5   has brought us here: from here we speak.

The sun stalks among these peaks to sight
the lake down aisles, long like a gun;
a ferryboat, lost by a century, toots
for trappers, the pelt of the mountains
10   rinsed in the sun and that sound.

Suppose a person far off to whom this lake
occurs: told a problem, he might hear a word
so dark he drowns an instant, and stands dumb
for the centuries of his country and the suave
15   hills beyond the stranger's sight.

Is this man dumb, then, for whom Chelan lives
in the wilderness? On the street you've seen
someone like a trapper's child pause,
and fill his eyes with some irrelevant flood—
20   a tide stops him, delayed in his job.

Permissive as a beach, he turns inland,
harks like a fire, glances through the dark
like an animal drinking, and arrives along that line
a lake has found far back in the hills
25   where what comes finds a brim gravity exactly requires.

Lake Chelan   In north-central Washington, sixty-five miles long and one to two miles wide—
one of the deepest lakes in the United States, 1419 feet.

Dylan Thomas (1914–1953)

The Force That Through the Green Fuse Drives the Flower

The force that through the green fuse drives the flower
Drives my green age; that blasts the roots of trees
Is my destroyer.
And I am dumb to tell the crooked rose
5   My youth is bent by the same wintry fever.

The force that drives the water through the rocks
Drives my red blood; that dries the mouthing streams
Turns mine to wax.
And I am dumb to mouth unto my veins
10   How at the mountain spring the same mouth sucks.

The hand that whirls the water in the pool
Stirs the quicksand; that ropes the blowing wind
Hauls my shroud sail.
And I am dumb to tell the hanging man
15   How of my clay is made the hangman's lime.

The lips of time leech to the fountain head;
Love drips and gathers, but the fallen blood
Shall calm her sores.
And I am dumb to tell a weather's wind
20   How time has ticked a heaven round the stars.

And I am dumb to tell the lover's tomb
How at my sheet goes the same crooked worm.

Green Fuse Perhaps a literal reference to the stem of the flower, but figuratively open to varied interpretation.

We Lying by Seasand

We lying by seasand, watching yellow
And the grave sea, mock who deride
Who follow the red rivers, hollow
Alcove of words out of cicada shade,
5   For in this yellow grave of sand and sea
A calling for colour calls with the wind
That's grave and gay as grave and sea
Sleeping on either hand.

The lunar silences, the silent tide
10 Lapping the still canals, the dry tide-master
    Ribbed between desert and water storm,
    Should cure our ills of the water
    With a one-coloured calm;
    The heavenly music over the sand
15 Sounds with the grains as they hurry
    Hiding the golden mountains and mansions
    Of the grave, gay, seaside land.
    Bound by a sovereign strip, we lie,
    Watch yellow, wish for wind to blow away
20 The strata of the shore and drown red rock;
    But wishes breed not, neither
    Can we fend off rock arrival,
    Lie watching yellow until the golden weather
    Breaks, O my heart's blood, like a heart and hill.

Poem in October

    It was my thirtieth year to heaven
Woke to my hearing from harbor and neighbor wood
    And the mussel pooled and the heron
        Priested shore
5   The morning beckon
With water praying and call of seagull and rook
And the knock of sailing boats on the net webbed wall
        Myself to set foot
        That second
10 In the still sleeping town and set forth.

    My birthday began with the water-
Birds and the birds of the winged trees flying my name
    Above the farms and the white horses
        And I rose
15   In rainy autumn
And walked abroad in a shower of all my days.
High tide and the heron dived when I took the road
        Over the border
        And the gates
20 Of the town closed as the town awoke.

10 *the still sleeping town* The village of Laugharne on the southwest coast of Wales, where
Dylan Thomas had his home for the last fifteen of his thirty-nine years.

A springful of larks in a rolling
Cloud and the roadside bushes brimming with whistling
  Blackbirds and the sun of October
      Summery
25   On the hill's shoulder,
Here were fond climates and sweet singers suddenly
Come in the morning where I wandered and listened
  To the rain wringing
     Wind blow cold
30   In the wood faraway under me.

Pale rain over the dwindling harbor
And over the sea wet church the size of a snail
  With its horns through mist and the castle
     Brown as owls
35   But all the gardens
Of spring and summer were blooming in the tall tales
Beyond the border and under the lark full cloud.
  There could I marvel
     My birthday
40   Away but the weather turned around.

It turned away from the blithe country
And down the other air and the blue altered sky
  Streamed again a wonder of summer
     With apples
45   Pears and red currants
And I saw in the turning so clearly a child's
Forgotten mornings when he walked with his mother
  Through the parables
     Of sun light
50   And the legends of the green chapels

And the twice told fields of infancy
That his tears burned my cheeks and his heart moved in mine.
  These were the woods the river and sea
     Where a boy
55   In the listening
Summertime of the dead whispered the truth of his joy
To the trees and the stones and the fish in the tide.
  And the mystery
     Sang alive
60   Still in the water and singingbirds.

And there could I marvel my birthday
Away but the weather turned around. And the true

Joy of the long dead child sang burning
    In the sun.
65   It was my thirtieth
Year to heaven stood there then in the summer noon
Though the town below lay leaved with October blood.
        O may my heart's truth
        Still be sung
70   On this high hill in a year's turning.

Do Not Go Gentle into That Good Night

Do not go gentle into that good night,
Old age should burn and rave at close of day;
Rage, rage against the dying of the light.

Though wise men at their end know dark is right,
5 Because their words had forked no lightning they
Do not go gentle into that good night.

Good men, the last wave by, crying how bright
Their frail deeds might have danced in a green bay,
Rage, rage against the dying of the light.

10 Wild men who caught and sang the sun in flight,
And learn, too late, they grieved it on its way,
Do not go gentle into that good night.

Grave men, near death, who see with blinding sight
Blind eyes could blaze like meteors and be gay,
15 Rage, rage against the dying of the light.

And you, my father, there on the sad height,
Curse, bless, me now with your fierce tears, I pray.
Do not go gentle into that good night.
Rage, rage against the dying of the light.

Fern Hill

Now as I was young and easy under the apple boughs
About the lilting house and happy as the grass was green,
    The night above the dingle starry,

Fern Hill A farm where as a boy Dylan Thomas spent country holidays, near Llangain in Wales. It was rented by James Jones, the husband of Dylan's Aunt Ann.   **3** *dingle* A small wooded valley.

        Time let me hail and climb

5   Golden in the heydays of his eyes,
And honoured among wagons I was prince of the apple towns
And once below a time I lordly had the trees and leaves
        Trail with daisies and barley
     Down the rivers of the windfall light.

10   And as I was green and carefree, famous among the barns
About the happy yard and singing as the farm was home,
      In the sun that is young once only,
        Time let me play and be
     Golden in the mercy of his means,
15   And green and golden I was huntsman and herdsman, the calves
Sang to my horn, the foxes on the hills barked clear and cold,
        And the sabbath rang slowly
     In the pebbles of the holy streams.

All the sun long it was running, it was lovely, the hay
20   Fields high as the house, the tunes from the chimneys, it was air
      And playing, lovely and watery
           And fire green as grass.
      And nightly under the simple stars
As I rode to sleep the owls were bearing the farm away,
25   All the moon long I heard, blessed among stables, the nightjars
      Flying with the ricks, and the horses
        Flashing into the dark.

And then to awake, and the farm, like a wanderer white
With the dew, come back, the cock on his shoulder: it was all
30   Shining, it was Adam and maiden,
        The sky gathered again
      And the sun grew round that very day.
So it must have been after the birth of the simple light
In the first, spinning place, the spellbound horses walking warm
35   Out of the whinnying green stable
        On to the fields of praise.

And honoured among foxes and pheasants by the gay house
Under the new made clouds and happy as the heart was long
      In the sun born over and over,
40   I ran my heedless ways,
     My wishes raced through the house high hay
And nothing I cared, at my sky blue trades, that time allows
In all his tuneful turning so few and such morning songs

25 *nightjars* Birds, such as whippoorwills and nighthawks.   **26** *ricks* Stacks of hay.

Before the children green and golden
45   Follow him out of grace,

Nothing I cared, in the lamb white days, that time would take me
Up to the swallow thronged loft by the shadow of my hand,
    In the moon that is always rising,
        Nor that riding to sleep
50   I should hear him fly with the high fields
And wake to the farm forever fled from the childless land.
Oh as I was young and easy in the mercy of his means,
    Time held me green and dying
    Though I sang in my chains like the sea.

John Ciardi   (1916–   )

The Gift

In 1945, when the keepers cried *kaput,*
Josef Stein, poet, came out of Dachau
like half a resurrection, his other
eighty pounds still in their invisible grave.

5 Slowly then the mouth opened and first
a broth, and then a medication, and then
a diet, and all in time and the knitting mercies,
the showing bones were buried back in flesh,

and the miracle was finished. Josef Stein,
10   man and poet, rose, walked, and could even
beget, and did, and died later of other causes
only partly traceable to his first death.

He noted—with some surprise at first—
that strangers could not tell he had died once.
15   He returned to his post in the library, drank his beer,
published three poems in a French magazine,

and was very kind to the son who at last was his.
In the spent of one night he wrote three propositions:
That Hell is the denial of the ordinary. That nothing lasts.
20   That clean white paper waiting under a pen

is the gift beyond history and hurt and heaven.

1 *kaput* Roughly, "we've had it," originally an expression from a game of cards.   **2** *Dachau*
Nazi concentration camp, eleven miles northwest of Munich.

Epitaph

Here, time concurring (and it does),
Lies Ciardi. If no kingdom come,
A kingdom was. Such as it was,
This one, beside it, is a slum.

Faces

Once in Canandaigua, hitchhiking from Ann Arbor
to Boston in the middle of December, and just
as dark came full on a stone-cracking
drill of wind that shot a grit of snow,
5 I was picked up outside an all-night diner
by a voice in a Buick. "Jump in," it said. "It's cold."

Four, five miles out, in the dead winter of nowhere
and black as the insides of a pig, we stopped.
"I turn off here."
          I looked around at nothing.
"The drive's up there," he said.
10   But when I was out,
he headed on, turned round, drove back, and stopped.
"You haven't thanked me for the ride," he said.
"Thanks," I said, shuffling to find a rock
I might kick loose and grab for just in case.
15 But he wasn't that kind of crazy. He just waved:
"You're welcome, brother. Keep the rest for change."
Then he pulled in his head and drove away—
back toward Canandaigua.
                  I thought about him
a good deal, you might say, out there in the sandblast
20 till a truck lit like a liner picked me up
one blue-black inch from frostbite.
And off and on for something like twenty years
I've found him in my mind, whoever he was,
whoever he is—I never saw his face,
25 only its shadow—but for twenty years
I've been finding faces that might do for his.
The Army was especially full of possibles,
but not to the point of monopoly. Any party
can spring one through a doorway. "How do you do?"
30 you say and the face opens and there you are
back in the winter blast.

               But why tell you?
It's anybody's world for the living in it:
You know as much about that face as I do.

Robert Lowell   (1917–   )

From **Mexico (10)**

No artist perhaps, you go beyond their phrases,
a girl too simple for this measured cunning. . . .
Take that day of baking on the marble veranda,
the roasting brown rock, the roasting brown grass, the breath
5   of the world risen like the ripe smoke of chestnuts,
a cleavage dropping miles to the valley's body;
and the following sick and thoughtful day
of the red flower, the hills, the valley, the Volcano—
this not the greatest thing, though great; the hours
10   of shivering, ache and burning, when we'd charged
so far beyond our courage—altitudes,
then the falling . . . falling back on honest speech:
infirmity, a food the flesh must swallow,
feeding our minds . . . the mind which is also flesh.

Lawrence Ferlinghetti   (1919–   )

The Pennycandystore Beyond the El

The pennycandystore beyond the El
is where I first
            fell in love
                   with unreality
5   Jellybeans glowed in the semi-gloom
of that september afternoon
A cat upon the counter moved among
                  the licorice sticks
        and tootsie rolls
10   and Oh Boy Gum

Outside the leaves were falling as they died

A wind had blown away the sun

A girl ran in
Her hair was rainy
15   Her breasts were breathless in the little room

Outside the leaves were falling
             and they cried
                   Too soon! too soon!

Pennycandystore   A store, typical of the 1920s and 1930s, in which pieces of candy were
sold for a penny.   **El**   Elevated railway.

Starting from San Francisco

Here I go again
crossing the country in coach trains
(back to my old
lone wandering)
5   All night Eastward . . . Upward
over the Great Divide and on
into Utah
over Great Salt Plain
and onward, rocking,
10 the white dawn burst
across mesas,
table-lands,
all flat, all laid away.
Great glary sun—
15 wood bridge over water. . . .
Later in still light, we still reel onward—
Onward?
Back and forth, across the Continent,
bang bang
20 by any wheel or horse,
any rail,
by car
by buggy
by stagecoach,
25 walking,
riding,
hooves pounding the Great Plains,
caravans into the night. Forever.
Into Wyoming.
30 All that day and night, rocking through it,
snow on steppes and plains of November,
roads lost in it—or never existent—
back in the beginning again, no People yet,
no ruts Westward yet
35 under the snow. . . .
Still more huge spaces we bowl through,
still untouched dark land—
Indomitable.
Horizons of mesas
40 like plains of Spain high up
in Don Quixote country—

6 *the Great Divide*   The Continental Divide, the great ridge of the Rocky Mts. that separates
rivers flowing east from those flowing west.   **41** *Don Quixote*   Hero of Cervantes' satiric masterpiece
Don Quixote (1615).

sharp eroded towers of bluffs
like windmills tilted,
"los molinos" of earth, abandoned—
45 Great long rectangular stone islands
sticking up on far plains, like forts
or immense light cargo ships
high on plains of water,
becalmed and rudderless,
50 props thrashing wheat,
stranded forever,
no one on those bridges. . . .
Later again, much later,
one small halfass town,
55 followed by one telephone wire
and one straight single iron road
hung to the tracks as by magnets
attached to a single endless fence,
past solitary pumping stations,
60 each with a tank, a car, a small house, a dog,
no people anywhere—
All hiding?
White Man gone home?
Must be a cowboy someplace. . . .
65 Birds flap from fences, trestles,
caw and caw their nothingness.
Stone church sticks up
quote Out of Nowhere unquote
This must be Interzone
70 between Heaven and Brooklyn.
Do they have a Classified Section
as in phonebooks
in the back of the Bibles here?
Otherwise they'd never find Anything.
75 Try Instant Zen. . . .
Still later again,
sunset and strange clouds like udders
rayed with light from below—
some God's hand sticks through,
80 black trees stand out.
The world is a winter farm—
Cradle we rocked out of—
prairie schooners into Pullmans,

---

44 *"los molinos"* The mills.   **75** *Zen* Zen Buddhism, which asserts that enlightenment or inner self-realization can be attained through meditation.   **83** *prairie schooners* Covered wagons used by pioneers in cross-country travel.   *Pullmans* Railroad sleeping cars.

their bright saloons sheeted in oblivion—
85 Wagon-lits—bedwagons over the prairies,
bodies nested in them,
hurtled through night,
inscrutable. . . .
Onward still . . . or Backward . . .
90 huge snow fields still, on and on,
still no one,
Indians all gone to Florida
or Cuba!
Train hoots at something
95 in the nowhere we still rock through,
Dingding crossroads flicker by,
Mining towns, once roaring,
now shrunk to the railhead,
streetlights stoned with loneliness
100 or lit with leftover sun
they drank too much of during the day. . . .
And at long last now
this world shrunk
to one lone brakeman's face
105 stuck out of darkness—
long white forehead
like bleached skull of cow—
huge black sad eyes—
high-peaked cloth cap, grey-striped—
100 swings his railroad lantern high, close up,
as our window whizzes by—
his figure splashed upon it,
slanted, muezzin-like,
very grave, very tall,
115 strange skeleton—
Who stole America?

Myself I saw in the window reflected.

---

113 *muezzin* · A Muslim crier who calls the hour of daily prayers.

Howard Nemerov (1920–)

The Town Dump

"The art of our necessities is strange,
That can make vile things precious."

A mile out in the marshes, under a sky
Which seems to be always going away
In a hurry, on that Venetian land threaded
With hidden canals, you will find the city
5 Which seconds ours (so cemeteries, too,
Reflect a town from hillsides out of town),
Where Being most Becomingly ends up
Becoming some more. From cardboard tenements,
Windowed with cellophane, or simply tenting
10 In paper bags, the angry mackerel eyes
Glare at you out of stove-in, sunken heads
Far from the sea; the lobster, also, lifts
An empty claw in his most minatory
Of gestures; oyster, crab, and mussel shells
15 Lie here in heaps, savage as money hurled
Away at the gate of hell. If you want results,
These are results.
                    Objects of value or virtue,
However, are also to be picked up here,
Though rarely, lying with bones and rotten meat,
20 Eggshells and mouldy bread, banana peels
No one will skid on, apple cores that caused
Neither the fall of man nor a theory
Of gravitation. People do throw out
The family pearls by accident, sometimes,
25 Not often; I've known dealers in antiques
To prowl this place by night, with flashlights, on
The off-chance of somebody's having left
Derelict chairs which will turn out to be
By Hepplewhite, a perfect set of six
30 Going to show, I guess, that in any sty
Someone's heaven may open and shower down
Riches responsive to the right dream; though
It is a small chance, certainly, that sends
The ghostly dealer, heavy with fly-netting

"**The art . . . precious**" The epigraph is from Shakespeare's *King Lear* (III, ii, 70–71).
13 *minatory* Menacing.   **29** *Hepplewhite* George Hepplewhite (d. 1786), English cabinetmaker
famed for the delicacy and beauty of his furniture design.

35 Over his head, across these hills in darkness,
    Stumbling in cut-glass goblets, lacquered cups,
    And other products of his dreamy midden
    Pencilled with light and guarded by the flies.

    For there are flies, of course. A dynamo
40 Composed, by thousands, of our ancient black
    Retainers, hums here day and night, steady
    As someone telling beads, the hum becoming
    A high whine at any disturbance; then,
    Settled again, they shine under the sun
45 Like oil-drops, or are invisible as night,
    By night.
                All this continually smoulders,
    Crackles, and smokes with mostly invisible fires
    Which, working deep, rarely flash out and flare,
    And never finish. Nothing finishes;
50 The flies, feeling the heat, keep on the move.

    Among the flies, the purifying fires,
    The hunters by night, acquainted with the art
    Of our necessities, and the new deposits
    That each day wastes with treasure, you may say
55 There should be ratios. You may sum up
    The results, if you want results. But I will add
    That wild birds, drawn to the carrion and flies,
    Assemble in some numbers here, their wings
    Shining with light, their flight enviably free,
60 Their music marvelous, though sad, and strange.

    37 *midden*   Dunghill, refuse heap.

The Dream of Flying Comes of Age

Remember those wingovers and loops and spins?
Forbidden. Heavy, powerful, and solemn,
Our scheduled transports keep the straight and level.
It's not the joystick now, but the control column.

The Blue Swallows

Across the millstream below the bridge
Seven blue swallows divide the air
In shapes invisible and evanescent,

Kaleidoscopic beyond the mind's
5 Or memory's power to keep them there.

"History is where tensions were,"
"Form is the diagram of forces."
Thus, helplessly, there on the bridge,
While gazing down upon those birds—
10 How strange, to be above the birds!—
Thus helplessly the mind in its brain
Weaves up relation's spindrift web,
Seeing the swallows' tails as nibs
Dipped in invisible ink, writing . . .

15 Poor mind, what would you have them write?
Some cabalistic history
Whose authorship you might ascribe
To God? to Nature? Ah, poor ghost,
You've capitalized your Self enough.
20 That villainous William of Occam
Cut out the feet from under that dream
Some seven centuries ago.
It's taken that long for the mind
To waken, yawn and stretch, to see
25 With opened eyes emptied of speech
The real world where the spelling mind
Imposes with its grammar book
Unreal relations on the blue
Swallows. Perhaps when you will have
30 Fully awakened, I shall show you
A new thing: even the water
Flowing away beneath those birds
Will fail to reflect their flying forms,
And the eyes that see become as stones
35 Whence never tears shall fall again.

O swallows, swallows, poems are not
The point. Finding again the world,
That is the point, where loveliness
Adorns intelligible things
40 Because the mind's eye lit the sun.

20 *William of Occam* English scholastic philosopher (c. 1300-1349) who all but closed the scholastic controversy over universals with his nominalistic doctrine that the real is always individual and that universals have no real existence but are only abstract terms.

Richard Wilbur   (1921–   )

The Death of a Toad

A toad the power mower caught,
Chewed and clipped of a leg, with a hobbling hop has got
To the garden verge, and sanctuaried him
Under the cineraria leaves, in the shade
5   Of the ashen heart-shaped leaves, in a dim,
Low, and a final glade.

The rare original heartsblood goes,
Spends on the earthen hide, in the folds and wizenings, flows
In the gutters of the banked and staring eyes. He lies
10   As still as if he would return to stone,
And soundlessly attending, dies
Toward some deep monotone,

Toward misted and ebullient seas
And cooling shores, toward lost Amphibia's emperies.
15   Day dwindles, drowning, and at length is gone
In the wide and antique eyes, which still appear
To watch, across the castrate lawn,
The haggard daylight steer.

14 *Amphibia's emperies*   An *empery* is the territory of an emperor or powerful ruler. *Amphibia*
is a class of cold-blooded vertebrate animals.

Philip Larkin   (1922–   )

Reasons for Attendance

The trumpet's voice, loud and authoritative,
Draws me a moment to the lighted glass
To watch the dancers—all under twenty-five—
Shifting intently, face to flushed face,
5 Solemnly on the beat of happiness.

—Or so I fancy, sensing the smoke and sweat,
The wonderful feel of girls. Why be out here?
But then, why be in there? Sex, yes, but what
Is sex? Surely, to think the lion's share
10 Of happiness is found by couples—sheer

Inaccuracy, as far as I'm concerned.
What calls me is that lifted, rough-tongued bell
(Art, if you like) whose individual sound
Insists I too am individual.
15 It speaks; I hear; others may hear as well,

But not for me, nor I for them; and so
With happiness. Therefore I stay outside,
Believing this; and they maul to and fro,
Believing that; and both are satisfied,
20 If no one has misjudged himself. Or lied.

James Dickey   (1923-   )

The Hospital Window

I have just come down from my father.
Higher and higher he lies
Above me in a blue light
Shed by a tinted window.
5 I drop through six white floors
And then step out onto pavement.

Still feeling my father ascend,
I start to cross the firm street,
My shoulder blades shining with all
10 The glass the huge building can raise.
Now I must turn round and face it,
And know his one pane from the others.

Each window possesses the sun
As though it burned there on a wick.
15 I wave, like a man catching fire.
All the deep-dyed windowpanes flash,
And, behind them, all the white rooms
They turn to the color of Heaven.

Ceremoniously, gravely, and weakly,
20 Dozens of pale hands are waving
Back, from inside their flames.
Yet one pure pane among these
Is the bright, erased blankness of nothing.
I know that my father is there,

25 In the shape of his death still living.
   The traffic increases around me
   Like a madness called down on my head.
   The horns blast at me like shotguns,
   And drivers lean out, driven crazy—
30 But now my propped-up father

   Lifts his arm out of stillness at last.
   The light from the window strikes me
   And I turn as blue as a soul,
   As the moment when I was born.
35 I am not afraid for my father—
   Look! He is grinning; he is not

   Afraid for my life, either,
   As the wild engines stand at my knees
   Shredding their gears and roaring,
40 And I hold each car in its place
   For miles, inciting its horn
   To blow down the walls of the world

   That the dying may float without fear
   In the bold blue gaze of my father.
45 Slowly I move to the sidewalk
   With my pin-tingling hand half dead
   At the end of my bloodless arm.
   I carry it off in amazement,

   High, still higher, still waving,
50 My recognized face fully mortal,
   Yet not; not at all, in the pale,
   Drained, otherworldly, stricken,
   Created hue of stained glass.
   I have just come down from my father.

Cherrylog Road

   Off Highway 106
   At Cherrylog Road I entered
   The '34 Ford without wheels,
   Smothered in kudzu,
5 With a seat pulled out to run
   Corn whiskey down from the hills,

---

4 kudzu   A twining, rapidly growing, hardy perennial with large leaves and purple flowers.

And then from the other side
Crept into an Essex
With a rumble seat of red leather
10 And then out again, aboard
A blue Chevrolet, releasing
The rust from its other color,

Reared up on three building blocks.
None had the same body heat;
15 I changed with them inward, toward
The weedy heart of the junkyard,
For I knew that Doris Holbrook
Would escape from her father at noon

And would come from the farm
20 To seek parts owned by the sun
Among the abandoned chassis,
Sitting in each in turn
As I did, leaning forward
As in a wild stock-car race

25 In the parking lot of the dead.
Time after time, I climbed in
And out the other side, like
An envoy or movie star
Met at the station by crickets.
30 A radiator cap raised its head,

Become a real toad or a kingsnake
As I neared the hub of the yard,
Passing through many states,
Many lives, to reach
35 Some grandmother's long Pierce-Arrow
Sending platters of blindness forth

From its nickel hubcaps
And spilling its tender upholstery
On sleepy roaches,
40 The glass panel in between
Lady and colored driver
Not all the way broken out,

8 Essex   A low-priced car, first made in 1919.   **35 Pierce-Arrow**   A large luxury car, first
made in 1914.

The back-seat phone
Still on its hook.
45 I got in as though to exclaim,
"Let us go to the orphan asylum,
John; I have some old toys
For children who say their prayers."

I popped with sweat as I thought
50 I heard Doris Holbrook scrape
Like a mouse in the southern-state sun
That was eating the paint in blisters
From a hundred car tops and hoods.
She was tapping like code,

55 Loosening the screws,
Carrying off headlights,
Sparkplugs, bumpers,
Cracked mirrors and gear-knobs,
Getting ready, already,
60 To go back with something to show

Other than her lips' new trembling
I would hold to me soon, soon,
Where I sat in the ripped back seat
Talking over the interphone,
65 Praying for Doris Holbrook
To come from her father's farm

And to get back there
With no trace of me on her face
To be seen by her red-haired father
70 Who would change, in the squalling barn,
Her back's pale skin with a strop,
Then lay for me

In a bootlegger's roasting car
With a string-triggered 12-gauge shotgun
75 To blast the breath from the air.
Not cut by the jagged windshields,
Through the acres of wrecks she came
With a wrench in her hand,

Through dust where the blacksnake dies
80 Of boredom, and the beetle knows
The compost has no more life.

Someone outside would have seen
The oldest car's door inexplicably
Close from within:

85 I held her and held her and held her,
Convoyed at terrific speed
By the stalled, dreaming traffic around us,
So the blacksnake, stiff
With inaction, curved back
90 Into life, and hunted the mouse

With deadly overexcitement,
The beetles reclaimed their field
As we clung, glued together,
With the hooks of the seat springs
95 Working through to catch us red-handed
Amidst the gray, breathless batting

That burst from the seat at our backs.
We left by separate doors
Into the changed, other bodies
100 Of cars, she down Cherrylog Road
And I to my motorcycle
Parked like the soul of the junkyard

Restored, a bicycle fleshed
With power, and tore off
105 Up Highway 106, continually
Drunk on the wind in my mouth,
Wringing the handlebar for speed,
Wild to be wreckage forever.

Encounter in the Cage Country

What I was would not work
For them all, for I had not caught
The lion's eye. I was walking down

The cellblock in green glasses   and came
5 At last to the place where someone was hiding
His spots in his black hide.

Unchangeably they were there,
Driven in as by eyes
Like mine, his darkness ablaze

10 In the stinking sun of the beast house.
Among the crowd, he found me
Out   and dropped his bloody snack

And came to the perilous edge
Of the cage, where the great bars tremble
15 Like wire. All Sunday ambling stopped,

The curved cells tightened around
Us all   as we saw he was watching only
Me. I knew the stage was set, and I began

To perform   first saunt'ring   then stalking
20 Back and forth like a sentry   faked
As if to run   and at one brilliant move

I made as though drawing a gun from my hip-
bone, the bite-sized children broke
Up   changing their concept of laughter,

25 But none of this changed his eyes, or changed
My green glasses. Alert, attentive,
He waited for what I could give him:

My moves   my throat   my wildest love,
The eyes behind my eyes. Instead, I left
30 Him, though he followed me right to the end

Of concrete. I wiped my face, and lifted off
My glasses. Light blasted the world of shade
Back under every park bush   the crowd

Quailed from me   I was inside and out
35 Of myself   and something was given a life-
mission to say to me hungrily over

And over and over   *your moves are exactly right*
For a few things in this world: we know you
When you come, Green Eyes, Green Eyes.

John Logan   (1923–   )

Spring of the Thief

But if I look the ice is gone from the lake
and the altered air
no longer fills with the small
terrible bodies of the snow.
5 Only once these late winter weeks
the dying flakes
fell instead as manna or as wedding rice
blooming in the light
about the bronze Christ
10 and the thieves. There these three
still hang, more than man-
sized and heavier than life
on a hill over the lake
where I walk
15 this Third Sunday of Lent.
I come from Mass
melancholy at its ancient story
of the unclean ghost
a man thought he'd lost.
20 It came back into his well-swept house
and at the final state that man
was worse than he began.
Yet again today
there is the faintest edge of green
25 to trees about St. Joseph's Lake.
Ah God if our confessions show contempt
because we let them free us of our guilt
to sin again
forgive us still . . . before the leaves . . .
30 before the leaves have formed
you can glimpse the Christ and Thieves
on top of the hill. One of them was saved.
That day the snow had seemed to drop like grace
upon the four of us,
35 or like the peace of intercourse,
suddenly I wanted to confess—
or simply talk.
I paid a visit to the mammoth Sacred Heart
Church, and found it shut.

---

9 *bronze* Cf. Daniel 2:39, "and yet a third kingdom of bronze, which shall rule over all the
earth."

40 Who locked him out or in?
   Is the name of God changing in our time?
   What is his winter name?
   Where was his winter home?
   Oh I've kept my love to myself before.
45 Even those ducks weave down the shore
   together, drunk with hope
   for the April water. One spring festival
   near here I stripped and strolled
   through a rain filled field.
50 Spread eagled on the soaking earth
   I let the rain
   move its audible little hands
   gently on my skin . . . let the dark rain
   raise up my love.
55 But why? I was alone
   and no one saw how ardent I grew.
   And when I rolled naked in the snow one night
   as St. Francis with his Brother Ass
   or a hard bodied Finn
60 I was alone. Underneath
   the howling January moon
   I knelt and dug my fist
   full of the cold winter sand
   and rubbed and
65 hid my manhood under it.
   Washed up at some ancient or half-heroic shore
   I was ashamed that I was naked there.
   Before Nausicaä and the saints. Before myself.
   But who took off my coat? Who put it on?
70 Who drove me home?
   Blessed be sin if it teaches men shame.
   Yet because of it we cannot talk
   and I am separated from myself.
   So what is all this reveling in snow and rain?
75 Or in the summer sun when the heavy gold
   body weeps with joy or grief or love?
   When we speak of God, is it God we speak of?
   Perhaps his winter home
   is in that field where I rolled or ran . . .
80 this hill where once the snow
   fell serene as rain.
   Oh I have walked around the lake

68 *Nausicaä* Gracious daughter of Alcinuous, king of the Phaeacians. She found Odysseus
when he swam ashore to Scheria, supplied him with clothes, and took him to her father's palace,
where he was welcomed.

when I was not alone—
sometimes with my wife have seen these swans
85   dip down their necks
graceful as a girl, showering white and wet!
I've seen their heads delicately turn.
Have gone sailing with my quiet, older son.
And once on a morning walk
90   a student who had just come back
in fall found a perfect hickory shell
among the bronze and red
leaves and purple flowers of the time
and put its white bread into my hand.
95   Ekelöf said there is a freshness
nothing can destroy in us—
not even we ourselves.
Perhaps that
Freshness is the changed name of God.
100   Where all the monsters also hide
I bear him in the ocean of my blood
and in the pulp of my enormous head.
He lives beneath the unkempt potter's grass
of my belly and chest.
105   I feel his terrible, aged heart
moving under mine . . . can see the shadows
of the gorgeous light
that plays at the edges of his giant eye . . .
or tell the faint press and hum
110   of his eternal pool of sperm.
Like sandalwood! *Like sandalwood*
the righteous man
perfumes the axe that falls on him.
The cords of elm, of cedar oak and pine
115   will pile again in fall.
The ribs and pockets of the barns will swell.
Winds and fires in the field rage
and again burn out each
of the ancient roots.
120   Again at last the late November snow
will fill those fields, change this hill,
throw these figures in relief
and raining on them
will transform
125   the bronze Christ's brow and cheek,
the white face and thigh of the thief.

95 *Ekelöf*   Gunnar Ekelöf (1907-1968), Swedish poet and critic.

Philip Booth   (1925–   )

Deer Isle

Out-island once, on a South slope
bare in March, I saw a buck
limp out of the spruce and snow
to ease his gut in a hummocky meadow.

5   He fed two rooted hours on the hope
of spring, browsed, and flicked back
into the trees, a big ghost
of what hunters tracked at first frost.

That was six winters ago. Today,
10   three hundred miles South, a commuter
trapped by a detour sign
at dusk, I trailed a reflecting line

of red arrows that took me the long way
home. Late, caught in the neuter
15   traffic, driven beyond where I wanted
to go, I braked by a slanted

orchard where six cars were stopped.
There were six does there, feeding on frozen
winesaps, fat and white-rumped
20   as the drivers who sat in their cars. One limped,

and I thought of that buck, equipped
to survive, on the island he'd chosen
to swim to. That coast, about now,
would lie gray: the raw salt snow

25   topping a man's hauled lobsterpots,
and sifting down through thick spruce
where the sweat on a run buck
would freeze. A man with no luck

but a gun would be hunting home cross-lots.
30   I was parked miles beyond choice,
miles from home on a blocked curve
in the dead mist of a thick suburban preserve.

Deer Isle   An island off the coast of Maine.

My guts clamped. I honked my way clear,
tramping the gas toward nowhere
35   but where home was. My wife understood.
If I didn't go now, I never would.

W. D. Snodgrass   (1926–   )

Lobsters in the Window

First, you think they are dead.
Then you are almost sure
One is beginning to stir.
Out of the crushed ice, slow
5   As the hands on a schoolroom clock,
He lifts his one great claw
And holds it over his head;
Now he is trying to walk.

But like a run-down toy;
10   Like the backward crabs we boys
Waded for in the creek,
Trapped in jars or a net,
And then took home to keep.
Overgrown, retarded, weak,
15   He is fumbling yet
From the deep chill of his sleep

As if, in a glacial thaw,
Some ancient thing should wake
Sore and cold and stiff,
20   Struggling to raise one claw
Like a defiant fist,
Yet wavering, as if
Starting to swell and ache
With that thick peg in the wrist.

25   I should wave back, I guess,
But still in his permanent clench,
He's fallen back with the mass
Heaped in their common trench
Who stir, but do not look out
30   Through the rainstreaming glass,
Hear what the newsboys shout,
Or see the raincoats pass.

Robert Bly (1926–)

Love Poem

When we are in love, we love the grass,
And the barns, and the lightpoles,
And the small mainstreets abandoned all night.

Solitude Late at Night in the Woods

1

The body is like a November birch facing the full moon
And reaching into the cold heavens.
In these trees there is no ambition, no sodden body, no leaves,
Nothing but bare trunks climbing like cold fire!

2

5 My last walk in the trees has come. At dawn
I must return to the trapped fields,
To the obedient earth.
The trees shall be reaching all the winter.

3

It is a joy to walk in the bare woods.
10 The moonlight is not broken by the heavy leaves.
The leaves are down, and touching the soaked earth,
Giving off the odor that partridges love.

Watching Television

Sounds are heard too high for ears,
From the body cells there is an answering bay;
Soon the inner streets fill with a chorus of barks.

We see the landing craft coming in,
5 The black car sliding to a stop,
The Puritan killer loosening his guns.

Wild dogs tear off noses and eyes
And run off with them down the street—
The body tears off its own arms and throws them into the air.

10 The detective draws fifty-five million people into his revolver,
    Who sleep restlessly as in an air raid in London;
    Their backs become curved in the sloping dark.

    The filaments of the soul slowly separate:
    The spirit breaks, a puff of dust floats up,
15 Like a house in Nebraska that suddenly explodes.

Anne Sexton   (1928–   )

Ringing the Bells

        And this is the way they ring
    the bells in Bedlam
    and this is the bell-lady
    who comes each Tuesday morning
5   to give us a music lesson
    and because the attendants make you go
    and because we mind by instinct,
    like bees caught in the wrong hive,
    we are the circle of the crazy ladies
10 who sit in the lounge of the mental house
    and smile at the smiling woman
    who passes us each a bell,
    who points at my hand
    that holds my bell, E flat,
15 and this is the gray dress next to me
    who grumbles as if it were special
    to be old, to be old,
    and this is the small hunched squirrel girl
    on the other side of me
20 who picks at the hairs over her lip,
    who picks at the hairs over her lip all day,
    and this is how the bells really sound,
    as untroubled and clean
    as a workable kitchen,
25 and this is always my bell responding
    to my hand that responds to the lady
    who points at me, E flat;
    and although we are no better for it,
    they tell you to go. And you do.

LeRoi Jones (Ameer Baraka)   (1934–   )

The People's Choice: The Dream Poems II

A comb or womb of what we lay down nightly
in. Sleeping there, outside the ordinary fact
of lie and death. But there, the tired cone
of black love, tilted heavy through head bone
5   cross and jack to lift the tired soul, crossed staves
of the daring failure's history. Secret cove
of spirit waves of time and loss crack flesh
and dream, he turns there so, cracks simple things
like love. What I, a singer, have for the world
10 is simple, deadly darkness closing down so hard,
is simple, in defense, a yielded portion of grace.

As people in
my life
are common blankness: hugged in the womb
15 of the trees or night's whispered geometries. As people,
to consider, Buddha's child, a bearded drunk
considered, in my head of hair the dark is there
and light it lays against my tongue. I feel no thing
but word, picture, conditioning . . . black tomb of possibility . . .
20 heart, dreams of stinking feet. I feel no single
treachery but what you are having been these few seconds
something like my self.

Leonard Cohen   (1936–   )

Suzanne

Suzanne takes you down
To her place near the river.
You can hear the boats go by,
You can stay the night beside her,
5   And you know that she's half-crazy
But that's why you want to be there,
And she feeds you tea and oranges
That come all the way from China,
And just when you mean to tell her
10 That you have no love to give her,
Then she gets you on her wave-length
And she lets the river answer
That you've always been her lover.

And you want to travel with her,
15 And you want to travel blind,
And you know that she can trust you
'Cause you've touched her perfect body
With your mind.

And Jesus was a sailor
20 When he walked upon the water
And he spent a long time watching
From a lonely wooden tower
And when he knew for certain
That only drowning men could see him,
25 He said, "All men shall be sailors, then,
Until the sea shall free them,"
But he, himself, was broken
Long before the sky would open.
Forsaken, almost human,
30 He sank beneath your wisdom
Like a stone.

And you want to travel with him,
And you want to travel blind,
And you think you'll maybe trust him
35 'Cause he touched your perfect body
With his mind.

Suzanne takes your hand
And she leads you to the river.
She is wearing rags and feathers
40 From Salvation Army counters,
And the sun pours down like honey
On our lady of the harbor;
And she shows you where to look
Among the garbage and the flowers.
45 There are heroes in the seaweed,
There are children in the morning,
They are leaning out for love,
And they will lean that way forever
While Suzanne, she holds the mirror.

50 And you want to travel with her,
You want to travel blind,
And you're sure that she can find you
'Cause she's touched her perfect body
With her mind.

Diane Wakoski   (1937–   )

Love Letter Postmarked Van Beethoven

for a man I love
more than I should,
intemperance being something
a poet cannot afford

I am too angry to sleep beside you,
you big loud symphony who fell asleep drunk;
I try to count sheep and instead
find myself counting the times I would like to shoot you
5   in the back,
your large body
with its mustaches that substitute for love
and its knowledge of motorcycle mechanics that substitutes
for loving me;
10   why aren't you interested in
my beautiful little engine?
It needs a tune-up tonight, dirty with the sludge of
anger, resentment,
and the pistons all sticky, the valves
15   afraid of the lapping you might do,
the way you would clean me out of your life.

I count the times your shoulders writhe
and you topple over
after I've shot you with my Thompson Contender
20   (using the .38-caliber barrel
        or else the one they recommend for shooting rattlesnakes).
I shoot you each time in that wide dumb back,
insensitive to me,
glad for the mild recoil of the gun
25   that relieves a little of my repressed anger
each time I discharge a bullet into you;
one for my father who deserted me and whom you masquerade as,
every night, when you don't come home
or even telephone to give me an idea of when to expect you;
30   the anguish of expectation in one's life
and the hours when the mind won't work, waiting
for the sound of footsteps on the stairs,
the key turning in the lock;
another bullet for my first lover,
35   a boy of 18

(but that was when I was 18 too)
who betrayed me and would not marry me.
You too, betrayer,
you who will not give me your name as even a token of affection;
40   another bullet,
and of course each time
the heavy sound of your body falling over in heavy shoes
a lumber jacket, and a notebook in which you write down
everything
45   but reality;
another bullet for those men
who said they loved me
and followed other women into their silky bedrooms
and kissed them behind curtains,
50   who offered toasts to other women,
making me feel ugly, undesirable;
anger, fury, the desire to cry or to shake you back
to the way you used to love me,
even wanted to,
55   knowing that I have no recourse,
that if I air my grievances you'll only punish me more
or tell me to leave,
and yet knowing that silent grievances
will erode my brain,
60   make pieces of my ability to love
fall off,
like fingers from a leprosied hand;
and I shoot another bullet into your back,
trying to get to sleep,
65   only wanting you to touch me with some gesture of affection;
this bullet for the bad husband who would drink late in bars
and not take me with him,
talking and flirting with other women,
and who would come home, without a friendly word, and sleep
70   celibate next to my hungry body;
a bullet for the hypocrites;
a bullet for my brother who could not love me without guilt;
a bullet for the man I love who never listens to me;
a bullet for the men who run my country without consulting me;
75   a bullet for the man who says I am a fool to expect anyone to listen to me;
a bullet for the man who wrote a love poem to me
and a year later threw it away, saying it was a bad poem;
If I were Beethoven, by now I'd have tried every
dissonant chord;
80   were I a good marksman, being paid to test this new Thompson
Contender, I'd have several dozen dead rattlers lying
along this path already;

instead, I am ashamed of my anger
at you
85   whom I love
whom I ask for so much more than you want to give.
A string quartet would be too difficult right now.
Let us have the first movement of the Moonlight Sonata
I will try counting the notes
90   instead of sheep.

Fire Island Poem

for Jan

I resist
my banker
              He tried
to persuade me of the ocean
5   next to him.
                    He whispers
in my ear
about the rustle of money
of the waves
10   that cut little sand cliffs out of the beach.
                                                I ride away
from him
with you,
              some launch cuts through my belly,
15   leaves scars like the stripes of tigers
to remind me
of deserted beaches, deserts in my life, men riding
their motorcycles in races
I could not qualify for.

20   Do you see how easily
I get tangled
                    like my long hair whipping strangers on the deck
                    of the boat taking us
                    to a burning island,
25   how easily
a man with the sun burning in his hair
draws me
into his life? And how I run away from his
betrayals
30   into the jukebox
              into the rudder of the boat

into the broken heads of fish he cannot look at
into an ocean where sea turtles swim
into the sun,
35   on the beach
planting trees that will not grow,
desperately jumping into waves for the ritual
washing away
of memories
40   like gold glints of mica in the sand.

Open Me Up
and I will show you a mirror.
You are enticed by the mirror
and don't care about me.

45   My banker comes.
He rescues me during a midnight sunset.
He has a dark mustache
black
and reminds me that I have to light the way down
50   a deep road
with my pale skin,
my hands that flash with foam from the waves.
I would tear this page out of my book
and give it to you

55   If you knew
how
to accept it.

Not all fire burns you, young man.
Sometimes it comes in the shape of an island
60   or a tiger,
a woman,
like me,
who needs, wants,
cannot be
65   possessed.
Try,
just try,
to put fire
in your pocket safely,
70   young man.

Bob Dylan   (1941–   )

Sad-Eyed Lady of the Lowlands

With your mercury mouth in the missionary times,
And your eyes like smoke and your prayers like rhymes,
And your silver cross, and your voice like chimes,
Oh, who among them do they think could bury you?
5   With your pockets well protected at last,
And your street-car visions which you place on the grass,
And your flesh like silk, and your face like glass,
Who among them do they think could carry you?
Sad-eyed lady of the lowlands,
10 Where the sad-eyed prophet says that no man comes,
My ware-house eyes, my Arabian drums,
Should I leave them by your gate,
Or, sad-eyed lady, should I wait?

With your sheets like metal and your belt like lace,
15 And your deck of cards missing the jack and the ace,
And your basement clothes and your hollow face,
Who among them can think he could outguess you?
With your silhouette when the sunlight dims
Into your eyes where the moonlight swims,
20 And your match-book songs and your gypsy hymns,
Who among them would try to impress you?
Sad-eyed lady of the lowlands,
Where the sad-eyed prophet says that no man comes,
My ware-house eyes, my Arabian drums,
25 Should I leave them by your gate,
Or, sad-eyed lady, should I wait?

The kings of Tyrus with their convict list
Are waiting in line for their geranium kiss,
And you wouldn't know it would happen like this,
30 But who among them really wants just to kiss you?
With your childhood flames on your midnight rug,
And your Spanish manners and your mother's drugs,
And your cowboy mouth and your curfew plugs,
Who among them do you think could resist you?
35 Sad-eyed lady of the lowlands,
Where the sad-eyed prophet says that no man comes,
My ware-house eyes, my Arabian drums,

---

27 *Tyrus*   Tyre, a Phoenician port, one of the great cities of the ancient world, famous for
its commerce. Located south of what is today Beirut, Lebanon.

Should I leave them by your gate,
Or, sad-eyed lady, should I wait?

40 Oh, the farmers and the businessmen, they all did decide
To show you the dead angels that they used to hide,
But why did they pick you to sympathize with their side?
Oh, how could they ever mistake you?
They wished you'd accepted the blame for the farm,
45 But with the sea at your feet and the phony false alarm,
And with the child of a hoodlum wrapped up in your arms,
How could they ever, ever persuade you?
Sad-eyed lady of the lowlands,
Where the sad-eyed prophet says that no man comes,
50 My ware-house eyes, my Arabian drums,
Should I leave them by your gate,
Or, sad-eyed lady, should I wait?

With your sheet-metal memory of Cannery Row,
And your magazine-husband who one day just had to go,
55 And your gentleness now, which you just can't help but show,
Who among them do you think would employ you?
Now you stand with your thief, you're on his parole
With your holy medallion which your fingertips fold,
And your saint-like face and your ghost-like soul,
60 Oh, who among them do you think could destroy you?
Sad-eyed lady of the lowlands,
Where the sad-eyed prophet says that no man comes,
My ware-house eyes, my Arabian drums,
Should I leave them by your gate,
65 Or, sad-eyed lady, should I wait?

53 *Cannery Row*   In his novel *Cannery Row* (1945) John Steinbeck describes Cannery Row as a street in Monterey, California, with sardine canneries of corrugated iron, honky-tonks, and flop-houses, inhabited by Everybody.

Biographical Notes

Matthew Arnold (1822—1888) was born in Laleham, Middlesex, the eldest son of Dr. Thomas Arnold, headmaster of Rugby. He entered Rugby in 1837 and graduated from Oxford in 1844. From 1851, the year in which he married, until two years before his death he held a position as inspector of schools. From 1857 to 1867 he held a chair in poetry at Oxford. Arnold lectured in the United States in 1883—1884, and in 1886. His poetical works include *The Strayed Reveller and Other Poems* (1849), *Empedocles on Etna and Other Poems* (1852), *Poems* (1853), and *Poems* (1869). His critical essays include *On Translating Homer* (1861), *On the Study of Celtic Literature* (1867), *Essays in Criticism* (1865, 1888), *Culture and Anarchy* (1869), and *Literature and Dogma* (1873).

W. H. Auden (1907—   ) was born in York, England, the son of a retired medical officer. He was educated at Gresham's School in Holt and at Oxford (1925—1928). From 1930 to 1935 he was a schoolteacher. In 1935 he married Erika Mann, daughter of novelist Thomas Mann; they later divorced. In 1939 Auden became an American citizen. He has taught at various colleges and universities in the United States and from 1956—1961 was Professor of Poetry at Oxford. His volumes of poems include *Poems* (1930), *The Orators* (1932), *Look Stranger* (1936), *Another Time* (1940), *The Double Man* (1941), *Collected Poetry* (1945), *The Age of Anxiety: A Baroque Eclogue* (1947), *Nones* (1951), *The Shield of Achilles* (1955), *Homage to Clio* (1960), *About the House* (1965), *Collected Shorter Poems 1927—1957* (1966), *City Without Walls and Other Poems* (1969), and *Collected Longer Poems* (1969). His other writing includes verse plays, translations, librettos, and two volumes of criticism, *The Dyer's Hand and Other Essays* (1962) and *Secondary Worlds* (1967).

William Blake (1757—1827) was born in London, the son of a hosier. At the age of ten he was sent to drawing school to develop a clearly apparent talent. He became a professional engraver and was a prolific artist. Blake married in 1782, but had no children. His poems *Songs of Innocence,* etched on copper with hand-colored decorations, were published in 1789, and *Songs of Experience* in 1794. He also wrote mystical and metaphysical works, including *Prophetic Books* (1793—1804). His reputation as both poet and artist has increased since his death.

Robert Bly (1926—   ) was born in western Minnesota, the son of a farmer. He attended St. Olaf College and Harvard, where he received his B.A. in 1950. He is the editor of The Seventies Press and *The Seventies* magazine, which changed their names with the new decade—thus both were formerly The Sixties. Bly is married, has two children, and lives on a farm near Madison, Minnesota. His translations include *Twenty Poems of Georg Trakl* (1961) with James Wright, *Twenty Poems of Pablo Neruda* (1968) with James

Wright, and *Forty Poems of Juan Ramon Jimenez* (1969). His poetic work includes two volumes of poems, *Silence in the Snowy Fields* (1962) and *The Light Around the Body* (1967). He received the National Book Award for the latter.

Louise Bogan (1897–1970) was born in Livermore Falls, Maine. She was educated at Mount St. Mary's Academy in Manchester, New Hampshire (1907–1909), and the Boston Girls' Latin School (1910–1915), and spent one year at Boston University. She married in 1916, was widowed with a small daughter in 1920, married again in 1925, and was divorced in 1937. After 1925 Bogan lived for the most part in New York, and from 1931 until her death she was a regular reviewer for *The New Yorker.* Her volumes of poems include *Body of This Death* (1923), *Dark Summer* (1929), *The Sleeping Fury* (1937), and *Collected Poems, 1923–1953* (1954). Her criticism is collected in *A Poet's Alphabet* (1970).

Philip Booth (1925–   ) was born in Hanover, New Hampshire, the son of an English professor at Dartmouth College. He attended the Hanover public schools and the Vermont Academy, served as a pilot in the United States Air Force in 1944–1945, and married in 1946. He is the father of three daughters. In 1948 Booth received his B.A. from Dartmouth and in 1949 his M.A. from Columbia. He has taught at Bowdoin, Dartmouth, and Wellesley, and since 1961 at Syracuse University, where he is Professor of English and Poet in Residence. His volumes of poems are *Letter from a Distant Land* (1957), *The Islanders* (1961), *Weathers and Edges* (1966), and *Margins* (1970).

Gwendolyn Brooks (1917–   ) was born in Topeka, Kansas, but her parents actually had their home in Chicago. Brought up in Chicago, she graduated from Englewood High School in 1934 and from Wilson Junior College in 1936. In 1939 she married Henry L. Blakely; they have two children. Brooks has taught at various colleges and universities in the Chicago area and in 1968 succeeded Carl Sandburg as Poet Laureate of Illinois. Her volumes of poems include *A Street in Bronzeville* (1945), *Annie Allen* (1949), *Bronzeville Boys and Girls* (1956), *The Bean Eaters* (1960), *Selected Poems* (1963), and *In the Mecca* (1968). She is also the author of a novel, *Maud Martha* (1953), and a volume of poetry and fiction, *The World of Gwendolyn Brooks* (1971).

Robert Browning (1812–1889) was born in the London suburb of Camberwell, the son of a clerk in the Bank of England. He eventually became the literary lion of London, so celebrated that he was practically a legend, but as a schoolboy he was a rebel and for years remained unrecognized as a poet. In fact, his family supported him until he was thirty-three years old and paid to publish his poetry, with hardly a return on their investment. Browning was in his fifties before he had a real reputation. *The Ring and the Book* (1868–1869), a poem of more than 21,000 lines dramatizing a murder in Renaissance Rome, vaulted him to final success. In 1846 he married Elizabeth Barrett, who was famous as a poet before he was. She was thirty-eight when in January of 1845 he wrote to her, "I love your poems, dear Miss Barrett, and I love you too."

William Cullen Bryant (1794–1878) was born in Cummington, Massachusetts, the son of a physician and scholar. He attended Williams College (1810–1811) and practiced law in Barrington, Massachusetts, from 1815 to 1825. He married in 1820 and was co-owner and coeditor of the New York *Evening Post* from 1829 until his death. Some of his early poems were published in *North American Review* in 1817, but his first book publication was *The Fountain, and Other Poems* in 1842. This was followed by *The Whitefooted Doe and Other Poems* (1844), *The Flood of Years* (1876), and *A Lifetime* (1877).

Robert Burns (1759–1796) was born in Alloway, Ayrshire, in Scotland, the son of a struggling farmer. He was educated by his father and worked as a farmer while writing poetry. He fell in love with Jean Armour in 1786 and, her father refusing to allow her to marry him, she bore him two sons out of wedlock. They were married in 1788 and settled on a farm at Ellisland, Dumfriesshire. In 1786 Burns published *Poems, Chiefly in the Scottish Dialect,* which met with substantial success; a second edition followed the next year. He contributed two hundred songs to James Johnson's *Scots Musical Museum* (1787–1797) and about one hundred songs to *Select Collection of Original Scotish Airs* (1793–1805).

George Gordon, Lord Byron (1788–1824) was born in London and became the sixth Lord Byron at the age of ten. He was educated at Harrow and at Trinity College, Cambridge, and began an extraordinarily successful literary career while still in his twenties. A combination of difficulties, centering on the breakup of his marriage to Annabella Milbanke and promiscuous relations with his half-sister Augusta, encouraged Byron to leave England in 1816. He never returned. The women awaiting him on the Continent included Claire Clairmont, who bore him a daughter, Allegra, and (in 1819) Teresa Guiccioli, wife of an Italian count. He settled down with Teresa in Ravenna and turned to the writing of *Don Juan,* of which sixteen cantos and a fragment were eventually finished. Byron joined revolutionaries in Greece and died of fever at Missolonghi at the age of thirty-six. His poetical work includes the satire *English Bards and Scotch Reviewers* (1809), the long narrative poem *Childe Harold's Pilgrimage* (1812), and *The Prisoner of Chillon* (1816).

Thomas Campion (1567–1620) was born in London, studied at Cambridge but left without a degree in 1584. He came to public attention as a poet in the mid-1590s. Campion was also a musician. In 1605 he received an M.D. degree from the University of Caen in France and probably returned to London shortly thereafter to practice medicine. In addition to his many songs and poems, he wrote masques for which he composed the music. Campion's work is collected in *The Works of Thomas Campion,* edited by Walter R. Davis (1967).

Lewis Carroll (Charles Lutwidge Dodgson) (1832–1898) was born at Daresbury parsonage, Cheshire, the son of a clergyman. He was educated at Rugby and at Oxford, from which he received his B.A. in 1854. From 1855 until 1881 he was mathematical lecturer at Oxford, where he published mathematical treatises such as *Euclid and His Modern Rivals* (1879). *Alice's Adventures in Wonderland* appeared in 1865 and *Through the Looking Glass* in 1872. Carroll's other literary works include the long nonsense poem *The Hunting of the Snark* (1876) and a novel, *Sylvie and Bruno* (1889).

Geoffrey Chaucer (c. 1343–1400) was born in London, the son of a prosperous vintner. He became a page in the service of the Countess of Ulster, whose account book for 1357 lists him as in her service. In 1366 he married Philippa Roet, the sister of John of Gaunt's first wife. He subsequently went abroad on diplomatic missions to Italy, Flanders, France, and Lombardy, where he met Boccaccio and perhaps Petrarch. For most of his career Chaucer was a civil servant to the Crown, working, for example, in such positions as comptroller of the customs and subsidy of wools. Over the years he received various pensions, but he also knew periods of poverty. In 1386 he was elected to Parliament from Kent. Chaucer was buried in what later became the Poet's Corner in Westminster Abbey. His chief works are *The Book of the Duchess* (1369), *The House of Fame* and *The Parliament of Fowls* (probably written between 1374 and 1382), *Troilus and Criseyda* (1385), and *The Canterbury Tales* (after 1387).

John Ciardi (1916–   ) was born in Boston, the son of a laborer, tailor, and insurance agent who was killed in an auto accident when Ciardi was three. Educated at Bates, Tufts, and the University of Michigan, he followed an academic career until 1961, when he resigned his position as Professor of English at Rutgers University. He lives in Metuchen, New Jersey, is married, and has three children. For over twenty-five years Ciardi has repaired to Vermont in August to direct the Bread Loaf Writers Conference. He has written a dozen books of poems, several children's books, and numerous essays, collected in *Manner of Speaking* (1963) and *Dialogue with an Audience* (1964). He is also a translater of Dante and an anthology editor.

Arthur Hugh Clough (1819–1861) was born in Liverpool, the son of a cotton merchant. He spent his childhood in Charleston, South Carolina, and was educated at Rugby and Oxford (B.A., 1841). Clough was a fellow at Oriel College, Oxford, from 1841 to 1848, but resigned because of his skepticism about the dogmas of the Church of England. His *Poems* appeared in 1862. Matthew Arnold commemorated his friendship with Clough in his poem "Thyrsis."

Leonard Cohen (1934–   ) was born in Montreal, Canada, the son of a clothing merchant. He attended Westmont Secondary School in Montreal and received his B.A. with a major in English from McGill University in 1955. His first volume of poetry, *Let Us Compare Mythologies,* was published in 1956. He is unmarried, but since 1960 has lived with a Norwegian divorcee and her son. His first record album, "The Songs of Leonard Cohen," appeared in 1968. Cohen is a vice-president of Stranger Music, Inc. His other volumes of poems include *The Spice-Box of Earth* (1961), *Flowers for Hitler* (1964), *Parasites of Heaven* (1966), and *Selected Poems: 1956–1968* (1968). He is also the author of two novels, *The Favorite Game* (1963) and *Beautiful Loser* (1966). A selection of his songs with music are collected in *Songs of Leonard Cohen* (1969).

Samuel Taylor Coleridge (1772–1834) was born in Ottery St. Mary, Devonshire, the son of a clergyman who died when Samuel was nine. From 1782 to 1790 he was a student at Christ's Hospital, a charity school in London, and from 1791 to 1793 at Jesus College, Cambridge, from which he fled to enlist in the Fifteenth Light Dragoons. Although he returned to Cambridge after his discharge in 1794, he never graduated. Coleridge married Sara Fricker in 1795, and they had three children. With Wordsworth he collaborated on the great collection of poems *Lyrical Ballads* (1798). By the early 1800s he had become an opium addict, and his last years were characterized by the deep sadness that his early poetry had seemed to anticipate. His *Biographia Literaria* (1817) has been a strong influence in modern literary criticism.

Stephen Crane (1871–1900) was born in Newark, New Jersey, the son of a Methodist minister. He was educated at Hudson River Military Institute, and spent one semester each at Lafayette College and Syracuse University. From 1890 to 1895 he was a freelance writer in New York City. Crane's first book of poems, *The Black Riders,* appeared in 1895, the same year in which his novel *The Red Badge of Courage* appeared. From 1896 to 1898 he was a war correspondent in Cuba and Greece. He married in 1897, lived in England, and died in Germany of tuberculosis. Crane's work includes the novel *Maggie: A Girl of the Streets* (1893) and the book of poems *War Is Kind* (1899).

Countee Cullen (1903–1946) was born in New York City and lived with his maternal grandmother until he was thirteen, when he was adopted by the Reverend Frederick A. Cullen, minister of a church in Harlem. He attended Dewitt Clinton High School and received his B.A. from New York University in 1925, the same year in which his first volume of poems, *Color,* was published. Cullen received his M.A. from Harvard in 1926. He served as an assistant editor of *Opportunity: Journal of Negro Life,* married in 1928 but was divorced a year later, and from 1929 until his death taught in the New York public schools. He married again in 1940. Cullen's other volumes of poems are *Copper Sun* (1927), *The Ballad of the Brown Girl* (1927), *The Black Christ* (1929), *The Medea and Other Poems* (1935), *My Nine Lives and How I Lost Them* (1942), and his selection *On These I Stand* (1947). He is also the author of a novel, *One Way to Heaven* (1931).

E. E. Cummings (1894–1962) was born in Cambridge, Massachusetts, the son of an English professor who later became a Congregationalist minister. He received his B.A. from Harvard in 1915 and his M.A. in 1916. During World War I he served as an ambulance driver in France and was unjustly imprisoned for three months, an occasion that led to his work *The Enormous Room* (1922). For several years after the war Cummings studied art in Paris, returning to New York in 1924, the year of his first marriage. He married again in 1927, and for the third time in 1932. In 1952–1953 as Norton Professor at Harvard he delivered informal comments published as *i: six nonlectures* (1953). His volumes of poems include *Tulips and Chimneys* (1923), *is 5* (1926), *no thanks* (1935), *1 x 1* (1944), and *Poems, 1923–1954* (1954).

Emily Dickinson (1830–1886) was born in Amherst, Massachusetts, the daughter of a lawyer and prominent member of the community. The signal fact of her life is that she spent the last thirty years of it for the most part indoors, at her family home in Amherst; that her personal life lacked a normal happiness is inescapable. She began to write poetry in the winter of 1861–1862. The poems she left number about 1700, only four of which appeared in her lifetime. A collection of her poems first appeared in 1890. The standard edition is *The Poems of Emily Dickinson,* edited by Thomas H. Johnson, in three volumes (1955).

John Donne (1572–1631) was born in London, the son of a wealthy hardware merchant. He was early a witty, cynical, secular love poet. Later, having been ordained in the Church of England in 1615 and made Dean of St. Paul's in 1621, he became a religious poet and an extraordinary preacher. Brought up a Roman Catholic, Donne left Oxford without a degree and studied law. He fell passionately in love with Anne More and married her when she was seventeen and he twenty-nine. Although he was forced into jail by her father, he enjoyed a model marriage of love and devotion, and had twelve children (five did not survive). Even though he at times knew poverty, and lost his wife in 1617, Donne saw God as merciful, and died in peace. In addition to his early poems, his poetic works include *Of the Progress of the Soule* (published 1633), *Divine Poems* (1607), *Epithalamium* (1613), and *Cycle of Holy Sonnets* (1618).

John Dryden (1631–1700) was born in Northhamptonshire, the son of Erasmus Dryden, a member of the landed gentry. His boyhood and young manhood occurred during the English Civil Wars. He became part of the Restoration, a royalist in politics until his death. Dryden's talents were varied. He was a literary critic, a dramatist, a poet, and a translator. His verse form was the heroic couplet, and he was a master satirist. He married, had three sons, became a convert to Roman Catholicism in 1686, and stuck by his religious conviction despite adversity. Dryden was buried in Westminster Abbey, not far from Chaucer. Some of his chief works include *An Essay of Dramatic Poesy* (1668), the plays *Marriage-à-la Mode* (1673) and *All for Love* (1678), the political satire *Absalom and Achitophel* (1681), the literary satire *Mac Flecknoe* (1682), and the satiric religious apologies *Religio Laici* (1682) and *The Hind and the Panther* (1687).

Bob Dylan (1941–   ) was born in Duluth, Minnesota, the son of Abraham Zimmerman, an appliance dealer. Following graduation from high school in 1960 Dylan attended the University of Minnesota for six months. His first record album, "Bob Dylan," appeared in 1961, his change of name drawn from the poet Dylan Thomas. He is married and the father of five children. Creator of a "folk rock" style, Dylan has composed hundreds of songs and recorded over a dozen albums.

Richard Eberhart (1904–   ) was born in Austin, Minnesota, the son of a businessman. He received his B.A. from Dartmouth in 1926 and also studied at St. John's College, Cambridge University, from which he received a B.A. in 1929 and an M.A. in 1933. From 1933 to 1941 he taught at St. Mark's preparatory school in Massachusetts. In 1941 he married Helen E. Butcher; they have two children. During World War II Eberhart served in the navy as an aerial gunnery instructor and rose to the rank of lieutenant commander. After the war he worked for six years for the Butcher Polish Company of Boston, and since 1956 he has been Professor of English and Poet in Residence at Dartmouth. Eight volumes of his poems, beginning with *A Bravery of Earth* (1930), are selectively collected in *Collected Poems 1930–1960*. His subsequent volumes of poems are *The Quarry* (1964), *Selected Poems 1930–1965* (1965), *Thirty-One Sonnets* (1967), and *Shifts of Being: Poems* (1968). Eberhart is also the author of *Collected Verse Plays* (1962).

T. S. Eliot (1888–1965) was born in St. Louis; his father was the president of the Hydraulic Press Brick Company, and his mother wrote a biography of the poet's grandfather, who founded Washington University, and also a dramatic poem on the life of Savonarola. Eliot was educated at Smith Academy in St. Louis and at Harvard, where he received his B.A. in 1910 and M.A. in 1911. He married in 1915, the same year in which "The Love Song of J. Alfred Prufrock" was published in Harriet Monroe's *Poetry* magazine. He settled in England in 1914 and in 1927 became a British subject. In the early twenties Eliot became associated with the publishing house of Faber and Faber and eventually he became a director of the firm. His early essays, *The Sacred Wood,* were first published in 1920, and the poem *The Waste Land* appeared in 1922. His poems of religious meditation, *Four Quartets* (written between 1935 and 1942), were issued in a single volume in 1943. Eliot's first wife died in 1947, and he married Esmé Valerie Fletcher in 1957. In 1948 Eliot was awarded the Nobel Prize for Literature. His five verse plays include *Murder in the Cathedral* (1935) and *The Cocktail Party* (1949). *Collected Poems, 1909–1962* was published in 1963.

Ralph Waldo Emerson (1803–1882) was born in Boston, the son of the minister of First Church. He graduated from Harvard in 1821, studied for the ministry, and became minister of the Second Church of Boston, Unitarian (1829–1832), resigning because of doctrinal differences. He visited Europe, meeting Wordsworth, Coleridge, and Thomas Carlyle, and maintained a friendship and correspondence with his fellow transcendentalist Carlyle for over forty years. In 1834 Emerson settled in Concord, Massachusetts. He married in 1835, preached in various churches, and began to deliver public lectures. His first published work was *Nature* (1836). In 1837 he delivered *The American Scholar* as the Phi Beta Kappa address at Harvard. From 1842 to 1844 he edited *The Dial.* In 1841 and 1844 Emerson published volumes of *Essays,* which gave him an international reputation. His volume *Poems* was published in 1846. A vigorous opponent of slavery, he gave numerous antislavery speeches. His other works include *Representative Men* (1850), *English Traits* (1856), *The Conduct of Life* (1860), the volume of poems *May-Day and Other Pieces* (1867), *Society and Solitude* (1870), and *Letters and Social Aims* (1876).

Lawrence Ferlinghetti (1919–   ) was born in Yonkers, New York, the son of an auctioneer. He received his B.A. from the University of North Carolina in 1941, his M.A. from Columbia in 1948, and the Doctorat de l'Université from the Sorbonne in 1951. During World War II he served in the navy, rising to the rank of lieutenant commander. Ferlinghetti married in 1951 and has two children. He is the founder and publisher of City Lights Books, having opened in 1951 the City Lights Bookstore in San Francisco, the first all-paperbound bookstore in the United States. His volumes of poems include *Pictures of the Gone World* (1955), *A Coney Island of the Mind* (1958), *Starting from San Francisco* (1961; enlarged and revised 1967), and *The Secret Meaning of Things* (1968). He is also the author of a novel, *Her* (1960), *Unfair Arguments with Existence: Seven Plays for a New Theatre* (1963), and *The Mexican Night: Travel Journal* (1970).

Edward Fitzgerald (1809–1883) was born at Bredfield, near Woodbridge, Suffolk, and educated at Bury St. Edmunds and at Cambridge (B.A., 1830). He settled in Woodbridge and thereafter led a quiet secluded life. He married in 1856 but he and his wife soon separated. Fitzgerald is known mainly for his translation of *The Rubáiyát of Omar Khayyám,* first published as an anonymous pamphlet in 1859. A new and enlarged edition was published in 1868 and he continued to work on the poem until 1879.

Stephen Foster (1826–1864) was born on his family's farm near Lawrenceville, Pennsylvania. Although he received little musical training, his natural gifts were visible at an early age. At the age of six he taught himself to play the clarinet; at fourteen he composed

"The Tioga Waltz." His first minstrel melodies were written in 1845. Foster moved to Cincinnati to work as a bookkeeper for his brother in 1846, the same year in which he composed "Oh! Susanna." He married in 1850 and settled in Pittsburgh to work as a composer. From 1860 until his death he lived in New York City, separating from his wife in 1861. Never a good businessman, Foster died in poverty. He left about 190 songs, for most of which he wrote the words as well as the music.

Robert Frost (1874—1963) was born in San Francisco, the son of a journalist. He graduated from high school in Lawrence, Massachusetts, and attended Dartmouth and Harvard. In 1895 he married Elinor White, whom he had known in high school. From 1900 until 1912 they lived on a farm in Derry, New Hampshire, and then moved to England, where they remained for three years. He published his first book of poems, *A Boy's Will,* in England in 1913. *North of Boston,* published a year later, made him famous. Frost lectured and read his poetry all over the United States. At the inauguration of President. John F. Kennedy in 1961 he presented his poem "The Gift Outright," despite a glaring sun which made it impossible for him to read and forced him to recite from memory. On his eighty-eighth birthday (March 26) President Kennedy presented him with a medal voted by Congress. Frost died in Boston the following January. His volumes of poems include *Mountain Interval* (1916), *New Hampshire* (1923), *West-Running Brook* (1928), *A Further Range* (1936), *A Witness Tree* (1942), and *Complete Poems of Robert Frost* (1949).

Thomas Gray (1716—1771) was born in London, the son of a prosperous exchange broker. He was educated at Eton and at Cambridge, where he lived from the early 1740s until he died. In 1757 he refused the post of poet laureate, and in 1768 he became a professor of history at Cambridge. An edition of his poems appeared in the same year.

Thomas Hardy (1840—1928) was born in Upper Bockhampton in Dorsetshire, the son of a master mason. He studied architecture but after 1867 devoted himself to literature. He wrote fourteen novels, which appeared between 1871 and 1895. Hardy married in 1874 and, his first wife having died, again in 1914. In the latter part of his career he concentrated on lyric poetry. His novels include *Far from the Madding Crowd* (1874), *The Return of the Native* (1878), *The Mayor of Casterbridge* (1886), *Tess of the D'Urbervilles* (1891), and *Jude the Obscure* (1895). His poetical works include *Wessex Poems* (1898), *Poems of the Past and Present* (1901), and *The Dynasts* (1904—1908), a poetic drama in three parts.

Robert Hayden (1913—   ) was born in Detroit, the son of a teamster and laborer. He received his B.A. from Wayne State University in 1942 and his M.A. from the University of Michigan in 1944. Extremely poor eyesight excluded him from military service during World War II. He married in 1940 and has one child, a married daughter. Hayden taught at the University of Michigan from 1944 to 1946, at Fisk University from 1946 to 1969, and since 1969 has been Professor of English at the University of Michigan. His first volume of poems, *Heart-Shape in the Dust,* was published by the Falcon Press in Detroit in 1940. His other volumes are *A Ballad of Remembrance* (1962), *Selected Poems* (1966), *Words in the Mourning Time* (1970), and *The Night-Blooming Cereus* (1972), a booklet in a special edition published by Paul Breman, Ltd., of London. He is also the editor of *Kaleidoscope: Poems by American Negro Poets* (1967).

George Herbert (1593–1633) was born at Montgomery Castle, Wales, the son of Sir Richard and Lady Magdalen Herbert. He attended Westminster School, received his B.A. from Cambridge in 1613 and M.A. in 1616, married in 1629, and was ordained a priest in the Anglican Church in 1630. He became rector of Fugglestone and the rural parish of Bemerton, Wiltshire. Herbert played the lute and composed musical accompaniments for some of his own poems. His poems were published posthumously in a volume entitled *The Temple* (1633).

Robert Herrick (1591–1674) was born in Cheapside, London, the seventh child of Nicholas Herrick, a goldsmith. He went to Cambridge, where he took his M.A. in 1620, and became a clergyman in 1623. Herrick was a royalist in politics, classical and hedonistic in temperament. He never married and published only one book of some 1400 poems in two sections *(Hesperides* and *Noble Numbers)* in 1648.

Gerard Manley Hopkins (1844–1889) was born in Stratford, Essex, the son of the head of a firm of actuaries. He was educated at Balliol College, Oxford, converted to Roman Catholicism, and became a Jesuit priest in 1877. When he entered the Jesuit novitiate in 1868 he destroyed all of the poetry he had written. What survives was written after 1876 and finally published in 1918 by his friend Robert Bridges. In his last years Hopkins was Professor of Greek at the Royal University, Dublin.

A. E. Housman (1859–1936) was born in Worcestershire, England, the son of a lawyer. He took a degree in classics at Oxford, became a professor of Latin in University College, London, in 1911, and was appointed Kennedy Professor of Latin in Trinity College, Cambridge—a position he held and gave distinction to until his death. His life was austere and scholarly. Although Housman published only a slender quantity of verse, anthologists seldom omit his work. His volumes of poems are *A Shropshire Lad* (1896), *Last Poems* (1922), and the posthumous *More Poems* (1936).

Langston Hughes (1902–1967) was born in Joplin, Missouri; his father was a storekeeper and his mother was a schoolteacher. He studied at Columbia University in 1921 and received his B.A. from Lincoln University in Pennsylvania in 1929. He worked at various jobs in New York, was a trans-Atlantic seaman, and worked in Paris as a cook in a Montmarte nightclub. Many of Hughes' poems have been set to music. His first volume of poems was *The Weary Blues* (1926). His other volumes include *Fine Clothes to the Jew* (1927), *Dear Lovely Death* (1931), *The Dream Keeper* (1932), *Shakespeare in Harlem* (1942), *Fields of Wonder* (1947), *One-Way Ticket* (1949), *Ask Your Mama* (1961), and *The Panther and the Lash* (1967). His diverse writing includes fiction and drama and the autobiographies *The Big Sea* (1940) and *I Wonder as I Wander* (1956).

Randall Jarrell (1914–1965) was born in Nashville, Tennessee, and educated at Vanderbilt University, from which he received his B.A. in 1935 and his M.A. in 1938. He taught at Kenyon College from 1937 to 1939 and at the University of Texas from 1939 to 1942. During World War II he served in the Army Air Force and subsequently taught at Sarah

Lawrence College, Princeton, and the Women's College of the University of North Carolina. From 1956 to 1958 he was Consultant in Poetry at the Library of Congress. He married in 1952, had two daughters, and died suddenly when struck by a car. Jarrell's volumes of poems include *Blood for a Stranger* (1942), *Little Friend, Little Friend* (1945), *Losses* (1948), *The Seven League Crutches* (1951), *The Woman at the Washington Zoo: Poems and Translations* (1960), and *The Lost World* (1965). His *Complete Poems* appeared in 1969. His criticism includes *Poetry and the Age* (1953) and *The Third Book of Criticism* (1969). Jarrell was also the author of a satirical novel of college life, *Pictures from an Institution* (1954), *A Sad Heart at the Supermarket: Essays and Fables* (1962), and three children's books, *The Gingerbread Rabbit* (1963), *The Bat-Poet* (1964), and *The Animal Family* (1965).

Robinson Jeffers (1887–1962) was born in Pittsburgh, Pennsylvania, the son of a theology professor. He visited Europe frequently in the 1890s and attended boarding schools in Switzerland and Germany from 1899 to 1903. He graduated from Occidental College in 1905 and did graduate work in various subjects until 1911. In 1912 he received a legacy which enabled him to devote himself to writing. Jeffers married in 1913 and had two children. In 1914 he settled at Tor House, which he built of sea cobbles, on Carmel Bay, south of Monterey, California, and he built of the same stone Hawk Tower, in which he did much of his writing. He lived at Tor House for the rest of his life. Jeffers' volumes of poems include *Californians* (1916), *Tamar and Other Poems* (1924), *Roan Stallion, Tamar, and Other Poems* (1925), *Dear Judas and Other Poems* (1929), *Solstice and Other Poems* (1935), *Such Counsels You Gave to Me and Other Poems* (1937), *Be Angry at the Sun* (1941), *The Double Axe and Other Poems* (1948), and *The Beginning and the End and Other Poems* (1963).

LeRoi Jones (Ameer Baraka) (1934–   ) was born in Newark, New Jersey, the son of a postal supervisor. He attended Rutgers University and then Howard University, from which he received his B.A. in 1954. He received an M.A. in philosophy from Columbia University, and an M.A. in German literature from the New School for Social Research. For over two years he served in the Strategic Air Command as a weatherman and gunner. He has two children by his first marriage and one by his second. In 1965 Jones founded the Black Arts Repertory Theatre in Harlem, and in 1966 he established a black community theater in Newark. His volumes of poems are *Preface to a Twenty Volume Suicide Note* (1961), *The Dead Lecturer* (1964), and *Black Magic Poetry* (1969). His plays include three in 1964, *The Dutchman, The Slave,* and *The Toilet,* and *Four Black Revolutionary Plays* (1969). Jones' fiction includes a semiautobiographical novel, *The System of Dante's Hell* (1965), and a book of short stories, *Tales* (1967), and his nonfiction includes *Blues People: Negro Music in White America* (1963), *Home: Social Essays* (1965), and *Black Music* (1968). He is coauthor with Billy Abernathy of *In Our Terribleness: Pictures of the Hip World* (1969).

Ben Jonson (1572–1637) was born in Westminster, the posthumous son of a minister. Educated at Westminster School, and a classical scholar in temperament, he became an actor and a dramatist in London, where his famous comedy *Every Man in His Humour* was produced in 1598. In the same year he killed an actor in a duel, was sent to jail, pleaded guilty of manslaughter, and was released by benefit of clergy. Jonson composed masques for the court of King James and published the first volume of the folio edition of his works in 1616.

John Keats (1795—1821) was born in London, the son of a livery-stable keeper. His short life was characterized by overwhelming distress which never entirely overwhelmed him. When he was eight his father fell from a horse and was killed. His mother died of tuberculosis, as did he and his brother Tom. Keats' love affair with Fanny Brawne, to whom he became engaged in 1819, brought him little final happiness. He died in Rome, where he had gone for his health. His work includes *Poems* (1817), *Endymion* (1818), and *Lamia and Other Poems* (1820).

Galway Kinnell (1927—   ) was born in Providence, Rhode Island. He received his B.A. from Princeton in 1948 and his M.A. from the University of Rochester in 1949. He has taught at various colleges and universities, including Alfred University, the University of Chicago, the University of Grenoble in France, and the University of Teheran in Iran. He lives with his second wife and their two children in Sheffield, Vermont. His volumes of poems are *What a Kingdom It Was* (1960), *Flower Herding on Mount Monadnock* (1964), *Body Rags* (1968), *First Poems 1946—1954* (1971), and *The Book of Nightmares* (1971). He is also the author of a novel, *Black Light* (1966), and of several translations including *The Poems of François Villon* (1965), poems by Yves Bonnefoy, *On the Motion and Immobility of Douve* (1968), and poems by Yvan Goll, *Lackawanna Elegy* (1970).

Philip Larkin (1922—   ) was born in Coventry, Warwickshire, England. He attended the King Henry VIII School in Coventry and received his B.A. from Oxford in 1943 and his M.A. in 1947. He is unmarried. Since 1955 he has been Librarian at the University of Hull. His volumes of poems are *The North Ship* (1946; new edition 1966), *XX Poems* (1951), *The Less Deceived* (1955), and *The Whitsun Weddings* (1964). Larkin is also the author of two novels, *Jill* (1946; revised edition 1964) and *A Girl in Winter* (1947), and *All What Jazz: A Record Diary 1961—1968* (1970).

C. Day Lewis (1904—1972) was born in Ballintagher, Ireland, the only child of a clergyman. He attended Sherborne School, in Sherborne, North Dorset, England, and in 1928 married the headmaster's daughter. They were divorced and he remarried in 1951. He attended Oxford and until 1935 held various teaching posts. Lewis secured financial independence by writing detective stories under the pseudonym of Nicholas Blake. From 1951 to 1956 he was Professor of Poetry at Oxford. He is a director of the publishing firm of Chatto and Windus and since 1968 has been England's Poet Laureate. Lewis's volumes of poems include *Beechen Vigil and Other Poems* (1925), *Transitional Poem* (1929), *From Feathers to Iron* (1931), *The Magnetic Mountain* (1933), *A Time to Dance and Other Poems* (1935), *Overtures to Death and Other Poems* (1938), *Poems in Wartime* (1940), *Word Over All* (1943), *Collected Poems* (1954), *The Gate and Other Poems* (1962), *Requiem for Living* (1964), and *The Room and Other Poems* (1965). His wide-ranging work includes fiction, criticism, and translations.

Vachel Lindsay (1879—1931) was born in Springfield, Illinois, the son of a physician. He attended Hiram College from 1897 until 1900 and the Chicago Art Institute from 1900 to 1903. In 1904—1905 he studied at the New York School of Art. Unable to sell any of his drawings, he tramped through the South chanting his poems in exchange for food and lodging. He later lectured and chanted his poems throughout the United States and, in 1920, at Oxford University. Lindsay married in 1925 and had two children. His death by suicide came in poverty in Springfield. His volumes of poems include *General William Booth Enters into Heaven and Other Poems* (1913), *The Congo and Other Poems* (1914), and *The Chinese Nightingale and Other Poems* (1917).

John Logan (1923–) was born in Red Oak, Iowa, the son of an accountant. He received his B.A. from Coe College in 1943 and his M.A. from the University of Iowa in 1949. He married in 1945, divorced in 1969, and is the father of nine children. From 1947 to 1951 he was a tutor at St. John's College in Annapolis, Maryland, and from 1951 to 1963 he taught at the University of Notre Dame. Since 1966 he has been Professor of English at the State University of New York in Buffalo. His volumes of poems are *Cycle for Mother Cabrini* (1955), *Ghosts of the Heart* (1960), *Spring of the Thief* (1963), and *The Zigzag Walk* (1969).

Richard Lovelace (1618–1658) was probably born in Holland, where his father, a member of an old Kentish family, was in the military service. He was educated at Oxford and devoted his fortune to the royalist cause during the English Civil War. In 1642 he was imprisoned in Gatehouse at Westminster, where he wrote "To Althea from Prison." Lovelace served in the French army and was wounded at Dunkirk in 1646. Imprisoned again upon returning to England, he prepared for the press his volume of poems *Lucasta* (1649). With the royalist cause lost, Lovelace spent his last years in physical and financial decline.

Robert Lowell (1917–) was born in Boston, the only child of a commander in the United States Navy. He grew up in Boston, attended St. Mark's preparatory school, and Harvard University. He transferred to Kenyon College, from which he graduated in 1940, the same year in which he married novelist Jean Stafford; they were divorced in 1948. In 1943 he served five months in federal prison for failure to obey the Selective Service Act. In 1949 he married the novelist and critic Elizabeth Hardwick; they have one daughter. Lowell has taught at various places, including Kenyon, Boston University, and Harvard. He lives in New York City. His volumes of poems include *Land of Unlikeness* (1944), *Lord Weary's Castle* (1946; with changes 1947), *Poems: 1938–1949* (1950), *The Mills of the Kavanaughs* (1951), *Life Studies* (1959), *Imitations* (1961), *For the Union Dead* (1964), *The Old Glory* (1965), *Near the Ocean* (1967), and *Notebook 1967–1968* (1969; revised and expanded 1970). His translations include *Phaedra* (1961), *The Voyage and Other Versions of Poems by Baudelaire* (1968), and *Prometheus Bound: Derived from Aeschylus* (1969).

Archibald MacLeish (1892–) was born in Glencoe, Illinois, the son of a successful Chicago merchant. He was educated at Hotchkiss, Yale (B.A., 1915), and Harvard (L.L.B., 1919). In 1916 he married Ada Hitchcock, a singer, and they had three sons and a daughter. From 1923 to 1928 he was in Paris writing poetry. In 1928 he settled on a farm in Farmington, Connecticut. From 1939 until 1944 he was Librarian of Congress, and until 1949 served in various government positions. In 1949 MacLeish became Boylston professor at Harvard. His volumes of poems include *The Happy Marriage* (1924), *The Pot* *of Earth* (1925), *Streets in the Moon* (1926), *Conquistador* (1932), *Land of the Free* (1938), and *Actfive and Other Poems* (1948). His half-dozen verse plays include *J.B.* (1957).

Louis MacNeice (1907–1963) was born in Belfast, Northern Ireland, the son of a clergyman. He was educated at Sherborne Preparatory School for Boys, Dorset (1917–1921), Marlborough College (1921–1926), and Oxford (1926–1930). He married in 1930, had one child, a son, and was divorced in 1936. He remarried in 1942 and had a daughter by his second marriage. From 1930 to 1936 he was lecturer in classics at the University of Birmingham. In 1937 MacNeice visited Iceland with W. H. Auden. From 1941 to 1954 he worked, with one eighteen-month interruption, as a scriptwriter and producer for the British Broadcasting Corporation. His volumes of poems include *Blind Fireworks* (1929), *Poems* (1935), *The Earth Compels* (1938), *Autumn Journal* (1939), *The Last Ditch* (1940), *Poems 1925–1940* (1940), *Plant and Phantom* (1941), *Collected Poems* (1949), *Ten Burnt Offerings* (1952), *Solstices* (1961), and *Collected Poems* (1967). His prose writing includes a collaboration with W. H. Auden on *Letters from Iceland* (1937), *Modern Poetry: A Personal Essay* (1938; second edition 1968), and *The Strings Are False: An Unfinished Autobiography* (1965). He is also the author of several plays and of a translation of Goethe's *Faust* (1951).

Christopher Marlowe (1564–1593) was born in Canterbury, the son of a shoemaker. He graduated from Cambridge, receiving his B.A. in 1584 and his M.A. in 1587. In London the theatrical company the Admiral's Men produced most of Marlowe's plays. *Tamburlaine the Great* was acted in 1587 or 1588, but not published until 1590; it established blank verse as the medium for later Elizabethan and Jacobean drama. Marlowe's other important plays are *The Tragedy of Dr. Faustus, The Jew of Malta,* and *Edward II.* He was killed in a tavern brawl in Deptford.

Andrew Marvell (1621–1678) was born in Winestead, Yorkshire, the son of a Calvinist preacher, and was educated at Cambridge. He missed the English Civil Wars (having traveled on the Continent from 1642 to 1646), but became an admirer of Cromwell and was appointed to assist Milton as Latin Secretary in 1657. He held that position until the Restoration, and then served in Parliament until his death. As a political writer Marvell vigorously opposed the government after the Restoration in pamphlets and satires. His poems, most of which were first published in 1681, are small in number but generally regarded as high in quality.

John Milton (1608–1674) was born in London, the son of a well-to-do scrivener who also composed music. He was destined to combine enormous learning with a passion for liberty. His education was the best—St. Paul's School in London, Christ College, Cambridge, five years of study at his father's country place (Horton, near Windsor), and then fifteen months abroad in 1638–1639. Milton was deeply involved in the Civil Wars that stretched from 1642 to 1651, an involvement reflected in the writing of pamphlets, including the famous argument for freedom of the press, *Areopagitica.* He also served as Cromwell's Latin Secretary. The Restoration of Charles II in 1660 shattered his dream of liberty, but not his spirit. Totally blind after 1651, Milton dictated *Paradise Lost* (which was published in 1667) to his secretaries and to his daughters from the first of his three marriages.

Marianne Moore (1887–1972) was born in St. Louis, Missouri, the daughter of an engineer, received her B.A. from Bryn Mawr in 1909, and studied for a year at Carlisle (Pennsylvania) Commercial College. From 1911 to 1915 she taught stenography at the Indian School in Carlisle. From 1921 to 1925 she was an assistant in the New York Public Library, and from 1926 to 1929 she was acting editor of the *Dial,* a magazine devoted to the arts. Moore never married. Her volumes of poems include *Poems* (1921), *The Pangolin and Other Verse* (1936), *What Are Years* (1941), *Collected Poems* (1951), and *O to Be a Dragon* (1959). *Predilections* (1955) is a selection of her critical articles.

Howard Nemerov (1920–   ) was born in New York, the son of the president and chairman of the board of the New York clothing store Russeks. He graduated in 1937 from the Fieldston School in New York, received his B.A. from Harvard in 1941, and during World War II served in the Royal Canadian Air Force and the United States Army Air Force in Canada and England. He married in 1944 and has three children. From 1946 to 1951 he was associate editor of the literary magazine *Furioso.* Nemerov has taught at Hamilton College, Bennington College, and Brandeis University, and since 1969 has been Professor of English at Washington University in St. Louis. His volumes of poems are *The Image and the Law* (1947), *Guide to the Ruins* (1950), *The Salt Garden* (1955), *Mirrors and Windows* (1958), *New and Selected Poems* (1960), *The Next Room of the Dream: Poems and Two Plays* (1962), and *The Blue Swallows* (1967). He is also the author of three novels, a volume of short stories, *A Commodity of Dreams and Other Stories* (1959), *Journal of the Fictive Life* (1965), and a critical study, *Poetry and Fiction: Essays* (1963).

Wilfred Owen (1893–1918) was born in Oswestry, Shropshire, the son of a railway worker. He attended the Birkenhead Institute in Liverpool from 1900 to 1907 and the Technical School in Shrewsbury, where his family settled. From 1911 to 1913 he was lay assistant to an Oxfordshire vicar. In 1913 he went to France and worked as an English tutor at the Berlitz School in Bordeaux. When England entered World War I Owen enlisted in the army and served in France from 1916 to 1917. Wounded, he was sent to England in June of 1917 and confined to a hospital in Scotland. He returned to France in August of 1918 and was killed in November, one week before Armistice Day, while crossing the Sambre Canal. There were twenty-three titles in his *Poems* (1920), which were edited and published by his friend Siegfried Sassoon.

Sylvia Plath (1932–1963) was born in Boston, the daughter of a professor of biology and scientific German at Boston University. She received her B.A. summa cum laude from Smith College in 1955, and her M.A. from Cambridge in 1957. In 1956 she married the English poet Ted Hughes. They had two children and were separated in 1962. Plath committed suicide in London on February 11, 1963. Her work includes the volumes of poems *The Colossus* (1960), *Ariel* (1965), and *Uncollected Poems* (1965), and a novel, *The Bell Jar* (1963).

Hyam Plutzik (1911–1962) was born in Brooklyn and brought up in Connecticut. He received his B.A. from Trinity College in 1932 and his M.A. from Yale in 1940. He served in the army from 1942 to 1945 and taught at the University of Rochester from 1946 until his death. Plutzik was married and the father of four children. His volumes of poems are *Aspects of Proteus* (1949), *Apples from Shinar* (1959), and *Horatio: A Poem* (1961).

Alexander Pope (1688—1744) was born in London, the son of a linen draper. He was four and a half feet tall but became a literary giant, the supreme master of the heroic couplet. A Roman Catholic in an England hostile to his faith, he, like his family, had to comply with a regulation forbidding papists to reside within ten miles of the city. In 1718 he settled near London in the village of Twickenham, where he lived until his death. He was the first English poet to know financial independence through his writings, specifically his translations of the *Iliad* (1715—1720) and *Odyssey* (1725—1726) of Homer. His other important works include *An Essay on Criticism* (1711), *The Rape of the Lock* (1712), *The Dunciad* (1728, 1742), and *An Essay on Man* (1733).

Sir Walter Ralegh (c. 1552—1618) was born at Hager Burton near Devon, the son of a country gentleman. Though he never set foot in North America, he sent an expedition which explored the coast from Florida to North Carolina in 1584, and he established a short-lived colony on Roanoke Island in 1585. The Queen banished him from her presence for four years, in part because he secretly married one of her maids, Elizabeth Throckmorton. With the accession of James I in 1603, Ralegh was stripped of his offices and estates, charged with conspiring against James, and sent to the Tower of London, where he lived with his wife and son until 1616 and composed his *History of the World* (1614). He was beheaded on October 26, 1618. About thirty of his poems survive.

Edwin Arlington Robinson (1869—1935) was born in Head Tide, Maine, the son of a businessman. He grew up in Gardiner, Maine, the "Tilbury Town" of his poems, attended Harvard from 1891 to 1893, and in 1896 settled in New York, where he printed the first two volumes of his poems, *The Torrent and the Night Before* (1896) and *The Children of the Night* (1897), at his own expense. The latter volume came to the attention of President Theodore Roosevelt, who had Robinson appointed to a clerkship in the United States Custom House in New York, a post which he held for five years. After 1911 he spent many summers at the MacDowell Colony in Peterborough, New Hampshire. Robinson never married. His other volumes of poems include *The Town Down the River* (1910), *The Man Against the Sky* (1916), *Merlin* (1917), *Lancelot* (1920), *Collected Poems* (1921), and *Tristram* (1927).

Theodore Roethke (1908—1963) was born in Saginaw, Michigan, the son of a florist who, with his uncle, owned a greenhouse. He received his B.A. from the University of Michigan in 1929 and his M.A. from the same institution in 1936. He taught at Lafayette College, Pennsylvania State College, Bennington College and, from 1947 until his death, at the University of Washington. Roethke married in 1953 and is survived by his wife; they had no children. His volumes of poems are *Open House* (1941), *The Lost Son and Other Poems* (1948), *Praise to the End* (1951), *The Waking: Poems 1933—1953* (1953), *Words for the Wind: The Collected Verse of Theodore Roethke* (1958), *I Am Says the Lamb* (1961), *Sequence, Sometimes Metaphysical, Poems* (1963), and *The Far Field* (1964). His *Collected Poems* appeared in 1966.

Christina Rossetti (1830—1894) was born in London, the youngest child of Gabriele Rossetti, an Italian poet and political refugee, and the sister of the poet Dante Gabriel Rossetti. Although she had two suitors, she refused to marry them because of religious differences. She devoted herself to the Anglican religion and to poetry and cared for her mother for many years. Rossetti visited France in 1861 and Italy in 1865. From 1871 until her death she was an invalid. Her poetical works include *Goblin Market and Other Poems* (1862), *The Prince's Progress and Other Poems* (1866), *A Pageant and Other Poems* (1881), and *New Poems* (1896).

Carl Sandburg (1878–1967) was born in Galesburg, Illinois, the son of a Swedish immigrant blacksmith. He left school at the age of thirteen, worked at many odd jobs in many places, and during the Spanish-American War served in the infantry in Puerto Rico. He attended Lombard College in Galesburg from 1898 to 1902 but did not graduate. Sandburg married in 1908 and was the father of three daughters. From 1910 to 1912 he was secretary to the mayor of Milwaukee and in 1913 he moved to Chicago, where he worked on the staff of the *Daily News*. His poem "Chicago" appeared in *Poetry* magazine in 1914. *Chicago Poems* was published in 1916 and *Cornhuskers* in 1918. Sandburg's other volumes of poems include *Smoke and Steel* (1920), *Slabs of the Sunburnt West* (1922), *Good Morning, America* (1928), and *The People, Yes* (1936). His biographies include *Abraham Lincoln, the Prairie Years* (1926), *Abraham Lincoln, the War Years* (1939), and the autobiography *Always the Young Strangers* (1953). He was also a folk singer, and the folk songs he sang are collected in *The American Songbag* (1927) and *Carl Sandburg's New American Songbag* (1950).

Anne Sexton (1928–   ) was born in Newton, Massachusetts, the daughter of a salesman, grew up in Wellesley, and attended Garland Junior College and Boston University. She married in 1948 and is the mother of two daughters. From 1961 to 1963 she was a scholar at the Radcliffe Institute for Independent Study. Her home is in Weston, Massachusetts. Her volumes of poems are *To Bedlam and Part Way Back* (1960), *All My Pretty Ones* (1962), *Selected Poems* (1964), *Live or Die* (1966), *Love Poems* (1969), and *Transformations* (1971).

William Shakespeare (1564–1616) was born at Stratford-on-Avon, the son of a glover and trader in farm products. He attended the free grammar school at Stratford, and in 1582 married Anne Hathaway of Stratford; they had three children. Shakespeare was living in London by 1592. He became a poet, actor, and dramatist whose plays were successes on the London stage, spent his last years in Stratford, and was buried there in the parish church. At the time of his death over half of his plays were still unpublished. The First Folio appeared in 1623.

Karl Shapiro (1913–   ) was born in Baltimore and attended the University of Virginia in 1932–1933 and Johns Hopkins from 1936 to 1939, but did not take a degree. He served in the army from 1941 to 1945, was Consultant in Poetry at the Library of Congress in 1946–1947, taught at Johns Hopkins from 1947 to 1950, and edited *Poetry* magazine from 1950 to 1956. He has been married twice, with three children by his first marriage. Shapiro taught at the University of Nebraska from 1956 to 1966, then for a year at the University of Illinois at Chicago Circle, and since 1967 he has been Professor of English at the University of California, Davis. His volumes of poems include *Poems* (1935), *Person Place and Thing* (1942), *V-Letter and Other Poems* (1944), *Trial of a Poet and Other Poems* (1947), *Poems 1940–1953* (1953), *Poems of a Jew* (1958), *The Bourgeois Poet* (1964), *White-Haired Lover* (1968), and *Selected Poems* (1968). His critical writing includes the blank verse *Essay on Rime* (1945), *Beyond Criticism* (1953; reprinted 1965 as *A Primer for Poets*), *In Defense of Ignorance* (1960), and *To Abolish Children and Other Essays* (1968).

Percy Bysshe Shelley (1792–1822) was born in Warnham, near Horsham, Sussex, an aristocrat whose lineage traced back to the fifteenth century, but at Eton and at Oxford he proved something of a rebel—being publicly expelled from the latter after the publication of his notorious pamphlet *The Necessity of Atheism.* He married Harriet Westbrook but in 1814 left her and their two children to elope to Switzerland with Mary Godwin, whom he married in 1816 after the death, apparently by suicide, of Harriet. Shelley's last years were spent in Italy. He died in a boating accident off the Italian coast, and his ashes were buried in the new Protestant cemetery in Rome. His major works include *Queen Mab* (1813), *Prometheus Unbound* (1818–1820), and *Adonais* (1821), his elegy on the death of John Keats.

W. D. Snodgrass (1926–   ) was born in Wilkinsburg, Pennsylvania, the son of an accountant. He attended Geneva College in Pennsylvania, spent three years in the navy (1944–1947), married in 1946, and graduated from the University of Iowa (B.A., 1949, M.A., 1951, M.F.A., 1953). He has taught at Cornell University, the University of Rochester, Wayne State University, and since 1968 at Syracuse University. Snodgrass lives with his third wife in Erieville, New York, and has three children by his previous marriages. His volumes of poems are *Heart's Needle* (1959) and *After Experience* (1968). He is also the author of *Gallows Songs* (1967), translations of the German lyric poet Christian Morgenstern.

William Stafford (1914–   ) was born in Hutchinson, Kansas, the son of a businessman who worked for a time as area manager for an oil company in Kansas. He received his B.A. from the University of Kansas in 1937, his M.A. from the same institution in 1946, and his Ph.D. from the University of Iowa in 1953. Stafford's first collection of poems, *West of Your City,* was published in 1960. His second, *Traveling Through the Dark,* won the 1963 National Book Award. Since 1948 he has taught at Lewis and Clark College in Port-land, Oregon. Stafford is married and has four children. In 1970–1971 he was Consultant in Poetry at the Library of Congress. His other volumes of poems are *The Rescued Year* (1966) and *Allegiances* (1970).

Wallace Stevens (1879–1955) was born in Reading, Pennsylvania, the son of a lawyer. He was educated at Harvard and New York University Law School, admitted to the New York bar in 1904, and practiced law in New York until 1916. From 1916 until his death he lived in Hartford, Connecticut, and was vice-president of the Hartford Accident and Indemnity Company from 1934. His first book of poems, *Harmonium,* was published in 1923 when he was forty-four. Stevens was married and had one child, a daughter. He was not interested in literary society. His poems are collected in *The Collected Poems of Wallace Stevens* (1954) and *Opus Posthumous* (1957).

Sir John Suckling (1609–1642) was born at Whitton, Middlesex, the son of Sir John Suckling, secretary of state to James I. He was admitted to Cambridge in 1623, inherited large estates from his father in 1627, and traveled on the Continent from 1628 to 1630.

Suckling invented the game of cribbage, wrote four poor plays which contained some good lyric poems, including "Why So Pale and Wan, Fond Lover?" (from *Aglaura*), and at the outbreak of the Civil War raised a troop of one hundred horse soldiers in support of the King. He had to flee to the Continent in 1641 and died in Paris, said by John Aubrey to have poisoned himself out of fear of poverty.

Alfred, Lord Tennyson (1809–1892) was born in Somersby, Lincolnshire, the son of an Anglican clergyman who educated his sons at home in Latin and Greek. Alfred's later education was at Trinity College, Cambridge. His early poems, published when he was in his twenties, were dealt with savagely by the critic John Wilson Croker, who may claim fame from the fact that he helped silence Tennyson for ten years. In 1842 Tennyson published the two-volume *Poems,* which established his reputation. In 1836 he became engaged to Emily Sellwood, but they could not marry until 1850, the year in which he succeeded William Wordsworth as England's Poet Laureate and in which he published the elegy on Arthur Henry Hallam, *In Memoriam.* Tennyson and his wife settled on the Isle of Wight. His poems on Arthurian legend, *The Idylls of the King,* first appeared in 1859, and in his last decades he enjoyed immense fame.

Dylan Thomas (1914–1953) was born in Swansea, Wales, the son of a teacher at Swansea Grammar School. He lived in Swansea until 1934, a period during which he wrote all of the poems in his first volume of poems, *18 Poems* (1934), and most of the poems in his second volume, *Twenty-Five Poems* (1936). In 1934 he settled in London, where as a struggling young poet he lived in poverty. In 1937 he married Caitlain Macnamara; they had three children. Thomas and his wife settled in a simple fisherman's cottage in Laugharne, Wales, in 1938. During World War II he did broadcasting work for the British Broadcasting Corporation. His fourth book of poems, *Deaths and Entrances* (1946), established him as a poet. From 1945 to 1949 he lived in England and in 1949 he returned to Laugharne, which was his home until his death. In 1950, 1952, and 1953 Thomas toured America giving poetry readings; he died in New York on his fourth American visit. His other volumes of poems include *The Map of Love* (1939), *In Country Sleep* (1952), and *Collected Poems* (1953). He is also the author of a verse play, *Under Milk Wood* (1954), and the prose works *Portrait of the Artist as a Young Dog* (1940) and *Adventures in the Skin Trade and Other Stories* (1955).

Diane Wakoski (1937–   ) was born in Whittier, California. Her father was a chief petty officer in the United States Navy, and her mother was a bookkeeper. Until she was thirteen, when her parents were divorced, she saw her father about once a year. She grew up in Orange County and graduated from Fullerton Union High School in 1955. Wakoski received her B.A. from the University of California at Berkeley in 1960 and has since lived in New York City. She married in 1965 and was divorced in 1967. After moving to New York she worked in a bookstore for three years, taught junior high school for three years, held a number of part-time jobs, and began to earn a living giving poetry readings on college and university campuses in 1967. Her volumes of poems are *Coins and Coffins* (1962), *Discrepancies and Apparitions* (1966), *The George Washington Poems* (1967), *Inside the Blood Factory* (1968), *The Magellanic Clouds* (1970), *The Motorcycle Betrayal Poems* (1971), and *Smudging* (1972).

Walt Whitman (1819–1892) was born on a farm in Long Island, the son of a carpenter. He went to school in Brooklyn, worked as an office boy, edited the Brooklyn *Eagle* (1846–1848), and finally gave up newspaper work to write poetry. The first edition of *Leaves of Grass,* privately printed, appeared in 1855. Whitman served in the Civil War as a male nurse, suffered a bad stroke in 1873, and lived thereafter with his brother in Camden, New Jersey. In his last years he enjoyed an American reputation and even made enough money to purchase a small house in Camden. Over the years he continuously revised and enlarged *Leaves of Grass,* the ninth and last edition appearing in 1891–1892.

William Carlos Williams (1883–1963) was born in Rutherford, New Jersey, the son of a New York businessman who was English-born and remained an English citizen. His mother, a Puerto Rican, had studied painting in Paris. Williams was educated at Horace Mann High School in New York and graduated from the University of Pennsylvania Medical School. His education also included school in Geneva, Switzerland and—after his internship in New York—at the University of Leipzig, where he specialized in pediatrics before settling in Rutherford to practice. He married in 1912, had two sons, and practiced medicine in Rutherford until his retirement in 1951. In addition to poetry—upon which his reputation is based—Williams' scores of books include short stories, novels, plays, and an autobiography. His volumes of poems include *Collected Earlier Poems* (1951), *Collected Later Poems* (revised edition 1963), and *Pictures from Brueghel and Other Poems* (1963).

William Wordsworth (1770–1850) was born in the beautiful English Lake District in the village of Cockermouth, Cumberland, the son of an attorney. After graduating from Cambridge he spent a year in France, had a love affair with Annette Vallon, who bore him a daughter, and returned to England before war broke out in 1793 between England and France—an event that made his revolutionary enthusiasm decline. With Coleridge he published the *Lyrical Ballads* in 1798. He settled with his sister Dorothy in the Lake Country, married Mary Hutchinson, had five children, and became a political conservative. Wordsworth became Poet Laureate in 1843, serving until his death.

Sir Thomas Wyatt (1503–1542) was born in Allington Castle, Kent, the residence of his father Sir Henry Wyatt. He was educated at St. John's College, Cambridge, where he received his B.A. in 1518 and M.A. in 1520, the year in which he married. He pursued a career at court which included going on diplomatic missions for Henry VIII, translated Petrarchan sonnets, pioneered the sonnet in England, and contributed over ninety sonnets, rondeaus, satires, and lyric poems to *Tottel's Miscellany* (1557).

William Butler Yeats (1865–1939) was a Protestant Irishman born in Dublin, the son of a painter. As a boy he spent much time at the home of his mother's parents in Sligo, a county in western Ireland where barren mountains overlook the sea and Celtic legends are in the air. His first volume of verse, *The Wanderings of Oisin and Other Poems,* was published in 1889, but his best poetry was written in his last thirty years. From 1899 to 1909 Yeats helped create an Irish national theater, the now-famous Abbey Theatre. In 1923 he won the Nobel Prize for Literature. After his marriage in 1917 he became interested in occult knowledge; his private mystic system was published in *The Vision* in 1925. He was greatly celebrated in his last years. His poetical work includes *The Wind Among the Reeds* (1899), *Responsibilities* (1914), *The Wild Swans at Coole* (1917), and *The Tower* (1927).

A Note on Listening

The availability of records and tapes of poets reading their own poems and of a variety of skilled readers or performers rendering their interpretations of poems has in recent years become more than ample. Caedmon Recordings of the Spoken Word, the Library of Congress, McGraw-Hill Sound Seminar Tapes, and Spoken Arts offer anthologies and individual readings in abundance and are likely to be available in English department or college and university library collections.

The two-record "Caedmon Treasury of Modern Poets Reading Their Own Poetry" (TC 2006) offers a good sample which includes Auden, Cummings, Eberhart, Eliot, Frost, MacLeish, MacNeice, Moore, Stevens, Dylan Thomas, Wilbur, Williams, and Yeats. The eighteen-record Spoken Arts "Treasury of 100 American Poets" (SA 1040–1057 or, boxed, SAP–18) is impressively comprehensive and includes all of the American poets just mentioned, as well as, for example, Sandburg, Jeffers, Bogan, Hughes, Cullen, Roethke, Shapiro, Jarrell, Ciardi, Lowell, Brooks, Nemerov, Ferlinghetti, Dickey, Booth, Snodgrass, Bly, Kinnell, Sexton, and Plath.

Caedmon also offers a two-record "Golden Treasury of English Poetry" (TC 2011), with selections ranging from Christopher Marlowe to Matthew Arnold. The readings are done by Claire Bloom, Eric Portman, and John Neville. Also of interest is Caedmon's "The Poetry of Robert Burns and Border Ballads" (TC 1103, cassette CDL 51103), which includes readings of the ballads "Sir Patrick Spens," "Edward," and "Get Up and Bar the Door," Caedmon's "The Child Ballads" (TC 1145 and 1146), and the Library of Congress "Child Ballads" (AAFS L57). Caedmon offers several Chaucer readings, "The Canterbury Tales General Prologue, in Middle English" (TC 1151, two-track tape CT2–1151, cassette CDL 51151), and readings of "The Pardoner's Tale" in both middle English (TC 1008, cassette CDL 51008) and modern English (TC 1130). For Chaucer pronunciation one should also note the authoritative Helge Kökeritz on the Lexington record "Beowulf, Chaucer" (5505). "Songs from the Plays of Shakespeare" sung and accompanied by musical instruments of the time are on Caedmon SRS 242.

Glossary of Critical Terms

ACCENT Relative emphasis or stress in the pronunciation of a syllable in a line of **verse**. *Metrical accent* is a regular pattern of accented or stressed and unaccented or unstressed syllables. *Word accent* is the spoken pattern of stressed and unstressed syllables; a dictionary indicates word accent when it tells how a word is to be pronounced. *Rhetorical accent* is the emphasis a speaker gives to a word because he views it as important.

ACROSTIC A poem in which the first letters of the individual lines spell out a word or words, usually related to the subject of the poem. Variations of the form use the last letters of lines, middle letters, letters running diagonally through the poem, or combinations of these.

ALEXANDRINE An **iambic hexameter** line. The **Spenserian stanza** ends with an alexandrine; for example:

Fierce wars and faithful loves shall moralize my song.

ALLEGORY A narrative in which character, action, and setting are used to express abstract meaning. Allegory is often defined as an extended metaphor; it derives from the Greek word *allegorein,* meaning to speak figuratively or in other terms. Spenser's *The Fairie Queene* and Bunyan's *Pilgrim's Progress* are well-known examples in English poetry and prose respectively.

ALLITERATION Repetition of consonant sounds at the beginning of words. Example: "Nor scar that whiter skin of hers than snow" (*Othello,* V, ii, 4). The term is also used more broadly to include the repetition of the initial consonant of internal syllables, or any pattern of consonant repetition. See **assonance.**

ALLUSION A reference to something outside the literary text itself, such as to a person, place, or event. Allusions are usually historical, literary, or mythological.

AMBIGUITY The use of a word or, more generally, of language in more senses than one at the same time. When skillfully used, ambiguity creates a richness and complexity of meaning. When unintended or unskillfully used, it becomes merely lack of clarity.

ANAPEST A metrical **foot** of two unaccented syllables followed by one accented syllable (⌣⌣ /).

APOSTROPHE Direct address to a person, object, or abstraction, either present or addressed as if present. "Roll on, thou deep and dark blue ocean, roll!" is the opening line of the apostrophe to the ocean in Byron's *Childe Harold's Pilgrimage* (Canto IV, stanza 179).

ARCHAISM A word or expression that is obsolete. Poets sometimes use archaisms deliberately for purposes of style. For example, in *The Rime of the Ancient Mariner* Coleridge uses such archaisms as "eftsoons" and "swound."

ASSONANCE Repetition of vowel sounds followed by different consonants. Example: "So sweet was ne'er so fatal. I must weep" (*Othello,* V, ii, 20). The vowel sound repeated may be either similar or identical. See **rhyme.**

BALLAD A narrative poem intended to be sung. The *folk* or *popular ballad* is usually anonymous and was originally transmitted orally. The *literary ballad* is usually the work of a single author deliberately using the popular ballad as his model. Coleridge's *The Rime of the Ancient Mariner* is a literary ballad.

BALLAD STANZA A four-line **stanza** alternating **iambic tetrameter** and **iambic trimeter**, usually rhyming *a b c b.*

BLANK VERSE Unrhymed **iambic pentameter**. Blank verse was introduced into English poetry about the middle of the sixteenth century by Henry Howard, Earl of Surrey, and was widely used in Elizabethan drama. It is the predominant **verse** form of Shakespeare's plays and Milton's poetry, and it has remained a significant verse form of poetry written in English.

CAESURA (CESURA) A main pause within a line of **verse**, usually indicated in **scansion** by vertical bars (‖). Example:

> Yet once more, ‖ O ye laurels, ‖ and once more
> Ye myrtles brown, ‖ with ivy never sere
> (John Milton, *Lycidas,* ll. 1-2).

CANTO A major division in a long poem, comparable to a prose chapter. Byron's *Don Juan* is divided into cantos.

CATALEXIS Omission of one or more final unaccented syllables in a line of **verse**.

CLICHÉ Any expression that has lost its freshness because of continued use, a trite expression. From the French *cliché,* a stereotype printing plate. Examples: "light as air," "bigger and better," "here today, gone tomorrow." Even phrases from Shakespeare may become clichés; for example, "starcrossed lovers" (*Romeo and Juliet,* Prologue, 6), and "Sweets to the sweet" (*Hamlet,* V, i, 266).

CLIMAX The highest point of interest in a narrative. A story is typically built to a point of crisis, which is followed immediately by a climax and then a resolution. A comparable pattern may be seen in many short poems that are not narratives.

CLOSED COUPLET See **couplet**.

CONCEIT A far-fetched comparison, an extended or elaborate metaphor. The term carries the sense of concept or idea and has nothing to do with *conceit* in the sense of vanity. A *metaphysical conceit* is conspicuously intellectual or ingenious, as is readily seen in the poetry of John Donne.

CONNOTATION The meaning or meanings which a word suggests or implies, as opposed to the meaning or meanings which it states. A dictionary definition of a word often includes connotation, but connotation also depends in part on the **context** in which a word is used. One connotation of the word *home,* for example, is that of a place about which we have a very deep feeling, but the simple statement, "I went home," might refer, for example, to where a person went at a given time, such as a vacation period.

CONSONANCE Repetition of consonant sounds. For example, *r* and *v* in, "To err is human, to forgive, divine" (Alexander Pope, *An Essay on Criticism,* l. 525).

CONSONANTAL RHYME See **rhyme**.

CONTEXT Everything surrounding a given unit (word, phrase, line, or more) of a literary work and modifying that unit's meaning while in turn being modified by it. More simply, the situation in which a phrase or line is spoken.

COUPLET A pair of consecutive rhyming lines, usually in the same **meter**; a two-line **stanza**. A *closed couplet* completes a thought—is syntactically complete—within the two lines. An *heroic couplet* is a pair of consecutive rhyming lines in **iambic pentameter**. Dryden's *Mac Flecknoe* and Pope's *The Rape of the Lock* are written in heroic couplets. Such couplets are called *heroic* because the form was widely used in English translations of heroic poems or epics from classical antiquity. *Heroic* is thus descriptive of function rather than of the **verse** form proper.

DACTYL A metrical **foot** of an accented syllable followed by two unaccented syllables ($/ \smile \smile$).

DENOTATION The meaning or meanings which a word states, as opposed to the meaning or meanings which it suggests or implies. Denotation tends to be specific, to refer to objects, facts, things.

DIDACTIC POEM A poem whose intent is to teach or to instruct, particularly in the area of moral virtue.

DIMETER   A line of two metrical feet.

DIRGE   A song or lyric poem expressing grief or mourning. A dirge is shorter and less formal than an **elegy.**

DOGGEREL   Verse that is clumsily written and trivial. Also, comic verse, burlesque.

DOUBLE RHYME   See **rhyme.**

DRAMATIC MONOLOGUE   A poem which is wholly the words of a single fictional character speaking to a silent listener. Examples of dramatic monologues are Browning's "My Last Duchess" and *Fra Lippo Lippi* and Eliot's "The Love Song of J. Alfred Prufrock."

ELEGY   A poem of mourning, usually **lyric** and reflective. In classical poetry, both Latin and Greek, the elegy was any serious meditation on a variety of subjects such as love, death, and war, written in **couplets** with the first line **dactylic hexameter** and the second line **pentameter.**

ELISION   The omission of part of a word for the sake of meter, as in "o'er" for "over," "ne'er" for "never," " 'tis" for "it is."

END-STOPPED LINE   A line of **verse** ending with a definite pause that also marks the end of a syntactical unit such as a phrase, clause, or sentence. Example:

> And now, unveiled, the Toilet stands
>   displayed,
> Each silver Vase in mystic order laid
> (Alexander Pope, *The Rape of the Lock,*
> I. 121-22).

ENJAMBMENT   A **run-on line,** as distinct from an **end-stopped line.** The sense of a run-on line requires no pause at the end, but rather carries into the next line. Example:

> Who would not sing for Lycidas? he
>   knew
> Himself to sing . . .
> (John Milton, *Lycidas,* II. 10-11).

EPIC   A long narrative poem usually written in an elevated style and about heroic characters. Milton's *Paradise Lost* is an epic.

EPIGRAM   A terse, polished, and often witty remark, in prose or **verse.** Example:

> A little learning is a dangerous thing;
> Drink deep, or taste not the Pierian
>   spring
> (Alexander Pope, *An Essay on Criticism,*
> II. 215-16).

EPITAPH   An inscription on a tomb, or commemorative verses written on the occasion of a person's death.

EPITHALAMION   A song or poem that celebrates a wedding; a marriage song in honor of bride and bridegroom. From the Greek, literally "at the bridal chamber."

EPITHET   A word or phrase used to describe an attribute or quality regarded as characteristic of a person or thing. Example: Dryden writes of Shadwell, "Thou last great prophet of tautology" (*Mac Flecknoe,* I. 30).

FALLING METER   Meter in which the unaccented syllables "fall away" from the accented syllables, that is, meter in which the accented syllable of each **foot** appears first. The **trochee** (/ ‿) and **dactyl** (/ ‿ ‿) are falling meters.

FEMININE ENDING   A line of **verse** ending with an unstressed syllable.

FEMININE RHYME   See **rhyme.**

FIGURE OF SPEECH   A general term used to define a great variety of departures from normal speech in order to gain special effects. Figurative language is nonliteral, rhetorical, metaphorical. Some common figures of speech are **apostrophe, hyperbole, irony, metaphor, metonymy, personification, simile,** and **synecdoche.**

FOOT   A metrical unit consisting of one accented and one or more unaccented syllables. In poetry written in English the common metrical feet are **iamb** (‿ /), **trochee** (/ ‿), **anapest** (‿ ‿ /), and **dactyl** (/ ‿ ‿), with the **spondee** (/ /) and **pyrrhic** (‿ ‿) considered substitutive.

FORM   A broad term used to describe the structure of a poem, the relation of all of its elements to each other and to the whole. *Form* is also used in reference to conventional arrangements of **meter** and **rhyme,** such as **ballad stanza, couplet, quatrain,** and **sonnet.**

FREE VERSE (VERS LIBRE) Poetry whose **rhythm** is based not on **meter** but rather on **accent** patterns related more directly to the spoken language. Although free verse shows a complex organization of sound and rhythm, it rarely includes **rhyme**. Most of the poems of Walt Whitman are written in free verse, which is common in twentieth-century poetry. But free verse may also be seen in Shakespeare's *Antony and Cleopatra* and Milton's *Samson Agonistes.*

GENRE A distinctive class or category of literary composition, a type of literature such as fiction, poetry, or drama.

HEPTAMETER A **verse** line of seven metrical feet.

HEROIC COUPLET See **couplet.**

HEXAMETER A **verse** line of six metrical feet.

HYMN A song of praise. From the Greek *hymnos,* a song in praise of gods or heroes. A hymn is also specifically a metrical composition adapted to be sung in a religious service. See Donne's "A Hymn to God the Father" and Shelley's "Hymn to Intellectual Beauty."

HYPERBOLE A **figure of speech** in which exaggeration or overstatement is used for the sake of emphasis. Example:

> Will all great Neptune's ocean wash this
> blood
> Clean from my hand? No, this my hand
> will rather
> The multitudinous seas incarnadine,
> Making the green one red
> (*Macbeth,* II, ii, 60-63).

IAMB A metrical **foot** of an unaccented syllable followed by an accented syllable ($\smile$/). Iambic **meter** is the most common meter of poetry written in English.

IDENTICAL RHYME See **rhyme.**

IMAGE A verbal representation of sense experience. Also, the response (mental picture) evoked by the verbal representation. Although an image stimulates sense perception, response to it is complex, involving

intellect, emotion, and related experience. In poetry the most common images involve comparisons and, more specifically, are usually **similes** and **metaphors.** For example, Eliot opens "The Love Song of J. Alfred Prufrock" with a simile comparing the evening to a hospital patient:

> Let us go then, you and I,
> When the evening is spread out against
> the sky
> Like a patient etherized upon a table.

In "Birches" Robert Frost uses an ice-enamel metaphor to describe birch trees loaded with ice on a sunny winter morning:

> They click upon themselves
> As the breeze rises, and turn many-
> colored
> As the stir cracks and crazes their
> enamel (ll. 7-9).

Although in poetry images are used to evoke all of the senses and to vivify experience, the sense of sight is the one evoked most often. In a broad sense the total experience of a poem is a complex or structured image.

IMAGERY **Images** regarded collectively.

INCREMENTAL REPETITION The device of repeating a **stanza** or **refrain** with a significant change or addition. Incremental repetition is typical of **ballads**; see, for example, "Edward." See also Tennyson's "Mariana."

INVERSION Reversal of normal word order as for purposes of **meter** or **rhyme.** Also, the use of a metrical **foot** opposite to the one required by the meter; for example, the substitution of a **trochee** for an **iamb.**

INVOCATION The poet's appeal to a god or muse for assistance in writing his work. Milton opens his epic *Paradise Lost* with an invocation which includes the explicit, "Sing, Heavenly Muse" (l. 6), and, "I thence Invoke thy aid to my adventurous song" (ll. 12-13).

IRONY Most simply defined, the use of words to convey the opposite of their literal meaning. But there are many shades of irony, and so it is more broadly defined as an expression marked by a deliberate contrast between the literal or apparent meaning and the intended meaning. These are definitions of *verbal irony. Irony of situation* occurs when the development of a situation is contrary to our expectations. *Dramatic irony* involves a discrepancy between what a character says and the author's **point of view** toward him, with the reader or spectator coming to share the author's point of view. See footnote 6 of Chapter 1, as well as Chapter 6.

ITALIAN SONNET   See **sonnet.**

JUXTAPOSITION   The placing of words, phrases, or other units of meaning next to each other in order to create meaning beyond that established by syntactical relationships. For example, in *The Rape of the Lock* Pope describes Belinda's dressing table: "Puffs, Powders, Patches, *Bibles,* Billet-doux" (I, 138, my italics).

KENNING   A formulaic **metaphor** characteristic of Old English poetry, usually a compound word or phrase. Some kennings from *Beowulf* are "the ringed prow" for ship, "the whale-road" for sea, and "the leavings of the file" for sword. The kenning is a good example of the use of **images** in poetry. See **image.**

LIMERICK   A humorous five-line poem of loosely **anapestic meter** and rhyming *a a b b a.* The name *limerick* is said to have come from the chorus of an old song mentioning the city of Limerick in Ireland. Example:

> An epicure dining at Crewe
> Found quite a large mouse in his stew.
> Said the waiter, "Don't shout,
> Or wave it about,
> Or the rest will be wanting one too!"

LYRIC   In ancient Greece, a poem intended to be sung or recited in accompaniment to a lyre (a stringed instrument resembling a harp). Now a general term for any poem that combines musicality and strong emotion, particularly emotion that is personal or subjective. **Songs, sonnets, odes, elegies,** and **hymns** are considered lyric poems.

LYRICS   The words of a song that is sung. *Song lyrics* range from poems that are particularly adapted to musical expression, such as Jonson's "Drink to Me Only with Thine Eyes" or Tennyson's "Sweet and Low," to prose that adapts to music. Similarly, song lyrics range in their language from a high degree of originality to the **cliché**-ridden.

MASCULINE RHYME   See **rhyme.**

METAPHOR   An implied comparison in which an identification is made between two normally unrelated objects (persons, things, actions, or the like). Example: He was a lion in battle. If the same comparison is stated directly, using explicit words of comparison such as *like* or *as,* then the comparison is called a **simile.** Example: He was like a lion in battle. The distinction between *simile* and *metaphor* is falling out of use, with *metaphor* being used as a general term to describe any comparison between two normally unrelated objects and, even more broadly, any use of figurative language; in this context the poem is an ordered or structured use of metaphor and is itself thought of as, finally, a metaphor. See **figure of speech** and **image.**

METER   The regular recurrence of patterns of accented and unaccented syllables. The basic metrical unit is the **foot** (one accented and one or more unaccented syllables), and the number of feet per line is indicated by the terms **monometer** (one foot per line), **dimeter** (two feet per line), **trimeter** (three feet per line), **tetrameter** (four feet per line), **pentameter** (five feet per line), **hexameter** (six feet per line), and so on. A line of poetry is metrically described by naming the kind and the number of feet it contains; for example, **iambic tetrameter, iambic pentameter, dactyllic hexameter.** See **accent, blank verse, caesura, couplet, end-stopped line, foot, form, free verse, inversion, rhythm, scansion, verse.**

METONYMY   A **figure of speech** in which the name of one thing is used to designate another thing to which it is related. Example: "the White House," meaning not the building but the President himself.

MOCK HEROIC   A poem in which the ordinary or trivial is treated in a grand or elevated style. Pope's *The Rape of the Lock* is a mock heroic.

MONOMETER   A line of one metrical foot.

MOTIF   A distinctive feature or element in the design of a literary work, a recurrent word, phrase, **image, theme,** pattern, or the like.

MUSE   In Greek mythology, the muses were the goddesses who presided over the arts. They were the nine daughters of Zeus and Mnemosyne, goddess of memory. Calliope was the muse of epic poetry, Clio of history, Erato of love poetry, Euterpe of music, Melpomene of tragedy, Polyhymnia of sacred poetry, Terpsichore of the dance, Thalia of comedy, and Urania of astronomy. *Muse* came to mean the power to which a poet looked for, and from which he received, his inspiration. See **invocation.**

MYTH   A story which has its roots in the culture of a people and which attempts to organize and to explain human experience in terms of certain fundamental or universal patterns. Myths attempt to explain, for example, creation, man's spiritual identity, and social, natural, and supernatural phenomena. Older myths usually involve the exploits of gods and heroes. A myth may be considered a metaphor of human experience. See **image** and **metaphor.**

NARRATIVE   A story, typically with plot, character, and setting.

NEAR-RHYME   See **rhyme.**

OBJECTIVE CORRELATIVE   A term used by T. S. Eliot in his essay "Hamlet and His Problems" (in *Selected Essays: 1917-1932,* London: Faber and Faber Ltd., 1932, p. 145): "The only way of expressing emotion in the form of art is by finding 'an objective correlative'; in other words, a set of objects, a situation, a chain of events which shall be the formula of that *particular* emotion . . . ."

OCTAVE   An eight-line **stanza.** Also, the eight-line first stanza of the Italian or Petrarchan **sonnet.**

ODE   In English, a **lyric** poem on a serious subject, usually formal in style and written in an elaborate **stanza** pattern for which there is no conventional form or model. The Pindaric ode originated with the three-part choric song of Greek drama. The first part, the *strophe,* was sung while the chorus moved from one side of the stage to the other; the second part, the *antistrophe,* as it moved back again; and the third part, the *epode,* while it stood still. The strophe and antistrophe were alike in stanza form and differed from the epode. The structure of

the Pindaric ode is seldom found in poetry written in English. In reference to poetry written in English, *ode* is not a strict term.

OFF RHYME   See **rhyme.**

ONOMATOPOEIA   The use of words in which sound seems to be or is made to be an imitation of sense. Examples: *crack, buzz, hush.* A well-known example from poetry is Alfred Noyes' "Tlot-tlot" in "The Highwayman" to suggest the sound of horses' hoofbeats. In *An Essay on Criticism* Pope generalizes the principle:

'Tis not enough no harshness gives
   offence;
The sound must seem an echo to the
   sense (ll. 364-65).

Pope then offers emphatic illustration of what he means. Onomatopoeia is a specific and relatively simple manifestation of poetry's complex appeal to the auditory imagination.

OTTAVA RIMA   An eight-line **stanza** of **iambic pentameter** rhyming *a b a b a b c c.* The stanza, perhaps originated by Boccaccio, was used by Italian writers and introduced into England in the sixteenth century. Examples of its use are Byron's *Don Juan* and Yeats' "Sailing to Byzantium."

OXYMORON   A **figure of speech** in which opposite or contradictory ideas or terms are combined; a form of **paradox.** Examples: sweet sorrow, darkness visible, the sound of silence.

PARADOX   A seeming contradiction that is nevertheless in some significant sense true. See footnote 5 of Chapter 1.

PARAPHRASE   A restatement of a passage in different words, usually to clarify meaning.

PARODY   An imitation of the style of an author in an exaggerated or humorous way. The **mock heroic** poem typically parodies the **epic** style. Lewis Carroll's "Father William" is an example of a parody of a bad poem, Robert Southey's "The Old Man's Comforts and How He Gained Them."

PASTORAL   A **genre** of poetry in which an idealized picture of rural life and character is presented in a conventional style. Theocritus and Virgil provide the classical models for pastoral poetry. Examples of pastoral poetry in English are Spenser's *The Shepherd's Calendar* and Pope's *Pastorals. Pastoral* is also used loosely to describe any poetry that presents a picture of rural life and praises its simplicity. Since pastoral poetry is strongly identified in terms of rural life as a convention (or set of conventions), a key critical question to be raised is whether or not pastoral poetry gets beyond its own convention and is shaped into a pleasing artistic whole.

PASTORAL ELEGY An **elegy** that uses **pastoral** conventions. Such conventions are, for example, the poet and the person for whom he mourns represented as shepherds, an **invocation** to the **muse**, all nature joining in the mourning for the dead shepherd, a rebuke to the guardian spirits of the dead shepherd for not having saved him, a procession of mourners and a catalogue of the flowers decking the bier, a general movement from "lamentation," apparently inconsolable grief, to "reconciliation," the assurance of life after death. Milton's *Lycidas* is a pastoral elegy that makes full use of pastoral conventions.

PENTAMETER A line of five metrical feet.

PERFECT RHYME See **rhyme.**

PERSONA The speaker or fictitious character imagined as speaking the words of a poem. From the Latin *persona,* a mask. The reader of a poem should not assume that the speaker is the poet himself in his identity from real life. A notorious example of such a confusion is the case of Robert Frost (see Chapter 4).

PERSONIFICATION A **figure of speech** in which human characteristics are attributed to inanimate objects, abstract ideas, or anything nonhuman. For example, in his Sonnet 10, John Donne addresses death as if it were a person: "Death, be not proud, though some have called thee Mighty and dreadful."

PETRARCHAN SONNET See **sonnet.**

POINT OF VIEW The attitude or complex of attitudes that a speaker has toward his subject. See Chapters 1 and 6.

PROSODY The systematic study of versification, including **meter, rhyme, rhythm, stanza** form, phonetic pattern, and the like.

PUN A play on words in which two or more meanings of a word fit the **context** in which it is being used. For example, in *Hamlet* Polonius puns elaborately on *tender.* One of his statements to Ophelia, "You'll tender me a fool" (I, iii, 109), has three distinct meanings: you will show yourself to me as a fool, you will show me to the world as a fool, and you will offer me an illegitimate child. In this example the pun is on a word with a single spelling. An example of a pun on a word with more than one spelling, that is, on words with different meanings but the same sound, is Hamlet's comment to Claudius, "I am too much in the sun," (I, ii, 67), meaning that he is in too much of the sunshine of the king's favor and that being his father's *son* and now Claudius' stepson is too much of the role of son for him.

PYRRHIC A metrical **foot** of two unaccented syllables(⌣ ⌣). Because the pyrrhic foot has no accented syllable, it cannot serve as the basis of a poetic **rhythm** and is generally considered a substitute for a metrical foot combining accented and unaccented syllables.

QUANTITATIVE VERSE **Verse** in which the metrical system is based on the length of time it takes to pronounce the syllables of the language, rather than on **accent.** Quantitative verse may be found in classical Greek and Latin, but it does not appear in poetry written in English. This is not to say that the poet writing in English ignores quantity as a factor, but rather that quantity is not a distinct basis of his metrical or rhythmic system.

QUATRAIN A four-line **stanza.**

REFRAIN A line or lines repeated at regular intervals in a poem, but usually at the end of a **stanza.** A refrain is characteristic of the **ballad** and is often used in song **lyrics.**

RHETORICAL QUESTION A question asked for the sake of emphasis rather than to evoke an answer that is usually obvious anyway. For example, Hamlet asks, "What is a man, If his chief good and market of his time Be but to sleep and feed?" (IV, iv, 33-35).

RHYME   The repetition or correspondence in two or more words between the final accented vowel and whatever sounds follow. Examples: toe-woe, sin-win, name-frame, flower-power, imploringly-adoringly. Rhymes with identical sounds such as these are called *true, exact, perfect.* Single-syllable rhyme, as in the first three examples, is called *masculine rhyme.* A rhyming accented syllable followed by one or more identical unaccented syllables, as in the last two examples, is called *feminine rhyme. Double rhyme* rhymes two syllables and *triple rhyme* rhymes three syllables. *Rhyme* at the ends of lines of poetry is called **end rhyme.** Example:

> All human things are subject to decay,
> And when Fate summons, monarchs
>   must obey
> (Dryden, *Mac Flecknoe,* ll. 1-2).

Rhyme within a line is called *internal rhyme.* Example: "Come from the holy *fire,* perne in a *gyre*" (Yeats, "Sailing to Byzantium," l. 19). Rhyme that does not involve an identity of vowel sounds but rather a similarity or approximation is called *near rhyme,* which is a general term comprehending such sound-repetition as **assonance, consonance,** and half rhyme. *Half rhyme,* also called *slant rhyme* or *off rhyme,* is rhyme in which the vowel sounds are similar but not identical, while the final consonant sounds, if any, are identical. Examples: too-potato, some-them, young-song, ear-despair, river-ever. Words which appear to rhyme because of their spelling but do not actually rhyme are called *eye rhyme.* Examples: tough, through, cough. See **assonance, consonance.**

RHYME ROYAL   A seven-line **stanza** of **iambic pentameter** rhyming *a b a b b c c.* Called **rhyme royal** in honor of James I of England, who wrote verses in the stanza. Chaucer used it extensively; for example, *The Man of Law's Tale* and *Troilus and Criseyde.* See Thomas Wyatt's "They Flee from Me."

RHYME SCHEME   The pattern formed by the end rhymes of all of the lines of a **stanza** or poem. The rhyming words are designated successively by the letters of the alphabet, a letter being repeated to show that a later word rhymes with an earlier one. Some rhyme schemes for a **quatrain** are, for example, *a b a b, a b b a, a b c b, a a b a.* For typical rhyme schemes of the Italian and English sonnet, see **sonnet.**

RHYTHM   Recurrence of **accent** or **stress.** Rhythm implies movement and flow in a succession of rising and falling sounds. When rhythm is systematic in terms of accent patterns it is called **meter.** When rhythm is not systematic in terms of accent patterns but is nevertheless emphatic it is called **free verse.** Rhythm is natural to man and altogether characteristic of language, whether spoken or written, poetry or prose, poetry being associated with rhythm that seems readily identifiable despite its complexity.

RIME   Alternate spelling for **rhyme.**

RISING METER   **Meter** in which the unaccented syllables "rise toward" the accented syllables, that is, meter in which the accented syllable of each **foot** appears last. The **iamb**($\smile$/) and the **anapest**($\smile\smile$/) are rising meters.

RUN-ON LINE   A line of poetry the sense of which requires no pause at the end but rather carries into the next line; **enjambment.**

SATIRE   A type of speaking and writing the object of which is to hold up folly or vice to ridicule, usually with corrective intent.

SCANSION   Descriptive analysis of the metrical patterns of a poem, whereby accented and unaccented syllables are marked and grouped into metrical feet. See **meter, rhythm.**

SECONDARY ACCENT OR STRESS   An **accent** or **stress** weaker than the primary accent or stress given to a syllable, but stronger than a syllable considered unaccented or unstressed. The middle-strength accent in a metrical system assumed to have three accents. Usually indicated by \. Example:
/$\smile$\ $\smile$ / $\smile$ /$\smile$/
Loveliest of trees, the cherry now
(A. E. Housman, "Loveliest of Trees").

SESTET   The last six lines of an Italian or Petrarchan **sonnet.** Also, a six-line **stanza** or poem.

SIMILE   See **metaphor.**

SLANT RHYME   See **rhyme.**

SOLILOQUY   A dramatic convention in which a character, alone on stage, speaks his thoughts aloud and is, of course, heard by the audience. See Hamlet's "To Be or Not to Be" and "How All Occasions Do Inform Against Me" soliloquies.

SONNET   A fourteen-line poem, usually in **iambic pentameter** and following, with minor variations, one of several fixed **rhyme schemes.** The *Italian* or *Petrarchan* sonnet is divided into an **octave** rhyming *a b b a a b b a* and a **sestet** in various combinations of two or three rhymes, such as *c d e c d e* or *c d c d c d.* A significant break in the meaning or overall movement of the Italian sonnet occurs between the octave and the sestet. The *English* or *Shakespearean* sonnet has three **quatrains** and a concluding **couplet,** rhyming *a b a b c d c d e f e f g g.* In general, the sonnet is a fixed **verse** form, readily identified, but with many variations in such things as **rhyme scheme, meter,** and thematic or dramatic organization.

SPENSERIAN STANZA   A nine-line **stanza** rhyming *a b a b b c b c c,* all lines **iambic pentameter** except the last, which is iambic **hexameter,** an **Alexandrine.** The stanza is named for Edmund Spenser, who created it for his poem *The Fairie Queene* (1590).

SPONDEE   A metrical **foot** of two accented syllables ($//$). Because the spondaic foot has no unaccented syllable, it cannot serve as the basis of a poetic **rhythm** and is generally considered a substitute for a metrical foot combining accented and unaccented syllables.

SPRUNG RHYTHM   A term coined by Gerard Manley Hopkins to describe his complex metrical system, in which the accented or stressed syllable is always considered as the beginning of the metrical **foot.** Any number of unstressed syllables, or none, may follow the stressed syllable. In sprung rhythm the time intervals between accents are approximately equal and the accent is intended to be "hit." The result is a **rhythm** that is emphatic, not unlike that of Old English poetry.

STANZA   A group of lines regarded as a unit, usually distinguished by number, met-rical pattern, and **rhyme scheme.** Poems are commonly divided according to stanza (Italian for stopping place) and often follow a single stanza pattern. The **couplet, tercet,** and **quatrain** are two-, three-, and four-line stanzas respectively. Some stanza forms are conventional and have their own names, such as **ottava rima, rhyme royal,** and **Spenserian stanza.** See separate entries and also **form, meter,** and **rhyme.**

STREAM OF CONSCIOUSNESS   A technique of dramatizing the mind through psychological association as an organizing principle, rather than through natural or logical movement in space. The term was coined by William James in his *Principles of Psychology* (1890). In prose fiction James Joyce's *Ulysses* (1922) is a landmark example. For an example of the technique in poetry see Eliot's "The Love Song of J. Alfred Prufrock."

STRESS   A synonym for **accent,** the relative emphasis in the pronunciation of a syllable in a line of **verse.**

STROPHE   See **ode.**

STRUCTURE   A general term referring to the relationship of all of the parts of a literary work to the whole and of the whole to all of the parts.

STYLE   A general term referring to that combination of distinctive features which gives a literary work an overall quality or identity, but usually with reference to manner of expression, *how* a writer says what he says, as opposed to *what* he is saying. Typical elements of style include diction, sentence structure, **rhythm,** figurative language, concreteness, abstraction, formality, informality. Such elements naturally overlap and interrelate in complex ways, making style an elusive concept.

SYLLABIC VERSE   **Verse** based on the number of syllables in a line rather than on **accent** or quantity.

SYMBOL   That which stands for something beyond itself. A word, for example, is a symbol in that it signifies an object, an event, an idea, or the like. But the object, event, or idea may, in turn, have a range of reference beyond itself. One meaning or symbolic signification of the word *light,* for example, is the illumination derived from any of a variety of sources, such as sunlight, daylight, candlelight, electric light, but light is also one of the most frequent symbols to be found in literature, suggesting all manner of things beyond itself: beneficence, the divine, inspiration, hope, joy, love, relationship, civilization, etc. A *conventional symbol* is one with a widely agreed-upon meaning; for example, a red light as a symbol of danger or of the necessity of bringing a vehicle to a stop. Poets typically use conventional symbols—just as they use words in their common meanings—as a point of departure for developing their own complex meanings, their own complex symbolism. In a broad sense a poem is an ordered or structured use of symbols and is itself thought of, finally, as a symbol. See **metaphor.**

SYNECDOCHE   A **figure of speech** in which the part stands for the whole, or the whole for the part. Examples: "sail" for "ship," "the law" for "a policeman." See **metonymy.**

TERCET   A three-line **stanza**. If all three lines end with the same **rhyme**, the tercet is a **triplet**. *Tercet* also denotes either of the two three-line groups in the **sestet** of an Italian **sonnet.**
TERZA RIMA   **Tercets** rhymed in the interlocking pattern *a b a, b c b, c d c, d e d.* Used by Dante in *The Divine Comedy.* See Shelley's "Ode to the West Wind."

TETRAMETER   A line of four metrical feet.

THEME   Topic or central idea. Used loosely to suggest subject, such as the themes of love, death, nature, beauty, relationship. More precisely, a one-sentence statement of the central idea of a literary work. The term *thesis* may be used as a synonym for theme, but suggests that the writer is trying to prove something. This is contrary to the normal intent of a work of art, which is concerned with the quality and complexity of human experience.

THEMATIC DEVELOPMENT   The **structure** of a poem defined in terms of **theme.**

THRENODY   A **dirge** or song of lamentation.

TONE   The attitude of a speaker or writer toward his subject, his audience, and himself. In spoken language tone is indicated through inflection, pitch, emphasis, gesture, and the like, as well as through diction, content, and **context**. In written language, by contrast, tone is more open to interpretation; it must to a greater degree be inferred by the reader. See **point of view.**

TRIMETER   A line of three metrical feet.

TRIPLE RHYME   See **rhyme.**

TRIPLET   A three-line **stanza** with a single **rhyme.**

TROCHEE   A metrical **foot** of one accented syllable followed by one unaccented syllable ($/\smile$).

TROPE   Another term for **figure of speech**. From the Greek *tropos,* a turn, hence a figure of speech involving the use of a word with a definite change in its *sense.*

TRUE RHYME   See **rhyme.**

UNDERSTATEMENT   A **figure of speech** in which less is said than is meant. The terms *litotes* (an affirmative expressed by the negation of its opposite; for example, not a dull poem) and *meiosis* are synonyms but are much less commonly used. An example of understatement is the last line of Robert Frost's "Birches": "One could do worse than be a swinger of birches." The poem makes clear that one could hardly do better.

VERS LIBRE   See **free verse.**

VERSE   A single line of poetry or, more generally, poetry as distinct from prose.

VERSE PARAGRAPH   A group of lines in a poem, set off by indentation, a space, or both, and representing a unit of development in the poem but *not* a metrical pattern or unit.

VERSIFICATION   See **prosody.**

VIRGULE   A slash or short slanting line (/) used to divide a line of poetry into feet or to indicate the division between one line of poetry and another.

VOICE The person speaking the words of a poem. Also, the manner in which the person speaks or is imagined to speak the words of a poem. The concept of voice emphasizes the range of possibilities both in the identification of the speaker of a poem and in his manner of speaking at any one time or in an overall way. Voice implies both the basic identity of a speaker and multifarious shades of meaning. See **persona** and **point of view.**

WEAK ENDING An unaccented syllable at the end of a line of poetry. In cases in which a metrical **accent** would fall on the syllable, it would not be accented in terms of sense or normal speech. See **rhyme.**

ZEUGMA A **figure of speech** in which a word is used to modify or to govern two or more words, although its use is grammatically or logically correct with only one. Example: She arrived in tears and on a motorcycle.

Index by Theme*

*Note: The indexes by theme and verse form are selective and suggestive, not comprehensive.

Index by Verse Form

Index by Author, Title, and First Line